CATALYST™
PRIME

SUPERB™

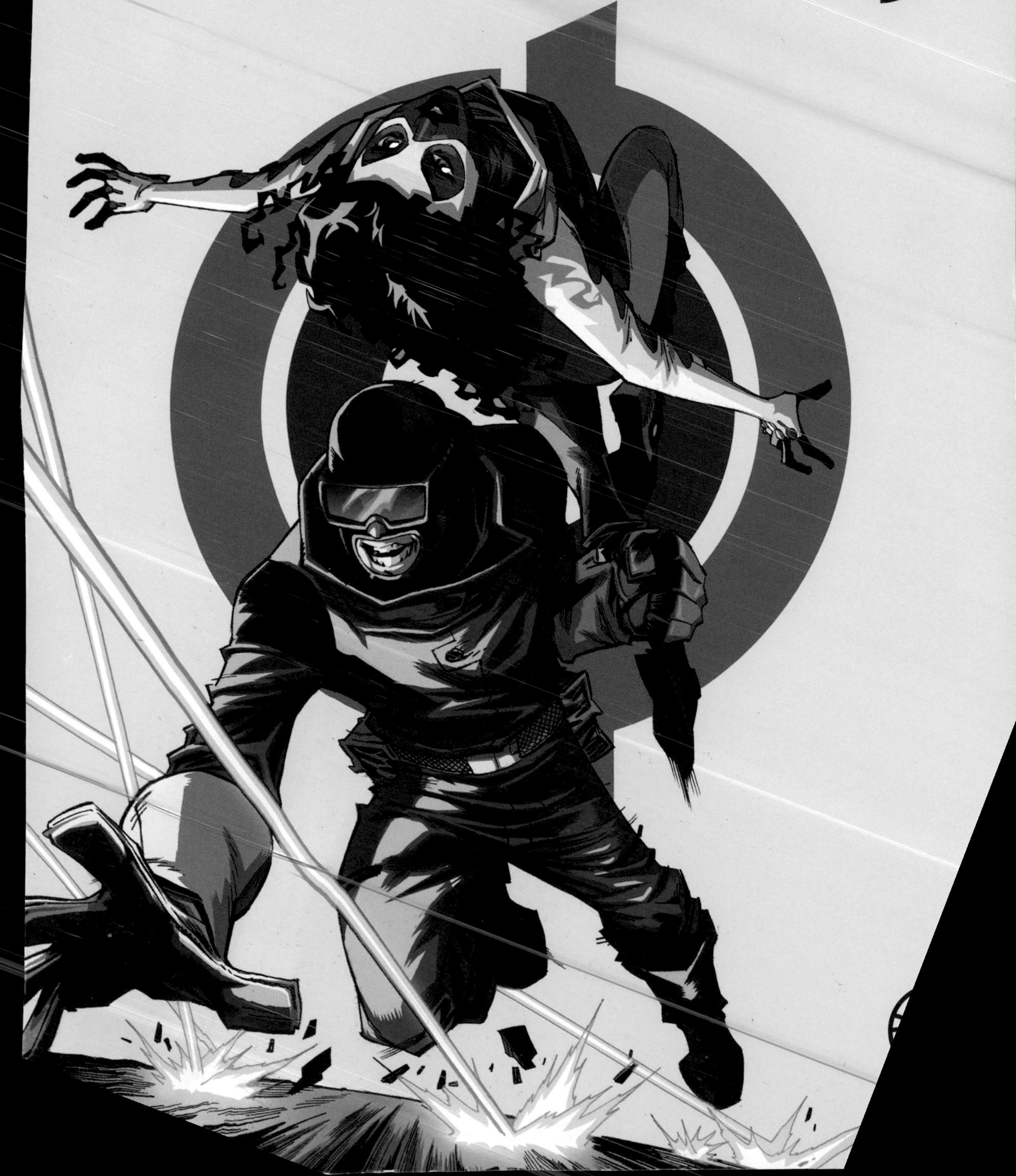

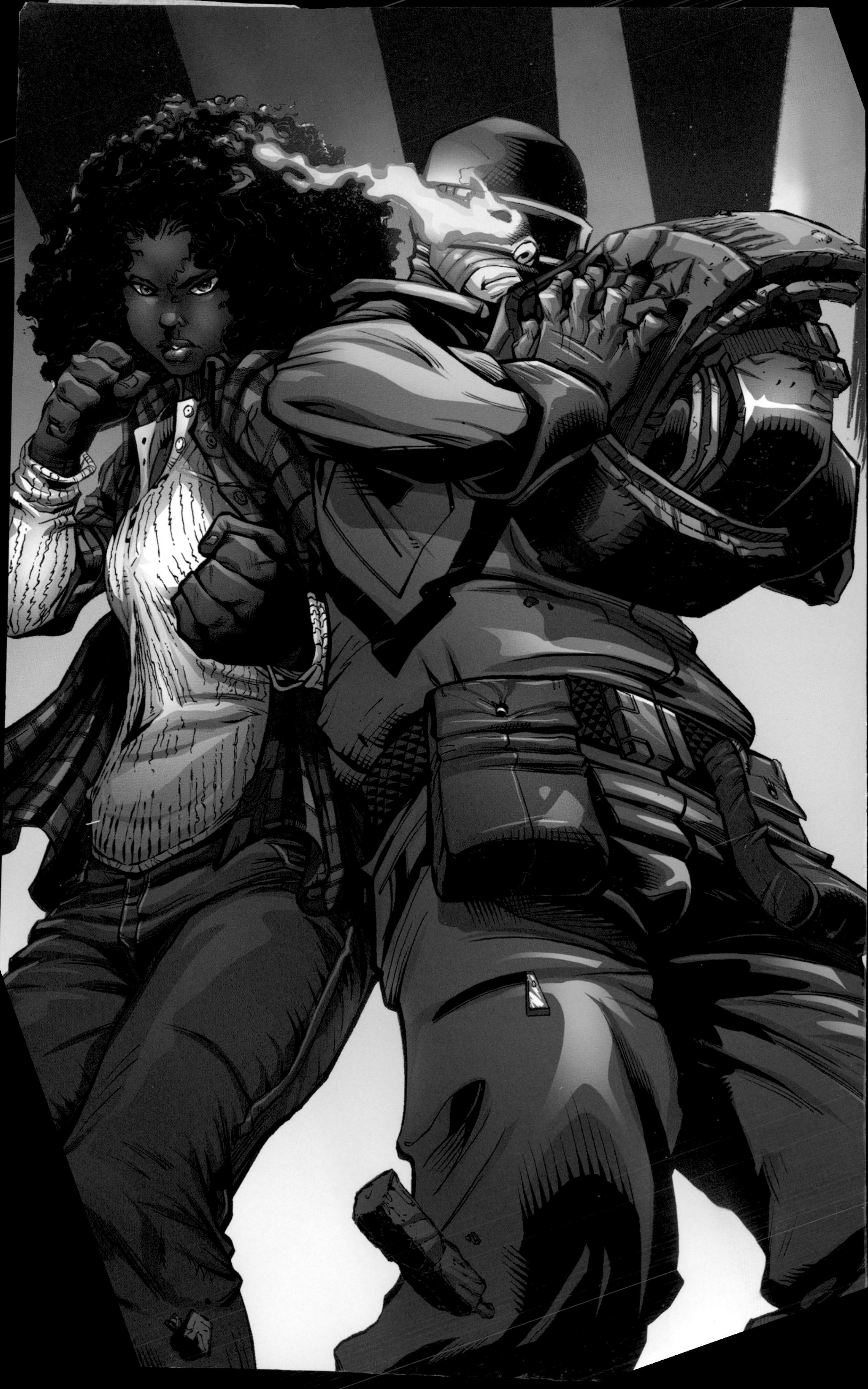

CATALYST™ PRIME

SUPERB™

"LIFE AFTER THE FALLOUT"

WRITTEN BY **DAVID F. WALKER** and **SHEENA C. HOWARD**
PENCILED BY **RAY-ANTHONY HEIGHT, ALITHA MARTINEZ,** and **ERIC BATTLE**
INKED BY **LEBEAU L. UNDERWOOD, ALITHA MARTINEZ,**
ERIC BATTLE, ROBIN RIGGS and **RAY-ANTHONY HEIGHT**
LETTERED BY **AW DESIGNS' TOM NAPOLITANO**
COLORED BY **CHRIS SOTOMAYOR** and **VERONICA GANDINI**

"THE EVENT"

WRITTEN BY **PRIEST** and
JOSEPH PHILLIP ILLIDGE
ILLUSTRATED BY **MARCO TURINI** and **WILL ROSADO**
LETTERED BY **ANDWORLD DESIGN**
COLORED BY **JESSICA KHOLINNE**

JOSEPH ILLIDGE - SENIOR EDITOR
DESIREE RODRIGUEZ - EDITORIAL ASSISTANT

COVER BY **RAY-ANTHONY HEIGHT** and **CHRIS SOTOMAYOR**

LION™ FORGE

ISBN 978-1-941302-40-8

Library of Congress Control Number: 2017951832

SUPERB™

CHAPTER 1

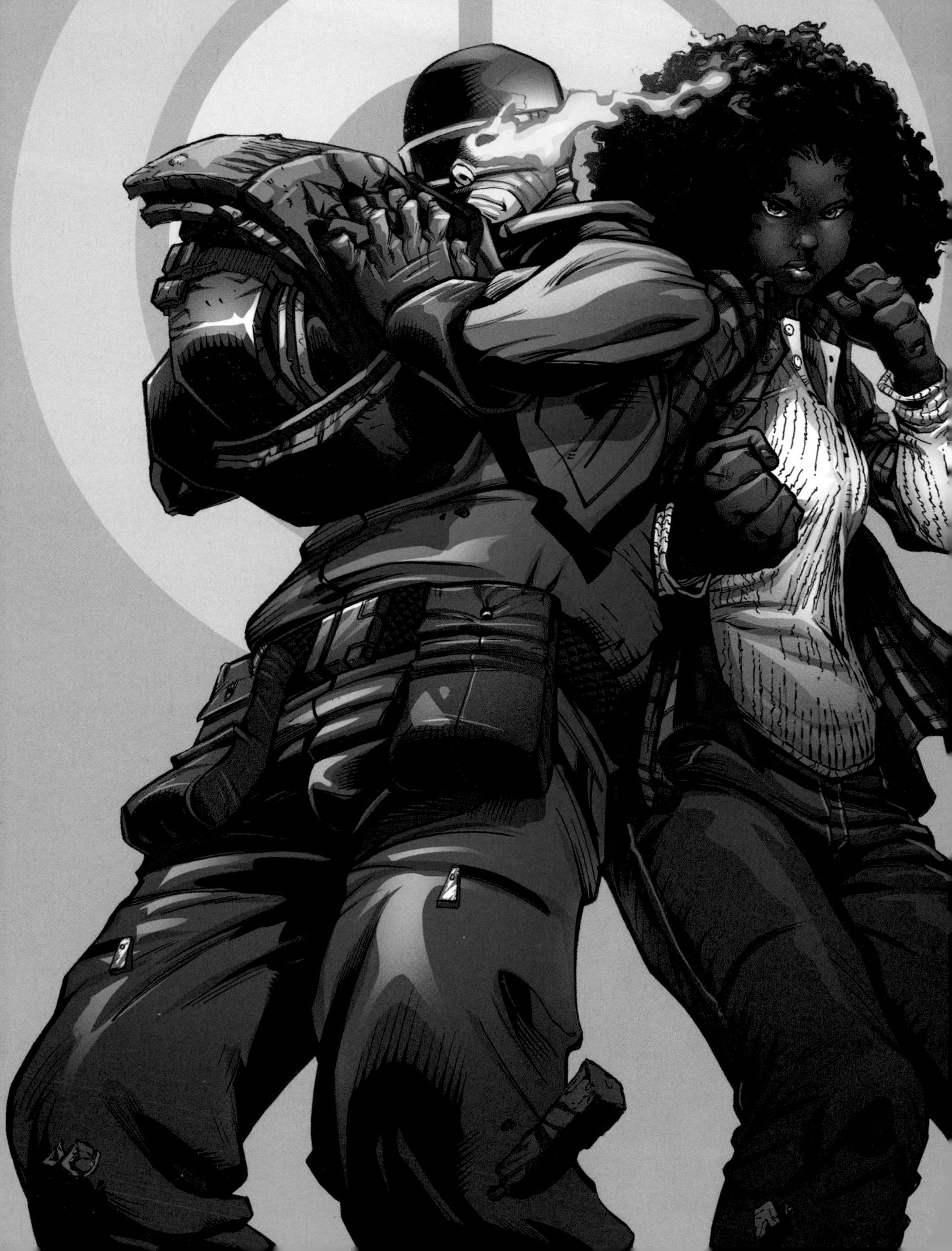

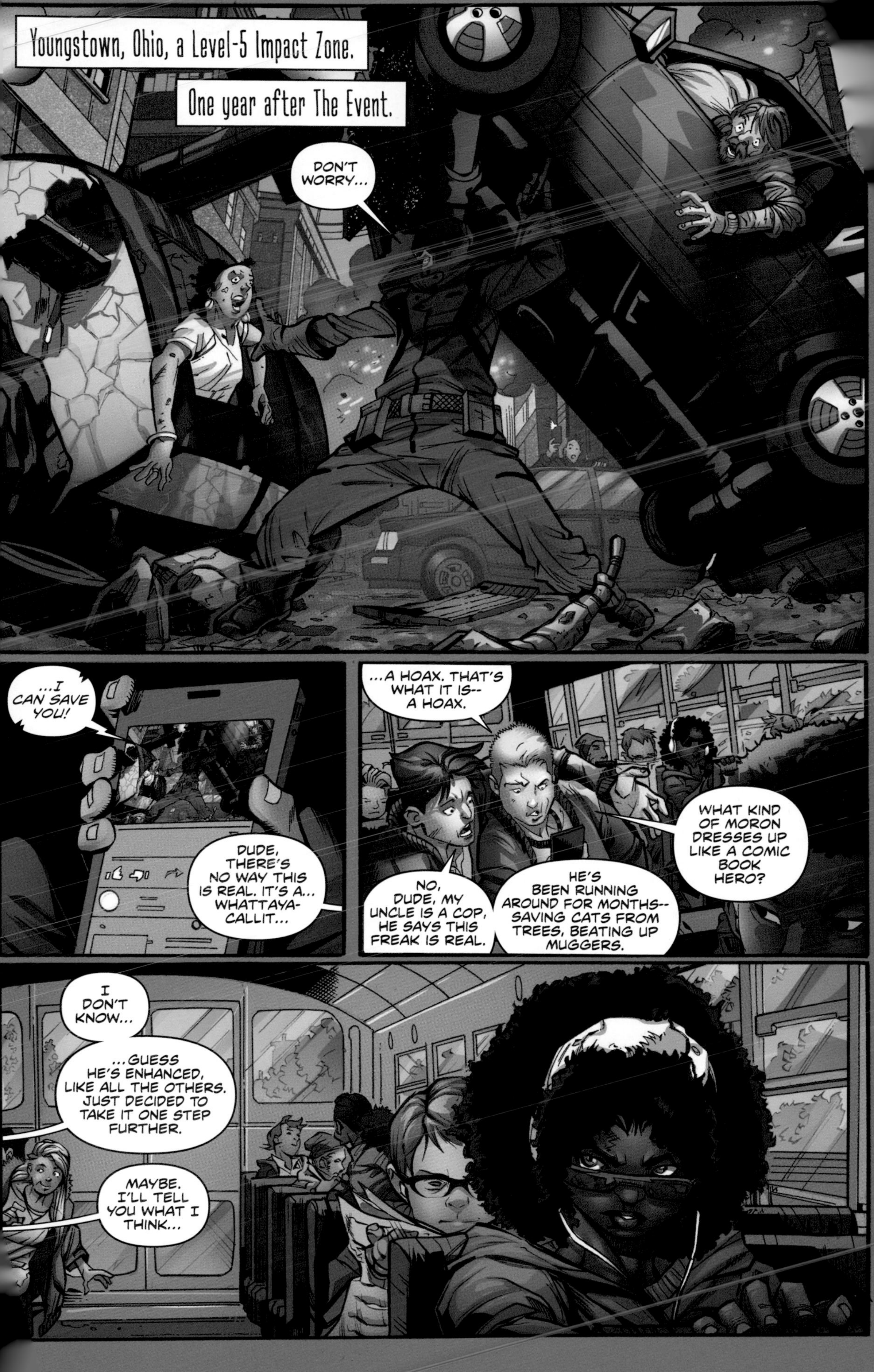
Youngstown, Ohio, a Level-5 Impact Zone.
One year after The Event.
DON'T WORRY...
...I CAN SAVE YOU!
DUDE, THERE'S NO WAY THIS IS REAL. IT'S A... WHATTAYA-CALLIT...
...A HOAX. THAT'S WHAT IT IS-- A HOAX.
NO, DUDE, MY UNCLE IS A COP, HE SAYS THIS FREAK IS REAL.
HE'S BEEN RUNNING AROUND FOR MONTHS-- SAVING CATS FROM TREES, BEATING UP MUGGERS.
WHAT KIND OF MORON DRESSES UP LIKE A COMIC BOOK HERO?
I DON'T KNOW...
...GUESS HE'S ENHANCED, LIKE ALL THE OTHERS. JUST DECIDED TO TAKE IT ONE STEP FURTHER.
MAYBE. I'LL TELL YOU WHAT I THINK...

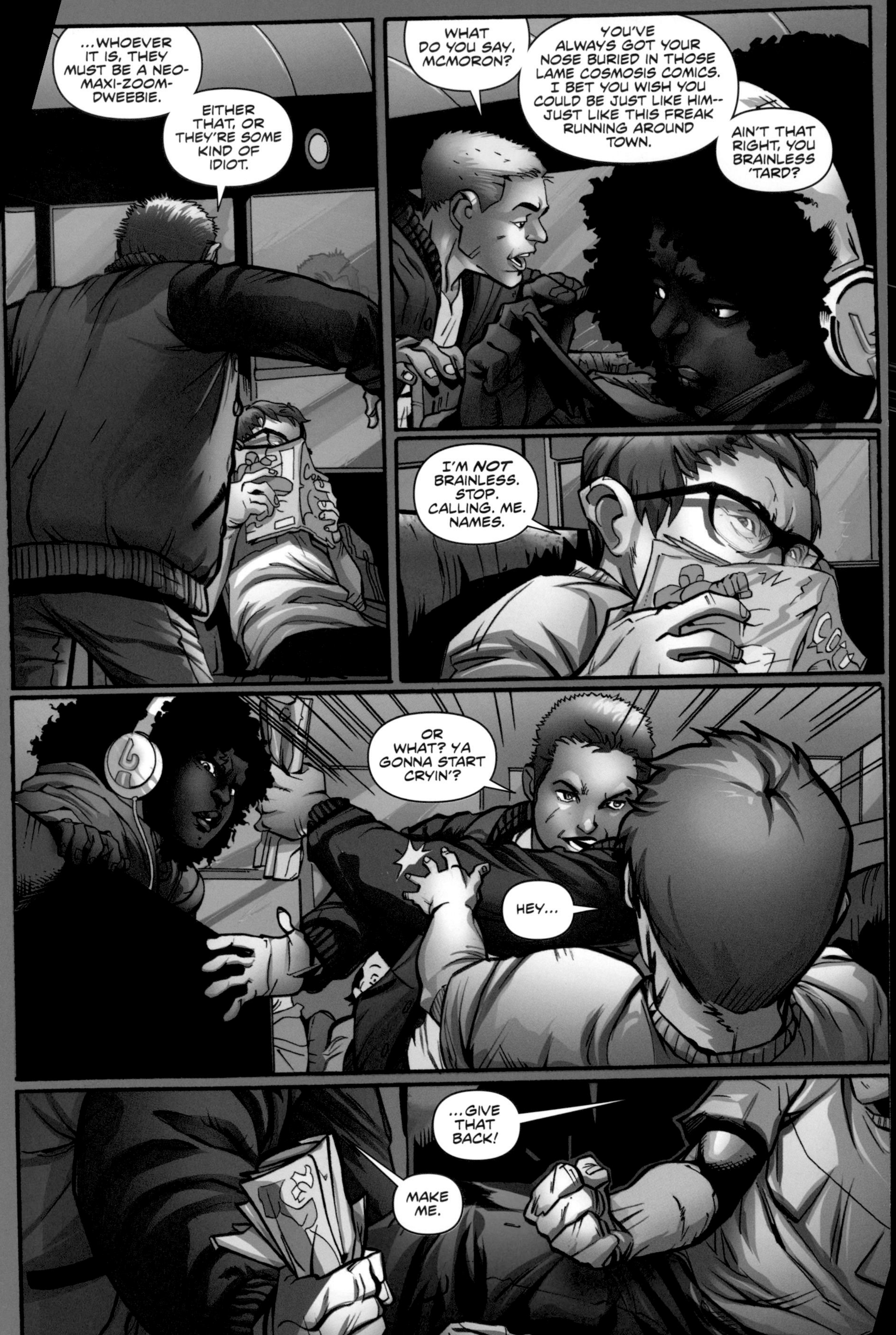
...WHOEVER IT IS, THEY MUST BE A NEO-MAXI-ZOOM-DWEEBIE.
EITHER THAT, OR THEY'RE SOME KIND OF IDIOT.
WHAT DO YOU SAY, MCMORON?
YOU'VE ALWAYS GOT YOUR NOSE BURIED IN THOSE LAME COSMOSIS COMICS. I BET YOU WISH YOU COULD BE JUST LIKE HIM-- JUST LIKE THIS FREAK RUNNING AROUND TOWN.
AIN'T THAT RIGHT, YOU BRAINLESS 'TARD?
I'M *NOT* BRAINLESS. STOP. CALLING. ME. NAMES.
OR WHAT? YA GONNA START CRYIN'?
HEY...
...GIVE THAT BACK!
MAKE ME.

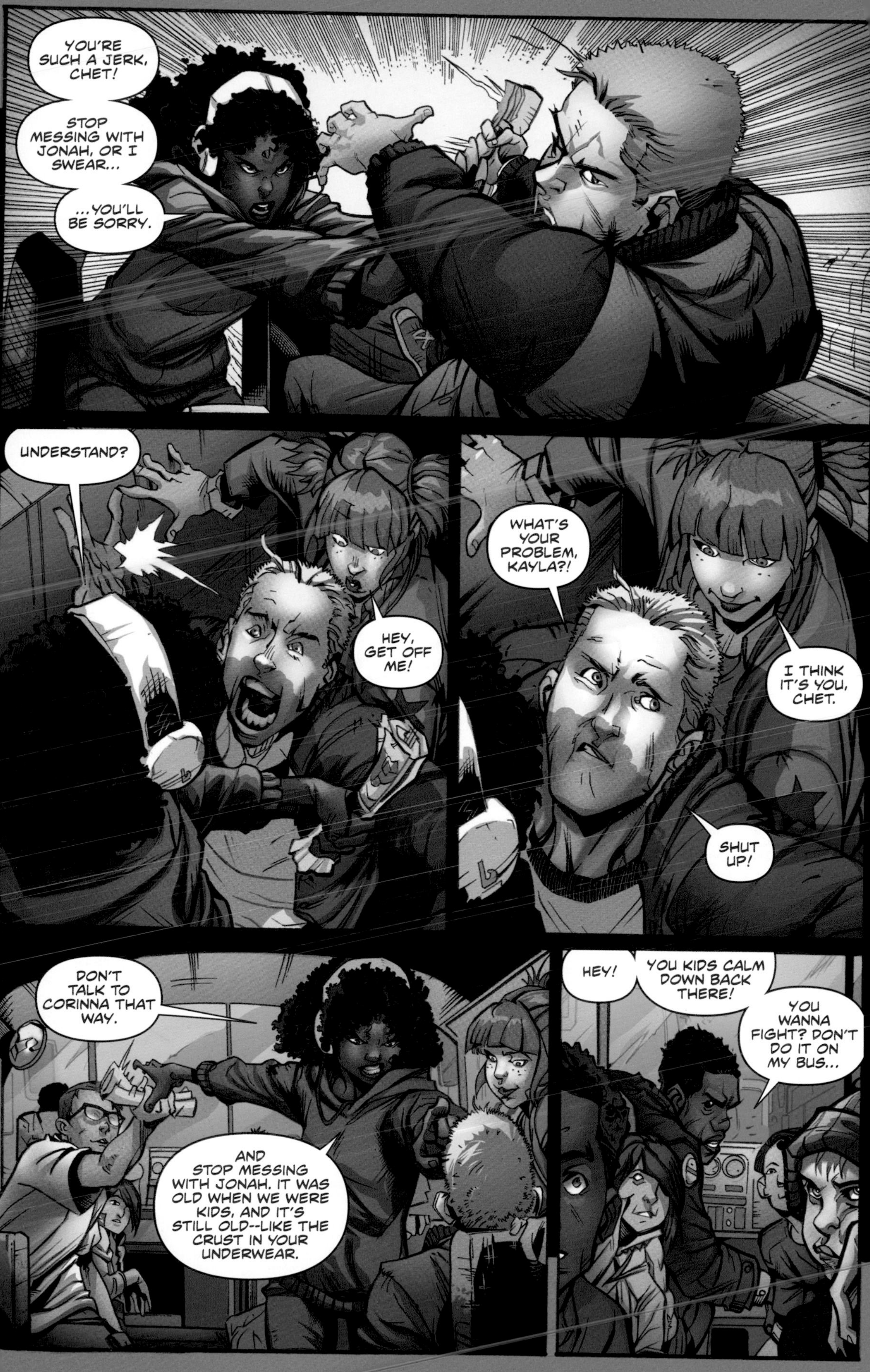
YOU'RE SUCH A JERK, CHET!
STOP MESSING WITH JONAH, OR I SWEAR...
...YOU'LL BE SORRY.
UNDERSTAND?
HEY, GET OFF ME!
WHAT'S YOUR PROBLEM, KAYLA?!
I THINK IT'S YOU, CHET.
SHUT UP!
DON'T TALK TO CORINNA THAT WAY.
AND STOP MESSING WITH JONAH. IT WAS OLD WHEN WE WERE KIDS, AND IT'S STILL OLD--LIKE THE CRUST IN YOUR UNDERWEAR.
HEY!
YOU KIDS CALM DOWN BACK THERE!
YOU WANNA FIGHT? DON'T DO IT ON MY BUS...

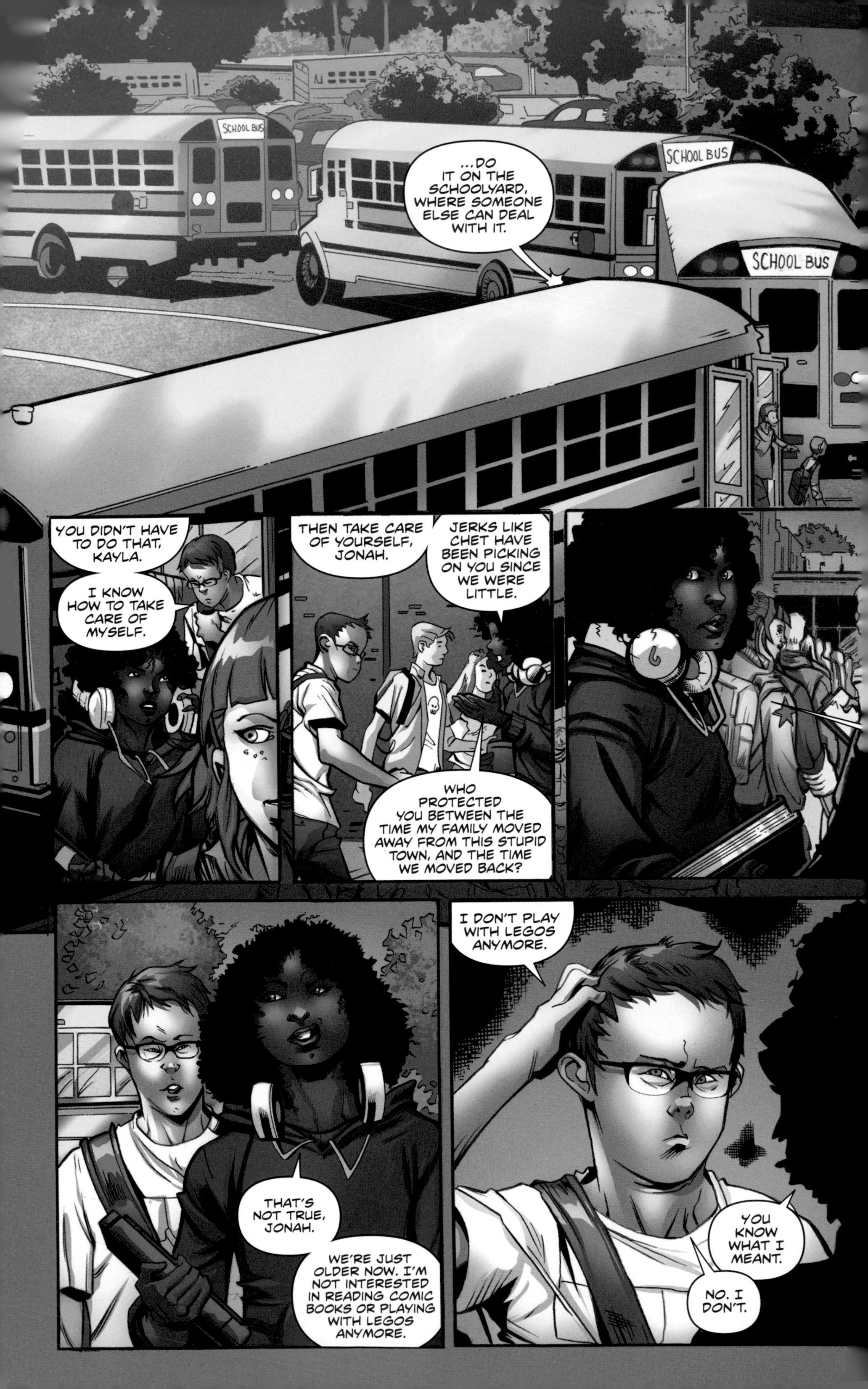
...DO IT ON THE SCHOOLYARD, WHERE SOMEONE ELSE CAN DEAL WITH IT.
SCHOOL BUS
SCHOOL BUS
SCHOOL BUS
YOU DIDN'T HAVE TO DO THAT, KAYLA.
I KNOW HOW TO TAKE CARE OF MYSELF.
THEN TAKE CARE OF YOURSELF, JONAH.
JERKS LIKE CHET HAVE BEEN PICKING ON YOU SINCE WE WERE LITTLE.
WHO PROTECTED YOU BETWEEN THE TIME MY FAMILY MOVED AWAY FROM THIS STUPID TOWN, AND THE TIME WE MOVED BACK?
THAT'S NOT TRUE, JONAH.
WE'RE JUST OLDER NOW. I'M NOT INTERESTED IN READING COMIC BOOKS OR PLAYING WITH LEGOS ANYMORE.
I DON'T PLAY WITH LEGOS ANYMORE.
YOU KNOW WHAT I MEANT.
NO. I DON'T.

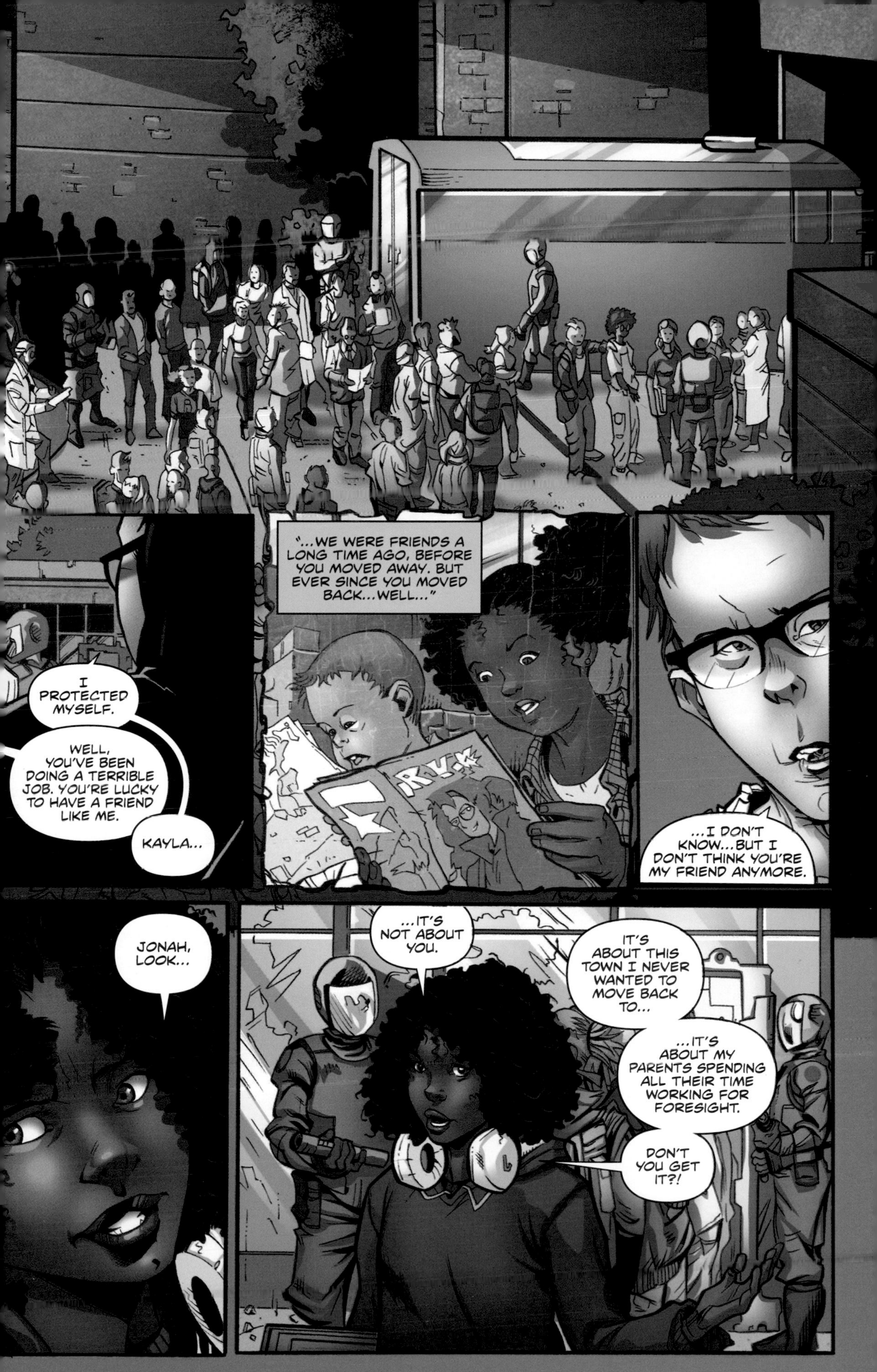
"...WE WERE FRIENDS A LONG TIME AGO, BEFORE YOU MOVED AWAY. BUT EVER SINCE YOU MOVED BACK...WELL..."
I PROTECTED MYSELF.
WELL, YOU'VE BEEN DOING A TERRIBLE JOB. YOU'RE LUCKY TO HAVE A FRIEND LIKE ME.
KAYLA...
...I DON'T KNOW...BUT I DON'T THINK YOU'RE MY FRIEND ANYMORE.
JONAH, LOOK...
...IT'S NOT ABOUT YOU.
IT'S ABOUT THIS TOWN I NEVER WANTED TO MOVE BACK TO...
...IT'S ABOUT MY PARENTS SPENDING ALL THEIR TIME WORKING FOR FORESIGHT.
DON'T YOU GET IT?!

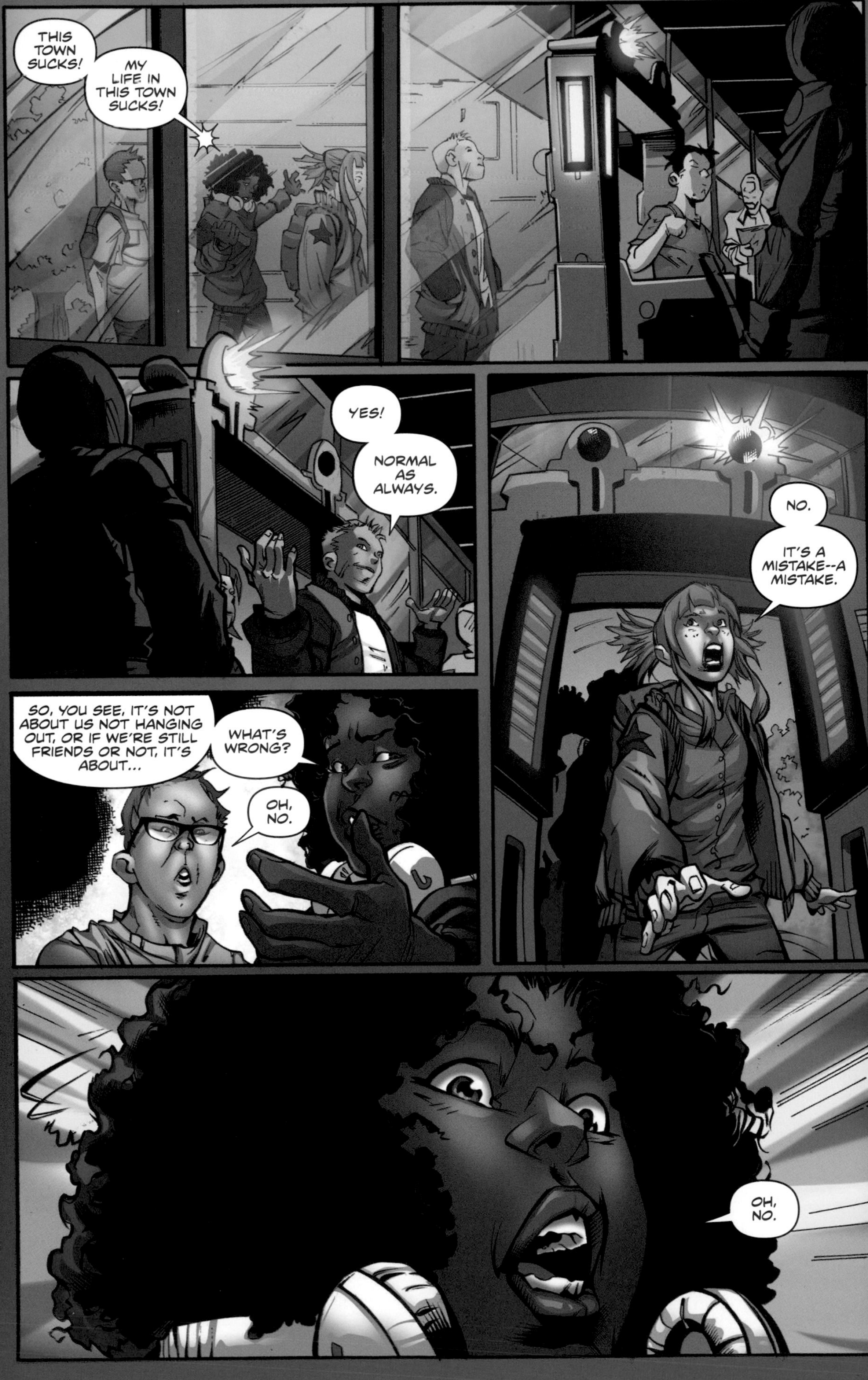
THIS TOWN SUCKS!
MY LIFE IN THIS TOWN SUCKS!
YES!
NORMAL AS ALWAYS.
NO.
IT'S A MISTAKE--A MISTAKE.
SO, YOU SEE, IT'S NOT ABOUT US NOT HANGING OUT, OR IF WE'RE STILL FRIENDS OR NOT, IT'S ABOUT...
WHAT'S WRONG?
OH, NO.
OH, NO.

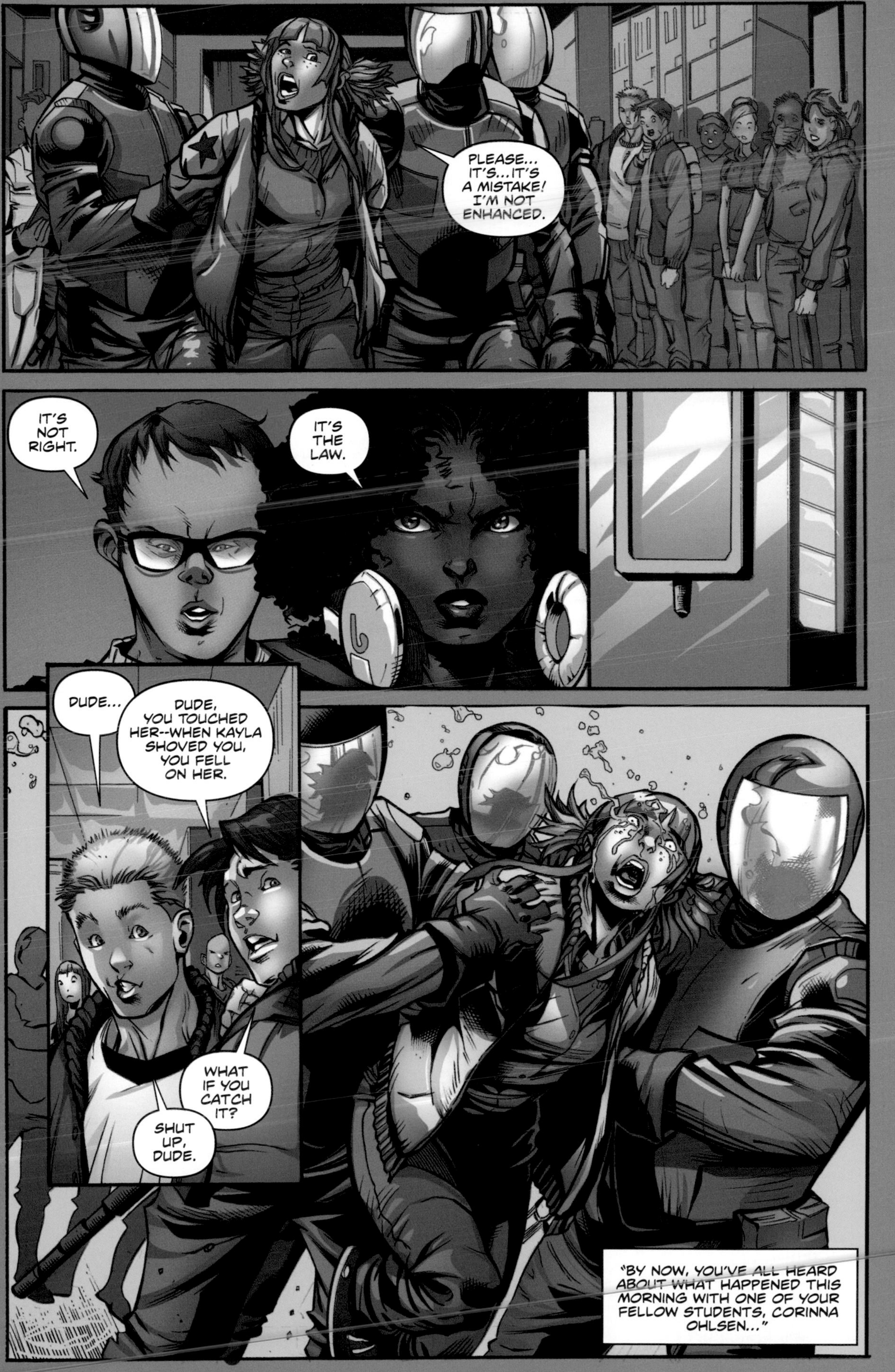
PLEASE... IT'S... IT'S A MISTAKE! I'M NOT ENHANCED.
IT'S NOT RIGHT.
IT'S THE LAW.
DUDE...
DUDE, YOU TOUCHED HER--WHEN KAYLA SHOVED YOU, YOU FELL ON HER.
WHAT IF YOU CATCH IT?
SHUT UP, DUDE.
"BY NOW, YOU'VE ALL HEARD ABOUT WHAT HAPPENED THIS MORNING WITH ONE OF YOUR FELLOW STUDENTS, CORINNA OHLSEN..."

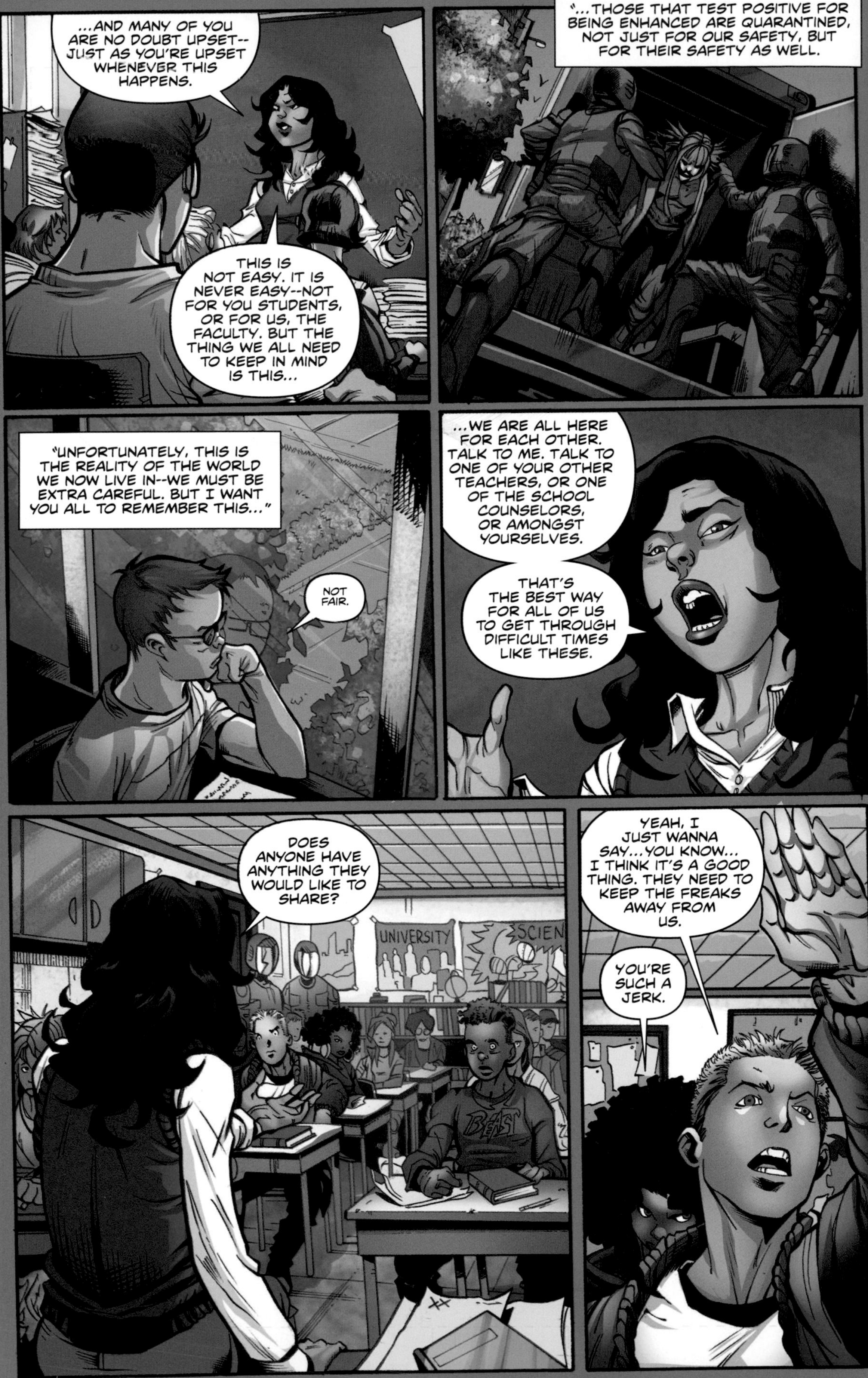
...AND MANY OF YOU ARE NO DOUBT UPSET--JUST AS YOU'RE UPSET WHENEVER THIS HAPPENS.
THIS IS NOT EASY. IT IS NEVER EASY--NOT FOR YOU STUDENTS, OR FOR US, THE FACULTY. BUT THE THING WE ALL NEED TO KEEP IN MIND IS THIS...
"...THOSE THAT TEST POSITIVE FOR BEING ENHANCED ARE QUARANTINED, NOT JUST FOR OUR SAFETY, BUT FOR THEIR SAFETY AS WELL.
"UNFORTUNATELY, THIS IS THE REALITY OF THE WORLD WE NOW LIVE IN--WE MUST BE EXTRA CAREFUL. BUT I WANT YOU ALL TO REMEMBER THIS..."
NOT FAIR.
...WE ARE ALL HERE FOR EACH OTHER. TALK TO ME. TALK TO ONE OF YOUR OTHER TEACHERS, OR ONE OF THE SCHOOL COUNSELORS, OR AMONGST YOURSELVES.
THAT'S THE BEST WAY FOR ALL OF US TO GET THROUGH DIFFICULT TIMES LIKE THESE.
DOES ANYONE HAVE ANYTHING THEY WOULD LIKE TO SHARE?
UNIVERSITY
YEAH, I JUST WANNA SAY...YOU KNOW... I THINK IT'S A GOOD THING. THEY NEED TO KEEP THE FREAKS AWAY FROM US.
YOU'RE SUCH A JERK.

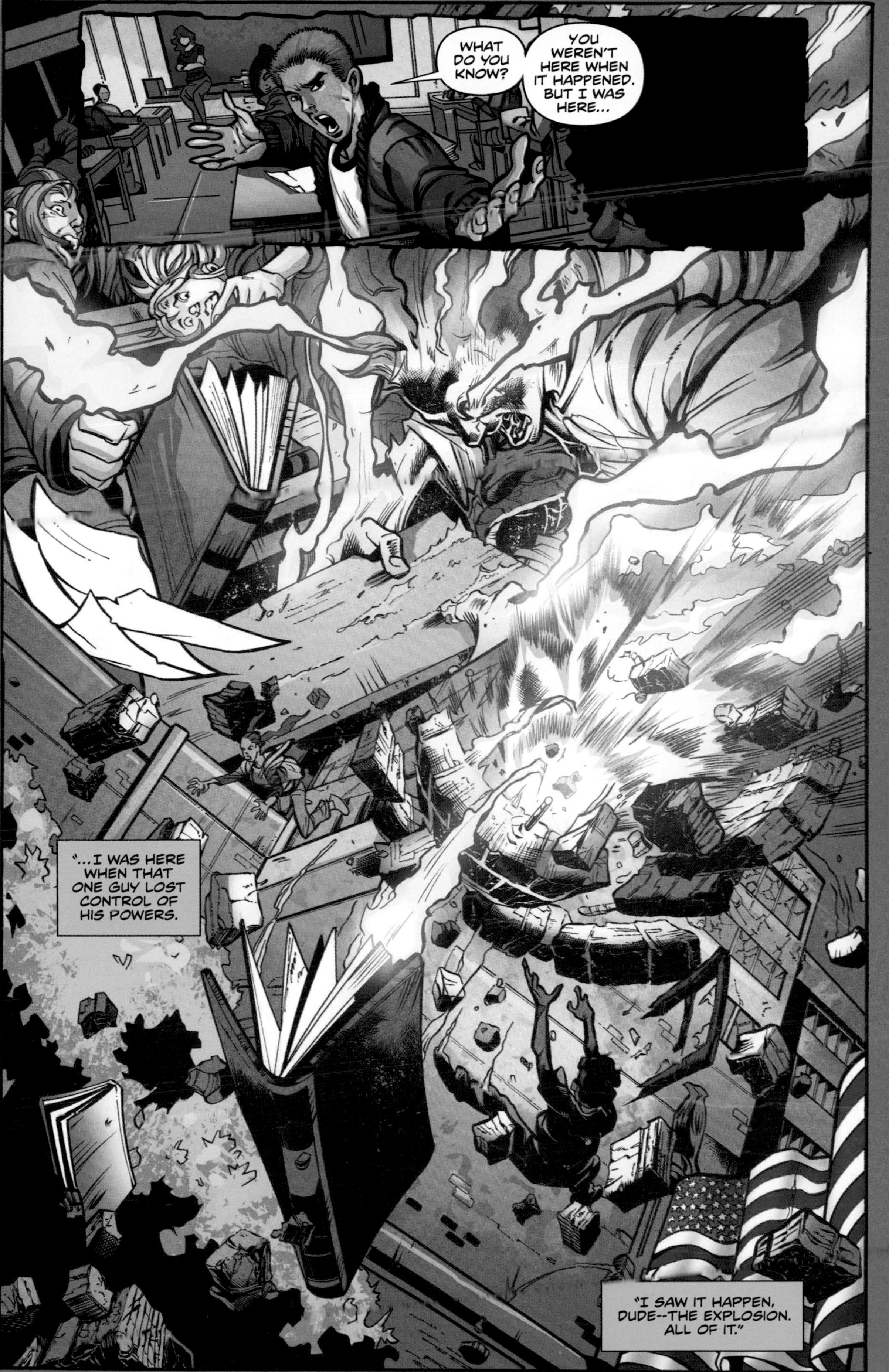
WHAT DO YOU KNOW?
YOU WEREN'T HERE WHEN IT HAPPENED. BUT I WAS HERE...
"...I WAS HERE WHEN THAT ONE GUY LOST CONTROL OF HIS POWERS.
"I SAW IT HAPPEN, DUDE--THE EXPLOSION. ALL OF IT."

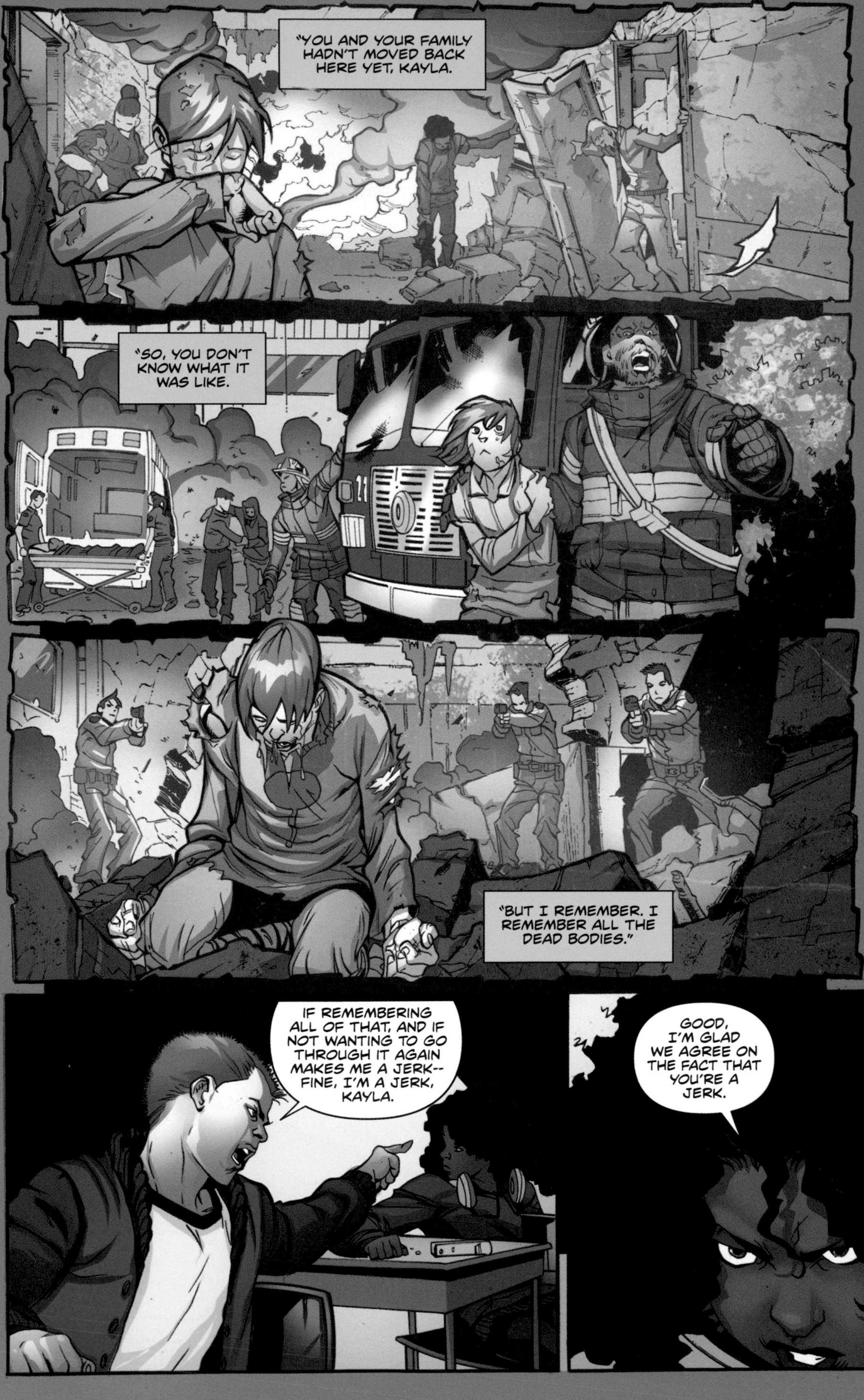
"YOU AND YOUR FAMILY HADN'T MOVED BACK HERE YET, KAYLA.
"SO, YOU DON'T KNOW WHAT IT WAS LIKE.
"BUT I REMEMBER. I REMEMBER ALL THE DEAD BODIES."
IF REMEMBERING ALL OF THAT, AND IF NOT WANTING TO GO THROUGH IT AGAIN MAKES ME A JERK-- FINE, I'M A JERK, KAYLA.
GOOD, I'M GLAD WE AGREE ON THE FACT THAT YOU'RE A JERK.

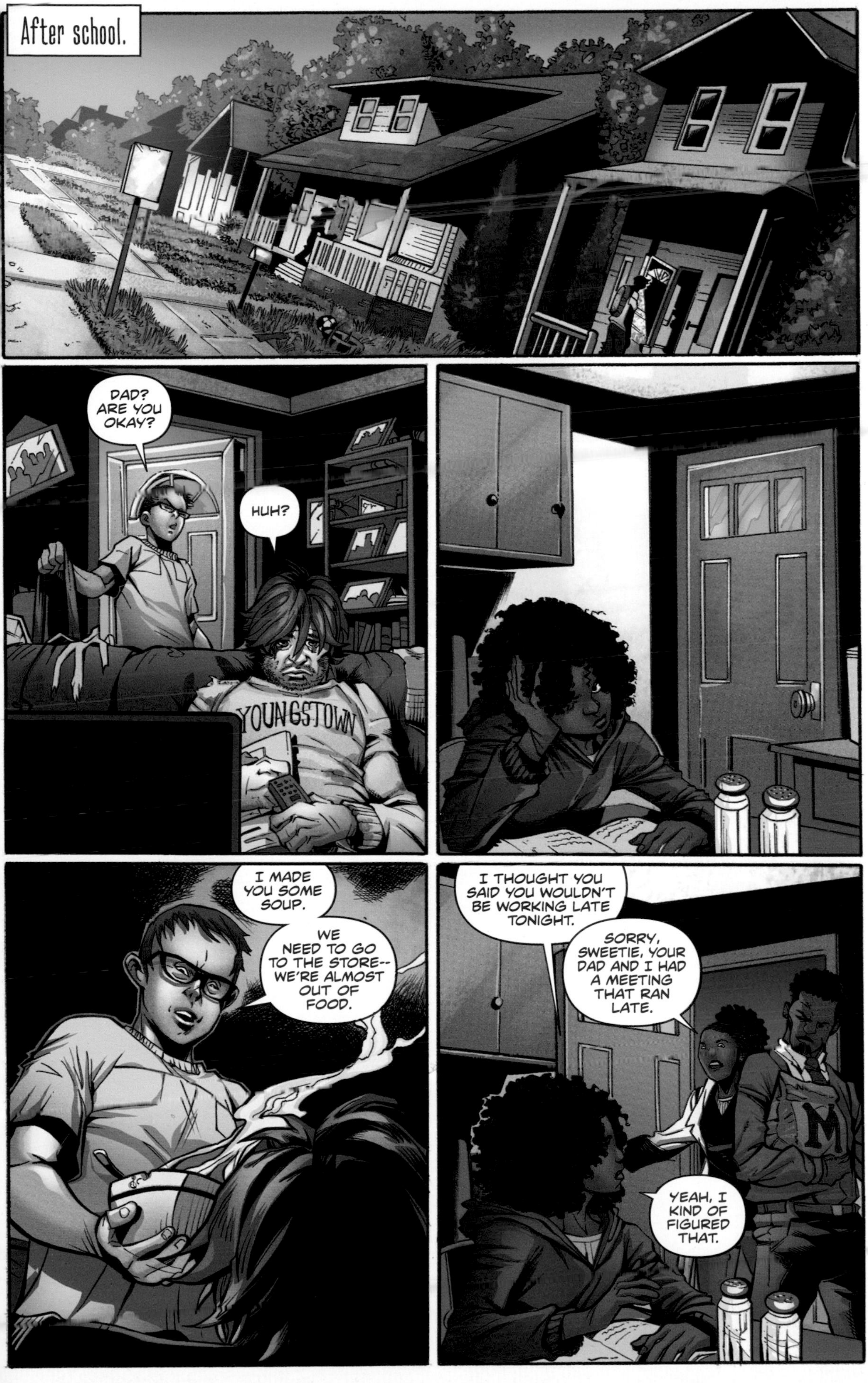
After school.
DAD? ARE YOU OKAY?
HUH?
YOUNGSTOWN
I MADE YOU SOME SOUP.
WE NEED TO GO TO THE STORE-- WE'RE ALMOST OUT OF FOOD.
I THOUGHT YOU SAID YOU WOULDN'T BE WORKING LATE TONIGHT.
SORRY, SWEETIE, YOUR DAD AND I HAD A MEETING THAT RAN LATE.
YEAH, I KIND OF FIGURED THAT.

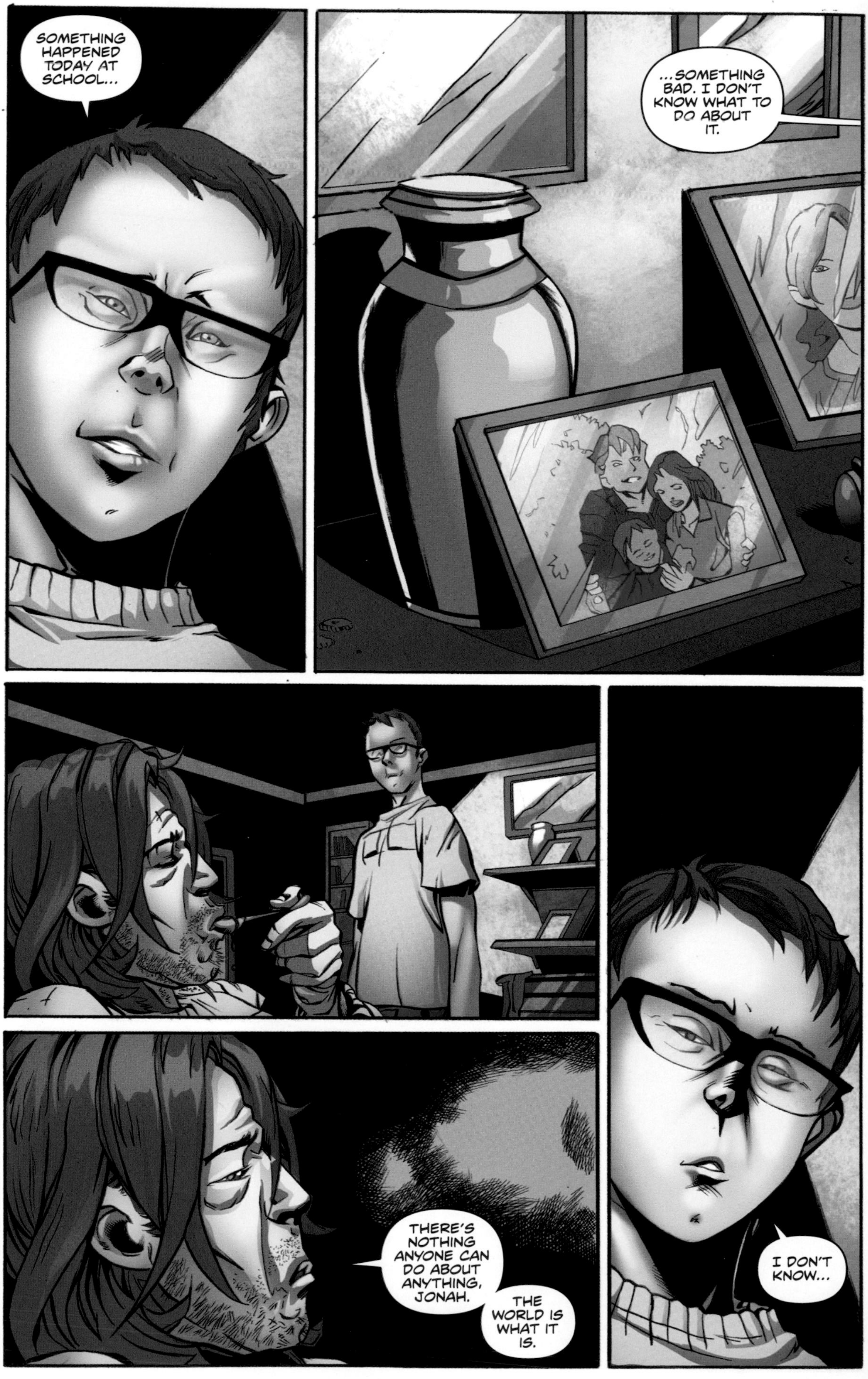
SOMETHING HAPPENED TODAY AT SCHOOL...
...SOMETHING BAD. I DON'T KNOW WHAT TO DO ABOUT IT.
THERE'S NOTHING ANYONE CAN DO ABOUT ANYTHING, JONAH.
THE WORLD IS WHAT IT IS.
I DON'T KNOW...

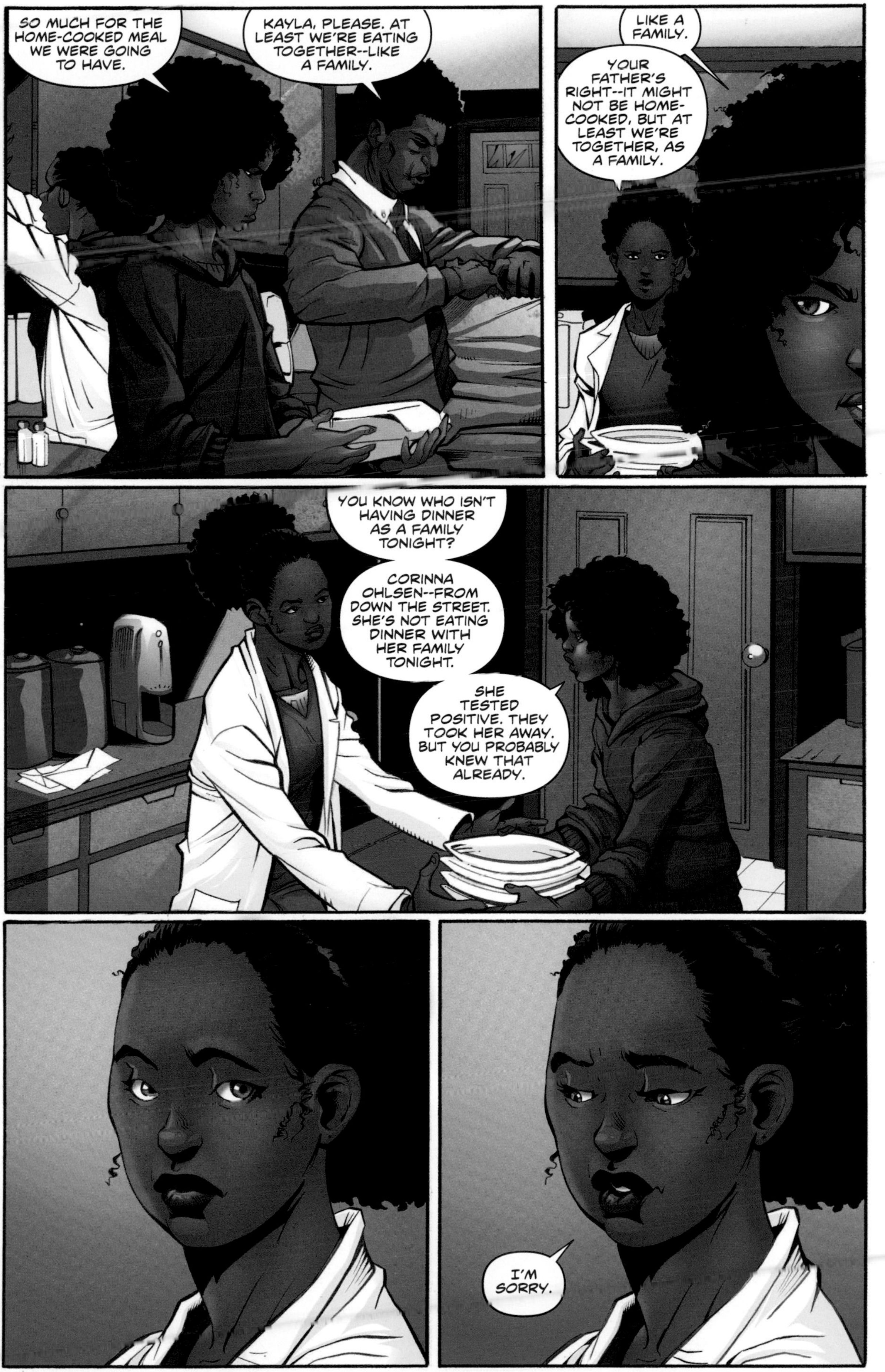
SO MUCH FOR THE HOME-COOKED MEAL WE WERE GOING TO HAVE.
KAYLA, PLEASE. AT LEAST WE'RE EATING TOGETHER--LIKE A FAMILY.
LIKE A FAMILY.
YOUR FATHER'S RIGHT--IT MIGHT NOT BE HOME-COOKED, BUT AT LEAST WE'RE TOGETHER, AS A FAMILY.
YOU KNOW WHO ISN'T HAVING DINNER AS A FAMILY TONIGHT?
CORINNA OHLSEN--FROM DOWN THE STREET. SHE'S NOT EATING DINNER WITH HER FAMILY TONIGHT.
SHE TESTED POSITIVE. THEY TOOK HER AWAY. BUT YOU PROBABLY KNEW THAT ALREADY.
I'M SORRY.

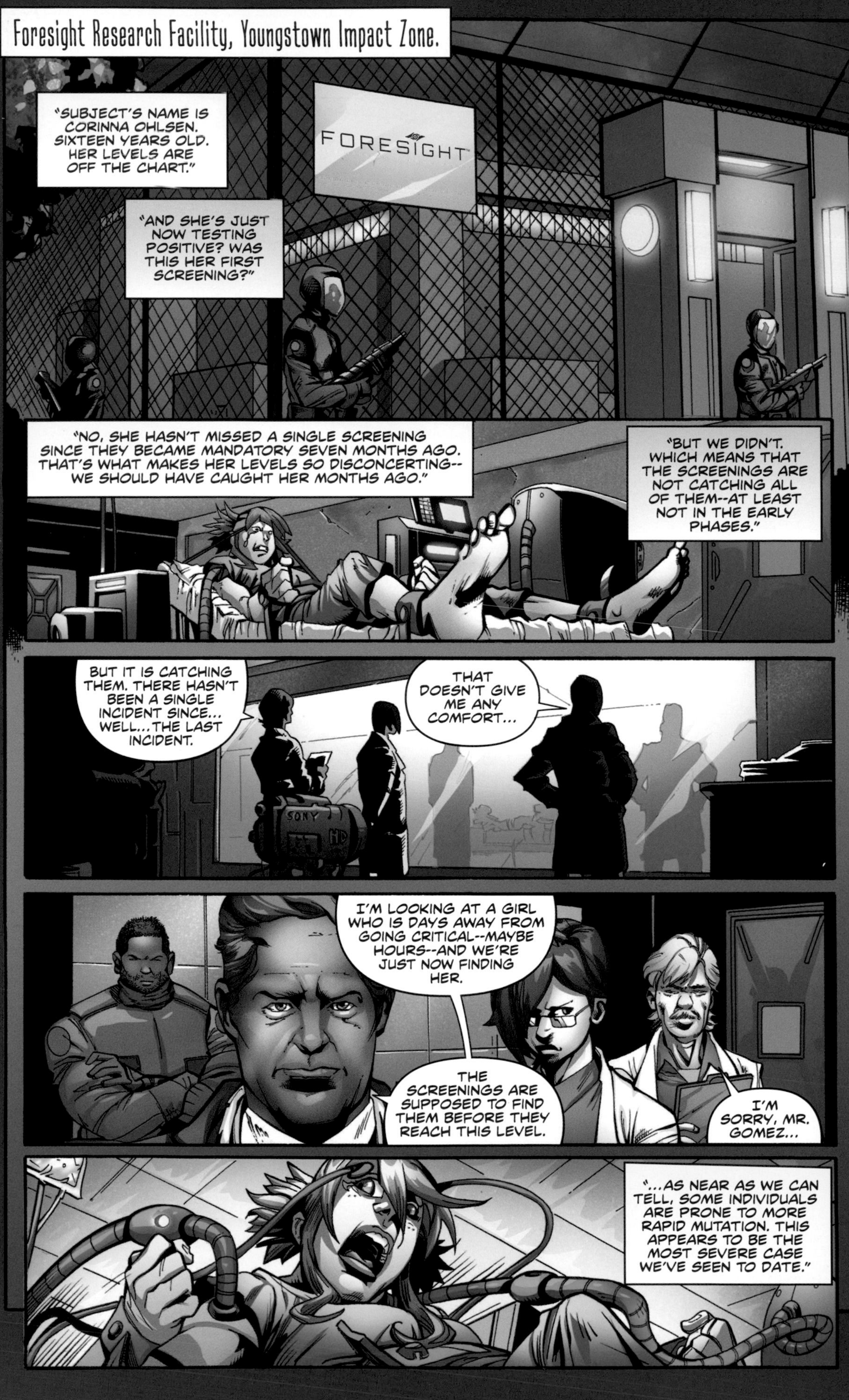
Foresight Research Facility, Youngstown Impact Zone.
"SUBJECT'S NAME IS CORINNA OHLSEN. SIXTEEN YEARS OLD. HER LEVELS ARE OFF THE CHART."
FORESIGHT
"AND SHE'S JUST NOW TESTING POSITIVE? WAS THIS HER FIRST SCREENING?"
"NO, SHE HASN'T MISSED A SINGLE SCREENING SINCE THEY BECAME MANDATORY SEVEN MONTHS AGO. THAT'S WHAT MAKES HER LEVELS SO DISCONCERTING-- WE SHOULD HAVE CAUGHT HER MONTHS AGO."
"BUT WE DIDN'T. WHICH MEANS THAT THE SCREENINGS ARE NOT CATCHING ALL OF THEM--AT LEAST NOT IN THE EARLY PHASES."
BUT IT IS CATCHING THEM. THERE HASN'T BEEN A SINGLE INCIDENT SINCE... WELL...THE LAST INCIDENT.
THAT DOESN'T GIVE ME ANY COMFORT...
SONY
HD
I'M LOOKING AT A GIRL WHO IS DAYS AWAY FROM GOING CRITICAL--MAYBE HOURS--AND WE'RE JUST NOW FINDING HER.
THE SCREENINGS ARE SUPPOSED TO FIND THEM BEFORE THEY REACH THIS LEVEL.
I'M SORRY, MR. GOMEZ...
"...AS NEAR AS WE CAN TELL, SOME INDIVIDUALS ARE PRONE TO MORE RAPID MUTATION. THIS APPEARS TO BE THE MOST SEVERE CASE WE'VE SEEN TO DATE."

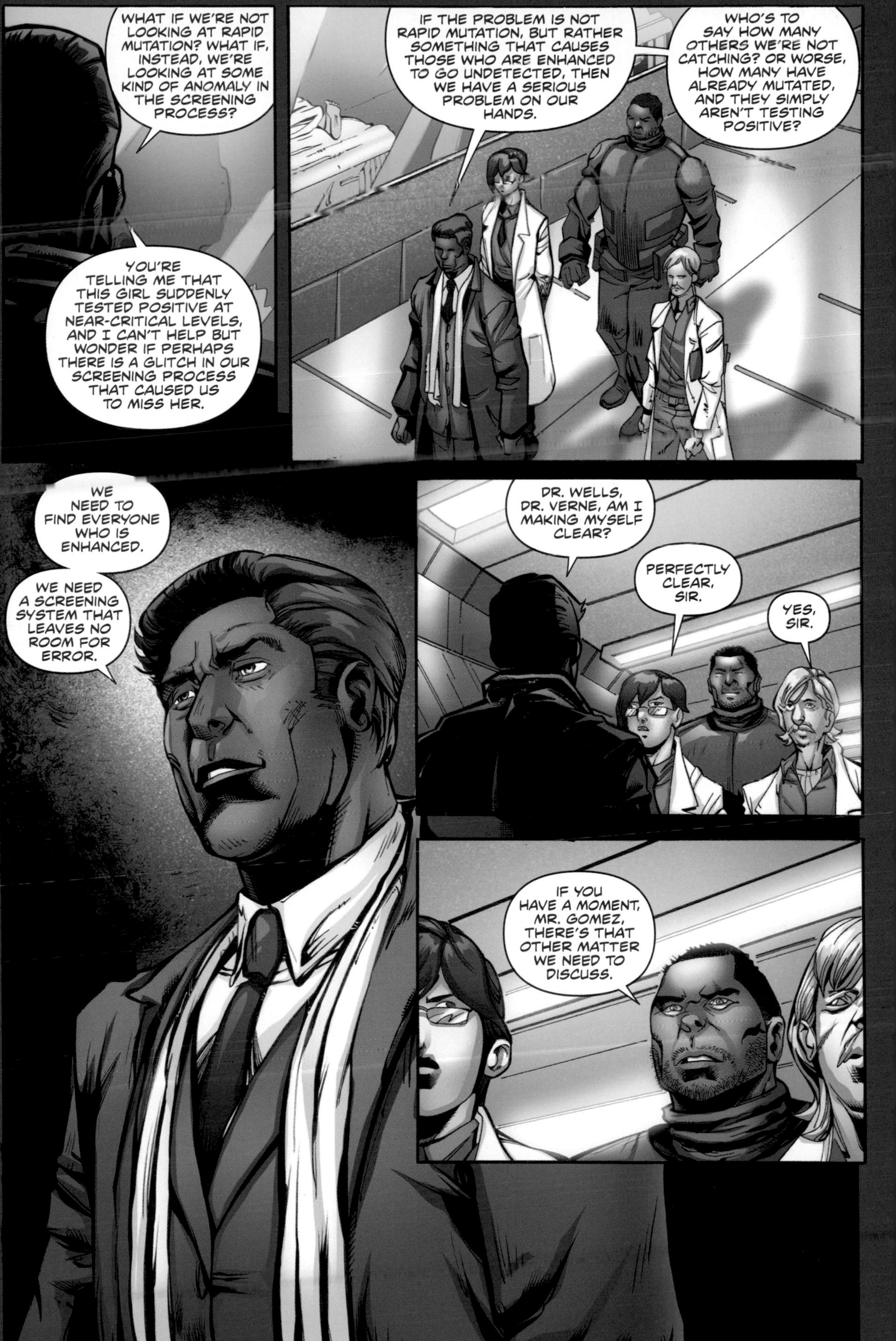
WHAT IF WE'RE NOT LOOKING AT RAPID MUTATION? WHAT IF, INSTEAD, WE'RE LOOKING AT SOME KIND OF ANOMALY IN THE SCREENING PROCESS?
YOU'RE TELLING ME THAT THIS GIRL SUDDENLY TESTED POSITIVE AT NEAR-CRITICAL LEVELS, AND I CAN'T HELP BUT WONDER IF PERHAPS THERE IS A GLITCH IN OUR SCREENING PROCESS THAT CAUSED US TO MISS HER.
IF THE PROBLEM IS NOT RAPID MUTATION, BUT RATHER SOMETHING THAT CAUSES THOSE WHO ARE ENHANCED TO GO UNDETECTED, THEN WE HAVE A SERIOUS PROBLEM ON OUR HANDS.
WHO'S TO SAY HOW MANY OTHERS WE'RE NOT CATCHING? OR WORSE, HOW MANY HAVE ALREADY MUTATED, AND THEY SIMPLY AREN'T TESTING POSITIVE?
WE NEED TO FIND EVERYONE WHO IS ENHANCED.
WE NEED A SCREENING SYSTEM THAT LEAVES NO ROOM FOR ERROR.
DR. WELLS, DR. VERNE, AM I MAKING MYSELF CLEAR?
PERFECTLY CLEAR, SIR.
YES, SIR.
IF YOU HAVE A MOMENT, MR. GOMEZ, THERE'S THAT OTHER MATTER WE NEED TO DISCUSS.

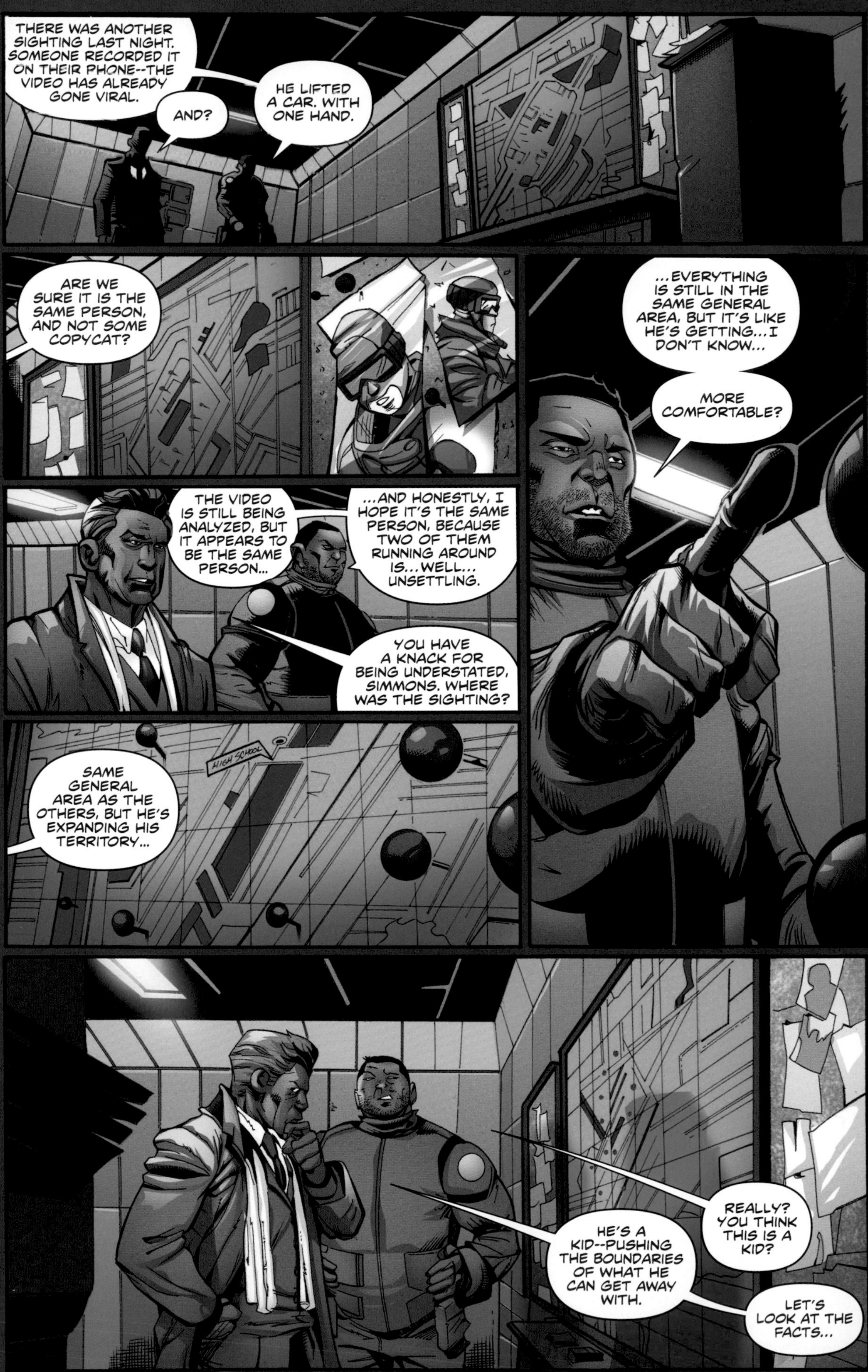
THERE WAS ANOTHER SIGHTING LAST NIGHT. SOMEONE RECORDED IT ON THEIR PHONE--THE VIDEO HAS ALREADY GONE VIRAL.
AND?
HE LIFTED A CAR. WITH ONE HAND.
ARE WE SURE IT IS THE SAME PERSON, AND NOT SOME COPYCAT?
THE VIDEO IS STILL BEING ANALYZED, BUT IT APPEARS TO BE THE SAME PERSON...
...AND HONESTLY, I HOPE IT'S THE SAME PERSON, BECAUSE TWO OF THEM RUNNING AROUND IS...WELL... UNSETTLING.
YOU HAVE A KNACK FOR BEING UNDERSTATED, SIMMONS. WHERE WAS THE SIGHTING?
HIGH SCHOOL
SAME GENERAL AREA AS THE OTHERS, BUT HE'S EXPANDING HIS TERRITORY...
...EVERYTHING IS STILL IN THE SAME GENERAL AREA, BUT IT'S LIKE HE'S GETTING...I DON'T KNOW...
MORE COMFORTABLE?
HE'S A KID--PUSHING THE BOUNDARIES OF WHAT HE CAN GET AWAY WITH.
REALLY? YOU THINK THIS IS A KID?
LET'S LOOK AT THE FACTS...

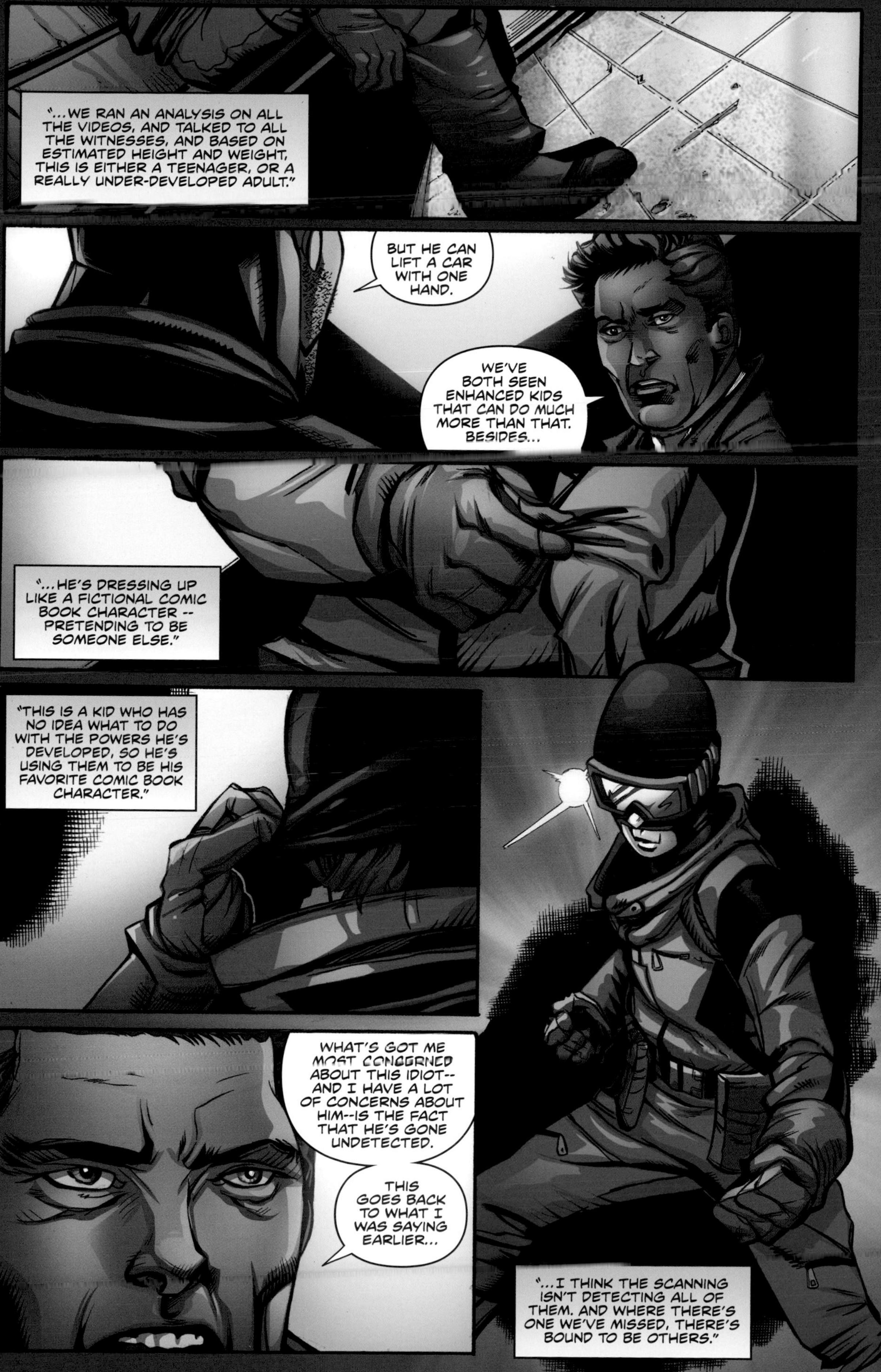
"...WE RAN AN ANALYSIS ON ALL THE VIDEOS, AND TALKED TO ALL THE WITNESSES, AND BASED ON ESTIMATED HEIGHT AND WEIGHT, THIS IS EITHER A TEENAGER, OR A REALLY UNDER-DEVELOPED ADULT."
BUT HE CAN LIFT A CAR WITH ONE HAND.
WE'VE BOTH SEEN ENHANCED KIDS THAT CAN DO MUCH MORE THAN THAT. BESIDES...
"...HE'S DRESSING UP LIKE A FICTIONAL COMIC BOOK CHARACTER -- PRETENDING TO BE SOMEONE ELSE."
"THIS IS A KID WHO HAS NO IDEA WHAT TO DO WITH THE POWERS HE'S DEVELOPED, SO HE'S USING THEM TO BE HIS FAVORITE COMIC BOOK CHARACTER."
WHAT'S GOT ME MOST CONCERNED ABOUT THIS IDIOT--AND I HAVE A LOT OF CONCERNS ABOUT HIM--IS THE FACT THAT HE'S GONE UNDETECTED.
THIS GOES BACK TO WHAT I WAS SAYING EARLIER...
"...I THINK THE SCANNING ISN'T DETECTING ALL OF THEM. AND WHERE THERE'S ONE WE'VE MISSED, THERE'S BOUND TO BE OTHERS."

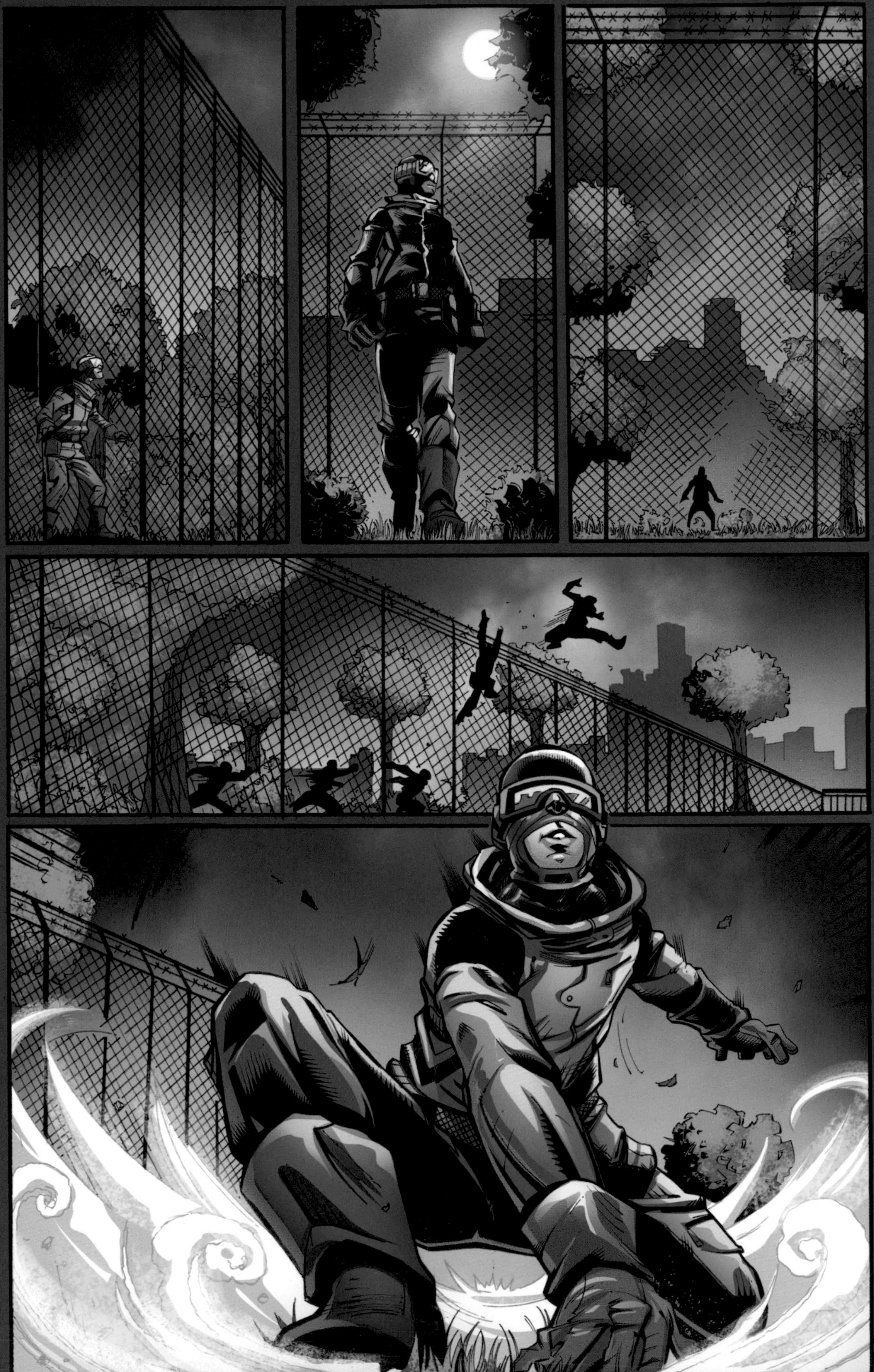

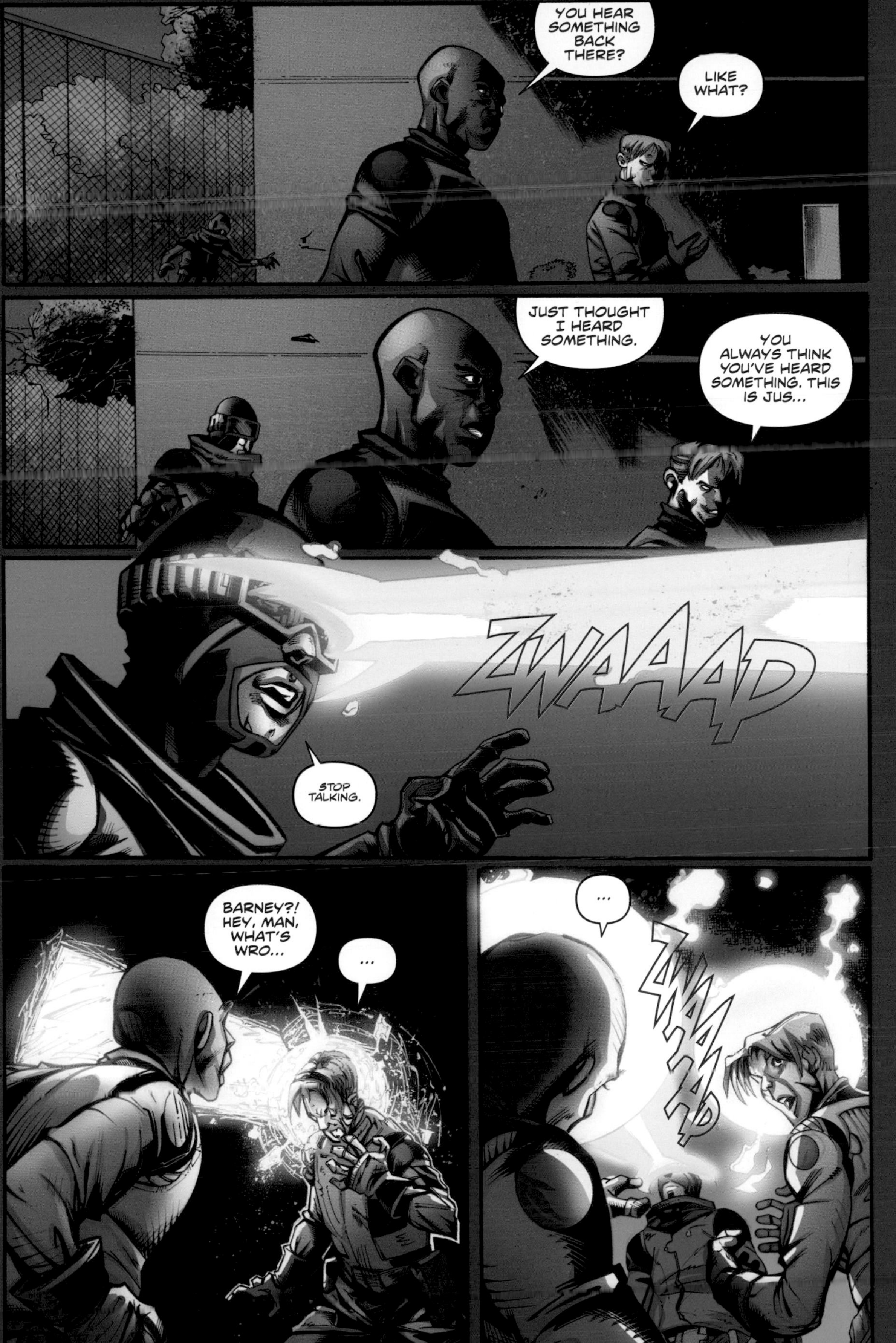

YOU HEAR SOMETHING BACK THERE?
LIKE WHAT?
JUST THOUGHT I HEARD SOMETHING.
YOU ALWAYS THINK YOU'VE HEARD SOMETHING. THIS IS JUS...
ZWAAAP
STOP TALKING.
BARNEY?! HEY, MAN, WHAT'S WRO...
...
...
ZWAAAAP

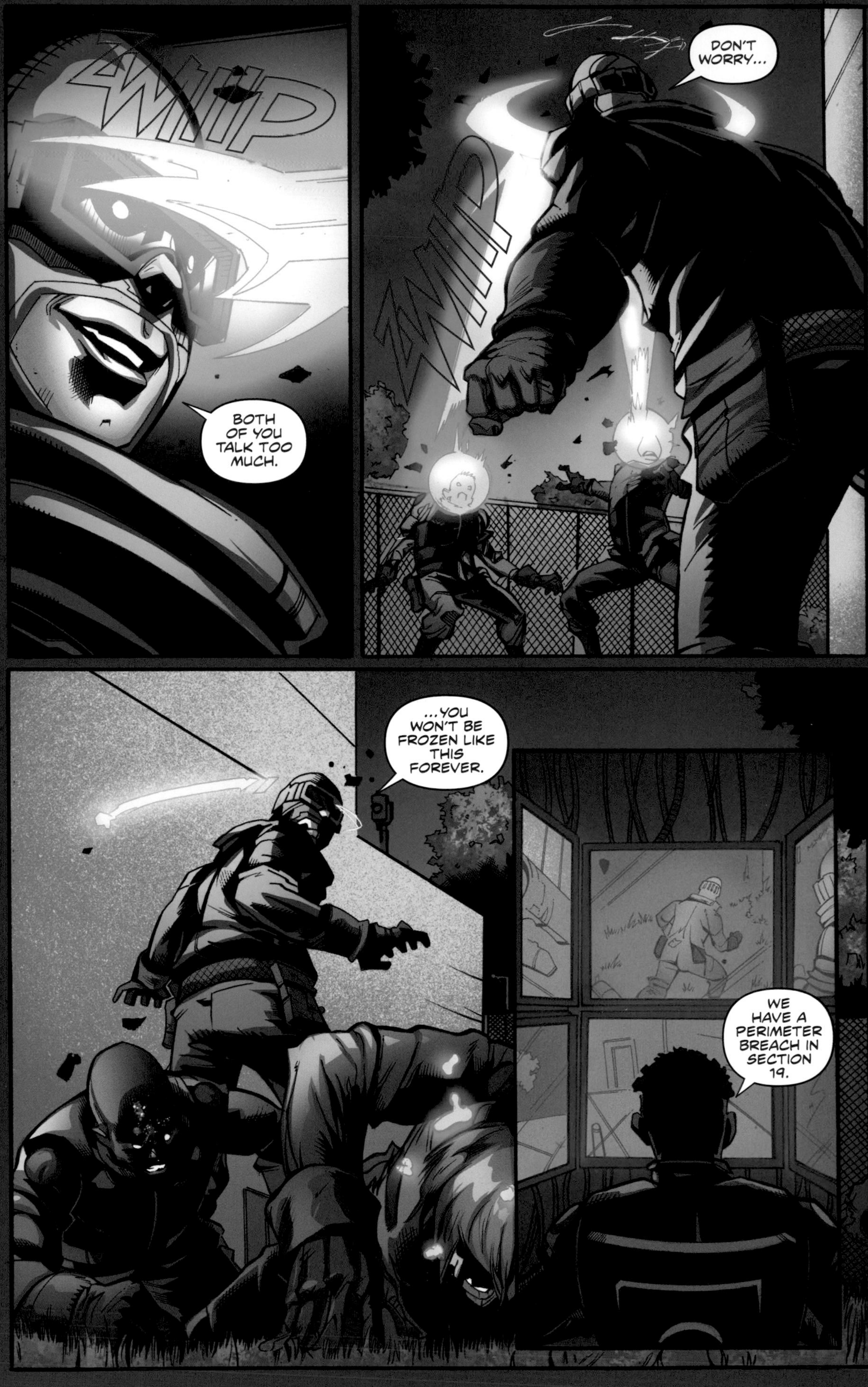
ZWIIP
BOTH OF YOU TALK TOO MUCH.
DON'T WORRY...
ZWIIP
...YOU WON'T BE FROZEN LIKE THIS FOREVER.
WE HAVE A PERIMETER BREACH IN SECTION 19.

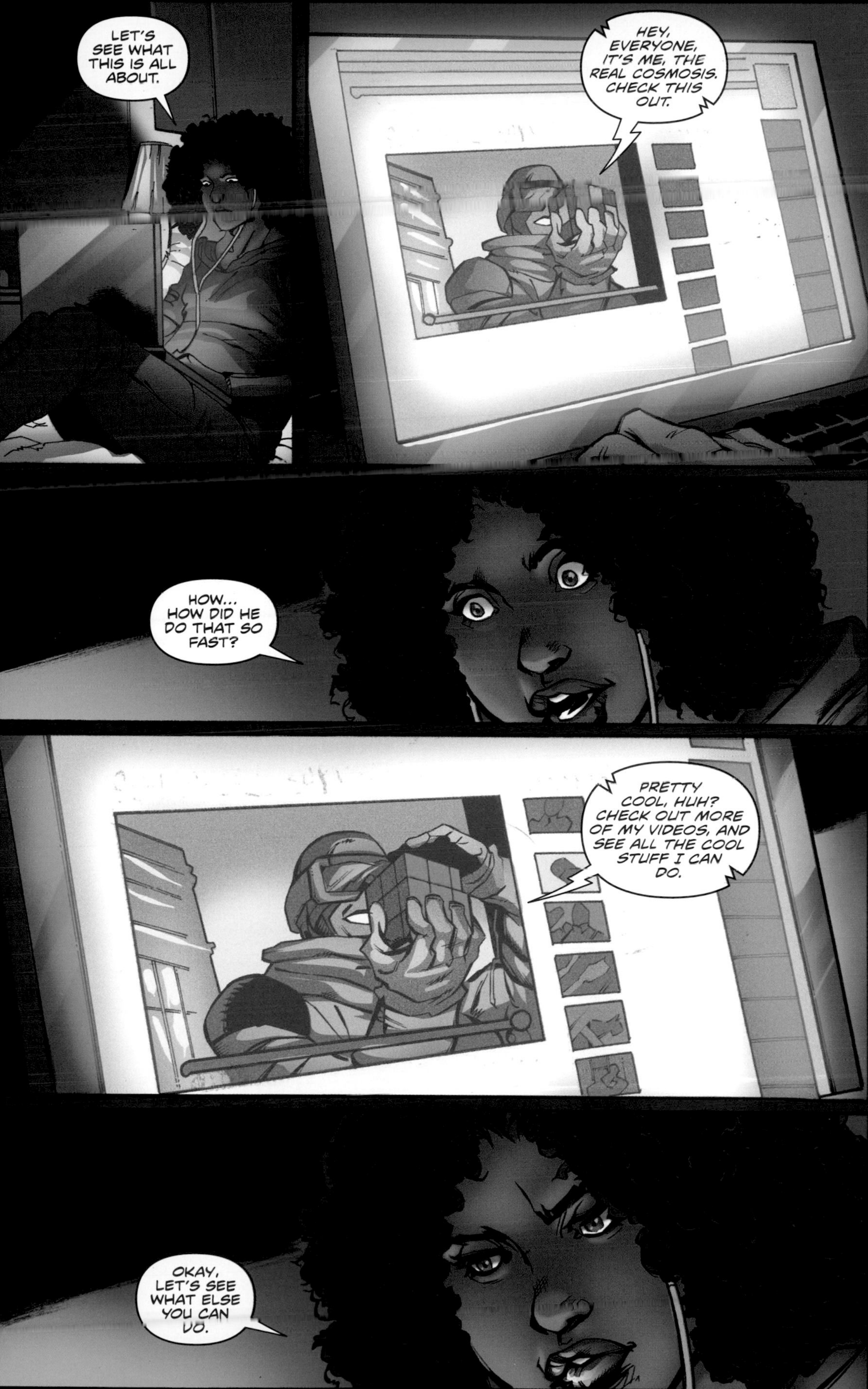
LET'S SEE WHAT THIS IS ALL ABOUT.
HEY, EVERYONE, IT'S ME, THE REAL COSMOSIS. CHECK THIS OUT.
HOW... HOW DID HE DO THAT SO FAST?
PRETTY COOL, HUH? CHECK OUT MORE OF MY VIDEOS, AND SEE ALL THE COOL STUFF I CAN DO.
OKAY, LET'S SEE WHAT ELSE YOU CAN DO.

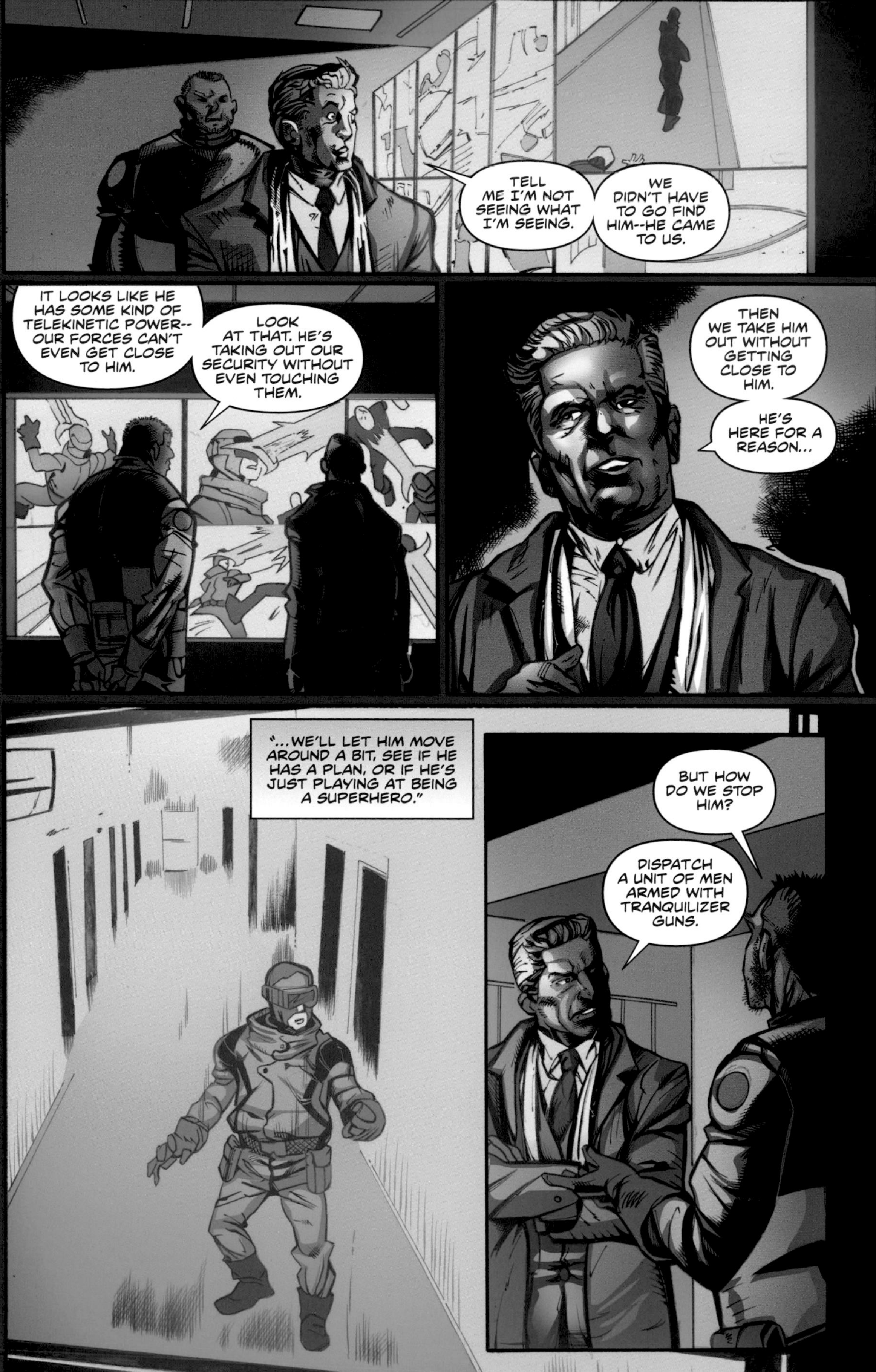
TELL ME I'M NOT SEEING WHAT I'M SEEING.
WE DIDN'T HAVE TO GO FIND HIM--HE CAME TO US.
IT LOOKS LIKE HE HAS SOME KIND OF TELEKINETIC POWER--OUR FORCES CAN'T EVEN GET CLOSE TO HIM.
LOOK AT THAT. HE'S TAKING OUT OUR SECURITY WITHOUT EVEN TOUCHING THEM.
THEN WE TAKE HIM OUT WITHOUT GETTING CLOSE TO HIM.
HE'S HERE FOR A REASON...
"...WE'LL LET HIM MOVE AROUND A BIT, SEE IF HE HAS A PLAN, OR IF HE'S JUST PLAYING AT BEING A SUPERHERO."
BUT HOW DO WE STOP HIM?
DISPATCH A UNIT OF MEN ARMED WITH TRANQUILIZER GUNS.

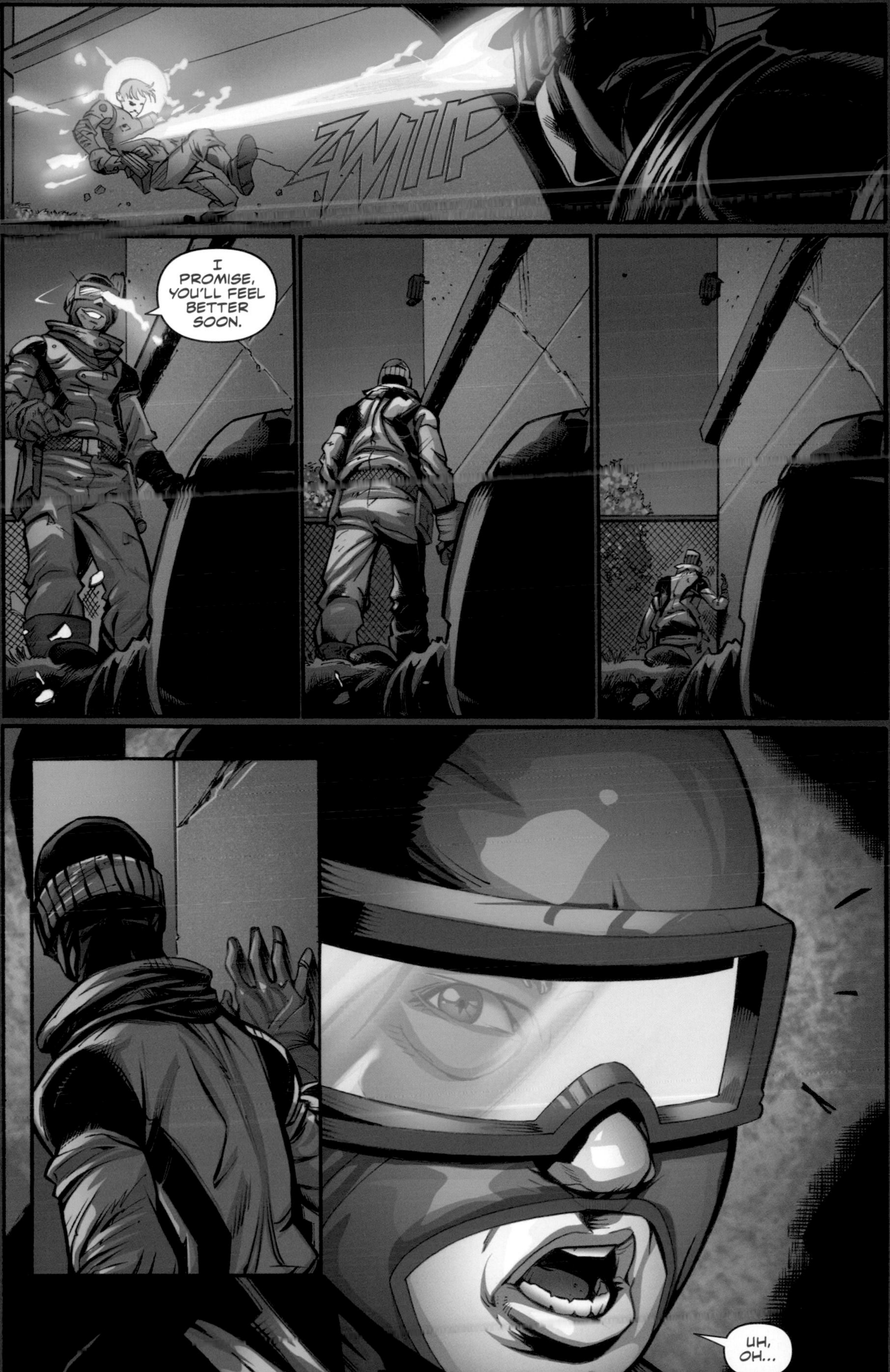
ZWIIP
I PROMISE, YOU'LL FEEL BETTER SOON.
UH, OH...

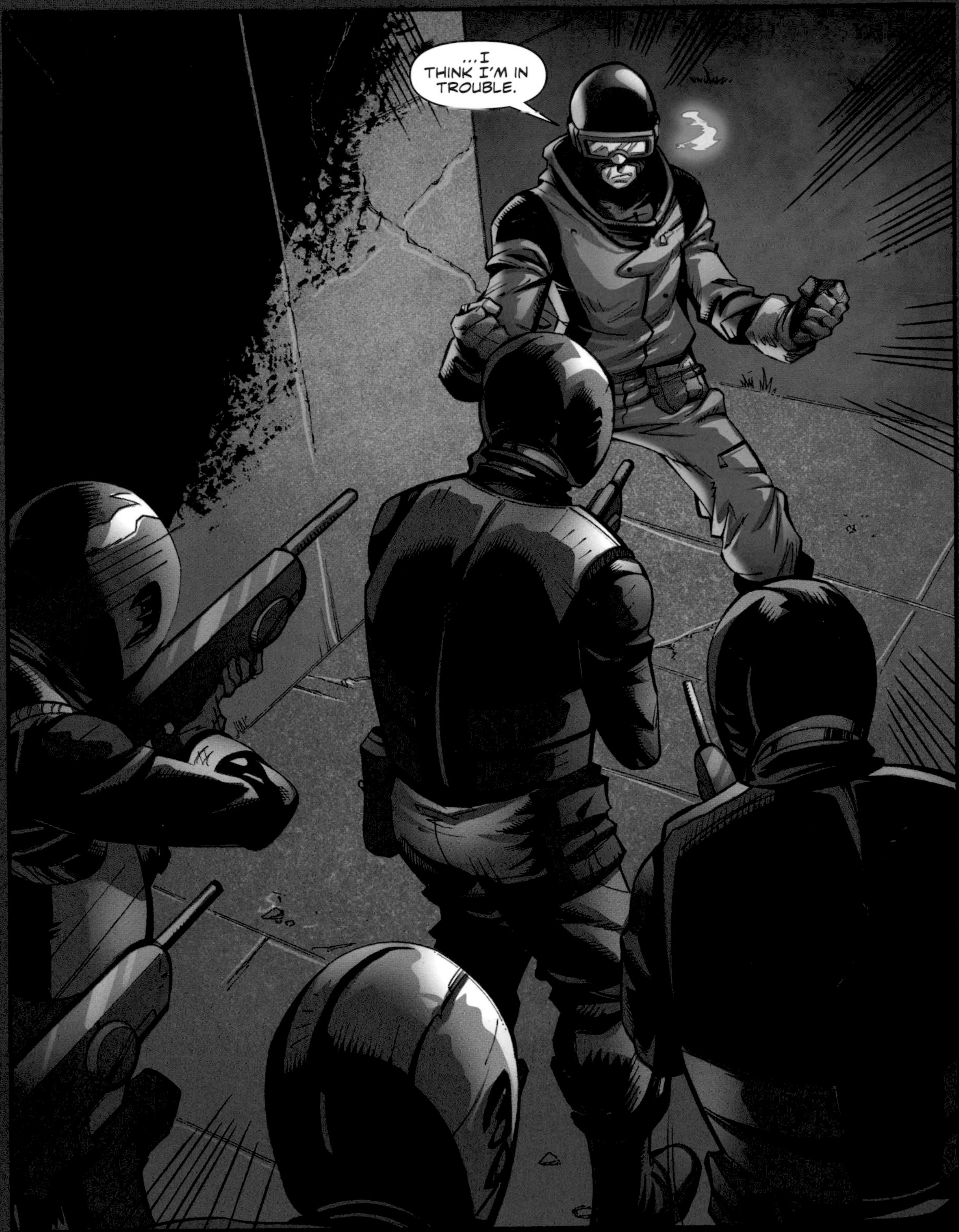
...I THINK I'M IN TROUBLE.

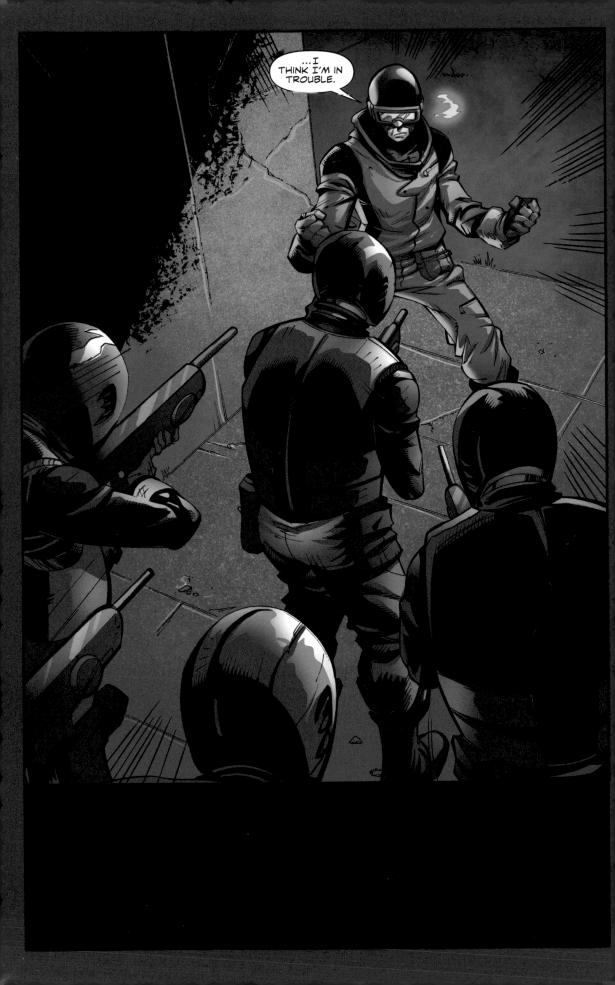

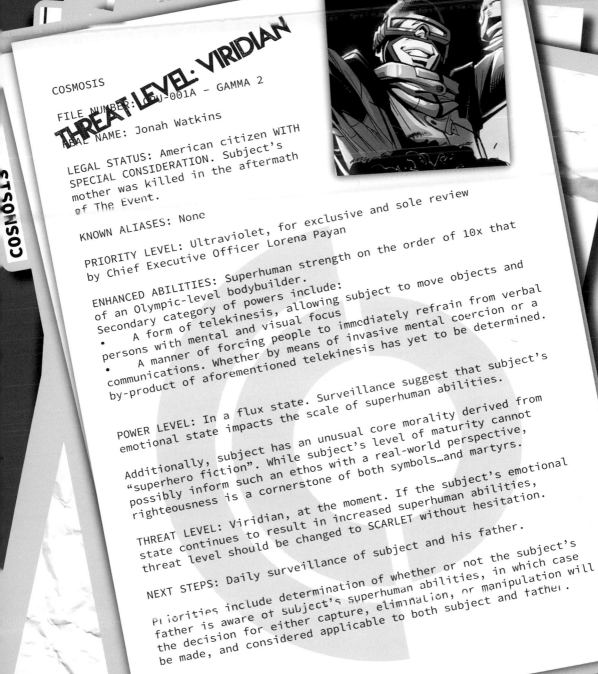

COSMOSIS

THREAT LEVEL: VIRIDIAN

FILE NUMBER: LCU-001A – GAMMA 2

REAL NAME: Jonah Watkins

LEGAL STATUS: American citizen WITH SPECIAL CONSIDERATION. Subject's mother was killed in the aftermath of The Event.

KNOWN ALIASES: None

PRIORITY LEVEL: Ultraviolet, for exclusive and sole review by Chief Executive Officer Lorena Payan

ENHANCED ABILITIES: Superhuman strength on the order of 10x that of an Olympic-level bodybuilder.
Secondary category of powers include:
• A form of telekinesis, allowing subject to move objects and persons with mental and visual focus
• A manner of forcing people to immediately refrain from verbal communications. Whether by means of invasive mental coercion or a by-product of aforementioned telekinesis has yet to be determined.

POWER LEVEL: In a flux state. Surveillance suggest that subject's emotional state impacts the scale of superhuman abilities.

Additionally, subject has an unusual core morality derived from "superhero fiction". While subject's level of maturity cannot possibly inform such an ethos with a real-world perspective, righteousness is a cornerstone of both symbols…and martyrs.

THREAT LEVEL: Viridian, at the moment. If the subject's emotional state continues to result in increased superhuman abilities, threat level should be changed to SCARLET without hesitation.

NEXT STEPS: Daily surveillance of subject and his father.

Priorities include determination of whether or not the subject's father is aware of subject's superhuman abilities, in which case the decision for either capture, elimination, or manipulation will be made, and considered applicable to both subject and father.

COSMOSIS

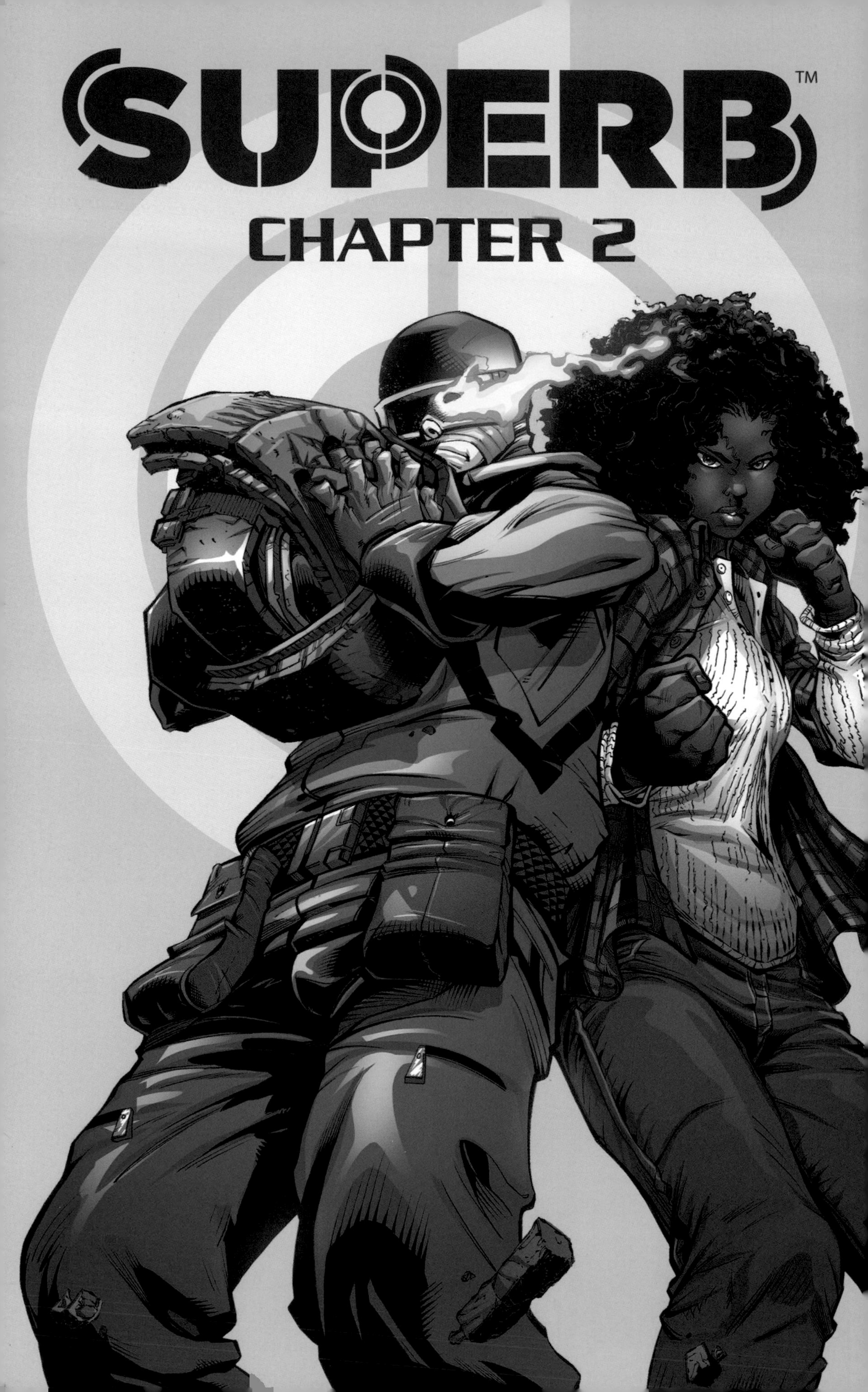
SUPERB™
CHAPTER 2

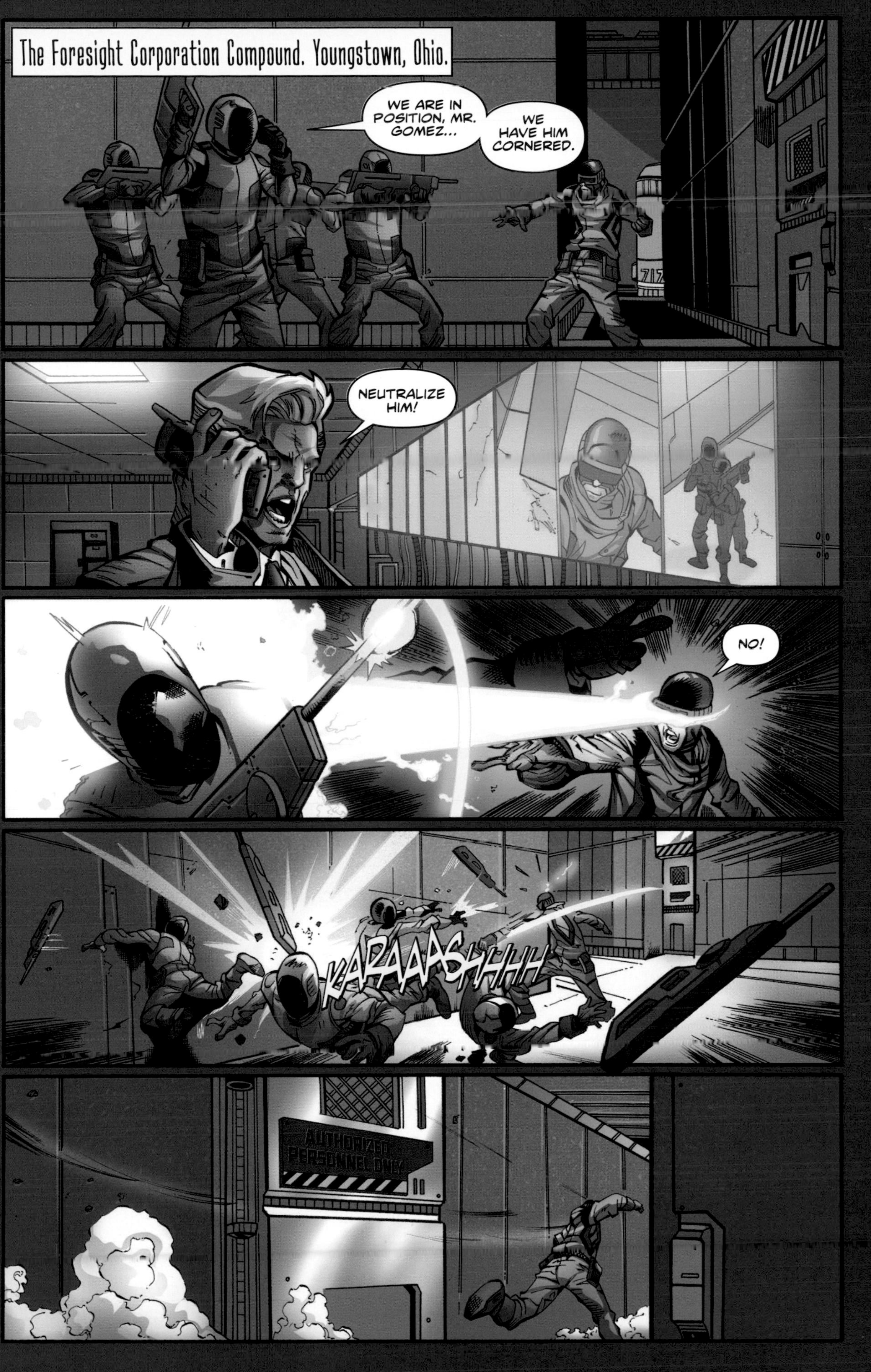

The Foresight Corporation Compound. Youngstown, Ohio.
WE ARE IN POSITION, MR. GOMEZ...
WE HAVE HIM CORNERED.
NEUTRALIZE HIM!
NO!
KARAAASHHHH
AUTHORIZED PERSONNEL ONLY

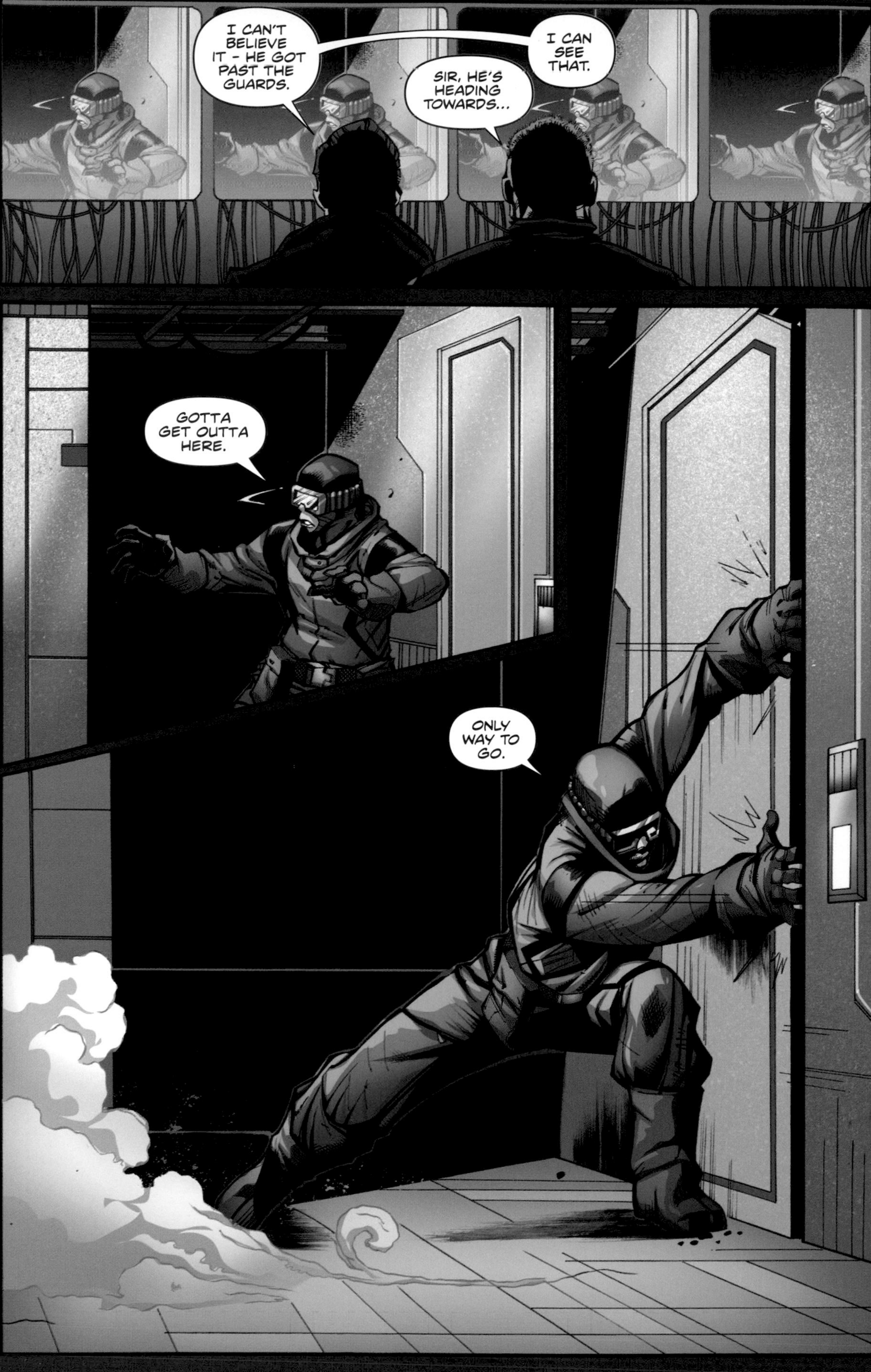
I CAN'T BELIEVE IT - HE GOT PAST THE GUARDS.
I CAN SEE THAT.
SIR, HE'S HEADING TOWARDS...
GOTTA GET OUTTA HERE.
ONLY WAY TO GO.

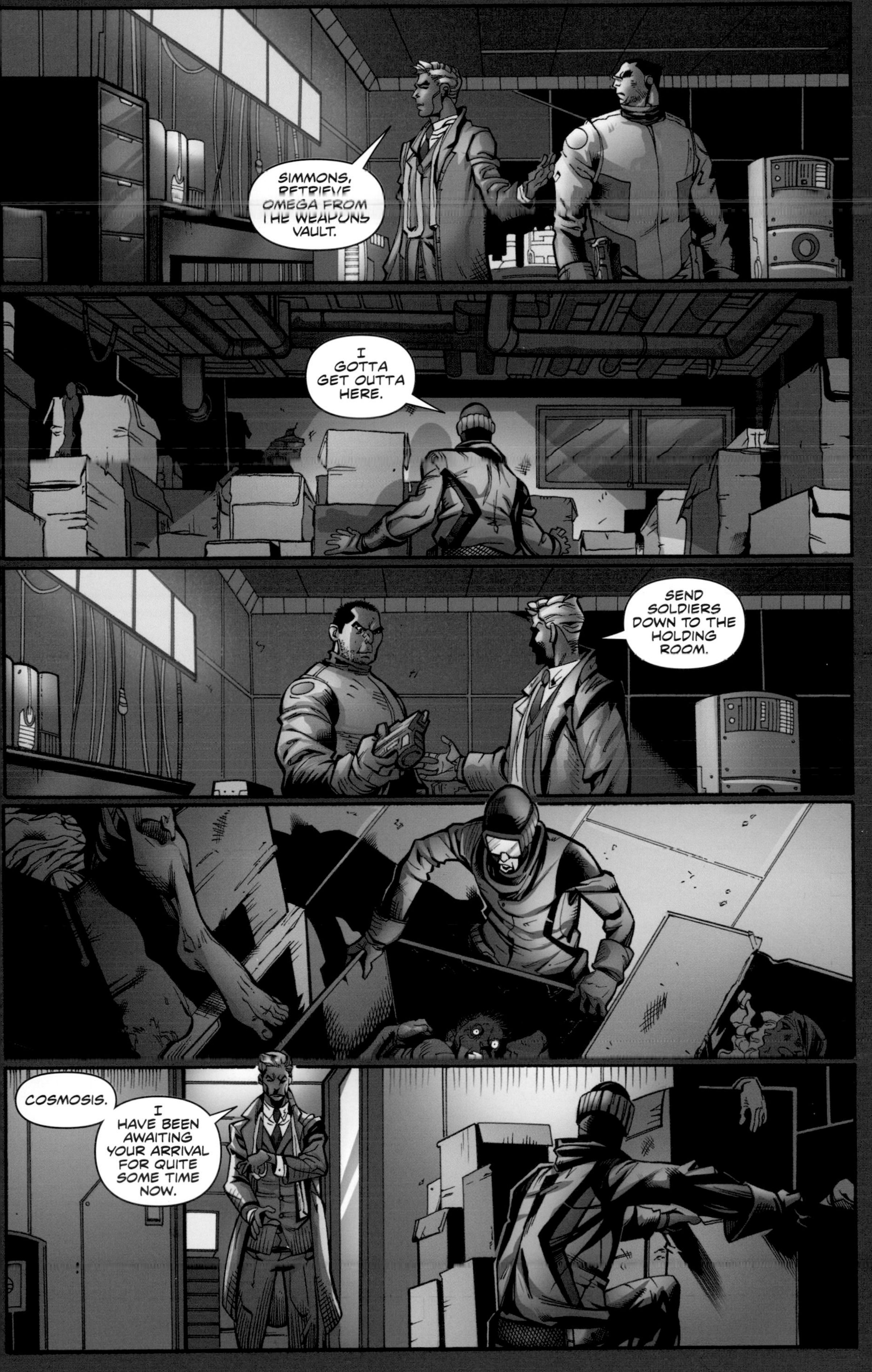
SIMMONS, RETRIEVE OMEGA FROM THE WEAPONS VAULT.
I GOTTA GET OUTTA HERE.
SEND SOLDIERS DOWN TO THE HOLDING ROOM.
COSMOSIS.
I HAVE BEEN AWAITING YOUR ARRIVAL FOR QUITE SOME TIME NOW.

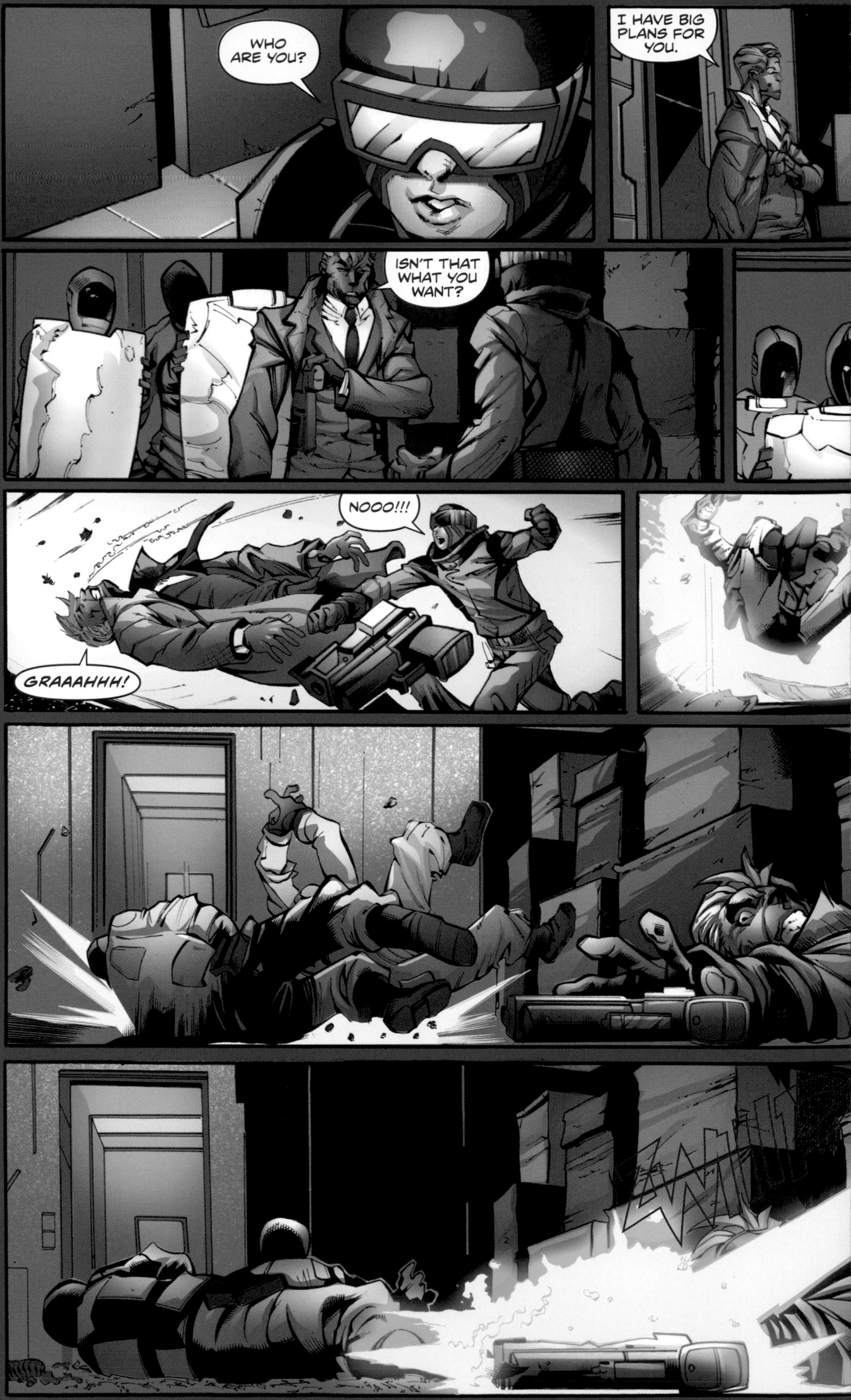
WHO ARE YOU?
I HAVE BIG PLANS FOR YOU.
ISN'T THAT WHAT YOU WANT?
NOOO!!!
GRAAAHHH!

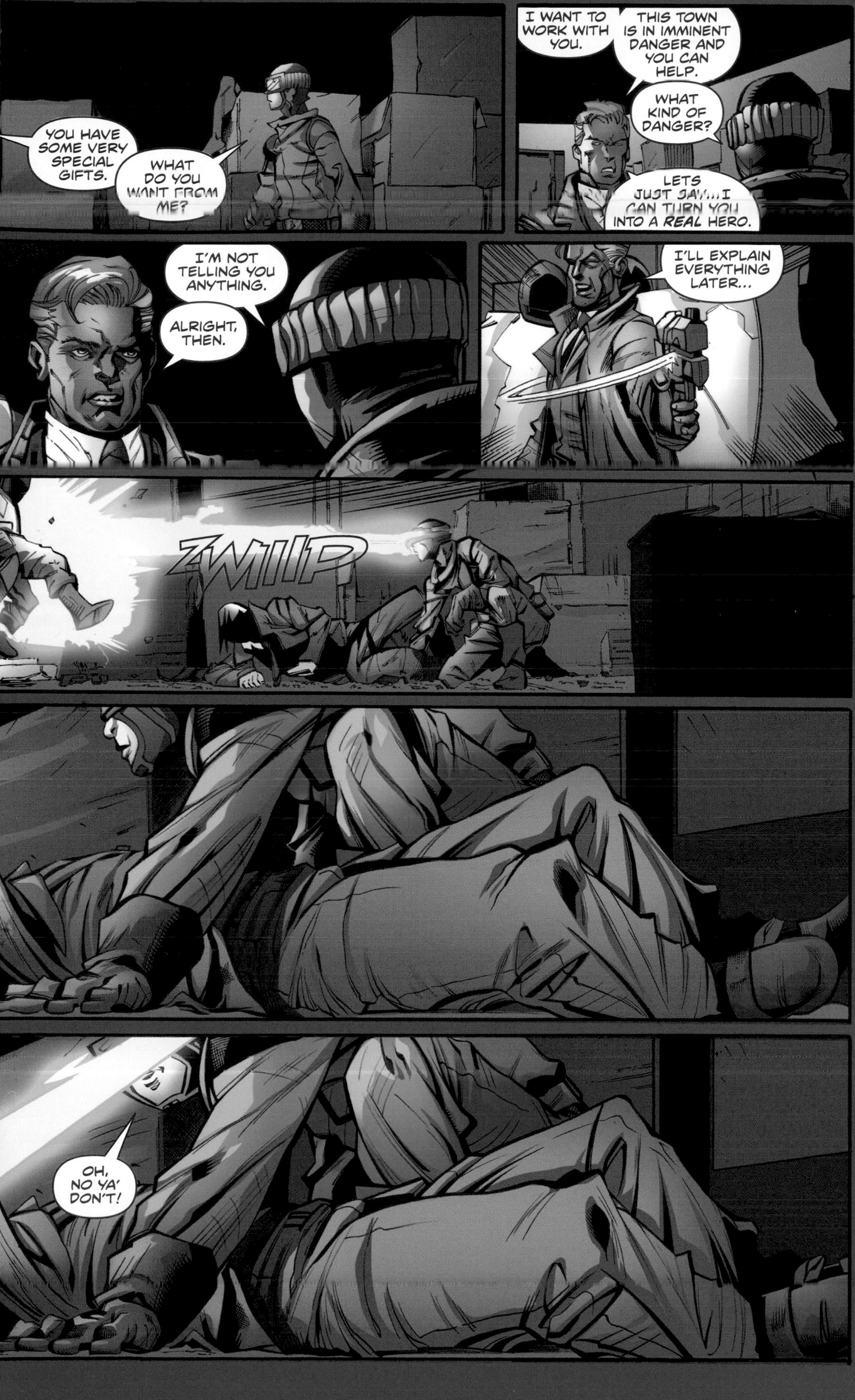
YOU HAVE SOME VERY SPECIAL GIFTS.
WHAT DO YOU WANT FROM ME?
I WANT TO WORK WITH YOU.
THIS TOWN IS IN IMMINENT DANGER AND YOU CAN HELP.
WHAT KIND OF DANGER?
LETS JUST SAY... I CAN TURN YOU INTO A *REAL* HERO.
I'M NOT TELLING YOU ANYTHING.
ALRIGHT, THEN.
I'LL EXPLAIN EVERYTHING LATER...
ZWIIIP
OH, NO YA' DON'T!

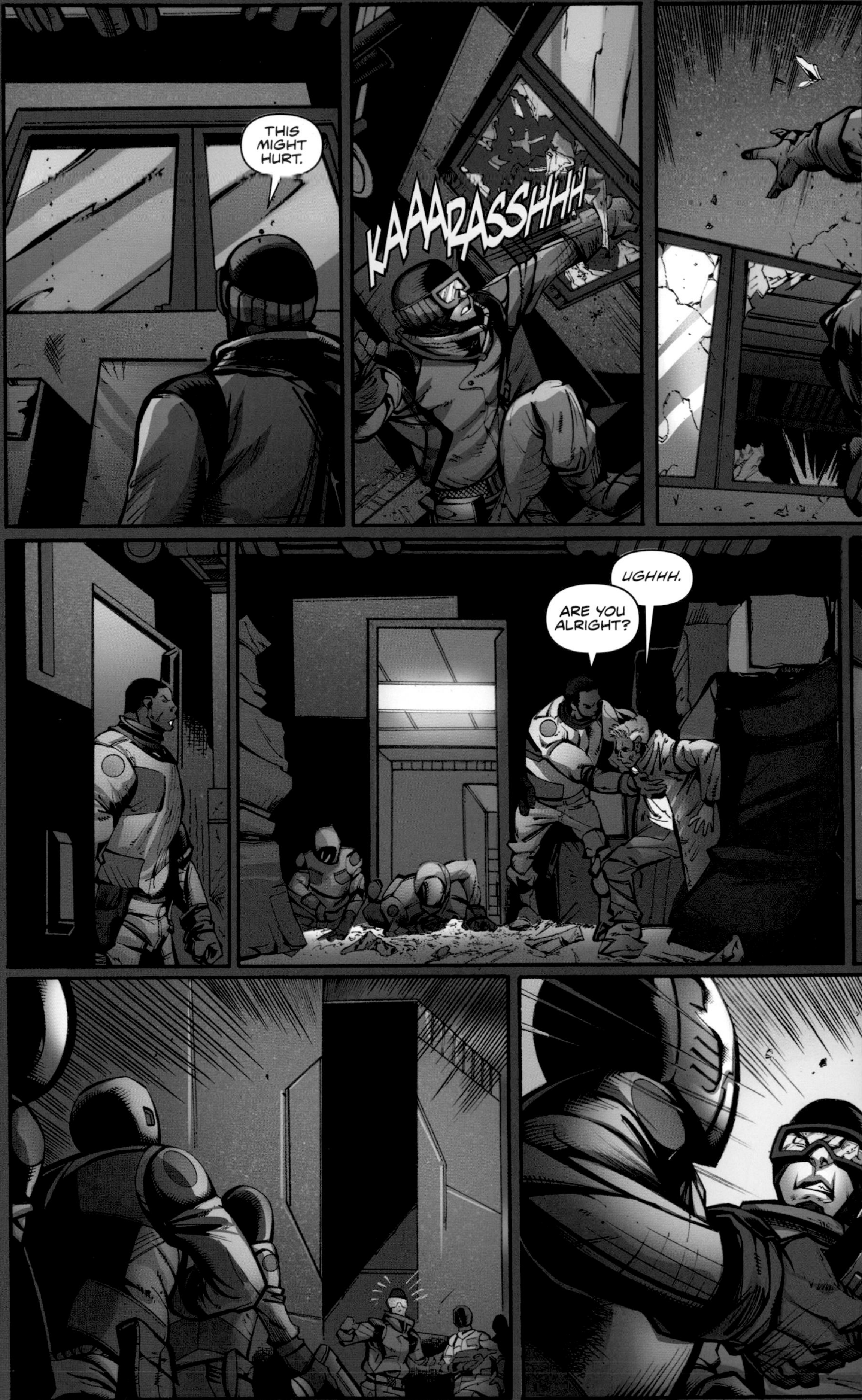
THIS MIGHT HURT.
KAAARASSHHH
UGHHH.
ARE YOU ALRIGHT?

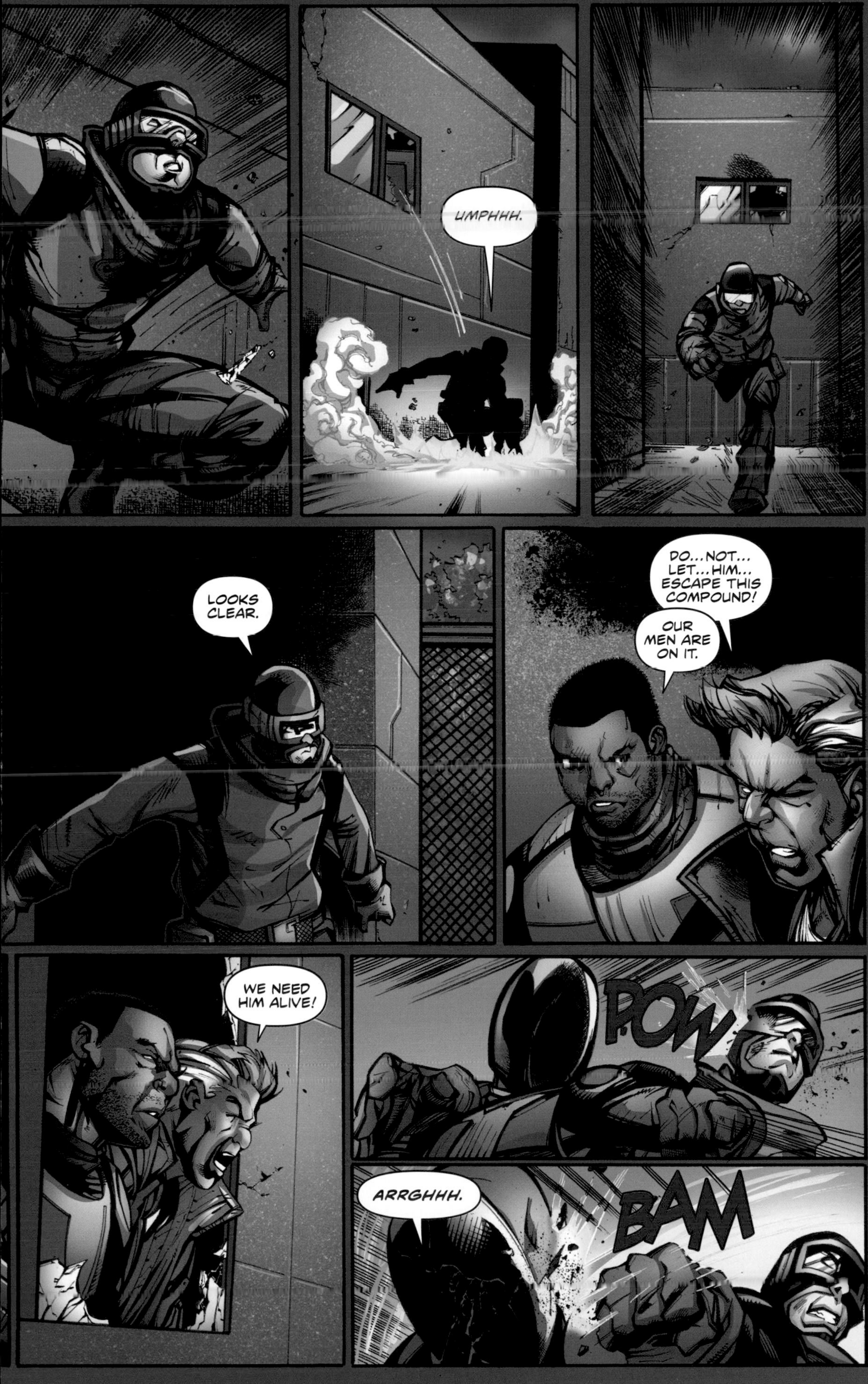
UMPHHH.
LOOKS CLEAR.
DO... NOT... LET... HIM... ESCAPE THIS COMPOUND!
OUR MEN ARE ON IT.
WE NEED HIM ALIVE!
POW
ARRGHHH.
BAM

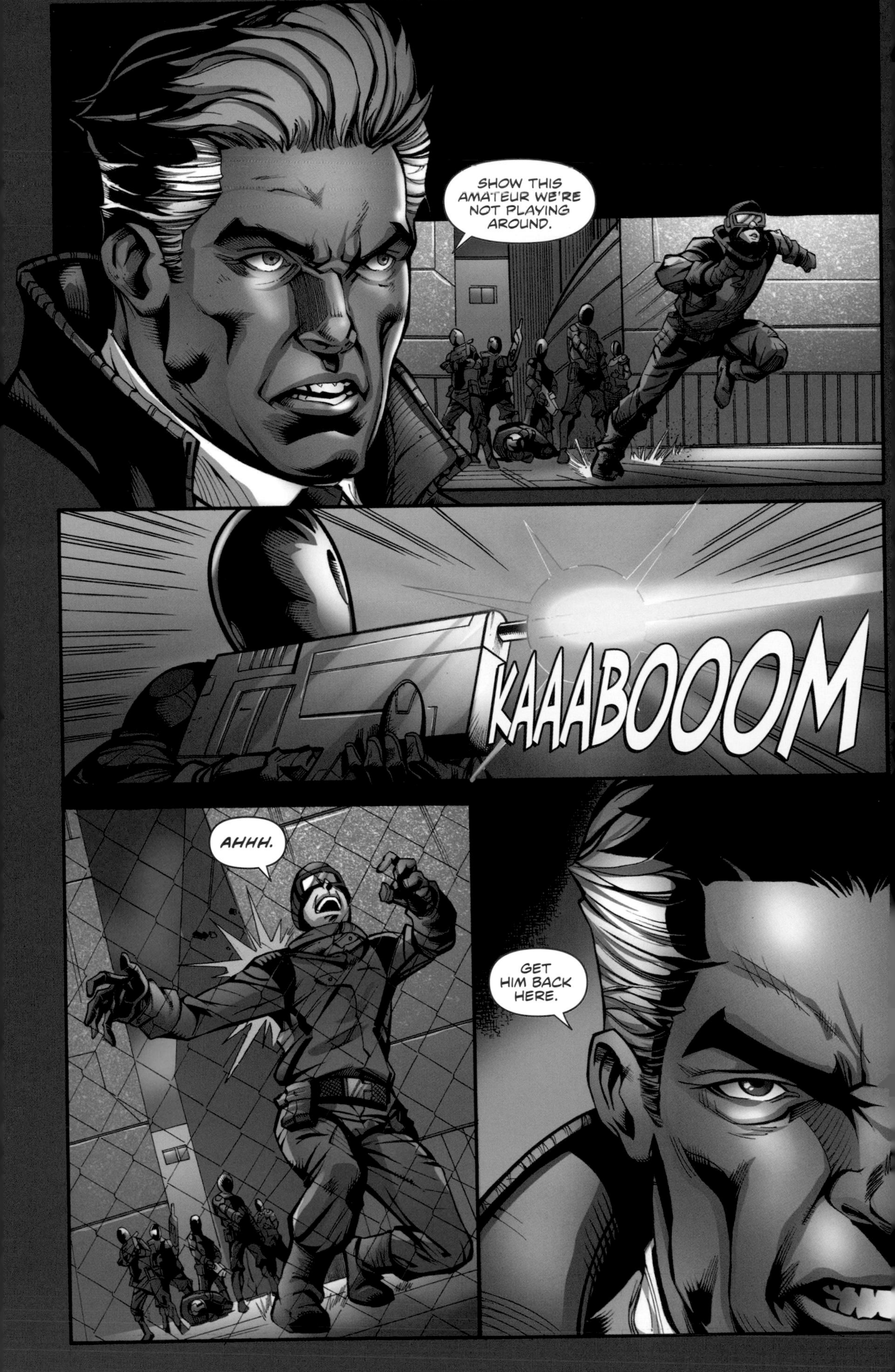
SHOW THIS AMATEUR WE'RE NOT PLAYING AROUND.
KAAABOOOM
AHHH.
GET HIM BACK HERE.

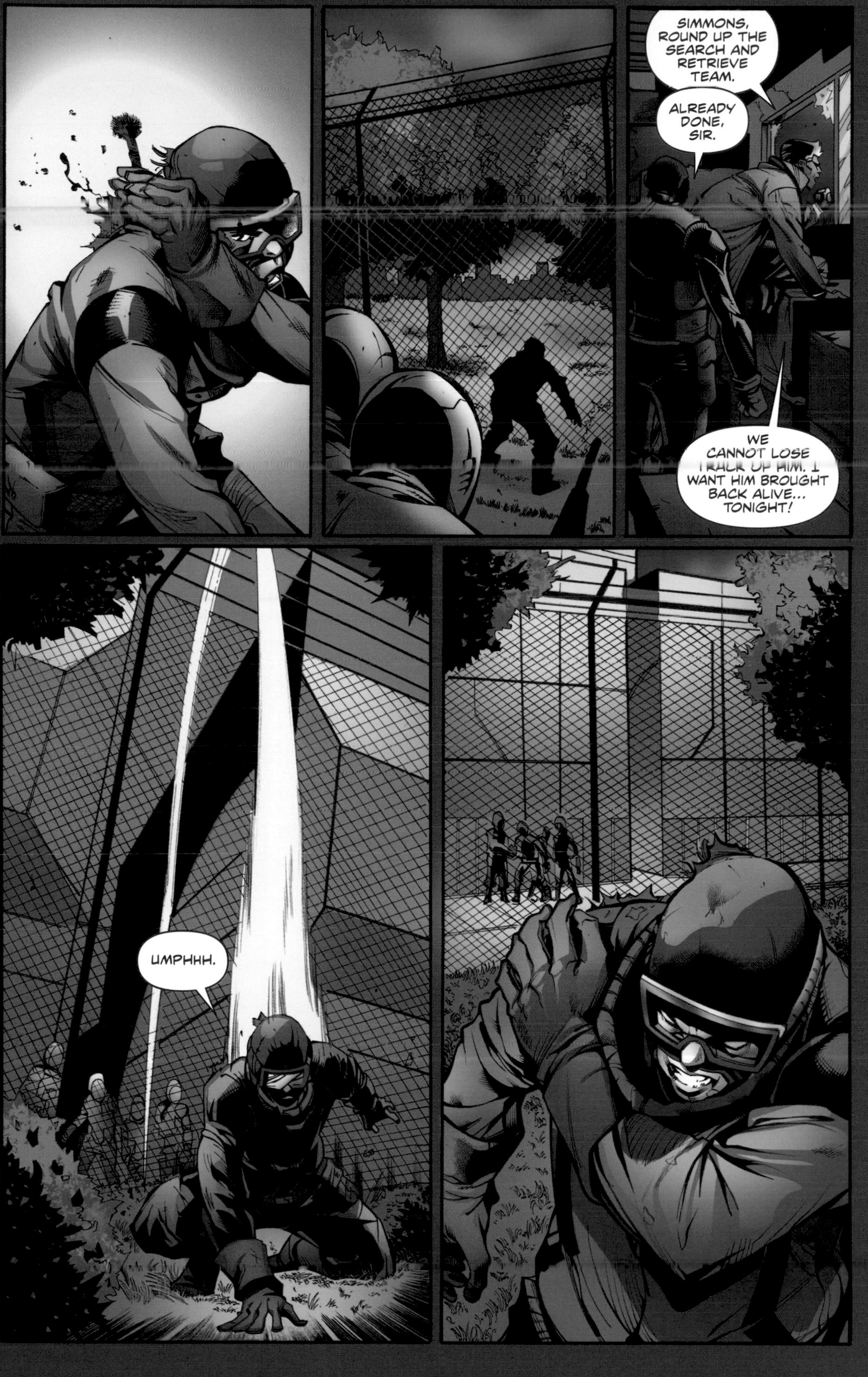
SIMMONS, ROUND UP THE SEARCH AND RETRIEVE TEAM.
ALREADY DONE, SIR.
WE CANNOT LOSE TRACK OF HIM. I WANT HIM BROUGHT BACK ALIVE... TONIGHT!
UMPHHH.

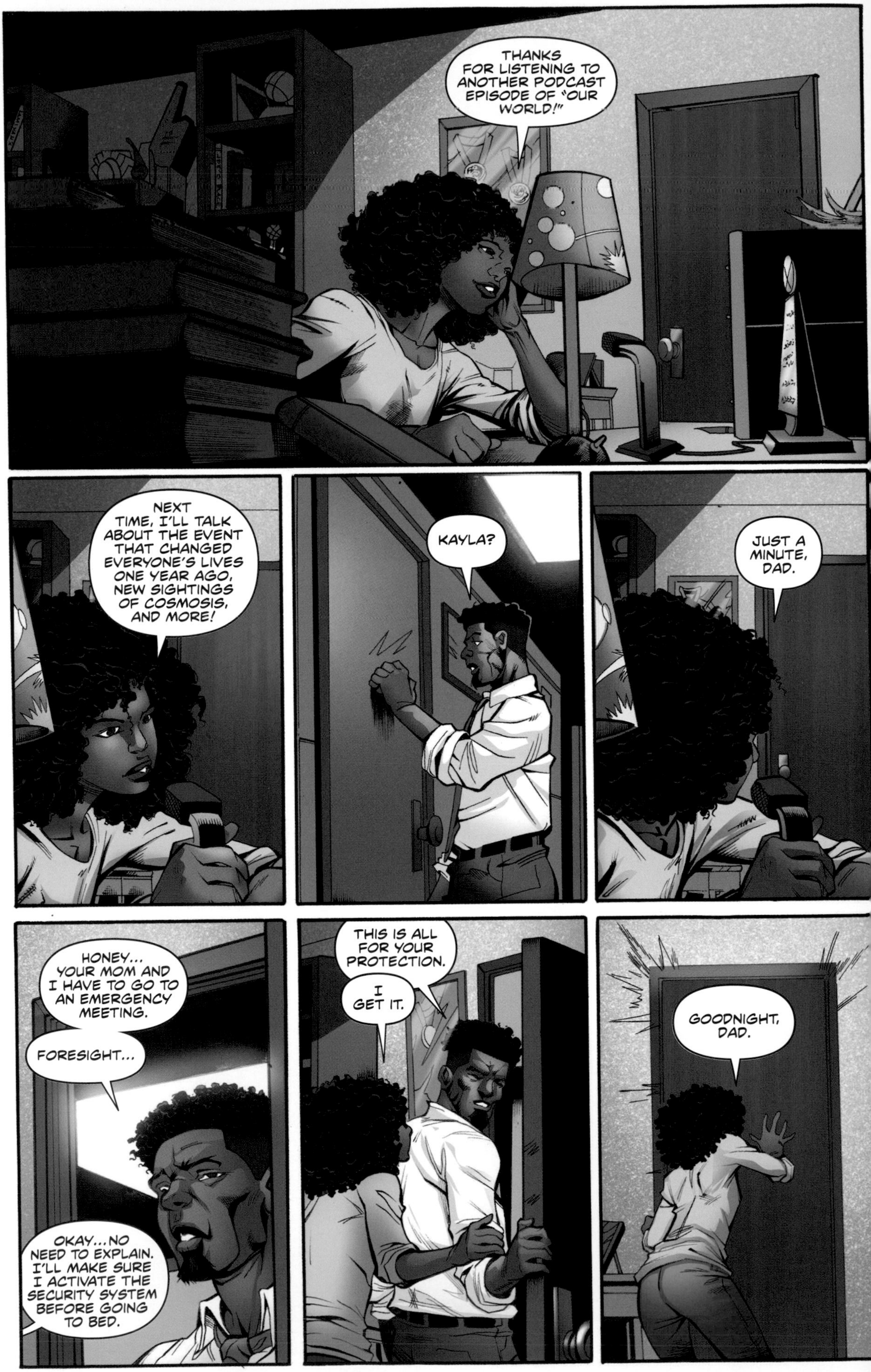
THANKS FOR LISTENING TO ANOTHER PODCAST EPISODE OF "OUR WORLD!"
NEXT TIME, I'LL TALK ABOUT THE EVENT THAT CHANGED EVERYONE'S LIVES ONE YEAR AGO, NEW SIGHTINGS OF COSMOSIS, AND MORE!
KAYLA?
JUST A MINUTE, DAD.
HONEY... YOUR MOM AND I HAVE TO GO TO AN EMERGENCY MEETING.
FORESIGHT...
OKAY...NO NEED TO EXPLAIN. I'LL MAKE SURE I ACTIVATE THE SECURITY SYSTEM BEFORE GOING TO BED.
THIS IS ALL FOR YOUR PROTECTION.
I GET IT.
GOODNIGHT, DAD.

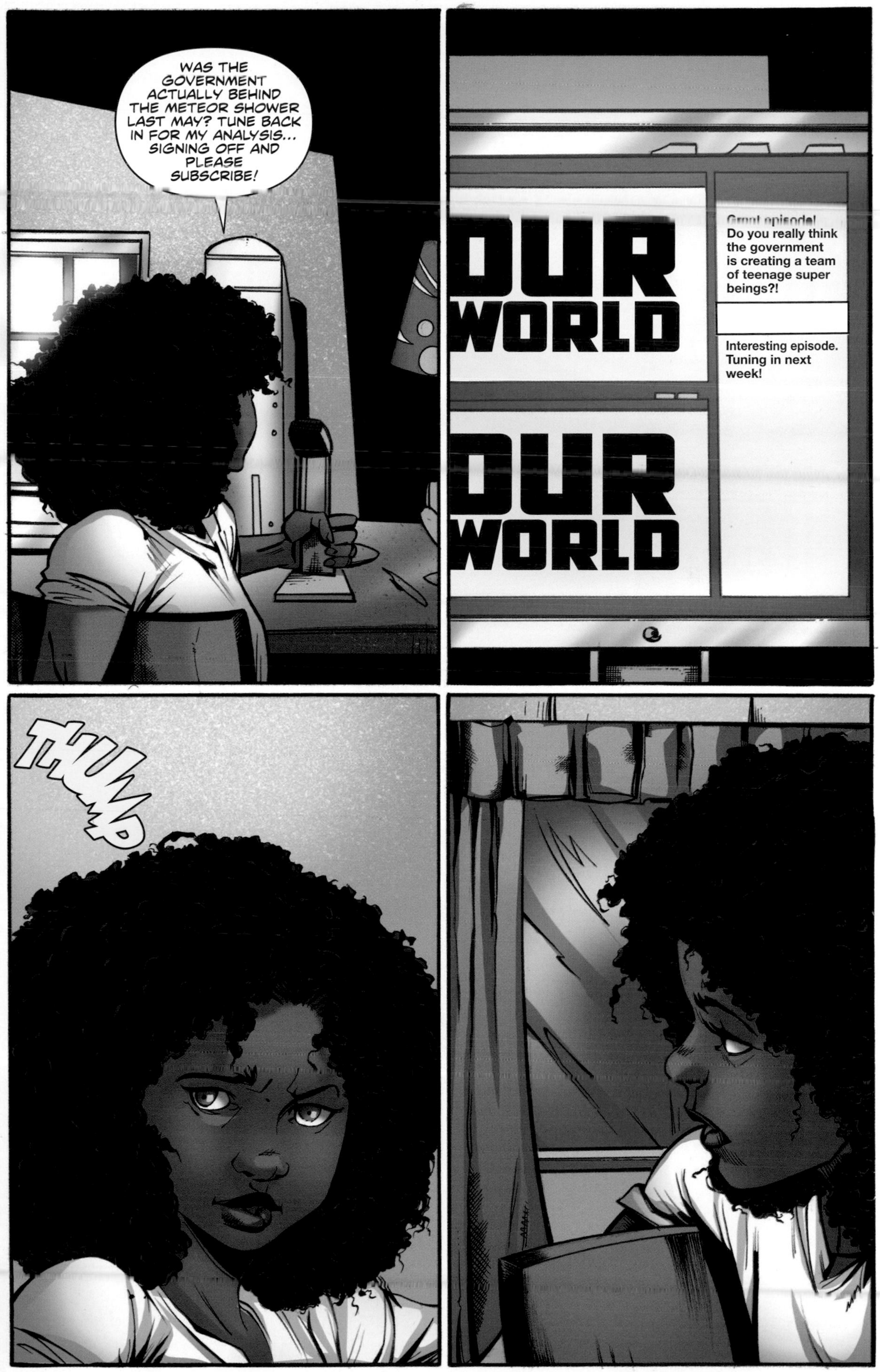
WAS THE GOVERNMENT ACTUALLY BEHIND THE METEOR SHOWER LAST MAY? TUNE BACK IN FOR MY ANALYSIS... SIGNING OFF AND PLEASE SUBSCRIBE!
OUR WORLD
Do you really think the government is creating a team of teenage super beings?!
Interesting episode. Tuning in next week!
OUR WORLD
THUMP

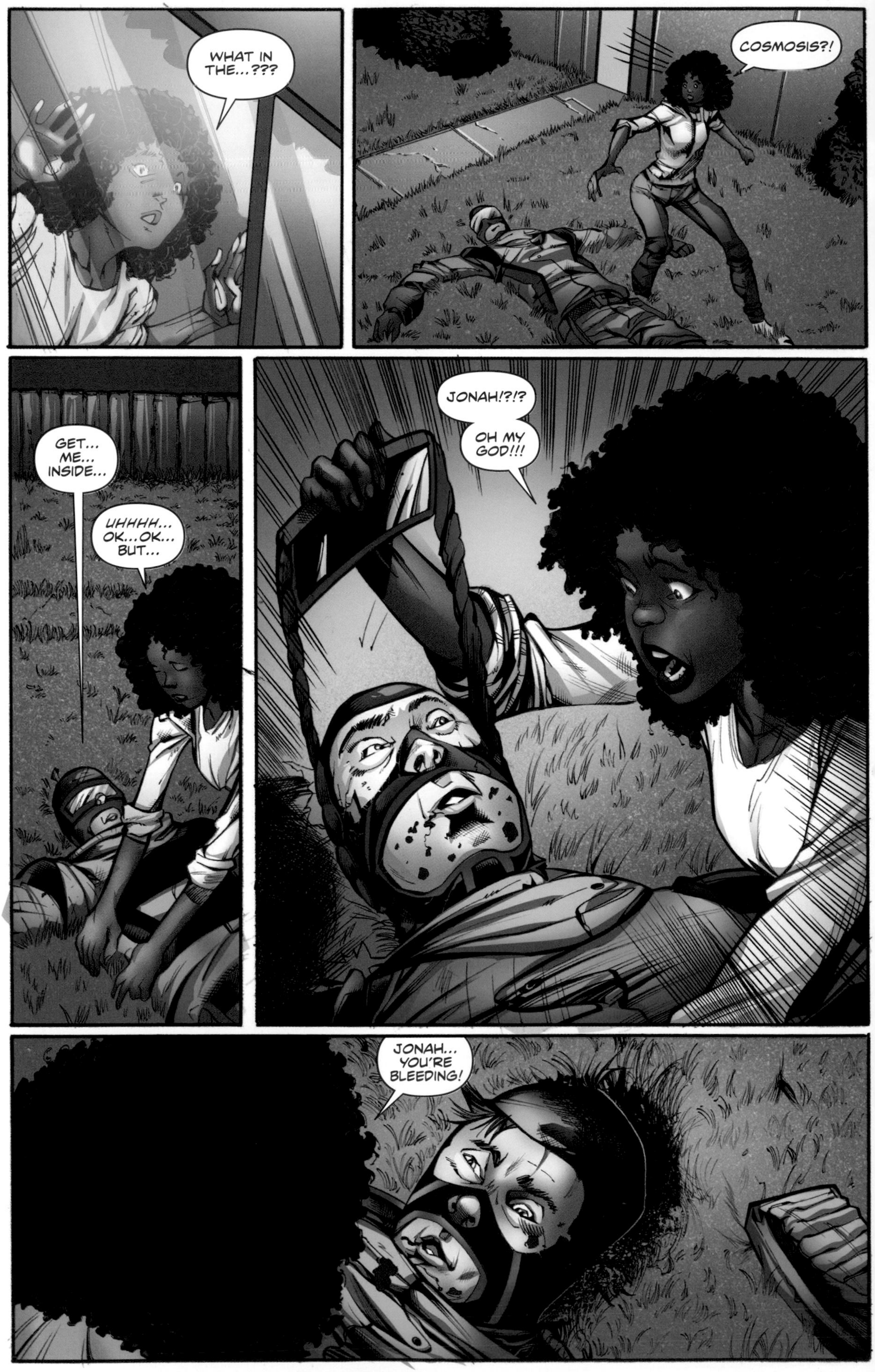
WHAT IN THE...???
COSMOSIS?!
GET... ME... INSIDE...
UHHHH... OK...OK... BUT...
JONAH!?!?
OH MY GOD!!!
JONAH... YOU'RE BLEEDING!

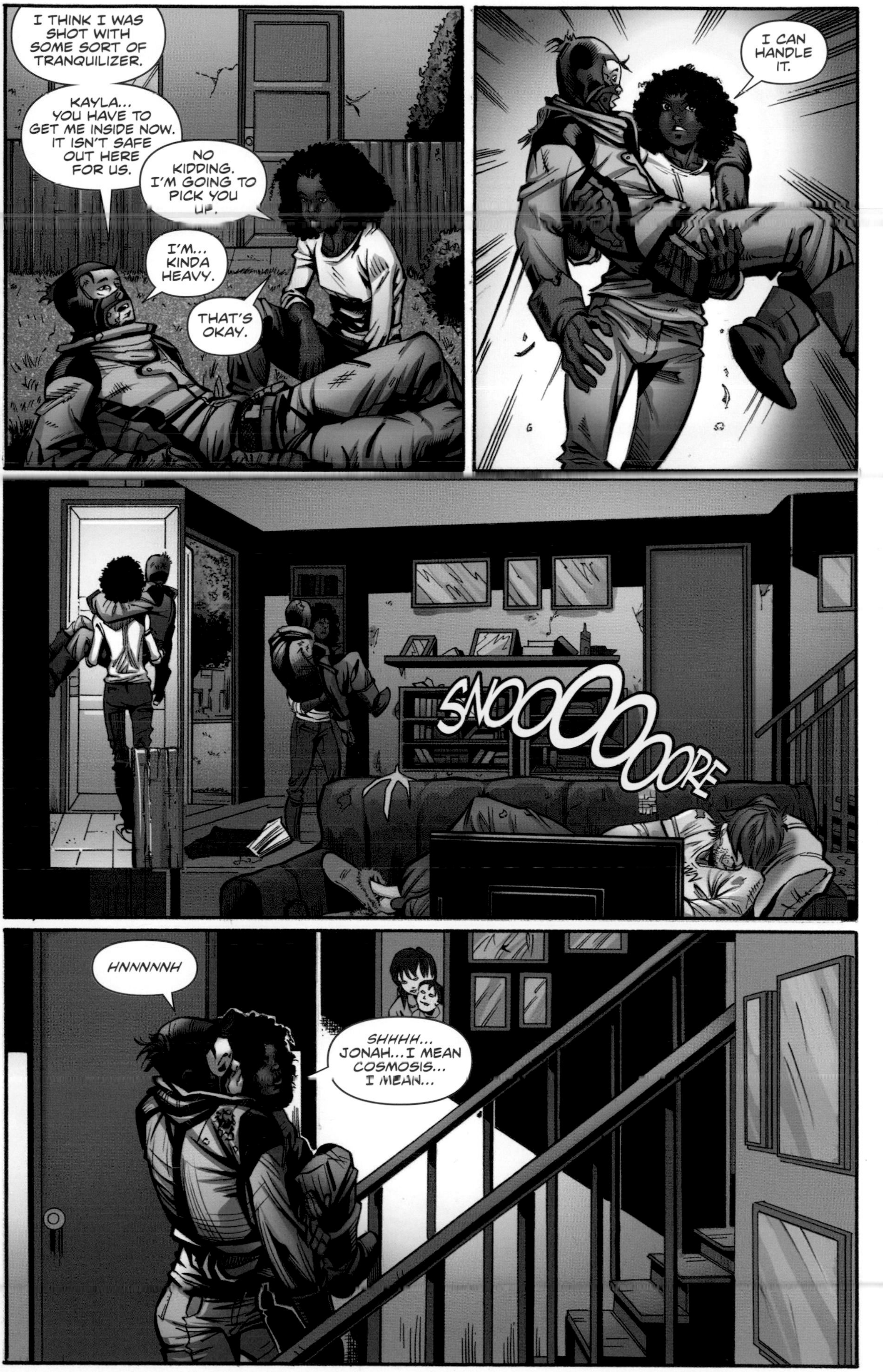
I THINK I WAS SHOT WITH SOME SORT OF TRANQUILIZER.
KAYLA... YOU HAVE TO GET ME INSIDE NOW. IT ISN'T SAFE OUT HERE FOR US.
NO KIDDING. I'M GOING TO PICK YOU UP.
I'M... KINDA HEAVY.
THAT'S OKAY.
I CAN HANDLE IT.
SNOOOOOOORE
HNNNNNH
SHHHH... JONAH... I MEAN COSMOSIS... I MEAN...

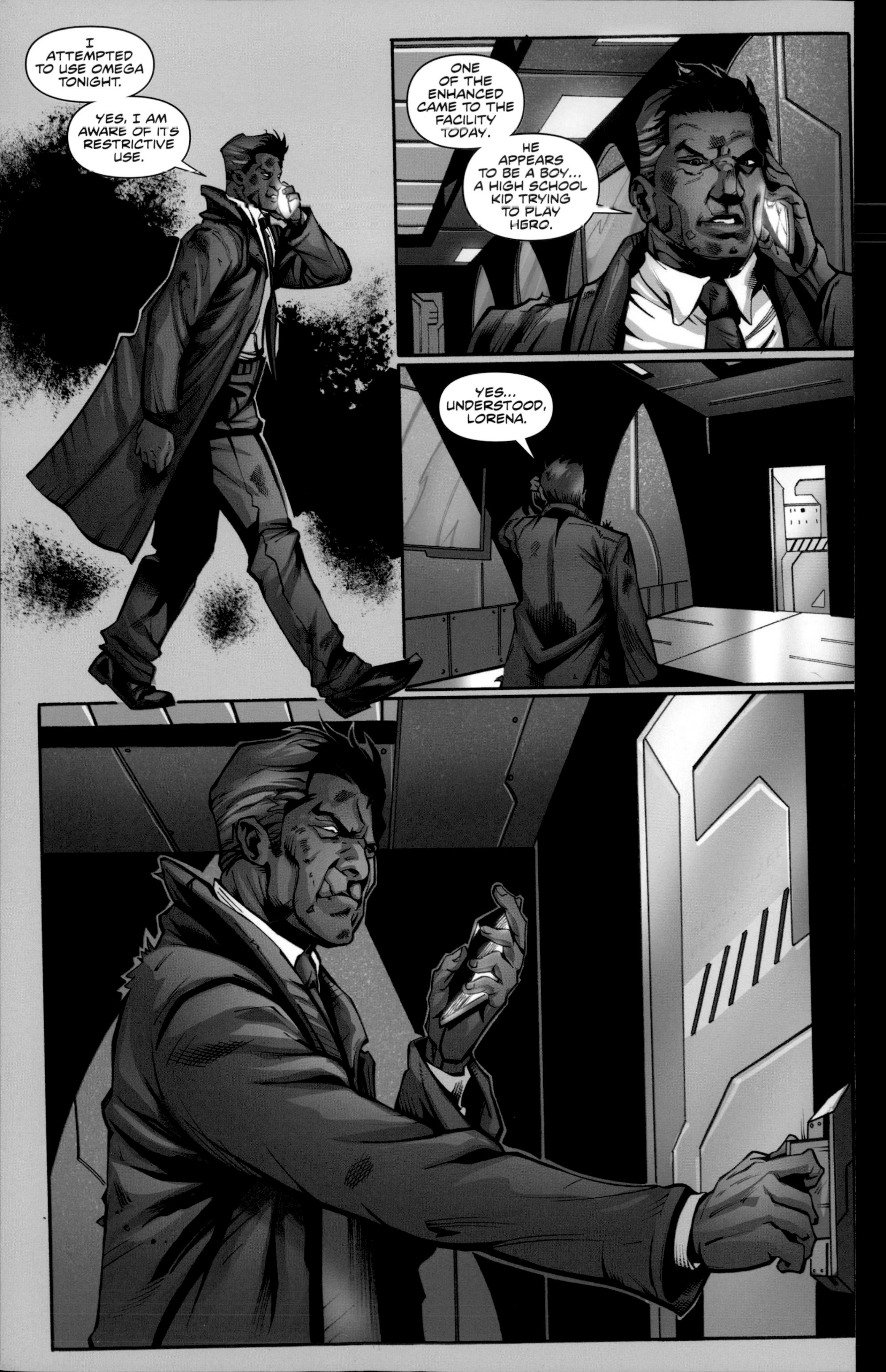
I ATTEMPTED TO USE OMEGA TONIGHT.
YES, I AM AWARE OF ITS RESTRICTIVE USE.
ONE OF THE ENHANCED CAME TO THE FACILITY TODAY.
HE APPEARS TO BE A BOY... A HIGH SCHOOL KID TRYING TO PLAY HERO.
YES... UNDERSTOOD, LORENA.

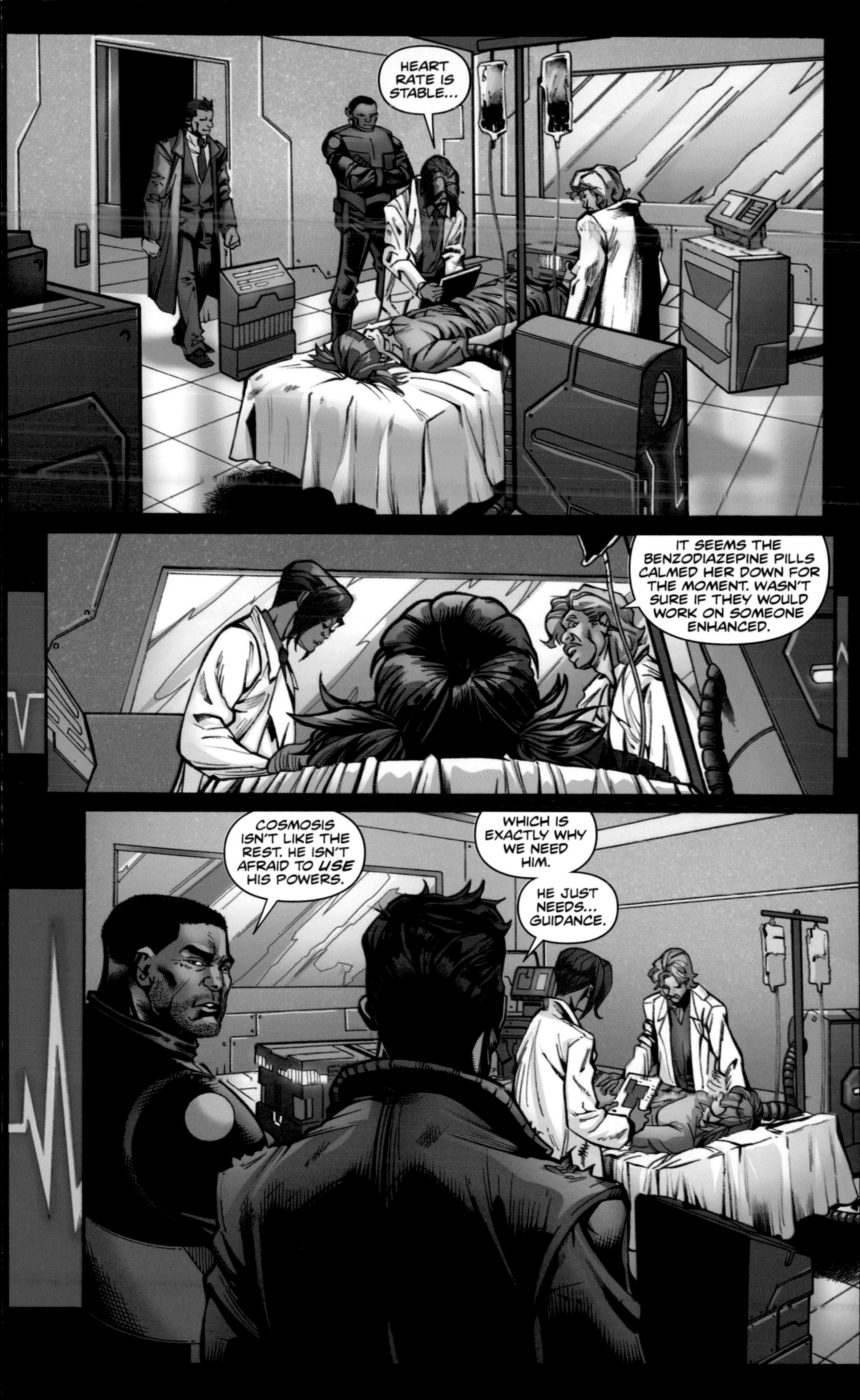
HEART RATE IS STABLE...
IT SEEMS THE BENZODIAZEPINE PILLS CALMED HER DOWN FOR THE MOMENT. WASN'T SURE IF THEY WOULD WORK ON SOMEONE ENHANCED.
COSMOSIS ISN'T LIKE THE REST. HE ISN'T AFRAID TO *USE* HIS POWERS.
WHICH IS EXACTLY WHY WE NEED HIM.
HE JUST NEEDS... GUIDANCE.

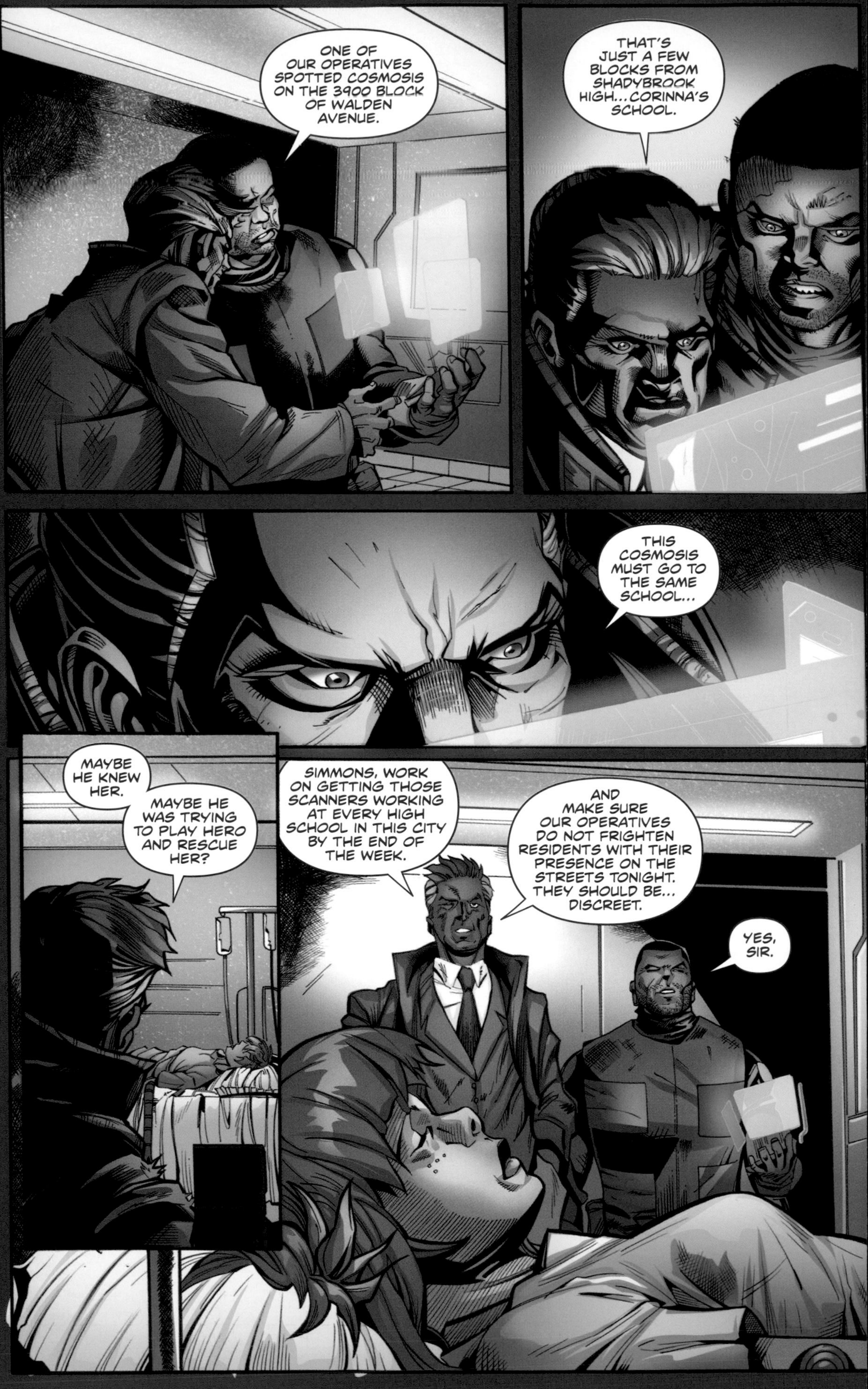
ONE OF OUR OPERATIVES SPOTTED COSMOSIS ON THE 3900 BLOCK OF WALDEN AVENUE.
THAT'S JUST A FEW BLOCKS FROM SHADYBROOK HIGH...CORINNA'S SCHOOL.
THIS COSMOSIS MUST GO TO THE SAME SCHOOL...
MAYBE HE KNEW HER.
MAYBE HE WAS TRYING TO PLAY HERO AND RESCUE HER?
SIMMONS, WORK ON GETTING THOSE SCANNERS WORKING AT EVERY HIGH SCHOOL IN THIS CITY BY THE END OF THE WEEK.
AND MAKE SURE OUR OPERATIVES DO NOT FRIGHTEN RESIDENTS WITH THEIR PRESENCE ON THE STREETS TONIGHT. THEY SHOULD BE... DISCREET.
YES, SIR.

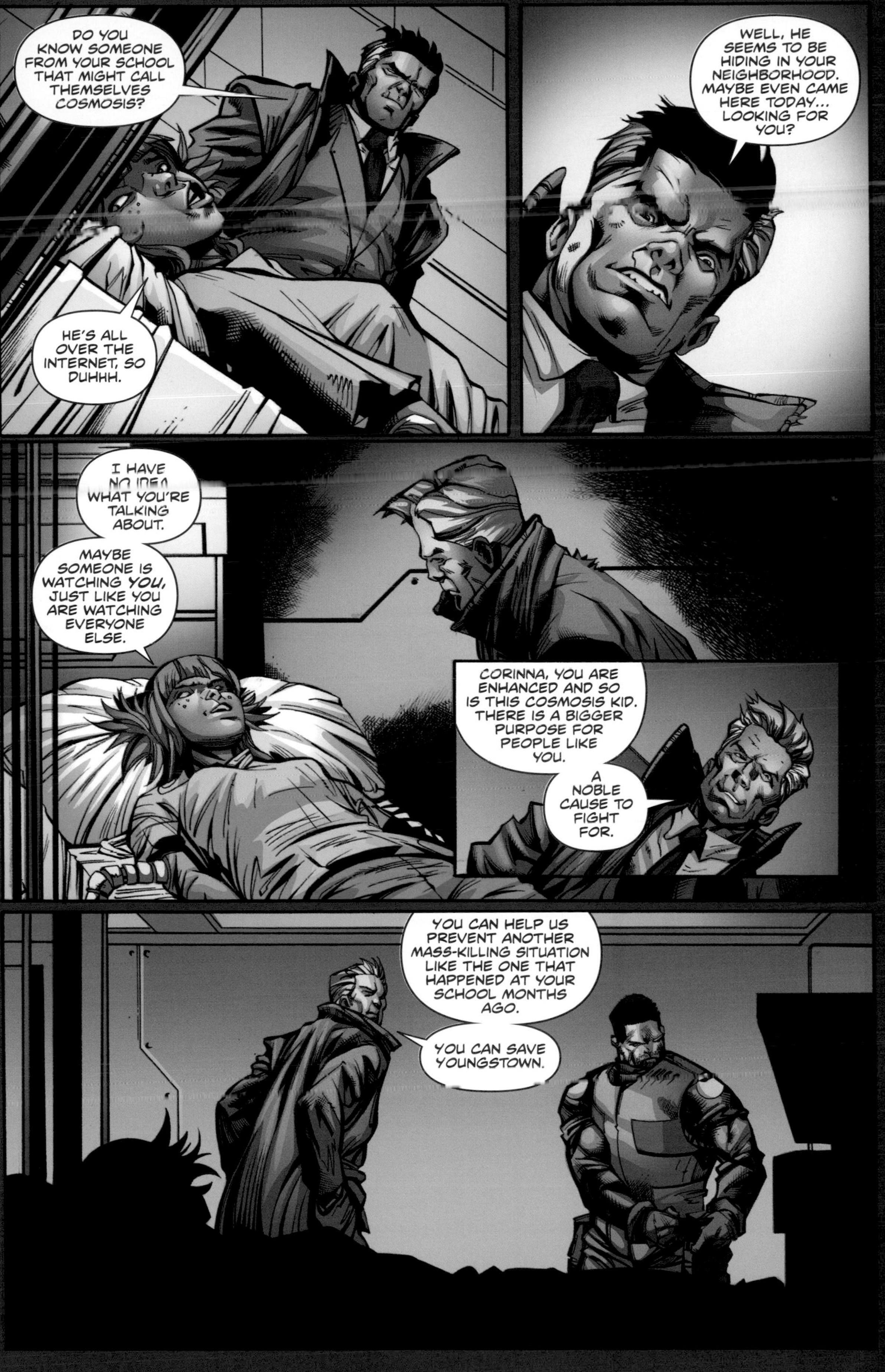
DO YOU KNOW SOMEONE FROM YOUR SCHOOL THAT MIGHT CALL THEMSELVES COSMOSIS?
HE'S ALL OVER THE INTERNET, SO DUHHH.
WELL, HE SEEMS TO BE HIDING IN YOUR NEIGHBORHOOD. MAYBE EVEN CAME HERE TODAY... LOOKING FOR YOU?
I HAVE NO IDEA WHAT YOU'RE TALKING ABOUT.
MAYBE SOMEONE IS WATCHING YOU, JUST LIKE YOU ARE WATCHING EVERYONE ELSE.
CORINNA, YOU ARE ENHANCED AND SO IS THIS COSMOSIS KID. THERE IS A BIGGER PURPOSE FOR PEOPLE LIKE YOU.
A NOBLE CAUSE TO FIGHT FOR.
YOU CAN HELP US PREVENT ANOTHER MASS-KILLING SITUATION LIKE THE ONE THAT HAPPENED AT YOUR SCHOOL MONTHS AGO.
YOU CAN SAVE YOUNGSTOWN.

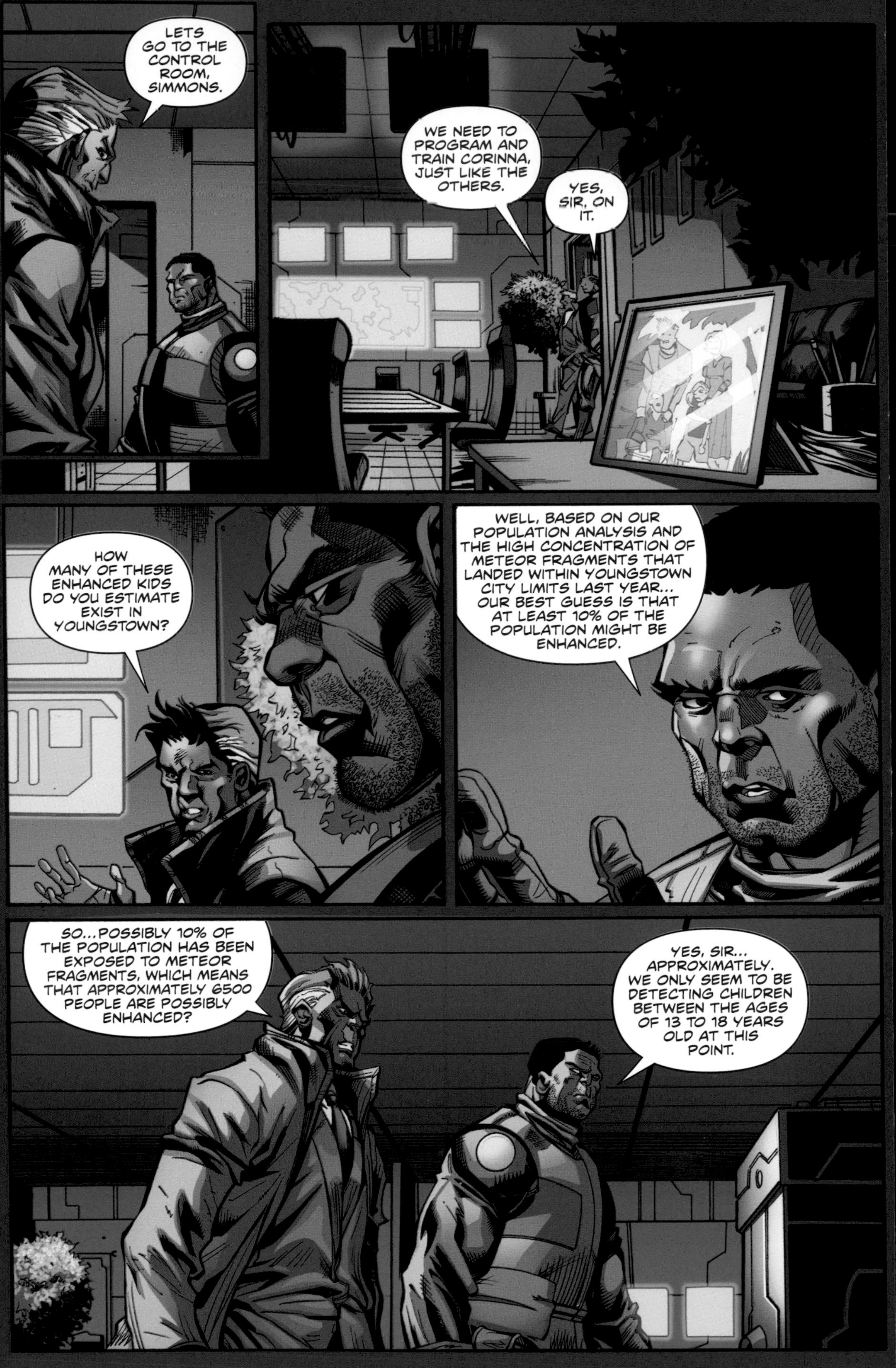
LETS GO TO THE CONTROL ROOM, SIMMONS.
WE NEED TO PROGRAM AND TRAIN CORINNA, JUST LIKE THE OTHERS.
YES, SIR, ON IT.
HOW MANY OF THESE ENHANCED KIDS DO YOU ESTIMATE EXIST IN YOUNGSTOWN?
WELL, BASED ON OUR POPULATION ANALYSIS AND THE HIGH CONCENTRATION OF METEOR FRAGMENTS THAT LANDED WITHIN YOUNGSTOWN CITY LIMITS LAST YEAR... OUR BEST GUESS IS THAT AT LEAST 10% OF THE POPULATION MIGHT BE ENHANCED.
SO...POSSIBLY 10% OF THE POPULATION HAS BEEN EXPOSED TO METEOR FRAGMENTS, WHICH MEANS THAT APPROXIMATELY 6500 PEOPLE ARE POSSIBLY ENHANCED?
YES, SIR... APPROXIMATELY. WE ONLY SEEM TO BE DETECTING CHILDREN BETWEEN THE AGES OF 13 TO 18 YEARS OLD AT THIS POINT.

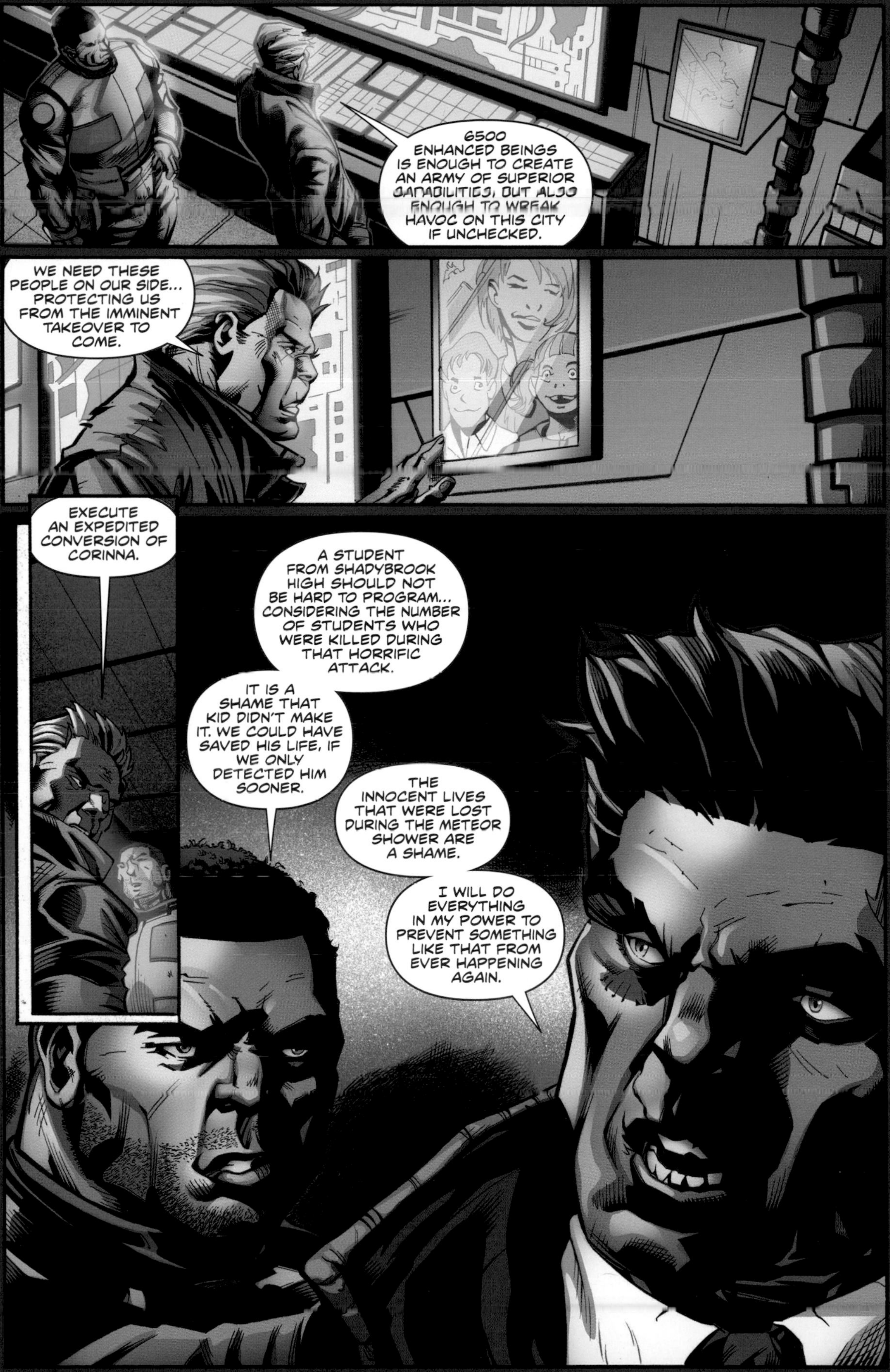
6500 ENHANCED BEINGS IS ENOUGH TO CREATE AN ARMY OF SUPERIOR CAPABILITIES, BUT ALSO ENOUGH TO WREAK HAVOC ON THIS CITY IF UNCHECKED.
WE NEED THESE PEOPLE ON OUR SIDE... PROTECTING US FROM THE IMMINENT TAKEOVER TO COME.
EXECUTE AN EXPEDITED CONVERSION OF CORINNA.
A STUDENT FROM SHADYBROOK HIGH SHOULD NOT BE HARD TO PROGRAM... CONSIDERING THE NUMBER OF STUDENTS WHO WERE KILLED DURING THAT HORRIFIC ATTACK.
IT IS A SHAME THAT KID DIDN'T MAKE IT. WE COULD HAVE SAVED HIS LIFE, IF WE ONLY DETECTED HIM SOONER.
THE INNOCENT LIVES THAT WERE LOST DURING THE METEOR SHOWER ARE A SHAME.
I WILL DO EVERYTHING IN MY POWER TO PREVENT SOMETHING LIKE THAT FROM EVER HAPPENING AGAIN.

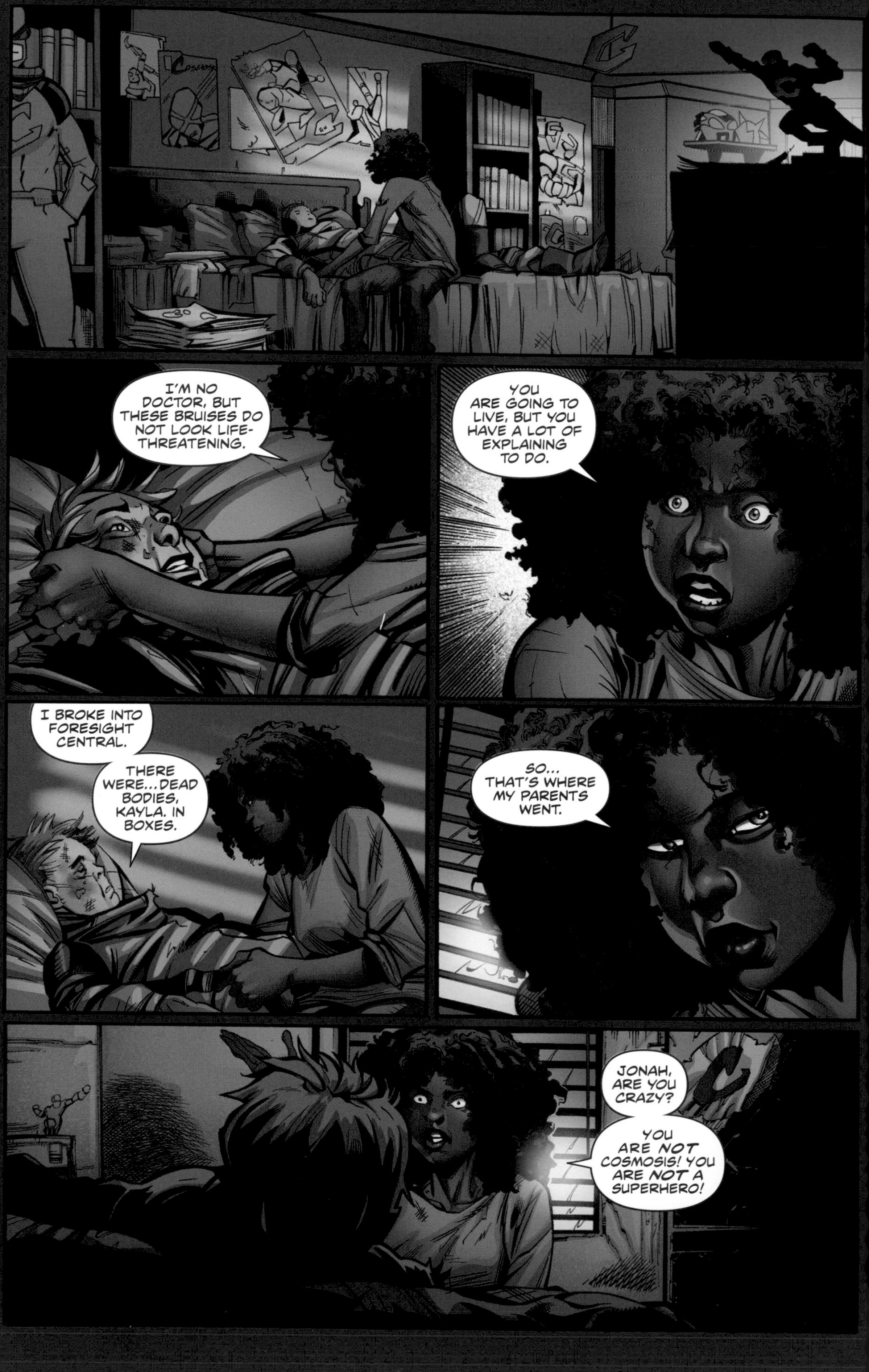
I'M NO DOCTOR, BUT THESE BRUISES DO NOT LOOK LIFE-THREATENING.
YOU ARE GOING TO LIVE, BUT YOU HAVE A LOT OF EXPLAINING TO DO.
I BROKE INTO FORESIGHT CENTRAL.
THERE WERE...DEAD BODIES, KAYLA. IN BOXES.
SO... THAT'S WHERE MY PARENTS WENT.
JONAH, ARE YOU CRAZY?
YOU ARE *NOT* COSMOSIS! YOU ARE *NOT* A SUPERHERO!

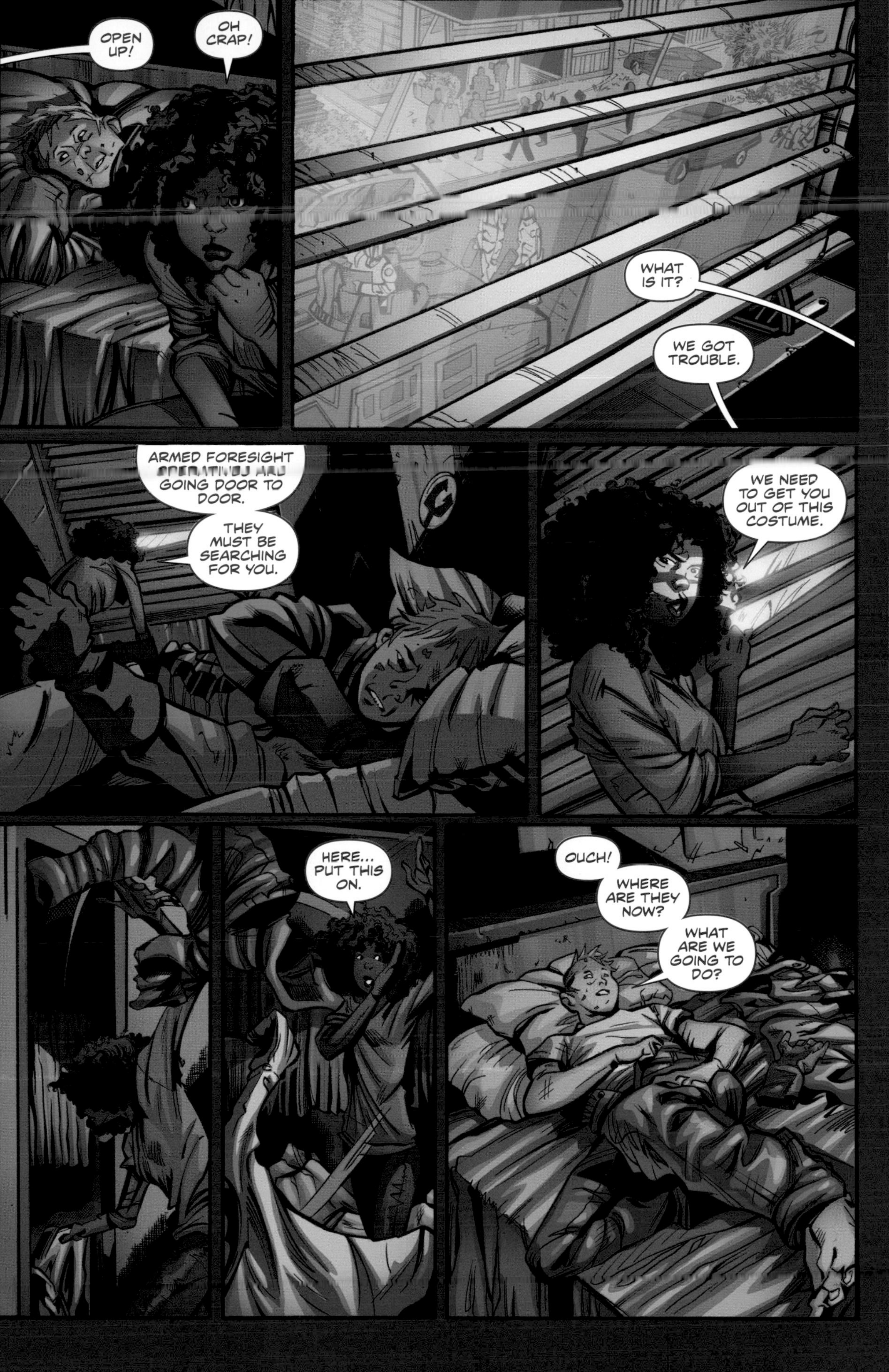
OPEN UP!
OH CRAP!
WHAT IS IT?
WE GOT TROUBLE.
ARMED FORESIGHT OPERATIVES ARE GOING DOOR TO DOOR.
THEY MUST BE SEARCHING FOR YOU.
WE NEED TO GET YOU OUT OF THIS COSTUME.
HERE... PUT THIS ON.
OUCH!
WHERE ARE THEY NOW?
WHAT ARE WE GOING TO DO?

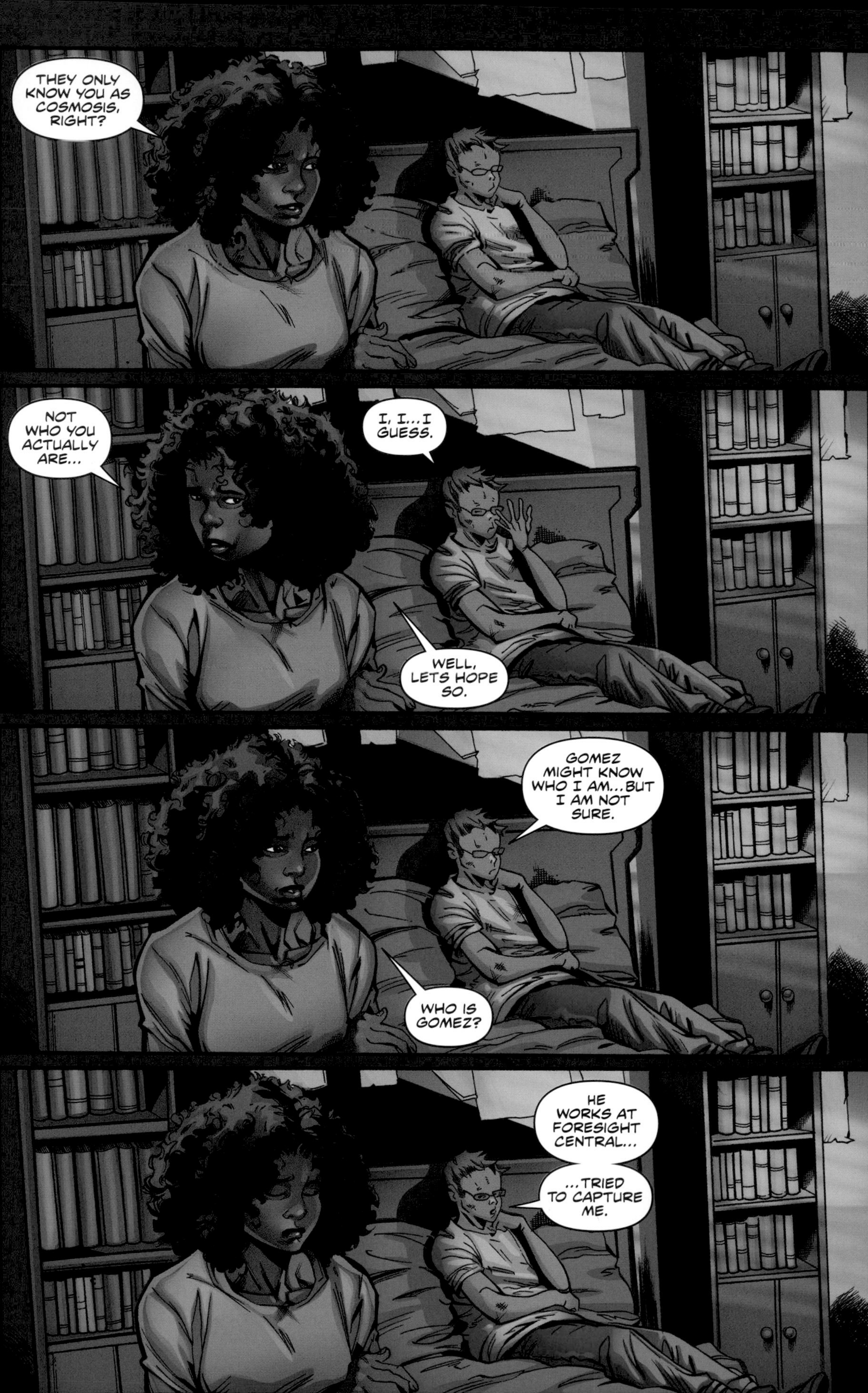
THEY ONLY KNOW YOU AS COSMOSIS, RIGHT?
NOT WHO YOU ACTUALLY ARE...
I, I...I GUESS.
WELL, LETS HOPE SO.
GOMEZ MIGHT KNOW WHO I AM...BUT I AM NOT SURE.
WHO IS GOMEZ?
HE WORKS AT FORESIGHT CENTRAL...
...TRIED TO CAPTURE ME.

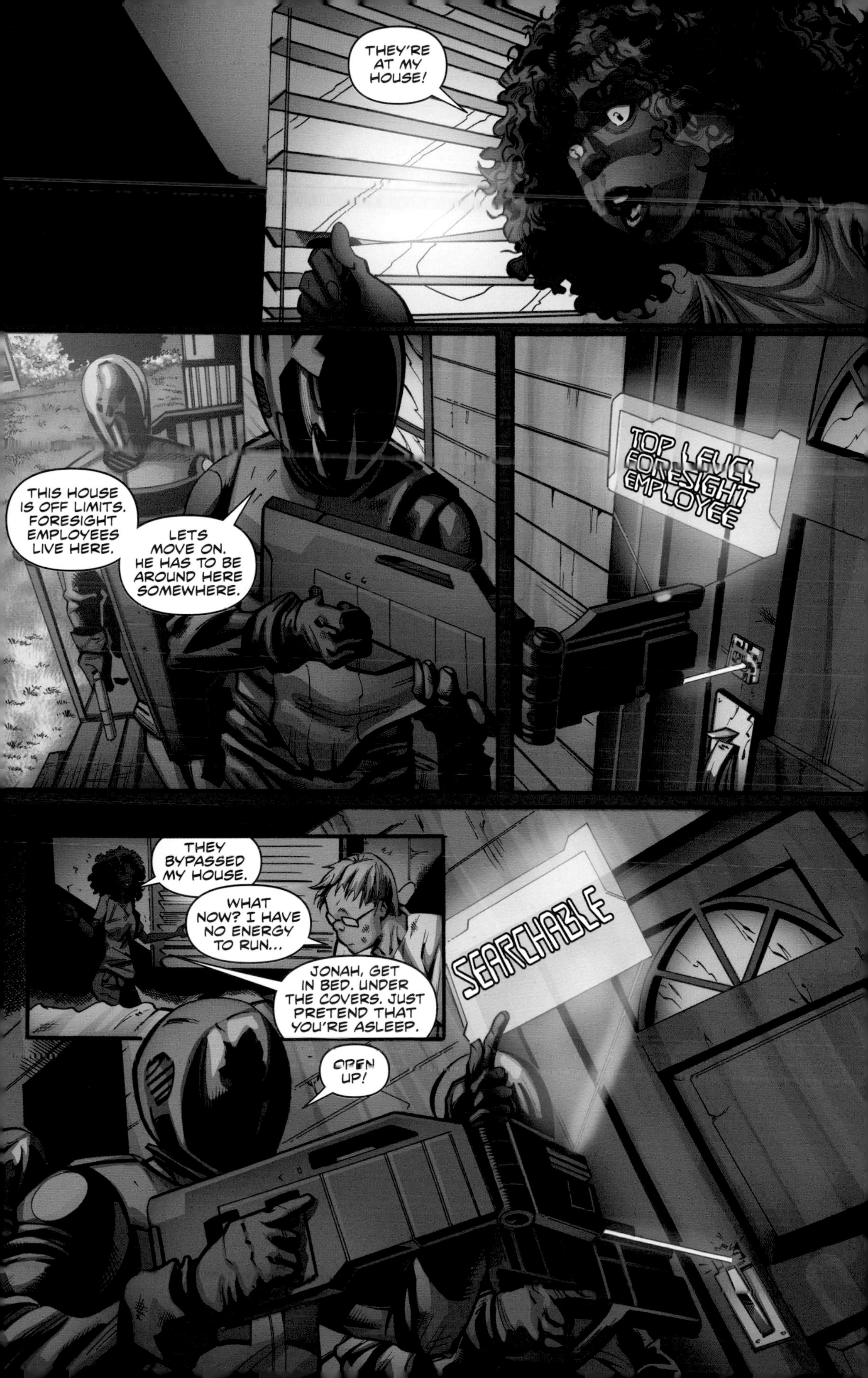
THEY'RE AT MY HOUSE!
THIS HOUSE IS OFF LIMITS. FORESIGHT EMPLOYEES LIVE HERE.
LETS MOVE ON. HE HAS TO BE AROUND HERE SOMEWHERE.
TOP LEVEL FORESIGHT EMPLOYEE
THEY BYPASSED MY HOUSE.
WHAT NOW? I HAVE NO ENERGY TO RUN...
JONAH, GET IN BED. UNDER THE COVERS. JUST PRETEND THAT YOU'RE ASLEEP.
SEARCHABLE
OPEN UP!

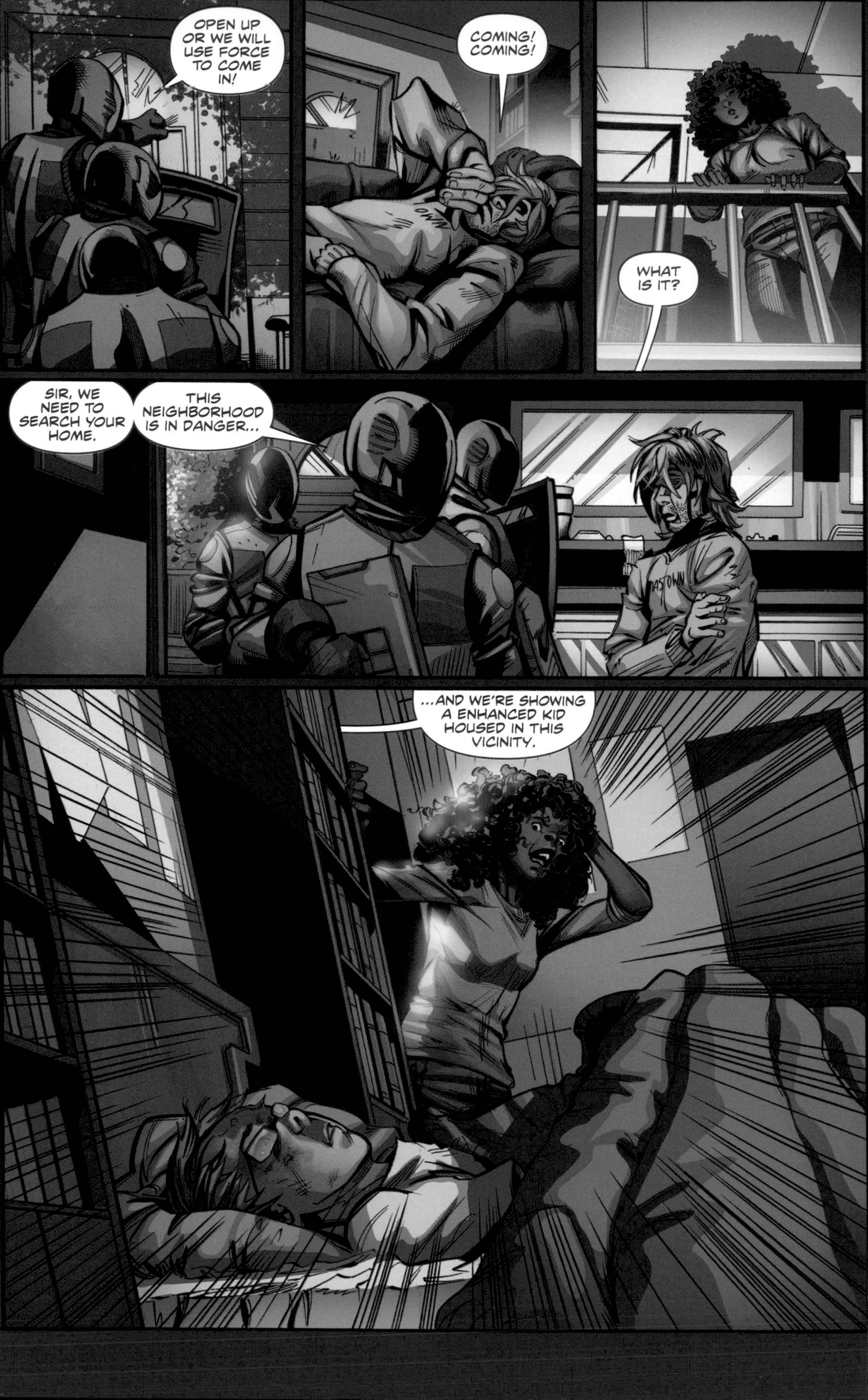
OPEN UP OR WE WILL USE FORCE TO COME IN!
COMING! COMING!
WHAT IS IT?
SIR, WE NEED TO SEARCH YOUR HOME.
THIS NEIGHBORHOOD IS IN DANGER...
...AND WE'RE SHOWING A ENHANCED KID HOUSED IN THIS VICINITY.

AMINA

Amina

THREAT LEVEL: VIRIDIAN

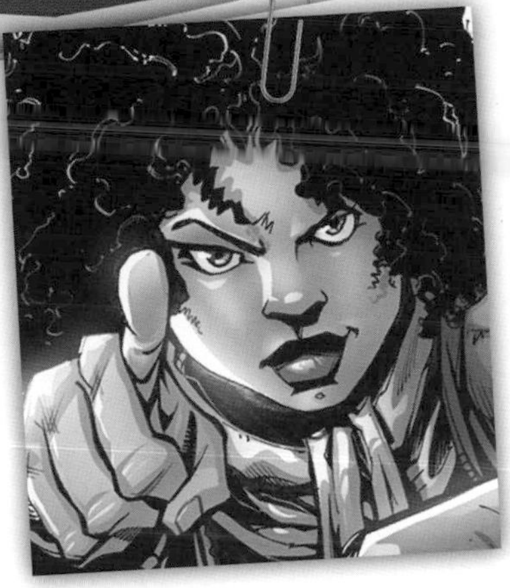

FILE NUMBER: CPU-001A - GAMMA

REAL NAME: Kayla Tate

LEGAL STATUS: American citizen WITH SPECIAL CONSIDERATION. Subject's parents are employees of Foresight Corp.

KNOWN ALIASES: None

PRIORITY LEVEL: Ultraviolet, for exclusive and sole review by Chief Executive Officer Lorena Payan

ENHANCED ABILITIES: Augmented physical abilities due to increased muscle power to superhuman levels, resulting in extraordinary strength, running speed (not in the same category as subject codename ACCELL), and jumping. Superhuman reflexes are an apparent by-product of subject's enhanced musculature, which paradoxically enough has not altered muscle density, but has improved muscle pliability, healing, and resiliency.

POWER LEVEL: At present, a few levels above Olympic athlete. However, subject's growth in formative years may lead to a parallel in development of superhuman abilities.

Additionally, subject has an exceptional capacity for determination and tenacity to investigate social matters of interest. A "potential crusader", for lack of a better term.

THREAT LEVEL: Viridian, at the moment. If the trio of emotional, experiential, and biochemical factors that impact human maturation also impact superhuman development, subject threat level should be changed to SCARLET without hesitation.

NEXT STEPS: Daily surveillance of subject and her parents.

Priorities include determination of whether or not the subject's parents are aware of her superhuman abilities, in which case the decision for either capture, elimination, or manipulation will be made, and be applicable to all parties.

SUPERB™

CHAPTER 3

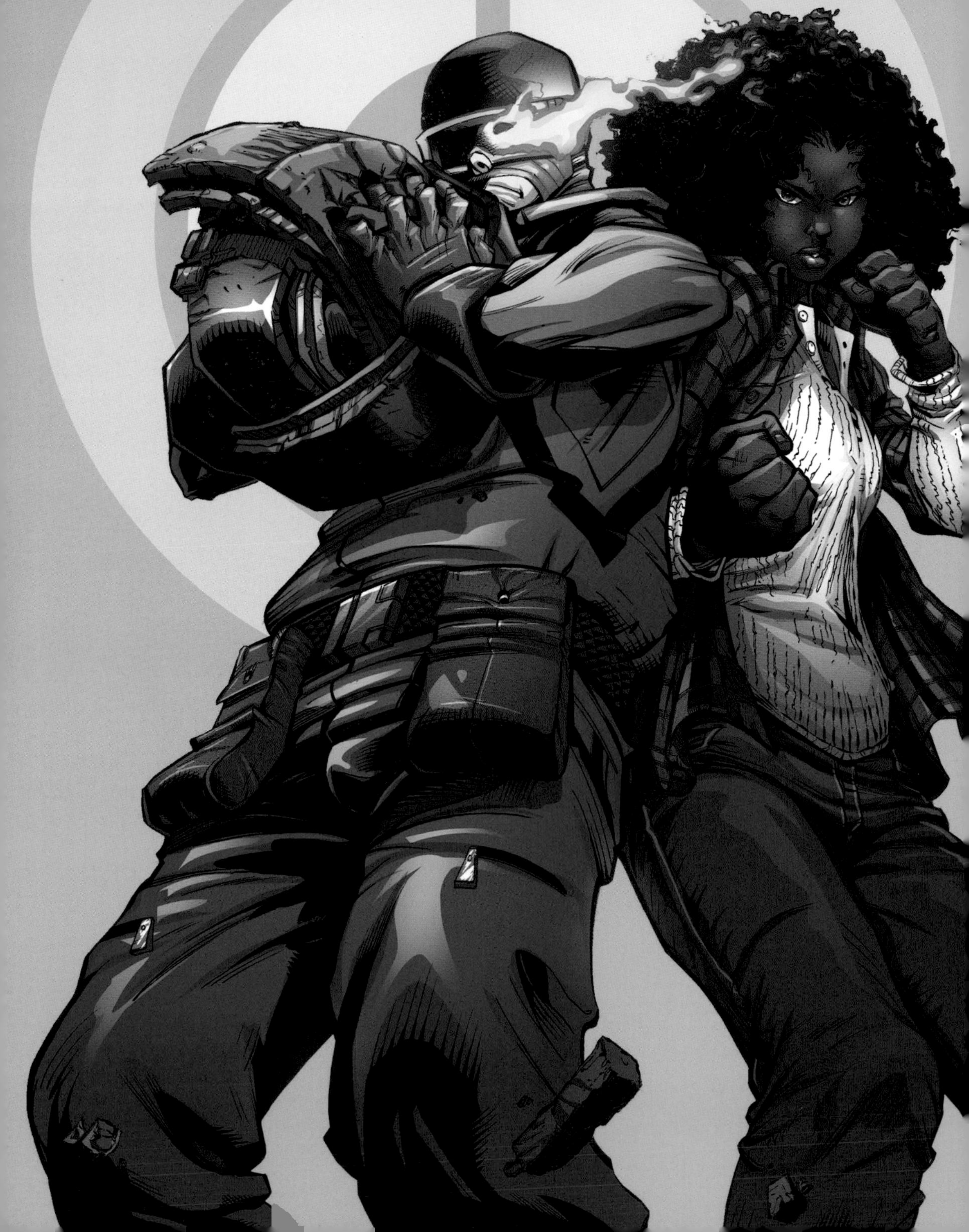

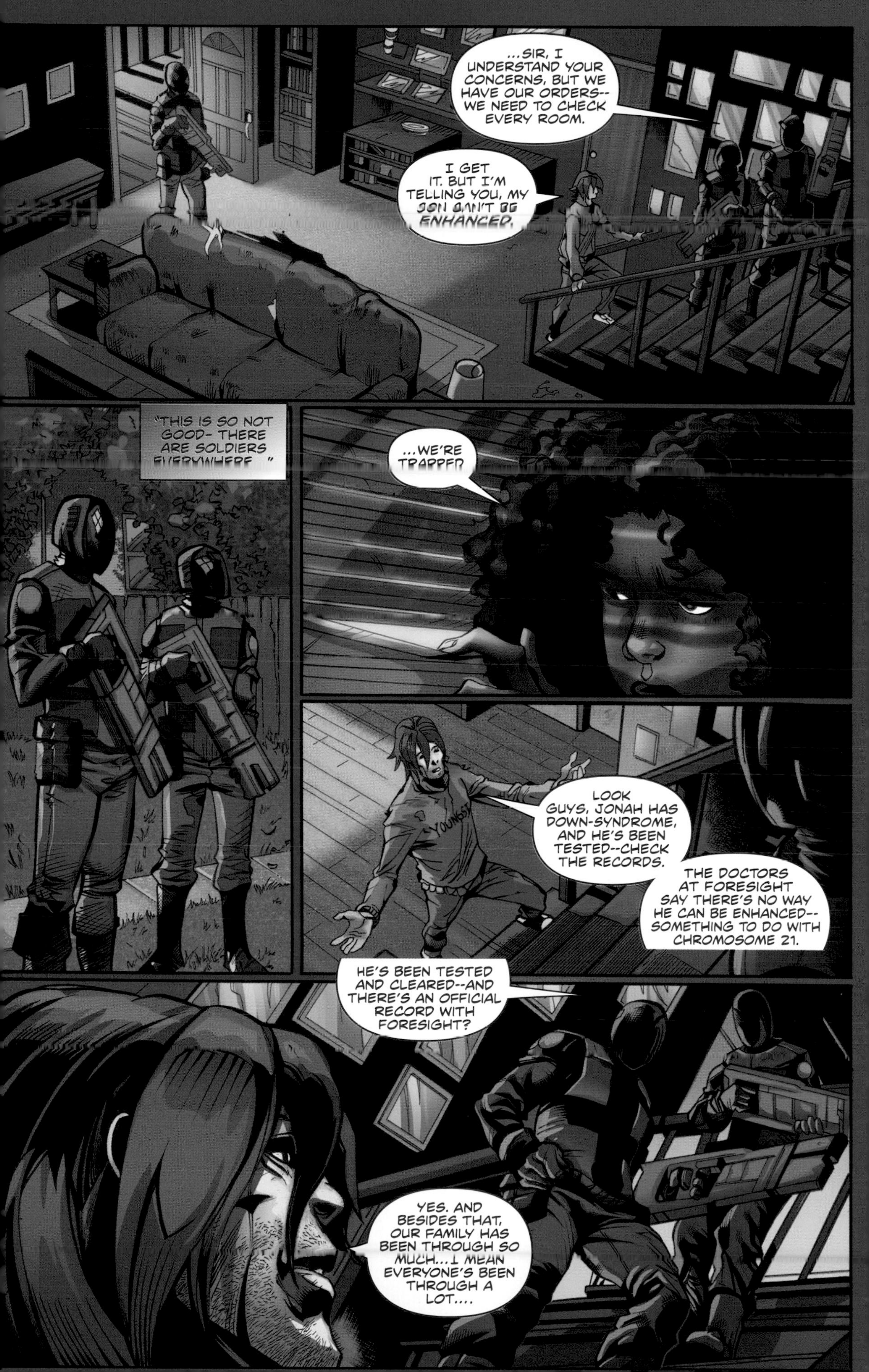
...SIR, I UNDERSTAND YOUR CONCERNS, BUT WE HAVE OUR ORDERS--WE NEED TO CHECK EVERY ROOM.
I GET IT. BUT I'M TELLING YOU, MY SON CAN'T BE ENHANCED.
"THIS IS SO NOT GOOD- THERE ARE SOLDIERS EVERYWHERE..."
...WE'RE TRAPPED
LOOK GUYS, JONAH HAS DOWN-SYNDROME, AND HE'S BEEN TESTED--CHECK THE RECORDS.
THE DOCTORS AT FORESIGHT SAY THERE'S NO WAY HE CAN BE ENHANCED--SOMETHING TO DO WITH CHROMOSOME 21.
HE'S BEEN TESTED AND CLEARED--AND THERE'S AN OFFICIAL RECORD WITH FORESIGHT?
YES. AND BESIDES THAT, OUR FAMILY HAS BEEN THROUGH SO MUCH... I MEAN EVERYONE'S BEEN THROUGH A LOT....

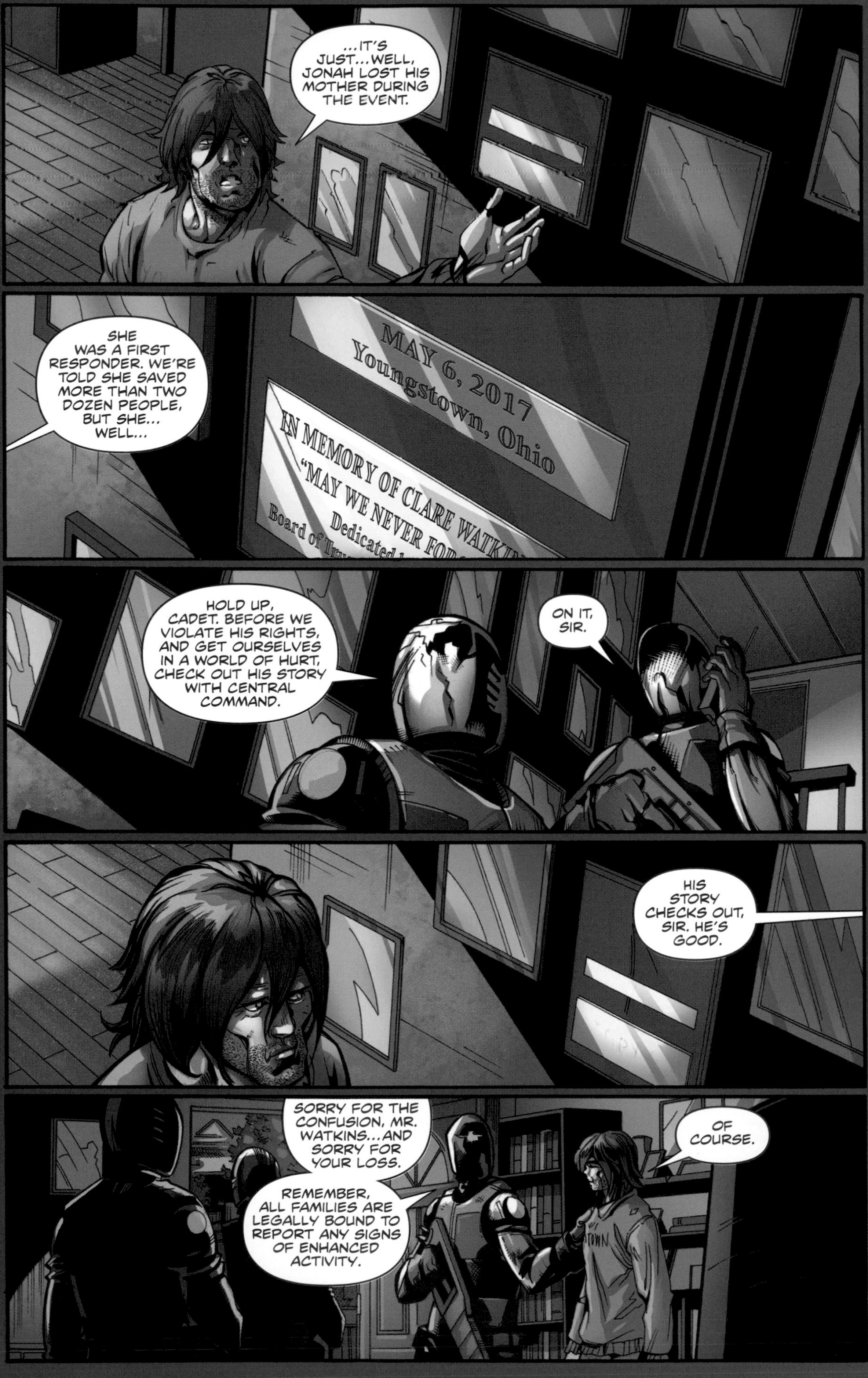
...IT'S JUST...WELL, JONAH LOST HIS MOTHER DURING THE EVENT.
SHE WAS A FIRST RESPONDER. WE'RE TOLD SHE SAVED MORE THAN TWO DOZEN PEOPLE, BUT SHE... WELL...
MAY 6, 2017
Youngstown, Ohio
IN MEMORY OF CLARE WATKI
"MAY WE NEVER FOR
Dedicated
Board of Tru
HOLD UP, CADET. BEFORE WE VIOLATE HIS RIGHTS, AND GET OURSELVES IN A WORLD OF HURT, CHECK OUT HIS STORY WITH CENTRAL COMMAND.
ON IT, SIR.
HIS STORY CHECKS OUT, SIR. HE'S GOOD.
SORRY FOR THE CONFUSION, MR. WATKINS...AND SORRY FOR YOUR LOSS.
REMEMBER, ALL FAMILIES ARE LEGALLY BOUND TO REPORT ANY SIGNS OF ENHANCED ACTIVITY.
OF COURSE.

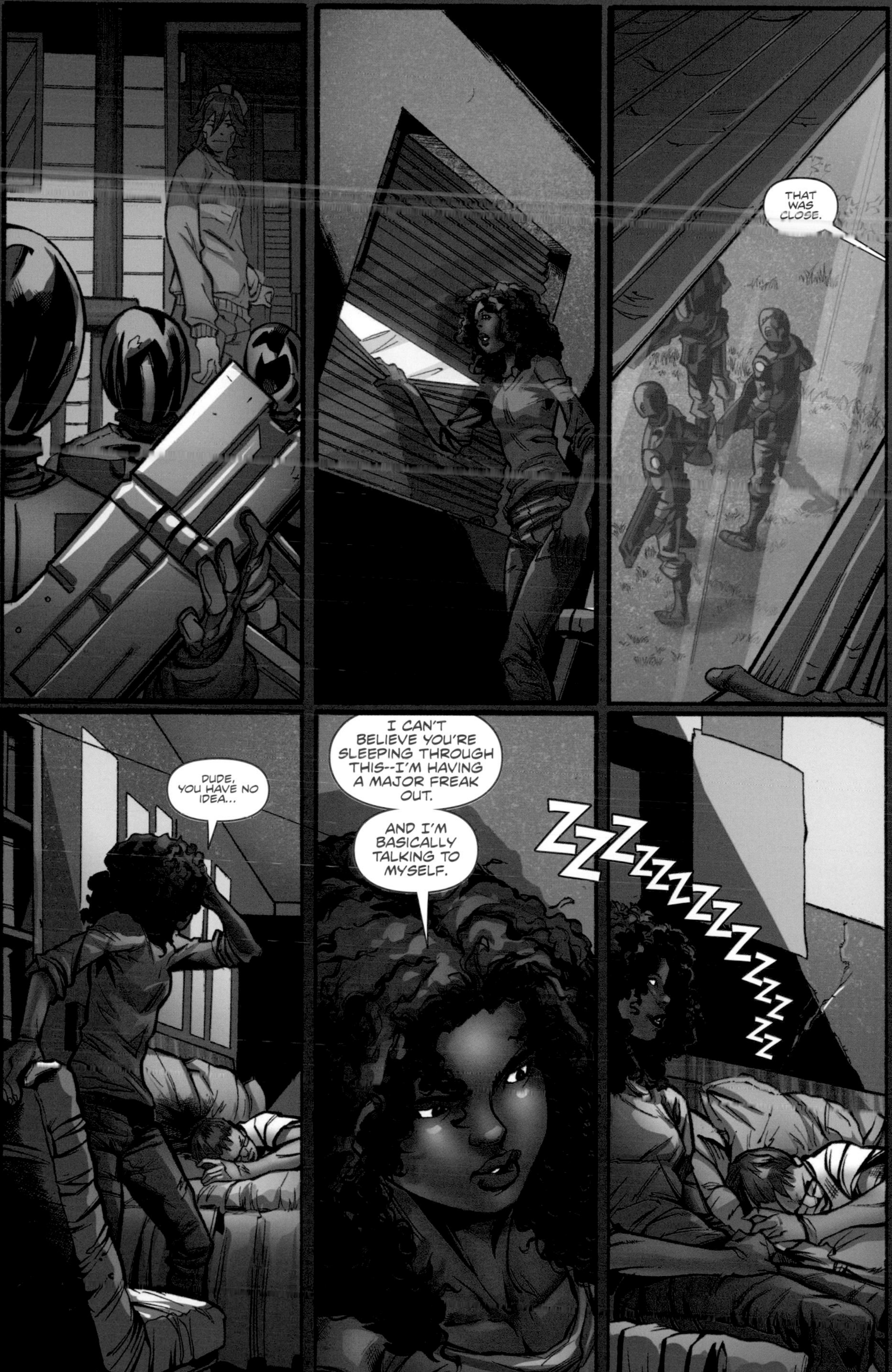
THAT WAS CLOSE.
DUDE, YOU HAVE NO IDEA...
I CAN'T BELIEVE YOU'RE SLEEPING THROUGH THIS--I'M HAVING A MAJOR FREAK OUT.
AND I'M BASICALLY TALKING TO MYSELF.
ZZZZZZZZZZZZZ

Foresight Compound, Youngstown, Ohio

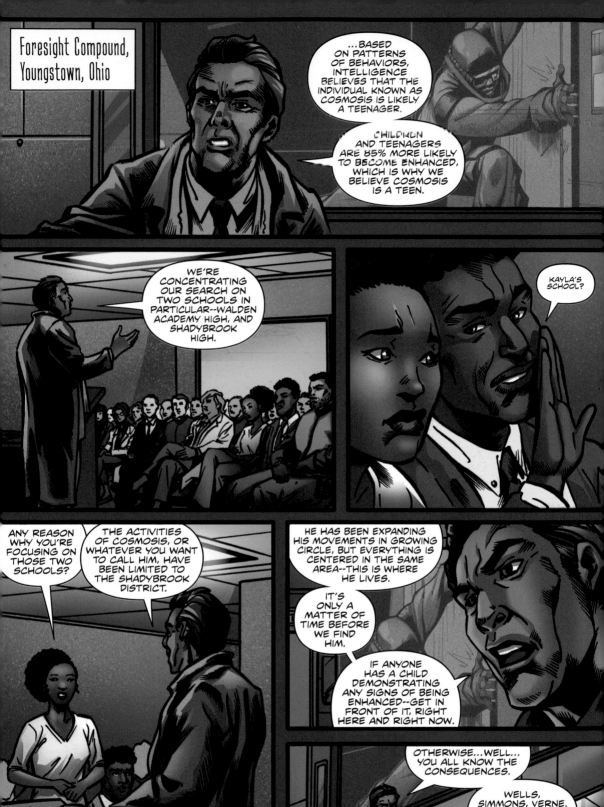

...BASED ON PATTERNS OF BEHAVIORS, INTELLIGENCE BELIEVES THAT THE INDIVIDUAL KNOWN AS COSMOSIS IS LIKELY A TEENAGER.

CHILDREN AND TEENAGERS ARE 85% MORE LIKELY TO BECOME ENHANCED, WHICH IS WHY WE BELIEVE COSMOSIS IS A TEEN.

WE'RE CONCENTRATING OUR SEARCH ON TWO SCHOOLS IN PARTICULAR--WALDEN ACADEMY HIGH, AND SHADYBROOK HIGH.

KAYLA'S SCHOOL?

ANY REASON WHY YOU'RE FOCUSING ON THOSE TWO SCHOOLS?

THE ACTIVITIES OF COSMOSIS, OR WHATEVER YOU WANT TO CALL HIM, HAVE BEEN LIMITED TO THE SHADYBROOK DISTRICT.

HE HAS BEEN EXPANDING HIS MOVEMENTS IN GROWING CIRCLE, BUT EVERYTHING IS CENTERED IN THE SAME AREA--THIS IS WHERE HE LIVES.

IT'S ONLY A MATTER OF TIME BEFORE WE FIND HIM.

IF ANYONE HAS A CHILD DEMONSTRATING ANY SIGNS OF BEING ENHANCED--GET IN FRONT OF IT, RIGHT HERE AND RIGHT NOW.

OTHERWISE...WELL... YOU ALL KNOW THE CONSEQUENCES.

WELLS, SIMMONS, VERNE. I NEED TO SPEAK WITH YOU PRIVATELY.

EVERYONE ELSE IS DISMISSED.

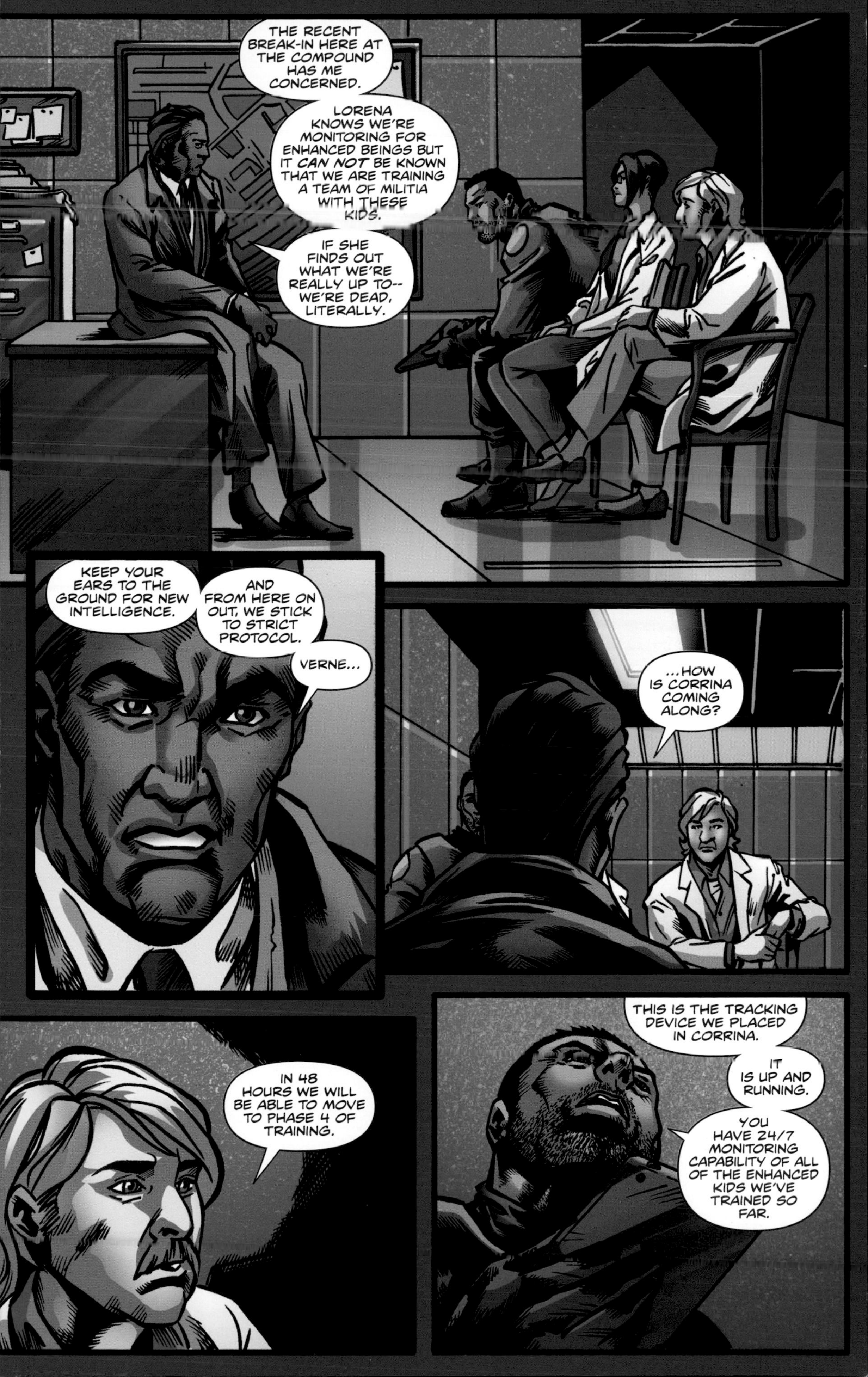
THE RECENT BREAK-IN HERE AT THE COMPOUND HAS ME CONCERNED.
LORENA KNOWS WE'RE MONITORING FOR ENHANCED BEINGS BUT IT *CAN NOT* BE KNOWN THAT WE ARE TRAINING A TEAM OF MILITIA WITH THESE KIDS.
IF SHE FINDS OUT WHAT WE'RE REALLY UP TO-- WE'RE DEAD, LITERALLY.
KEEP YOUR EARS TO THE GROUND FOR NEW INTELLIGENCE.
AND FROM HERE ON OUT, WE STICK TO STRICT PROTOCOL.
VERNE...
...HOW IS CORRINA COMING ALONG?
IN 48 HOURS WE WILL BE ABLE TO MOVE TO PHASE 4 OF TRAINING.
THIS IS THE TRACKING DEVICE WE PLACED IN CORRINA.
IT IS UP AND RUNNING.
YOU HAVE 24/7 MONITORING CAPABILITY OF ALL OF THE ENHANCED KIDS WE'VE TRAINED SO FAR.

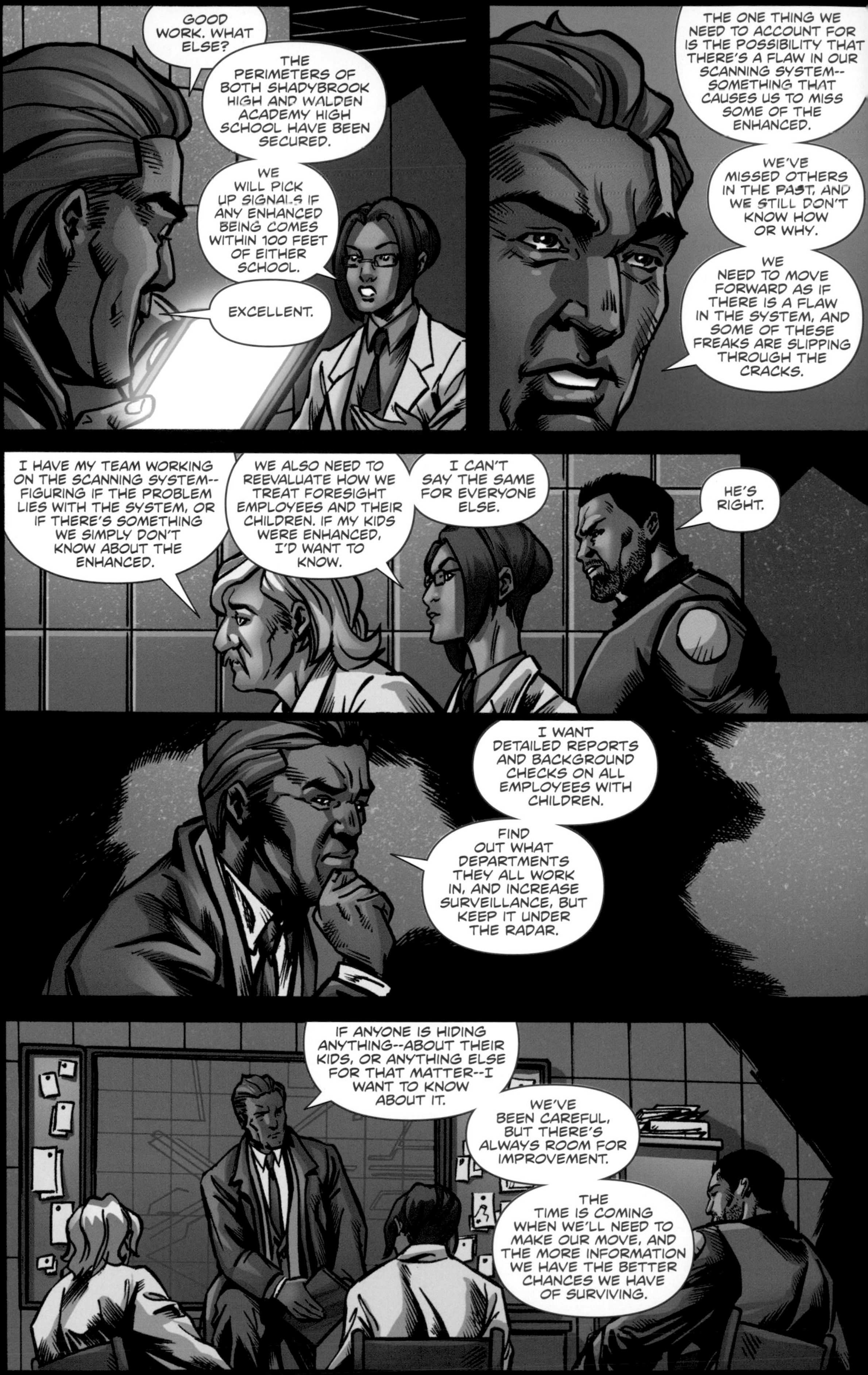
GOOD WORK. WHAT ELSE?
THE PERIMETERS OF BOTH SHADYBROOK HIGH AND WALDEN ACADEMY HIGH SCHOOL HAVE BEEN SECURED.
WE WILL PICK UP SIGNALS IF ANY ENHANCED BEING COMES WITHIN 100 FEET OF EITHER SCHOOL.
EXCELLENT.
THE ONE THING WE NEED TO ACCOUNT FOR IS THE POSSIBILITY THAT THERE'S A FLAW IN OUR SCANNING SYSTEM--SOMETHING THAT CAUSES US TO MISS SOME OF THE ENHANCED.
WE'VE MISSED OTHERS IN THE PAST, AND WE STILL DON'T KNOW HOW OR WHY.
WE NEED TO MOVE FORWARD AS IF THERE IS A FLAW IN THE SYSTEM, AND SOME OF THESE FREAKS ARE SLIPPING THROUGH THE CRACKS.
I HAVE MY TEAM WORKING ON THE SCANNING SYSTEM--FIGURING IF THE PROBLEM LIES WITH THE SYSTEM, OR IF THERE'S SOMETHING WE SIMPLY DON'T KNOW ABOUT THE ENHANCED.
WE ALSO NEED TO REEVALUATE HOW WE TREAT FORESIGHT EMPLOYEES AND THEIR CHILDREN. IF MY KIDS WERE ENHANCED, I'D WANT TO KNOW.
I CAN'T SAY THE SAME FOR EVERYONE ELSE.
HE'S RIGHT.
I WANT DETAILED REPORTS AND BACKGROUND CHECKS ON ALL EMPLOYEES WITH CHILDREN.
FIND OUT WHAT DEPARTMENTS THEY ALL WORK IN, AND INCREASE SURVEILLANCE, BUT KEEP IT UNDER THE RADAR.
IF ANYONE IS HIDING ANYTHING--ABOUT THEIR KIDS, OR ANYTHING ELSE FOR THAT MATTER--I WANT TO KNOW ABOUT IT.
WE'VE BEEN CAREFUL, BUT THERE'S ALWAYS ROOM FOR IMPROVEMENT.
THE TIME IS COMING WHEN WE'LL NEED TO MAKE OUR MOVE, AND THE MORE INFORMATION WE HAVE THE BETTER CHANCES WE HAVE OF SURVIVING.

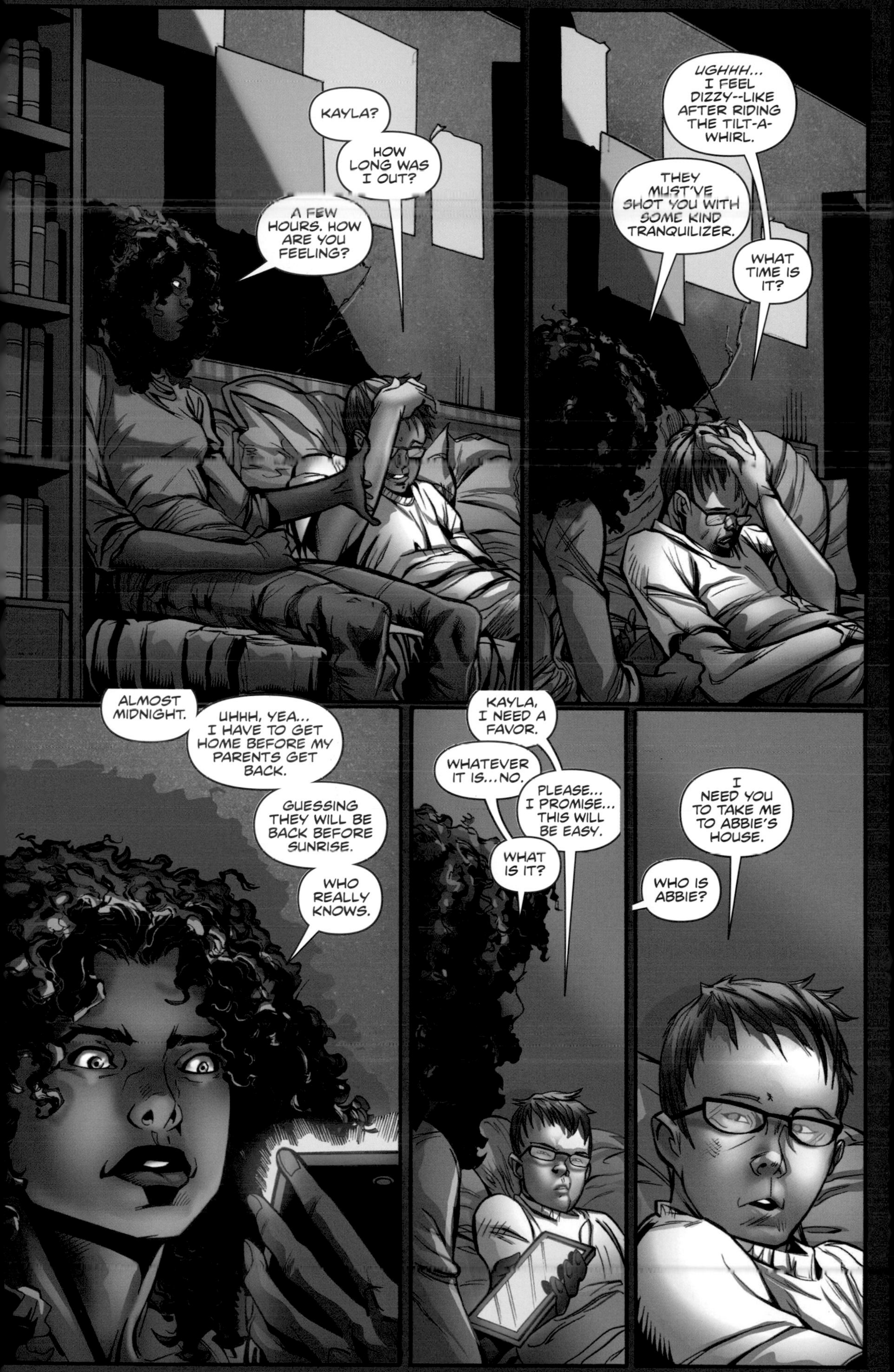
KAYLA?
HOW LONG WAS I OUT?
A FEW HOURS. HOW ARE YOU FEELING?
UGHHH... I FEEL DIZZY--LIKE AFTER RIDING THE TILT-A-WHIRL.
THEY MUST'VE SHOT YOU WITH SOME KIND TRANQUILIZER.
WHAT TIME IS IT?
ALMOST MIDNIGHT.
UHHH, YEA... I HAVE TO GET HOME BEFORE MY PARENTS GET BACK.
GUESSING THEY WILL BE BACK BEFORE SUNRISE.
WHO REALLY KNOWS.
KAYLA, I NEED A FAVOR.
WHATEVER IT IS...NO.
PLEASE... I PROMISE... THIS WILL BE EASY.
WHAT IS IT?
I NEED YOU TO TAKE ME TO ABBIE'S HOUSE.
WHO IS ABBIE?

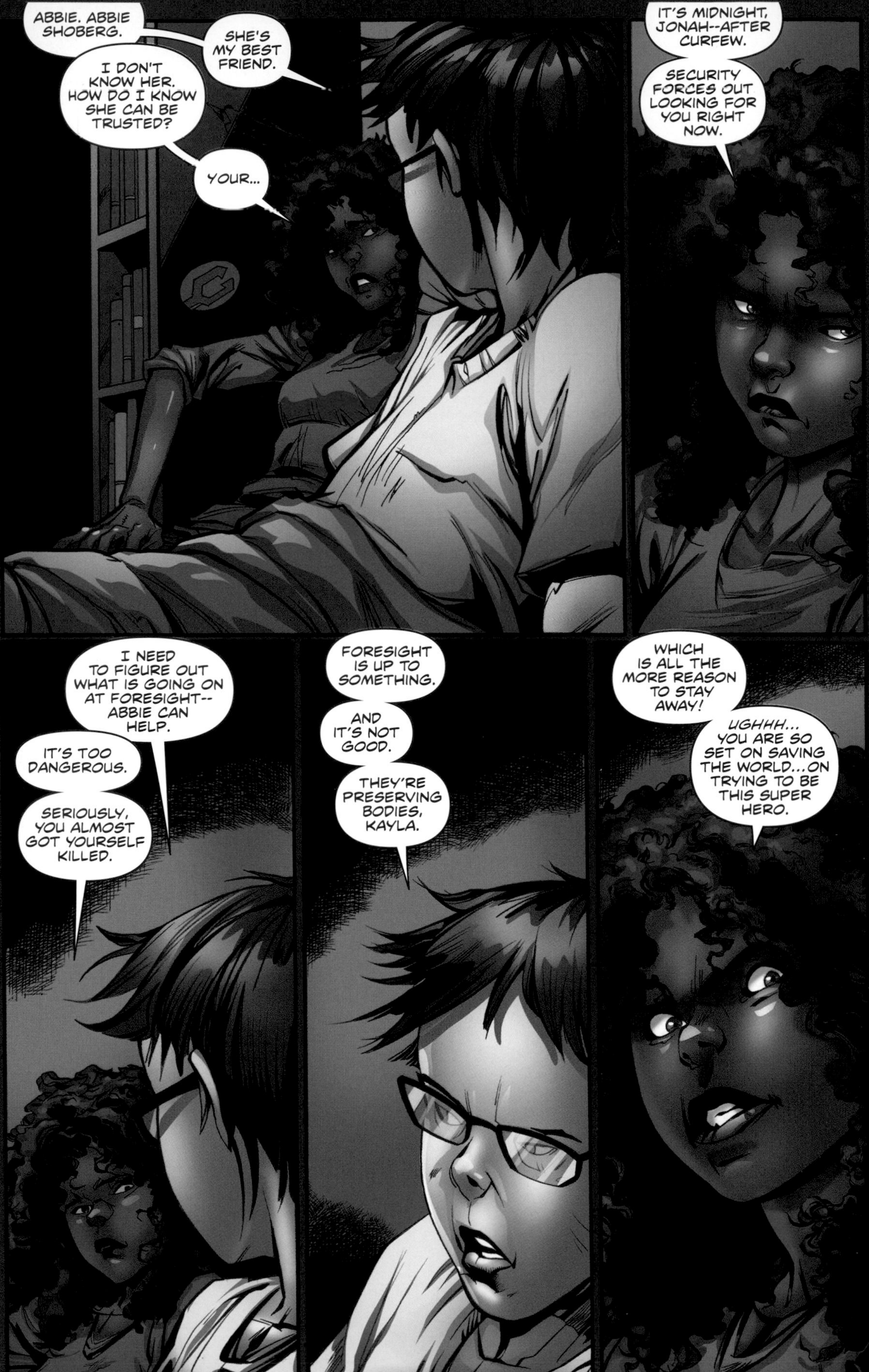
ABBIE. ABBIE SHOBERG.
SHE'S MY BEST FRIEND.
I DON'T KNOW HER. HOW DO I KNOW SHE CAN BE TRUSTED?
YOUR...
IT'S MIDNIGHT, JONAH--AFTER CURFEW.
SECURITY FORCES OUT LOOKING FOR YOU RIGHT NOW.
I NEED TO FIGURE OUT WHAT IS GOING ON AT FORESIGHT--ABBIE CAN HELP.
IT'S TOO DANGEROUS.
SERIOUSLY, YOU ALMOST GOT YOURSELF KILLED.
FORESIGHT IS UP TO SOMETHING.
AND IT'S NOT GOOD.
THEY'RE PRESERVING BODIES, KAYLA.
WHICH IS ALL THE MORE REASON TO STAY AWAY!
UGHHH... YOU ARE SO SET ON SAVING THE WORLD...ON TRYING TO BE THIS SUPER HERO.

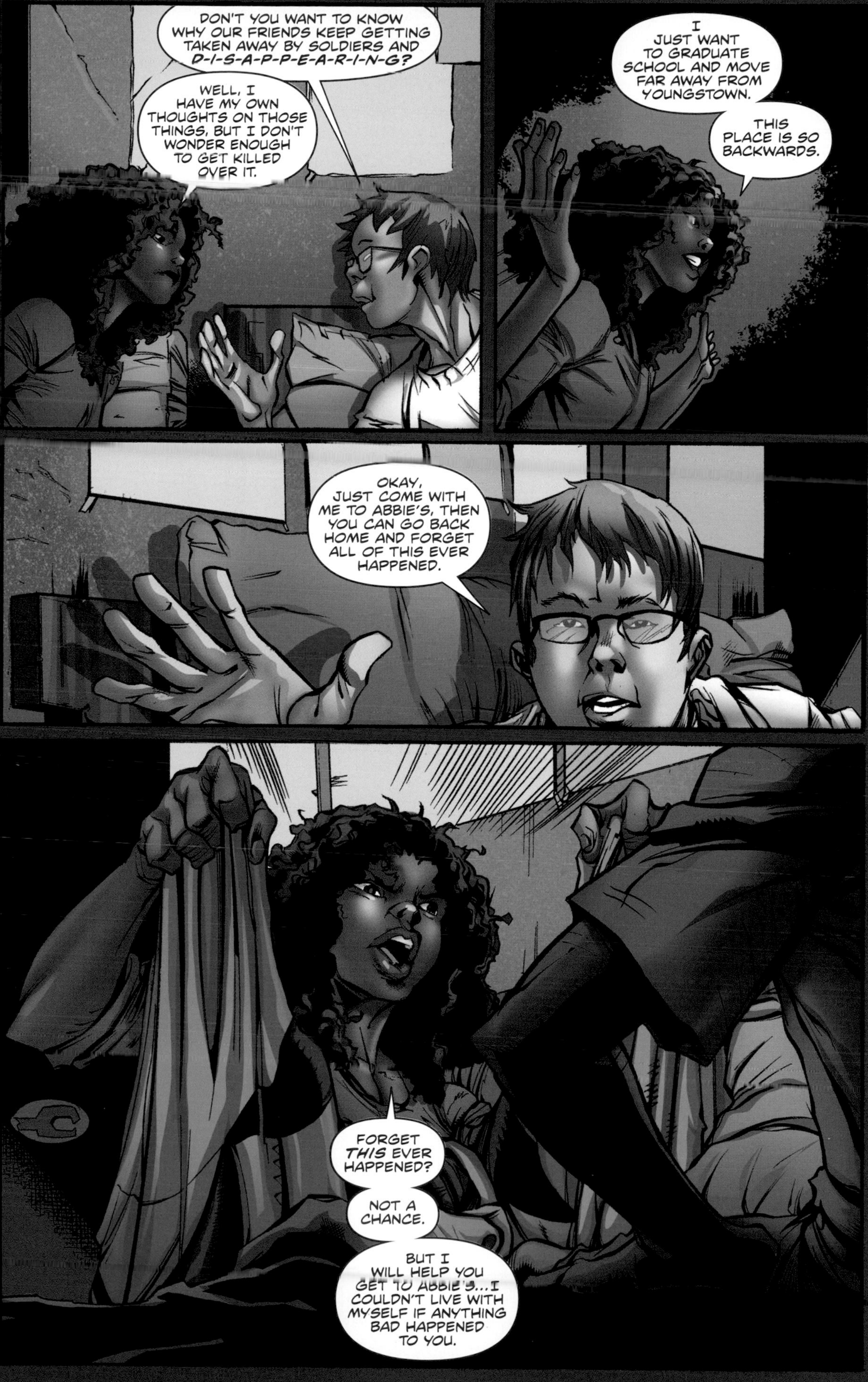
DON'T YOU WANT TO KNOW WHY OUR FRIENDS KEEP GETTING TAKEN AWAY BY SOLDIERS AND D-I-S-A-P-P-E-A-R-I-N-G?
WELL, I HAVE MY OWN THOUGHTS ON THOSE THINGS, BUT I DON'T WONDER ENOUGH TO GET KILLED OVER IT.
I JUST WANT TO GRADUATE SCHOOL AND MOVE FAR AWAY FROM YOUNGSTOWN.
THIS PLACE IS SO BACKWARDS.
OKAY, JUST COME WITH ME TO ABBIE'S, THEN YOU CAN GO BACK HOME AND FORGET ALL OF THIS EVER HAPPENED.
FORGET THIS EVER HAPPENED?
NOT A CHANCE.
BUT I WILL HELP YOU GET TO ABBIE'S... I COULDN'T LIVE WITH MYSELF IF ANYTHING BAD HAPPENED TO YOU.

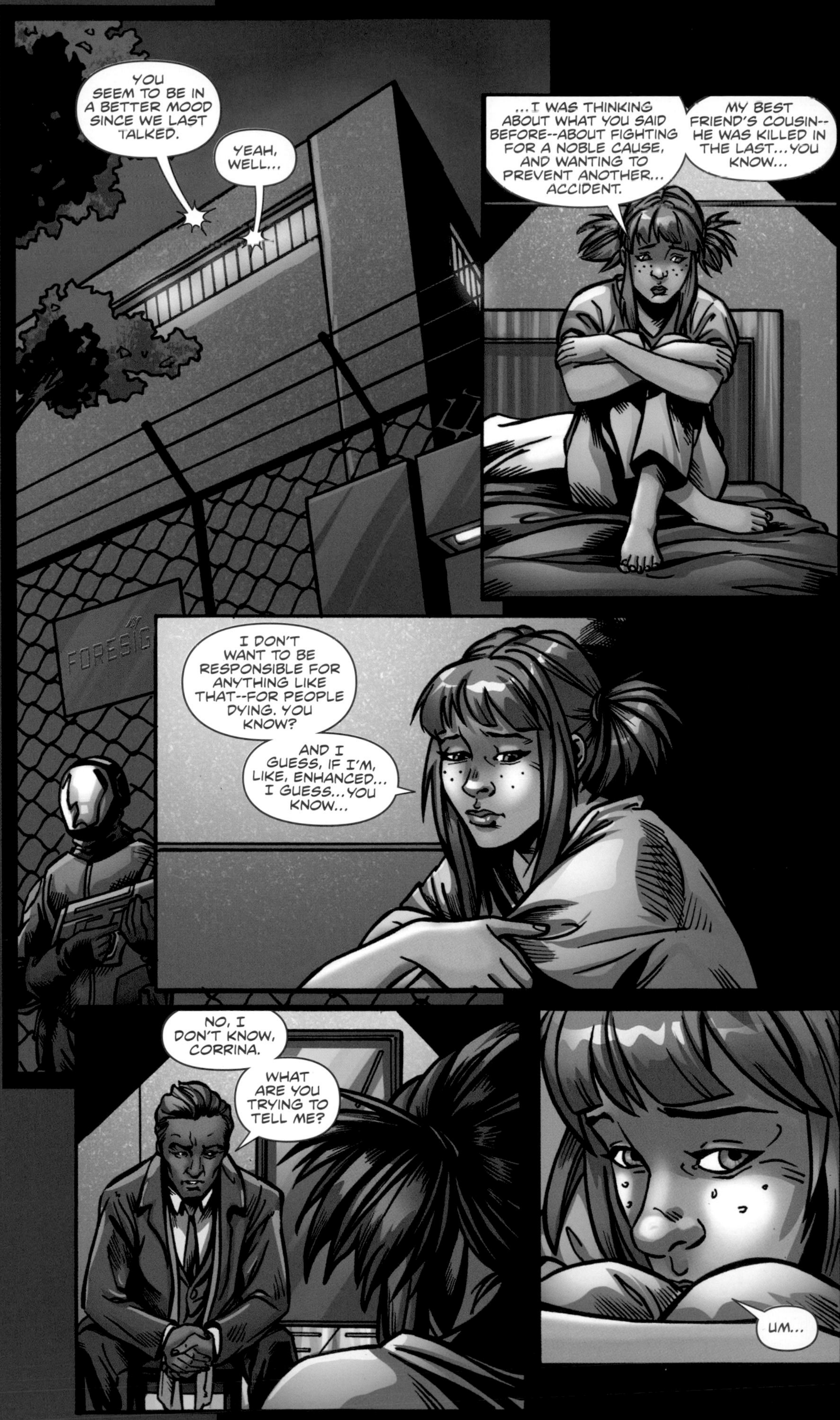
YOU SEEM TO BE IN A BETTER MOOD SINCE WE LAST TALKED.
YEAH, WELL...
...I WAS THINKING ABOUT WHAT YOU SAID BEFORE--ABOUT FIGHTING FOR A NOBLE CAUSE, AND WANTING TO PREVENT ANOTHER... ACCIDENT.
MY BEST FRIEND'S COUSIN--HE WAS KILLED IN THE LAST...YOU KNOW...
FORESIG
I DON'T WANT TO BE RESPONSIBLE FOR ANYTHING LIKE THAT--FOR PEOPLE DYING. YOU KNOW?
AND I GUESS, IF I'M, LIKE, ENHANCED... I GUESS...YOU KNOW...
NO, I DON'T KNOW, CORRINA.
WHAT ARE YOU TRYING TO TELL ME?
UM...

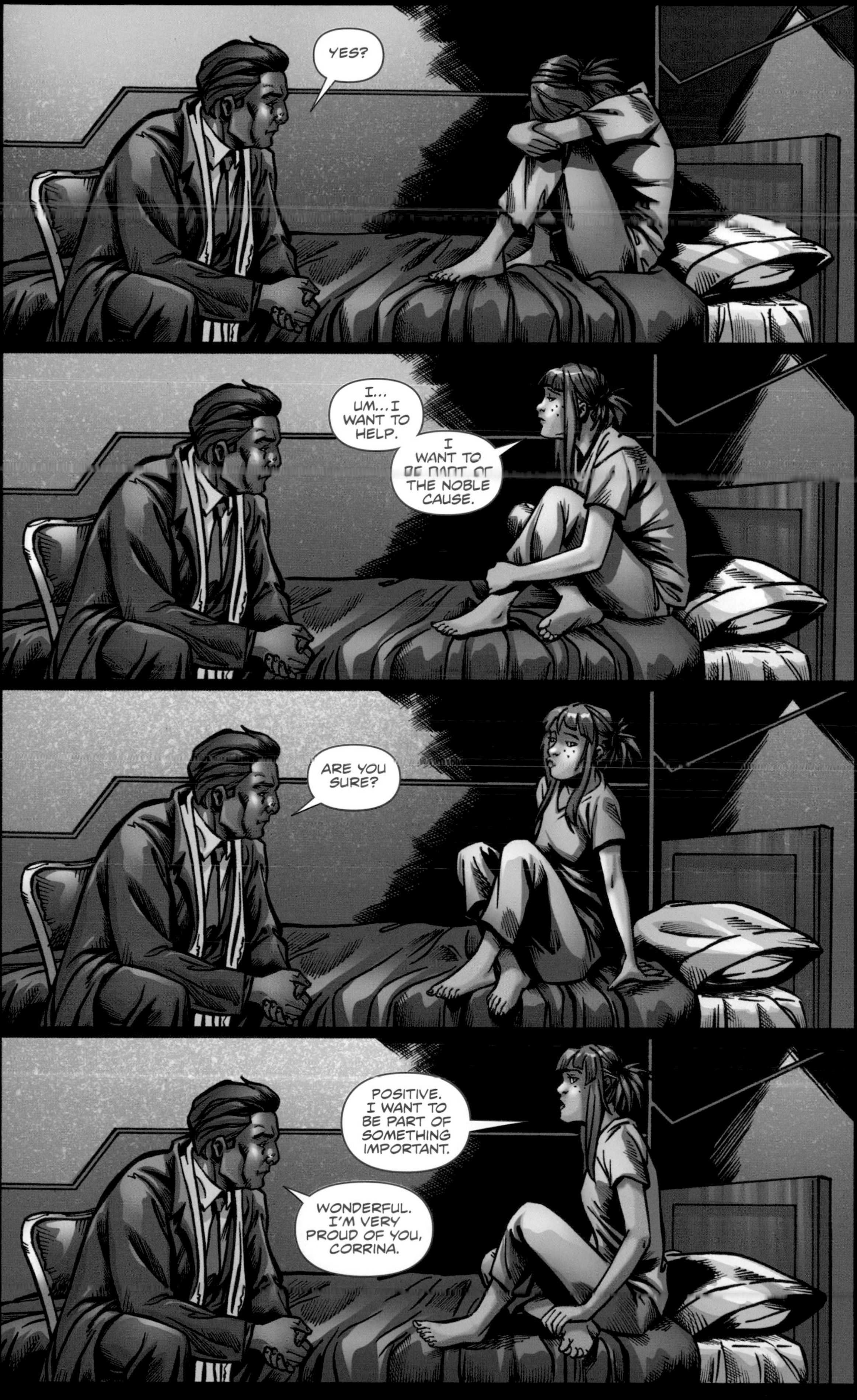
YES?
I... UM...I WANT TO HELP.
I WANT TO BE PART OF THE NOBLE CAUSE.
ARE YOU SURE?
POSITIVE. I WANT TO BE PART OF SOMETHING IMPORTANT.
WONDERFUL. I'M VERY PROUD OF YOU, CORRINA.

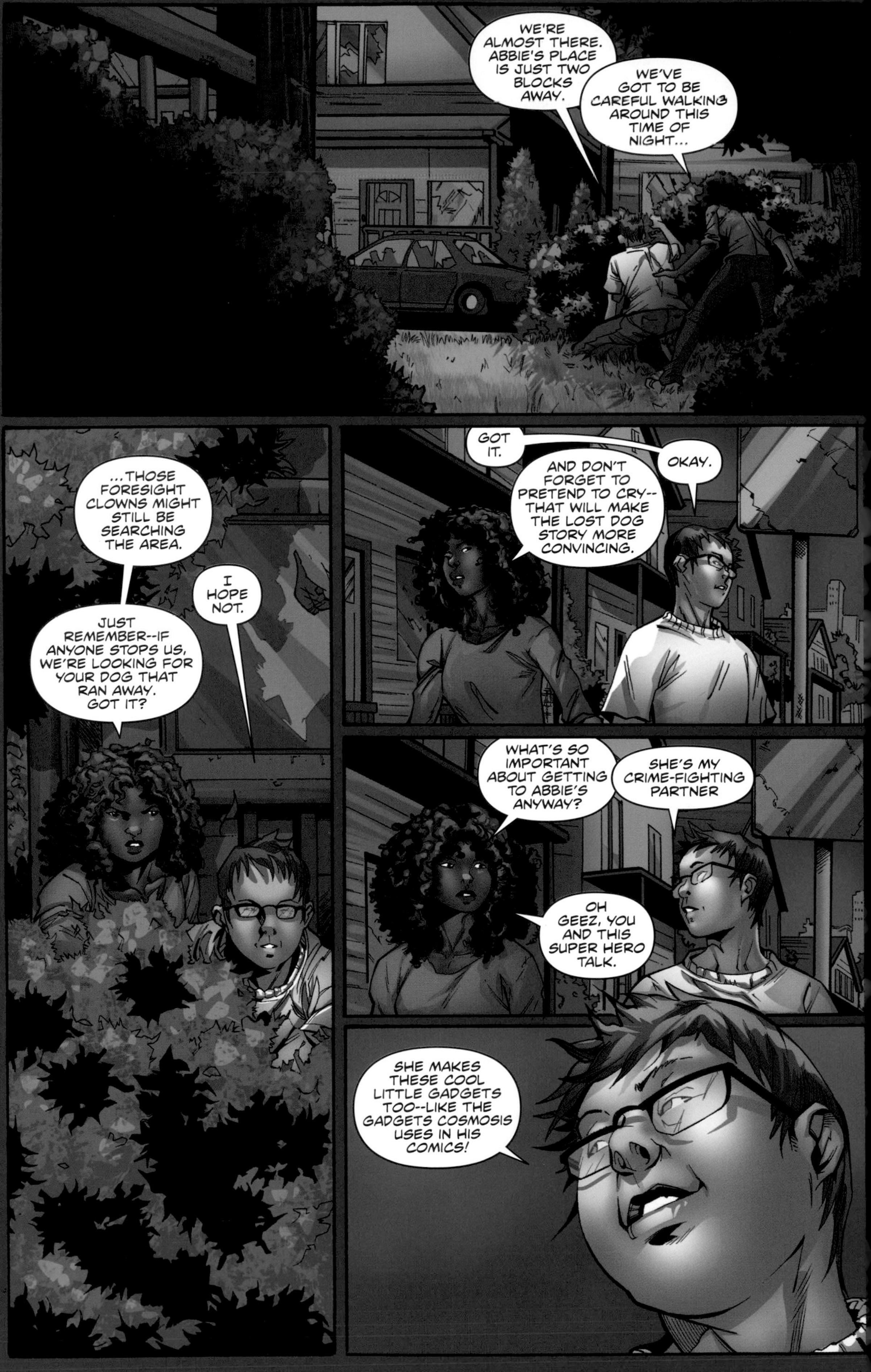

WE'RE ALMOST THERE. ABBIE'S PLACE IS JUST TWO BLOCKS AWAY.
WE'VE GOT TO BE CAREFUL WALKING AROUND THIS TIME OF NIGHT...
...THOSE FORESIGHT CLOWNS MIGHT STILL BE SEARCHING THE AREA.
I HOPE NOT.
JUST REMEMBER--IF ANYONE STOPS US, WE'RE LOOKING FOR YOUR DOG THAT RAN AWAY. GOT IT?
GOT IT.
OKAY.
AND DON'T FORGET TO PRETEND TO CRY--THAT WILL MAKE THE LOST DOG STORY MORE CONVINCING.
WHAT'S SO IMPORTANT ABOUT GETTING TO ABBIE'S ANYWAY?
SHE'S MY CRIME-FIGHTING PARTNER
OH GEEZ, YOU AND THIS SUPER HERO TALK.
SHE MAKES THESE COOL LITTLE GADGETS TOO--LIKE THE GADGETS COSMOSIS USES IN HIS COMICS!

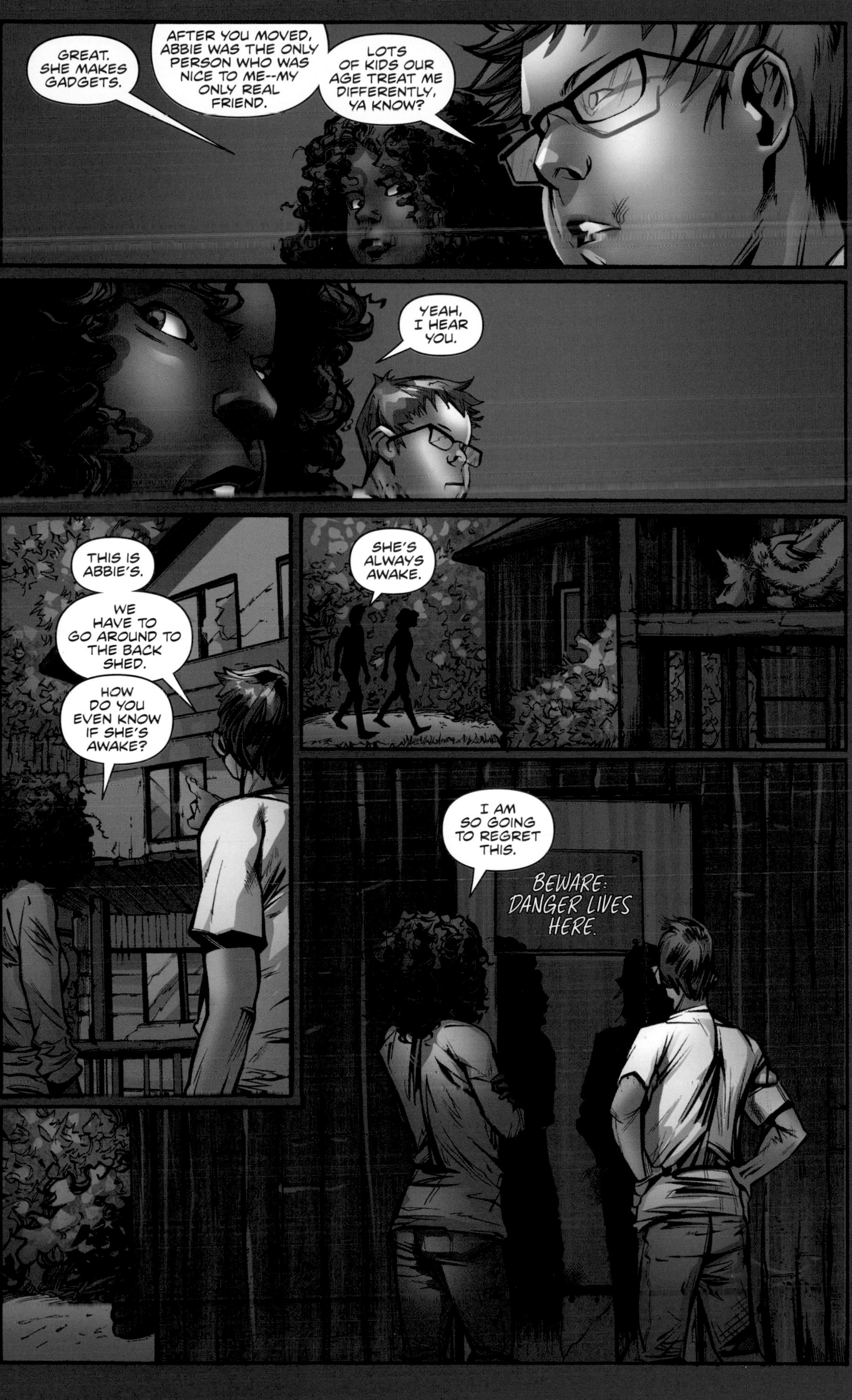
GREAT. SHE MAKES GADGETS.
AFTER YOU MOVED, ABBIE WAS THE ONLY PERSON WHO WAS NICE TO ME--MY ONLY REAL FRIEND.
LOTS OF KIDS OUR AGE TREAT ME DIFFERENTLY, YA KNOW?
YEAH, I HEAR YOU.
THIS IS ABBIE'S.
WE HAVE TO GO AROUND TO THE BACK SHED.
HOW DO YOU EVEN KNOW IF SHE'S AWAKE?
SHE'S ALWAYS AWAKE.
I AM SO GOING TO REGRET THIS.
BEWARE: DANGER LIVES HERE.

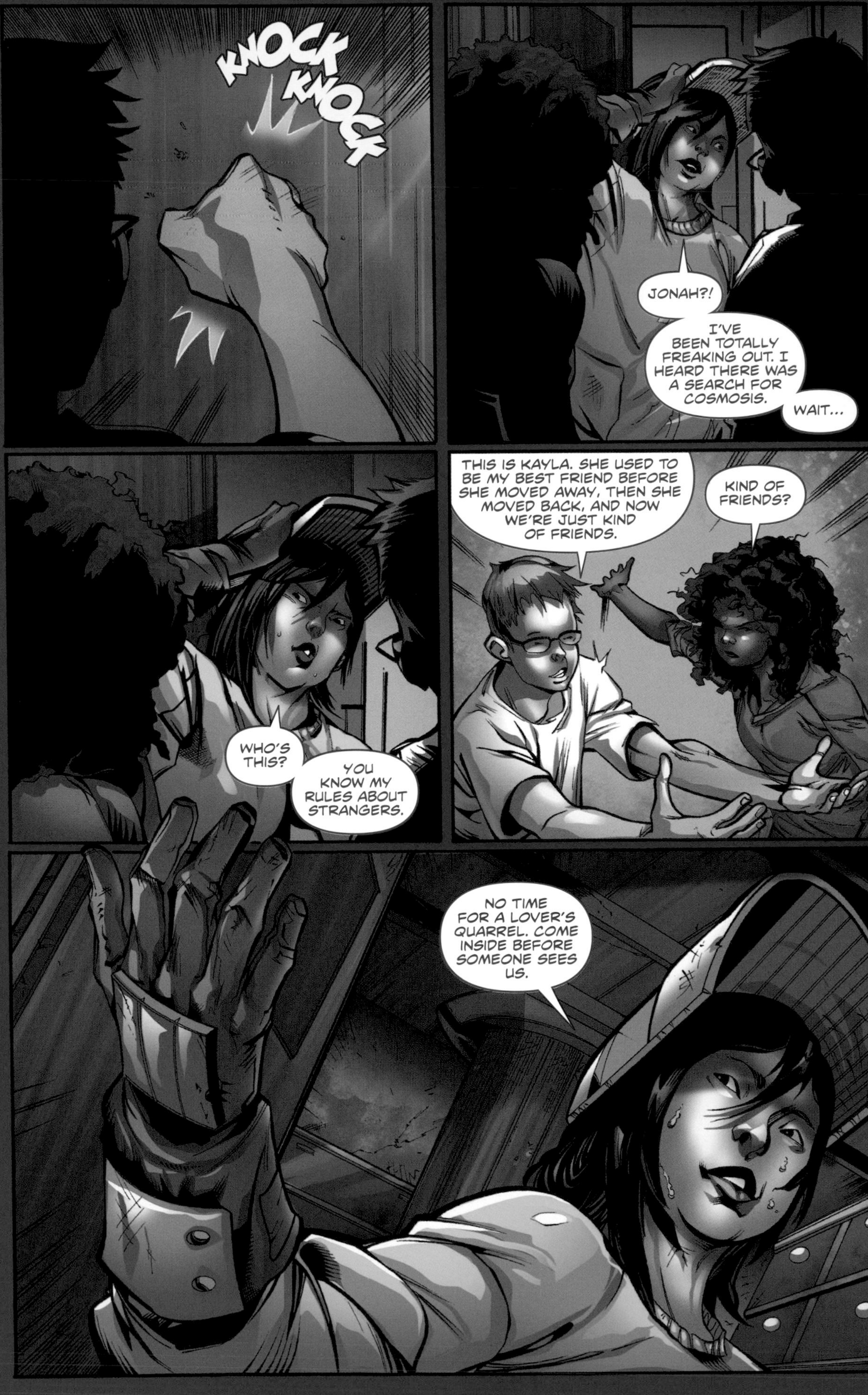
KNOCK KNOCK
JONAH?!
I'VE BEEN TOTALLY FREAKING OUT. I HEARD THERE WAS A SEARCH FOR COSMOSIS.
WAIT...
WHO'S THIS?
YOU KNOW MY RULES ABOUT STRANGERS.
THIS IS KAYLA. SHE USED TO BE MY BEST FRIEND BEFORE SHE MOVED AWAY, THEN SHE MOVED BACK, AND NOW WE'RE JUST KIND OF FRIENDS.
KIND OF FRIENDS?
NO TIME FOR A LOVER'S QUARREL. COME INSIDE BEFORE SOMEONE SEES US.

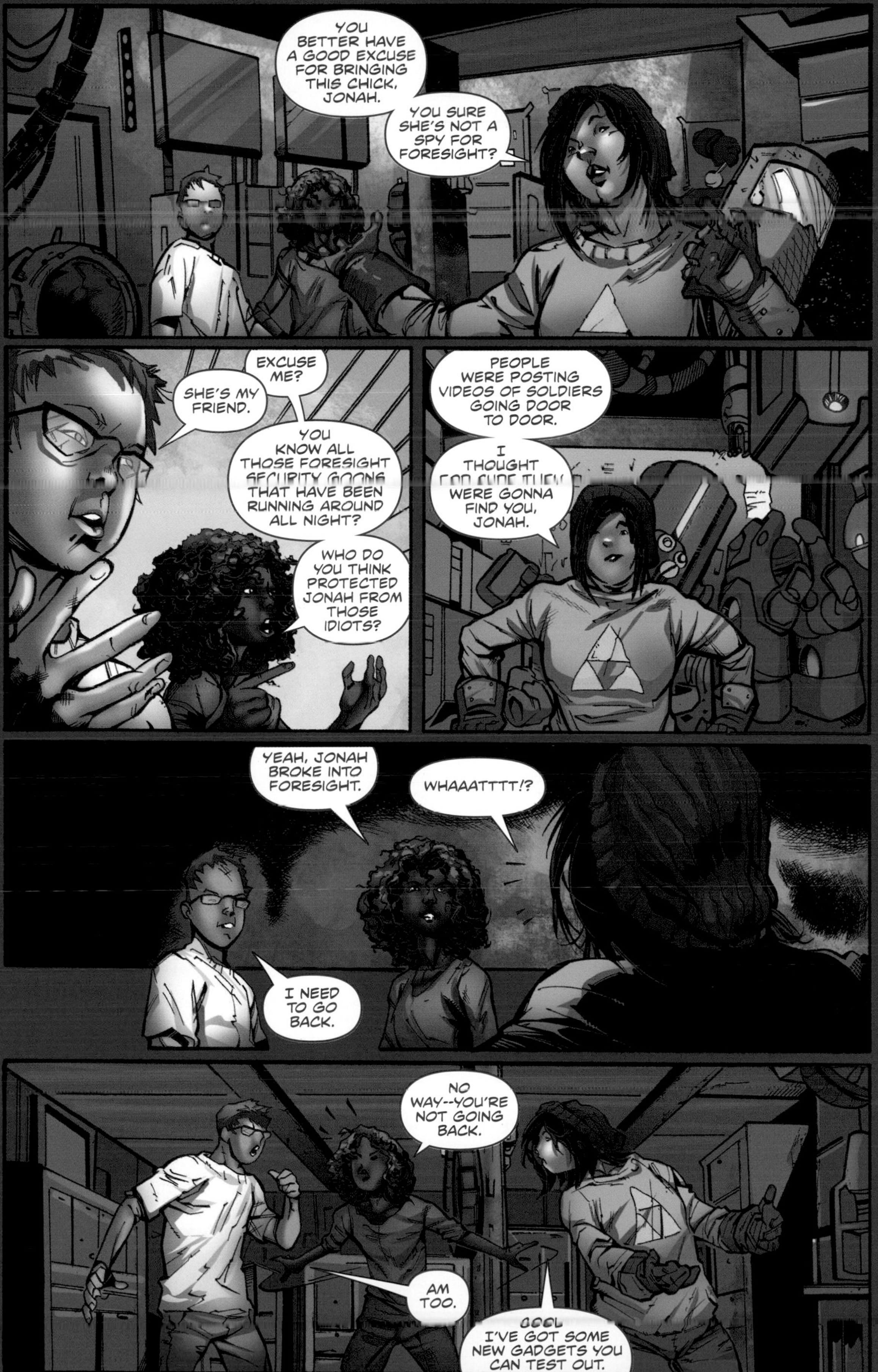
YOU BETTER HAVE A GOOD EXCUSE FOR BRINGING THIS CHICK, JONAH.
YOU SURE SHE'S NOT A SPY FOR FORESIGHT?
SHE'S MY FRIEND.
EXCUSE ME?
YOU KNOW ALL THOSE FORESIGHT SECURITY GOONS THAT HAVE BEEN RUNNING AROUND ALL NIGHT?
WHO DO YOU THINK PROTECTED JONAH FROM THOSE IDIOTS?
PEOPLE WERE POSTING VIDEOS OF SOLDIERS GOING DOOR TO DOOR.
I THOUGHT
WERE GONNA FIND YOU, JONAH.
YEAH, JONAH BROKE INTO FORESIGHT.
WHAAATTTT!?
I NEED TO GO BACK.
NO WAY--YOU'RE NOT GOING BACK.
AM TOO.
COOL
I'VE GOT SOME NEW GADGETS YOU CAN TEST OUT.

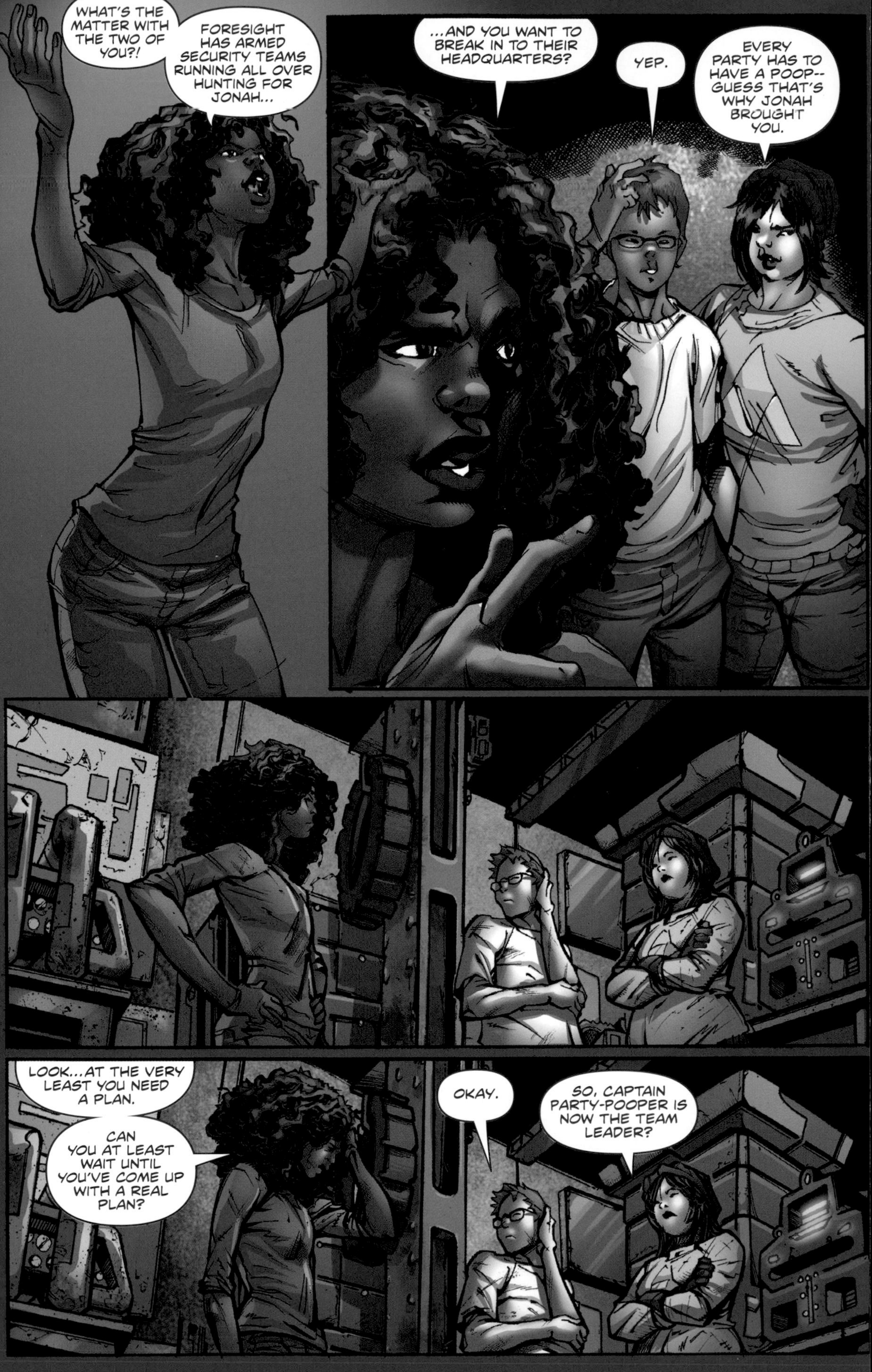
WHAT'S THE MATTER WITH THE TWO OF YOU?!
FORESIGHT HAS ARMED SECURITY TEAMS RUNNING ALL OVER HUNTING FOR JONAH...
...AND YOU WANT TO BREAK IN TO THEIR HEADQUARTERS?
YEP.
EVERY PARTY HAS TO HAVE A POOP-- GUESS THAT'S WHY JONAH BROUGHT YOU.
LOOK...AT THE VERY LEAST YOU NEED A PLAN.
CAN YOU AT LEAST WAIT UNTIL YOU'VE COME UP WITH A REAL PLAN?
OKAY.
SO, CAPTAIN PARTY-POOPER IS NOW THE TEAM LEADER?

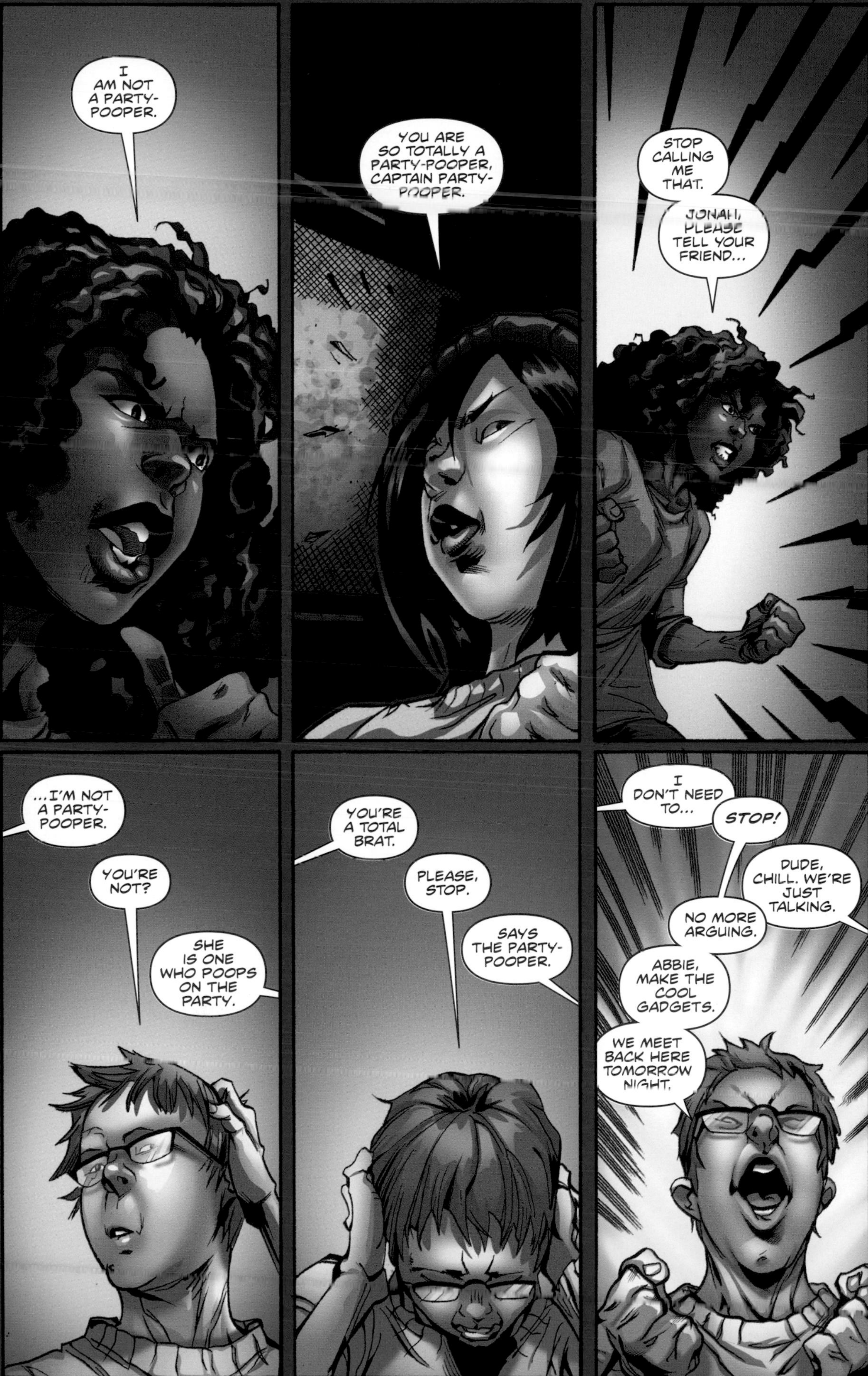
I AM NOT A PARTY-POOPER.
YOU ARE SO TOTALLY A PARTY-POOPER, CAPTAIN PARTY-POOPER.
STOP CALLING ME THAT.
JONAH, PLEASE TELL YOUR FRIEND...
...I'M NOT A PARTY-POOPER.
YOU'RE NOT?
SHE IS ONE WHO POOPS ON THE PARTY.
YOU'RE A TOTAL BRAT.
PLEASE, STOP.
SAYS THE PARTY-POOPER.
I DON'T NEED TO...
STOP!
DUDE, CHILL. WE'RE JUST TALKING.
NO MORE ARGUING.
ABBIE, MAKE THE COOL GADGETS.
WE MEET BACK HERE TOMORROW NIGHT.

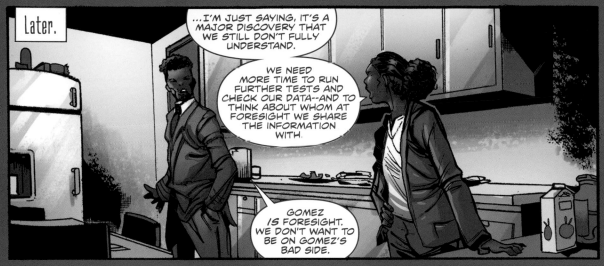

...I'M JUST SAYING, IT'S A MAJOR DISCOVERY THAT WE STILL DON'T FULLY UNDERSTAND.

WE NEED MORE TIME TO RUN FURTHER TESTS AND CHECK OUR DATA--AND TO THINK ABOUT WHOM AT FORESIGHT WE SHARE THE INFORMATION WITH.

GOMEZ IS FORESIGHT. WE DON'T WANT TO BE ON GOMEZ'S BAD SIDE.

WE'LL BE PUTTING OURSELVES IN DANGER, INCLUDING KAYLA IF THIS GETS OUT ANYMORE THAN IT ALREADY HAS.

GOMEZ DOESN'T KNOW THE FORMULA MIXTURE AND QUANTITIES UNLESS WE TELL HIM.

HE ONLY KNOWS THAT WE'VE FIGURED OUT WHY BODIES AREN'T DECOMPOSING.

HE'S DANGEROUS.

IF HE KNOWS WE UNDERSTAND WHY HUMANS AFFECTED BY METEORS DON'T DECOMPOSE...

...THEN HE PROBABLY KNOWS WE CAN CREATE HUMANS THAT DON'T DECOMPOSE.

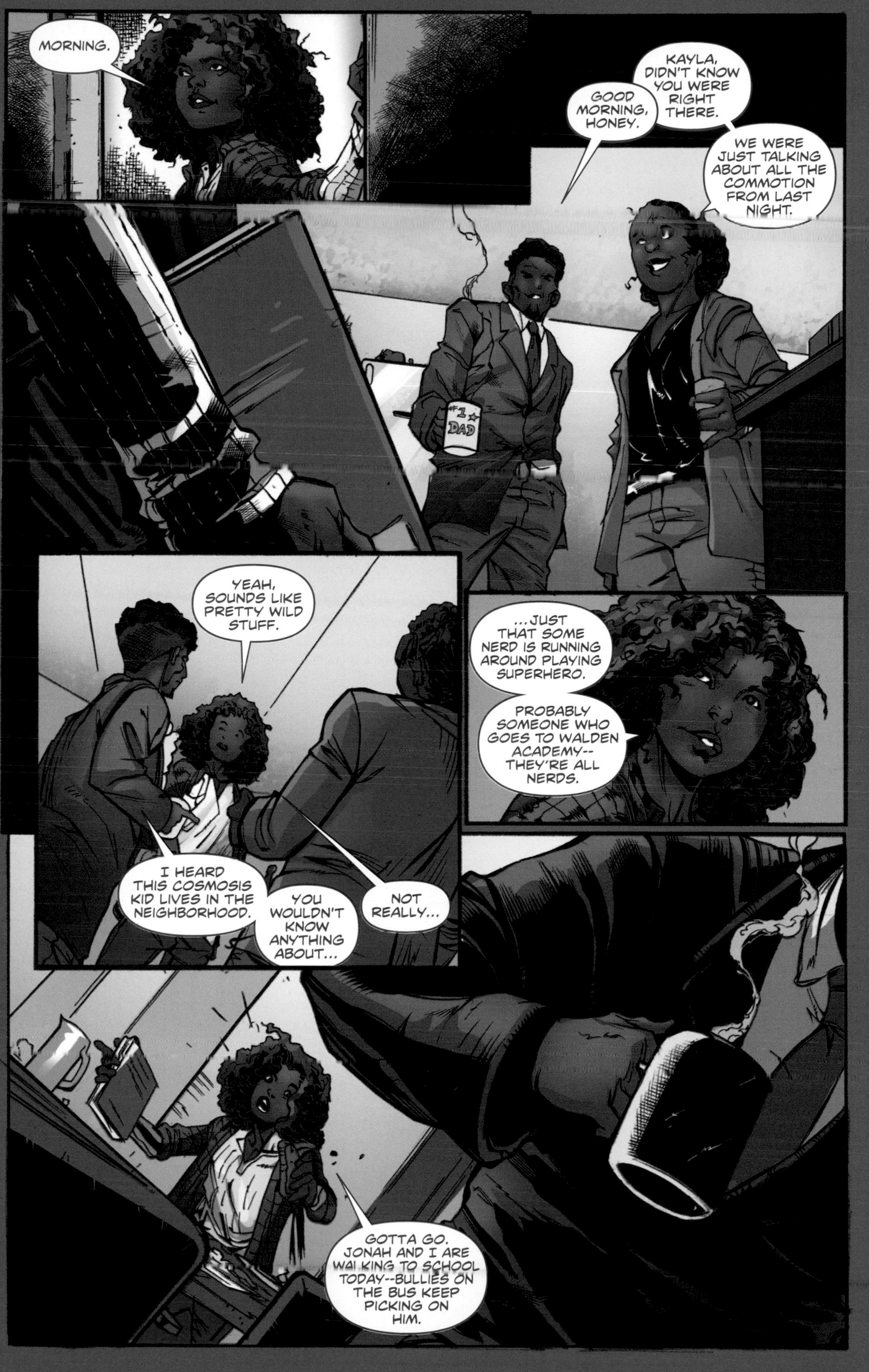
MORNING.
KAYLA, DIDN'T KNOW YOU WERE RIGHT THERE.
GOOD MORNING, HONEY.
WE WERE JUST TALKING ABOUT ALL THE COMMOTION FROM LAST NIGHT.
YEAH, SOUNDS LIKE PRETTY WILD STUFF.
I HEARD THIS COSMOSIS KID LIVES IN THE NEIGHBORHOOD.
YOU WOULDN'T KNOW ANYTHING ABOUT...
NOT REALLY...
...JUST THAT SOME NERD IS RUNNING AROUND PLAYING SUPERHERO.
PROBABLY SOMEONE WHO GOES TO WALDEN ACADEMY--THEY'RE ALL NERDS.
GOTTA GO. JONAH AND I ARE WALKING TO SCHOOL TODAY--BULLIES ON THE BUS KEEP PICKING ON HIM.

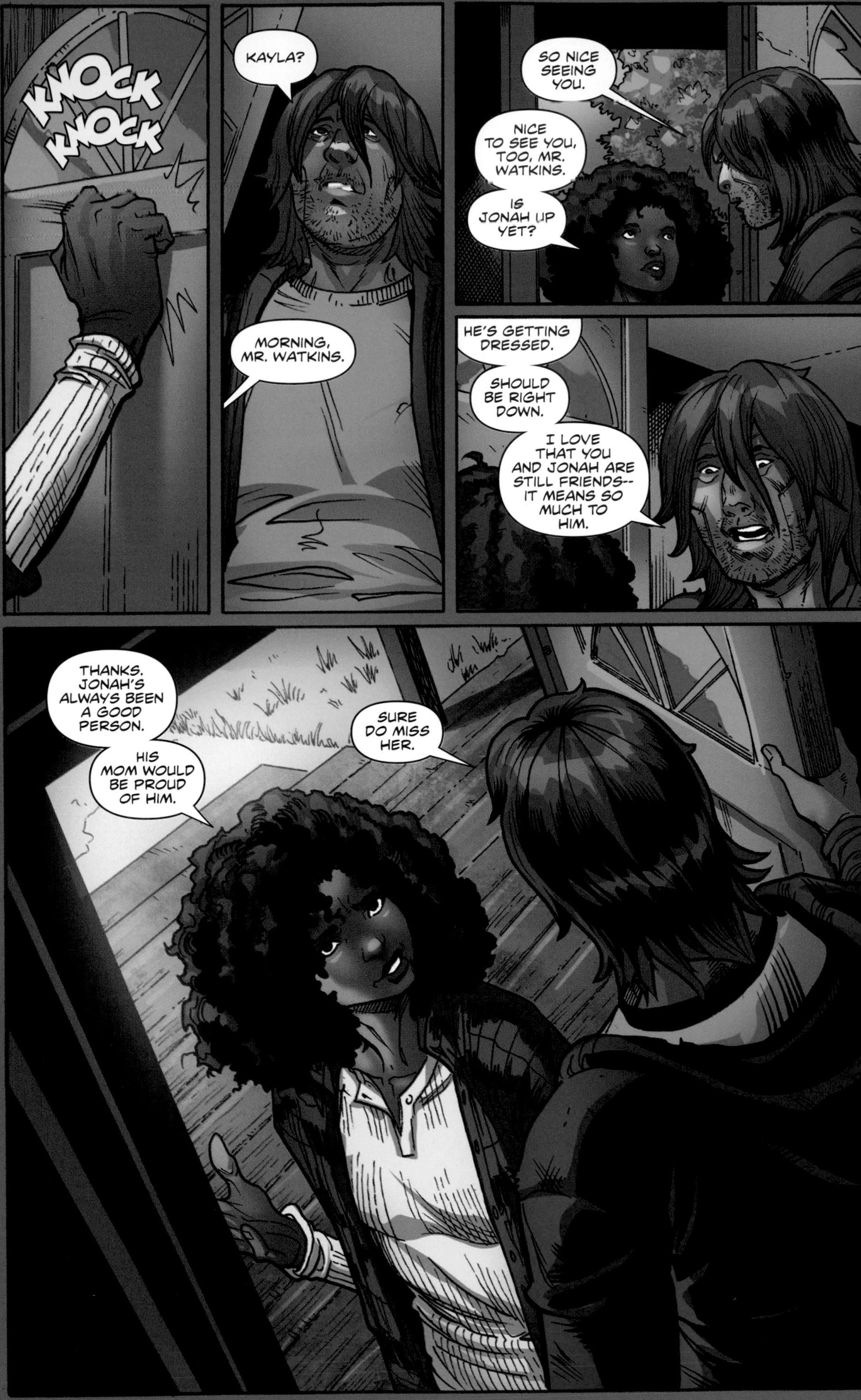
KNOCK KNOCK
KAYLA?
MORNING, MR. WATKINS.
SO NICE SEEING YOU.
NICE TO SEE YOU, TOO, MR. WATKINS.
IS JONAH UP YET?
HE'S GETTING DRESSED.
SHOULD BE RIGHT DOWN.
I LOVE THAT YOU AND JONAH ARE STILL FRIENDS-- IT MEANS SO MUCH TO HIM.
THANKS. JONAH'S ALWAYS BEEN A GOOD PERSON.
HIS MOM WOULD BE PROUD OF HIM.
SURE DO MISS HER.

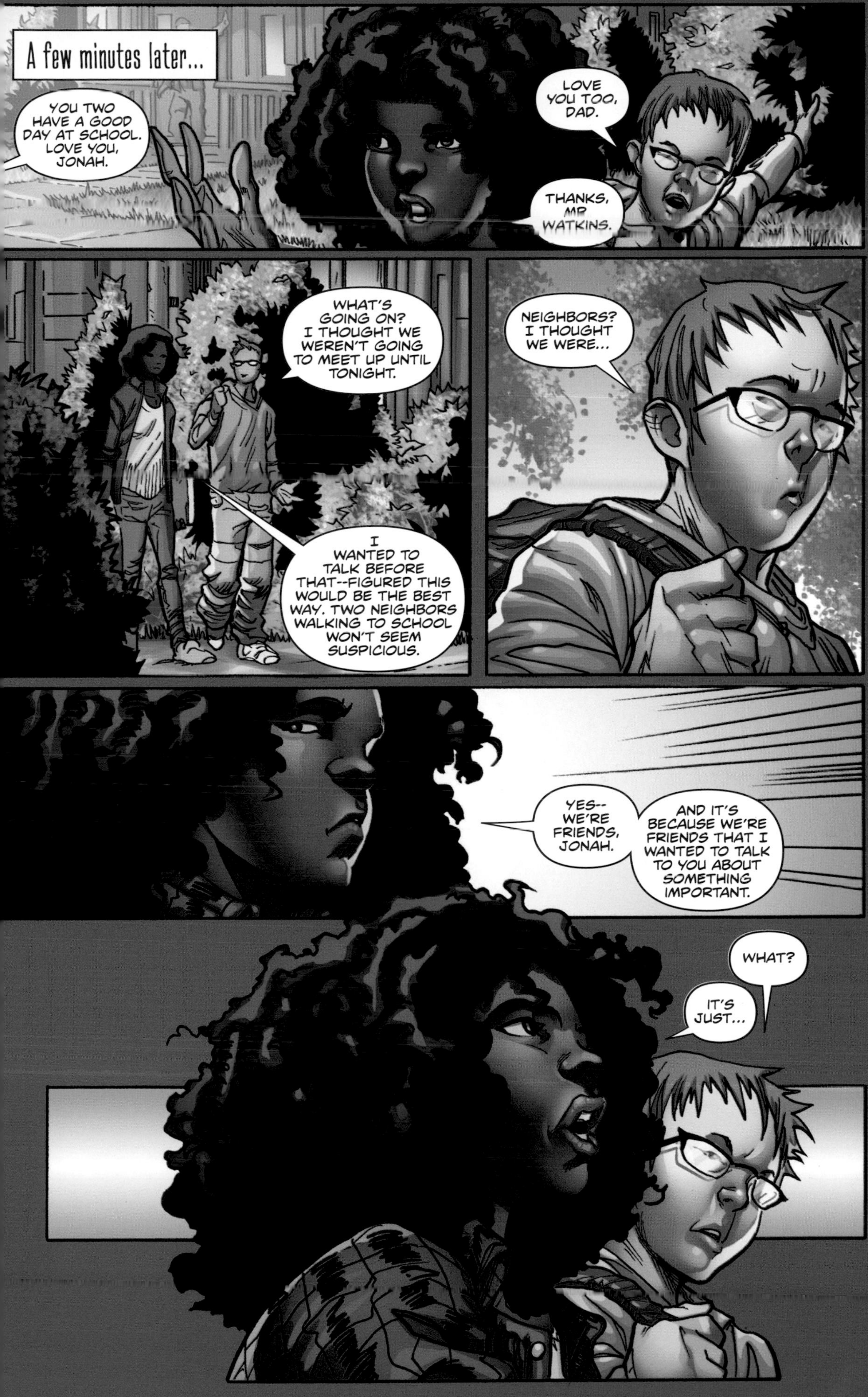
A few minutes later...
YOU TWO HAVE A GOOD DAY AT SCHOOL. LOVE YOU, JONAH.
LOVE YOU TOO, DAD.
THANKS, MR WATKINS.
WHAT'S GOING ON? I THOUGHT WE WEREN'T GOING TO MEET UP UNTIL TONIGHT.
I WANTED TO TALK BEFORE THAT--FIGURED THIS WOULD BE THE BEST WAY. TWO NEIGHBORS WALKING TO SCHOOL WON'T SEEM SUSPICIOUS.
NEIGHBORS? I THOUGHT WE WERE...
YES-- WE'RE FRIENDS, JONAH.
AND IT'S BECAUSE WE'RE FRIENDS THAT I WANTED TO TALK TO YOU ABOUT SOMETHING IMPORTANT.
WHAT?
IT'S JUST...

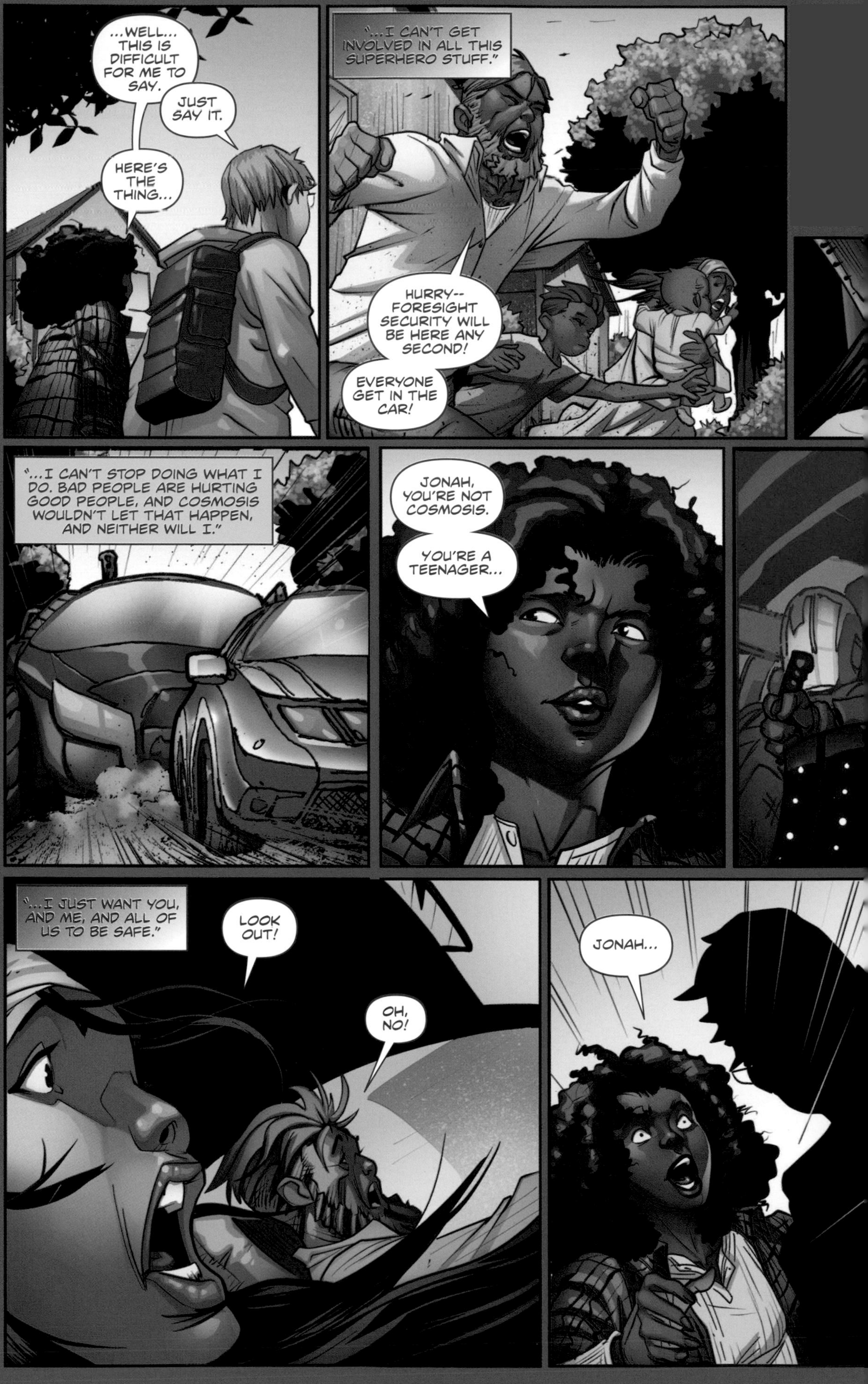
...WELL... THIS IS DIFFICULT FOR ME TO SAY.
JUST SAY IT.
HERE'S THE THING...
"...I CAN'T GET INVOLVED IN ALL THIS SUPERHERO STUFF."
HURRY-- FORESIGHT SECURITY WILL BE HERE ANY SECOND!
EVERYONE GET IN THE CAR!
"...I CAN'T STOP DOING WHAT I DO. BAD PEOPLE ARE HURTING GOOD PEOPLE, AND COSMOSIS WOULDN'T LET THAT HAPPEN, AND NEITHER WILL I."
JONAH, YOU'RE NOT COSMOSIS.
YOU'RE A TEENAGER...
"...I JUST WANT YOU, AND ME, AND ALL OF US TO BE SAFE."
LOOK OUT!
OH, NO!
JONAH...

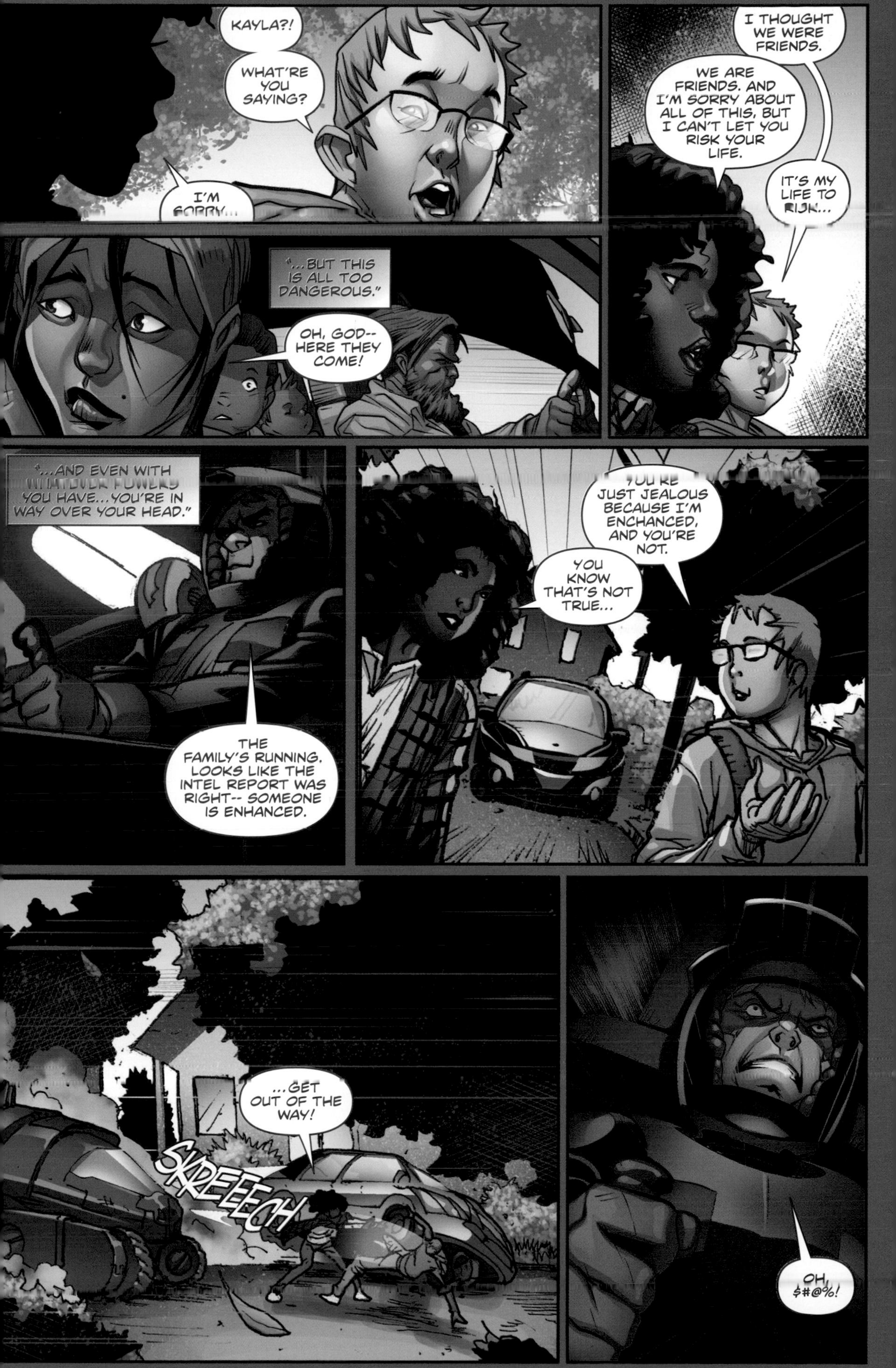

KAYLA?!
WHAT'RE YOU SAYING?
I'M
I THOUGHT WE WERE FRIENDS.
WE ARE FRIENDS. AND I'M SORRY ABOUT ALL OF THIS, BUT I CAN'T LET YOU RISK YOUR LIFE.
IT'S MY LIFE TO
"...BUT THIS IS ALL TOO DANGEROUS."
OH, GOD-- HERE THEY COME!
"...AND EVEN WITH
YOU HAVE...YOU'RE IN WAY OVER YOUR HEAD."
THE FAMILY'S RUNNING. LOOKS LIKE THE INTEL REPORT WAS RIGHT-- SOMEONE IS ENHANCED.
JUST JEALOUS BECAUSE I'M ENCHANCED, AND YOU'RE NOT.
YOU KNOW THAT'S NOT TRUE...
...GET OUT OF THE WAY!
SKREEEECH
OH, $#@%!

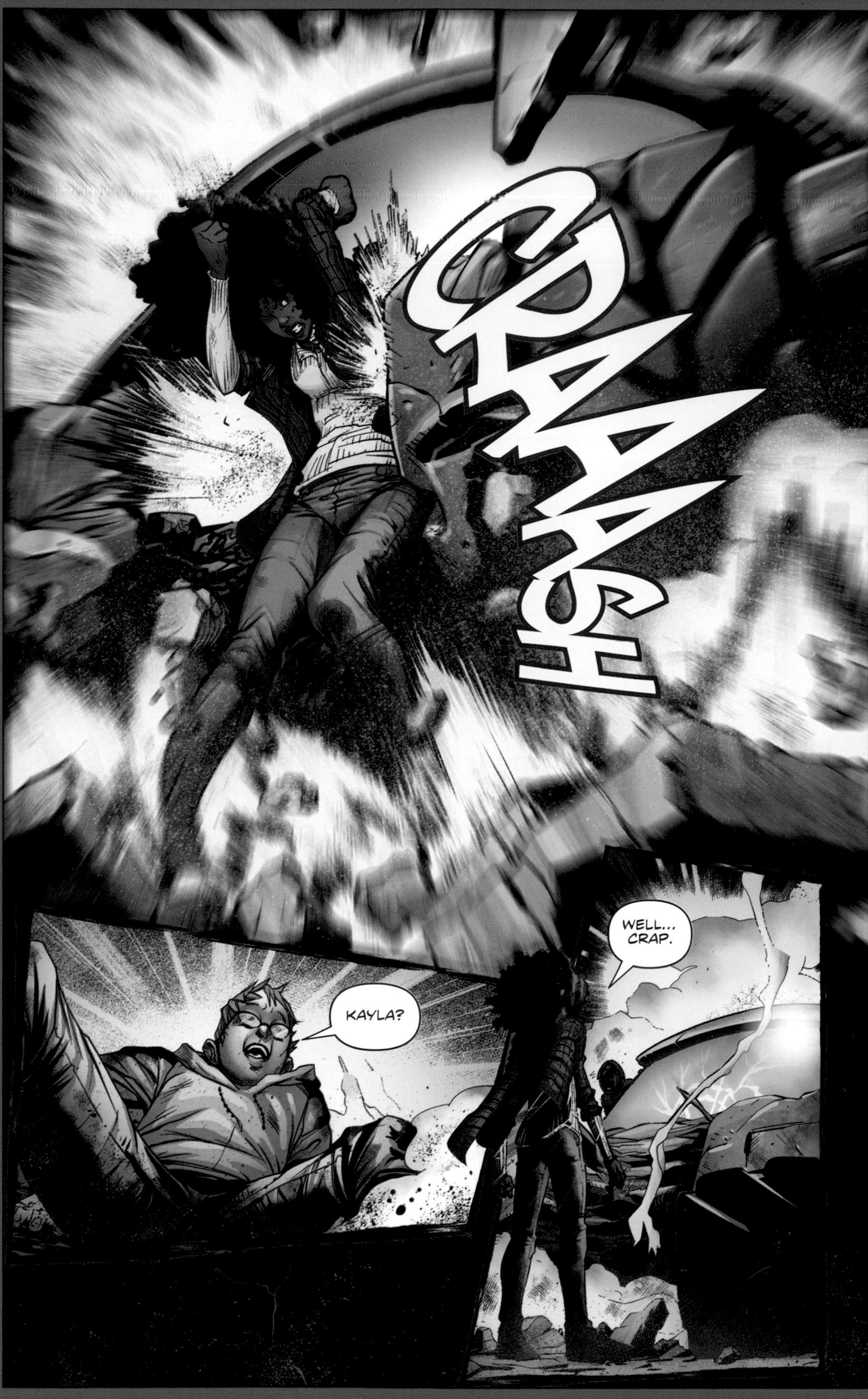
CRAAASH
KAYLA?
WELL... CRAP.

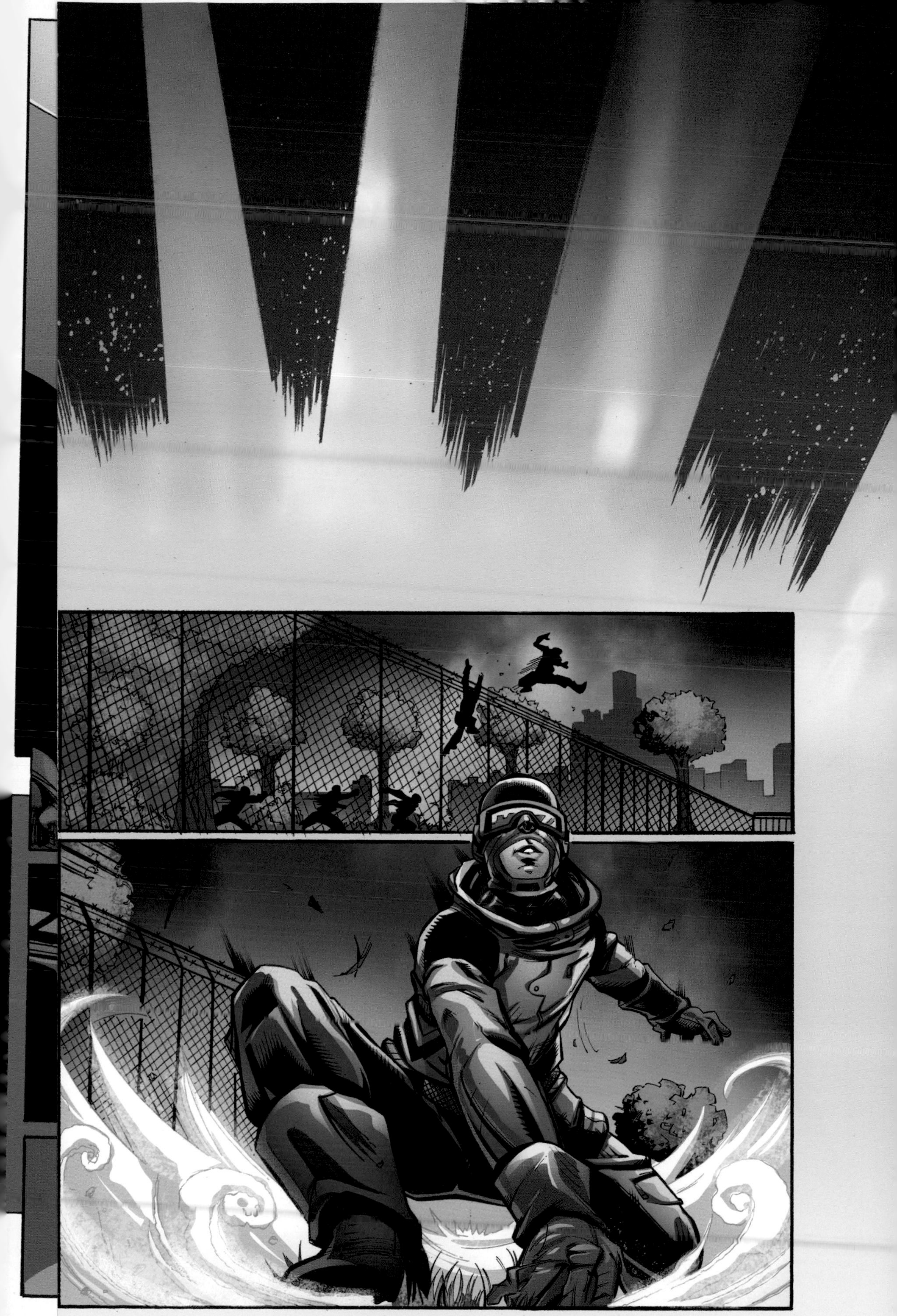

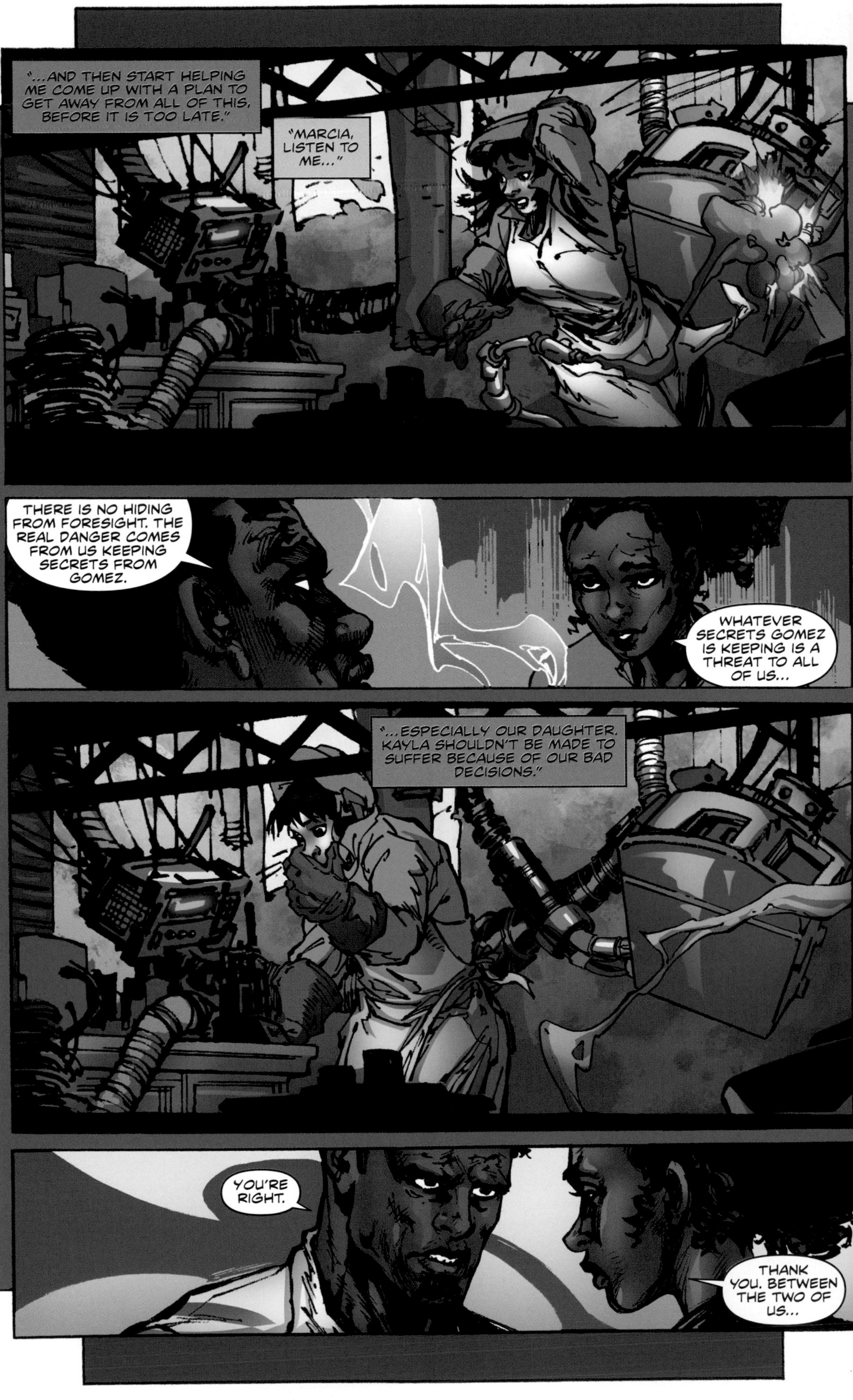
"...AND THEN START HELPING ME COME UP WITH A PLAN TO GET AWAY FROM ALL OF THIS, BEFORE IT IS TOO LATE."
"MARCIA, LISTEN TO ME..."
THERE IS NO HIDING FROM FORESIGHT. THE REAL DANGER COMES FROM US KEEPING SECRETS FROM GOMEZ.
WHATEVER SECRETS GOMEZ IS KEEPING IS A THREAT TO ALL OF US...
"...ESPECIALLY OUR DAUGHTER. KAYLA SHOULDN'T BE MADE TO SUFFER BECAUSE OF OUR BAD DECISIONS."
YOU'RE RIGHT.
THANK YOU. BETWEEN THE TWO OF US...

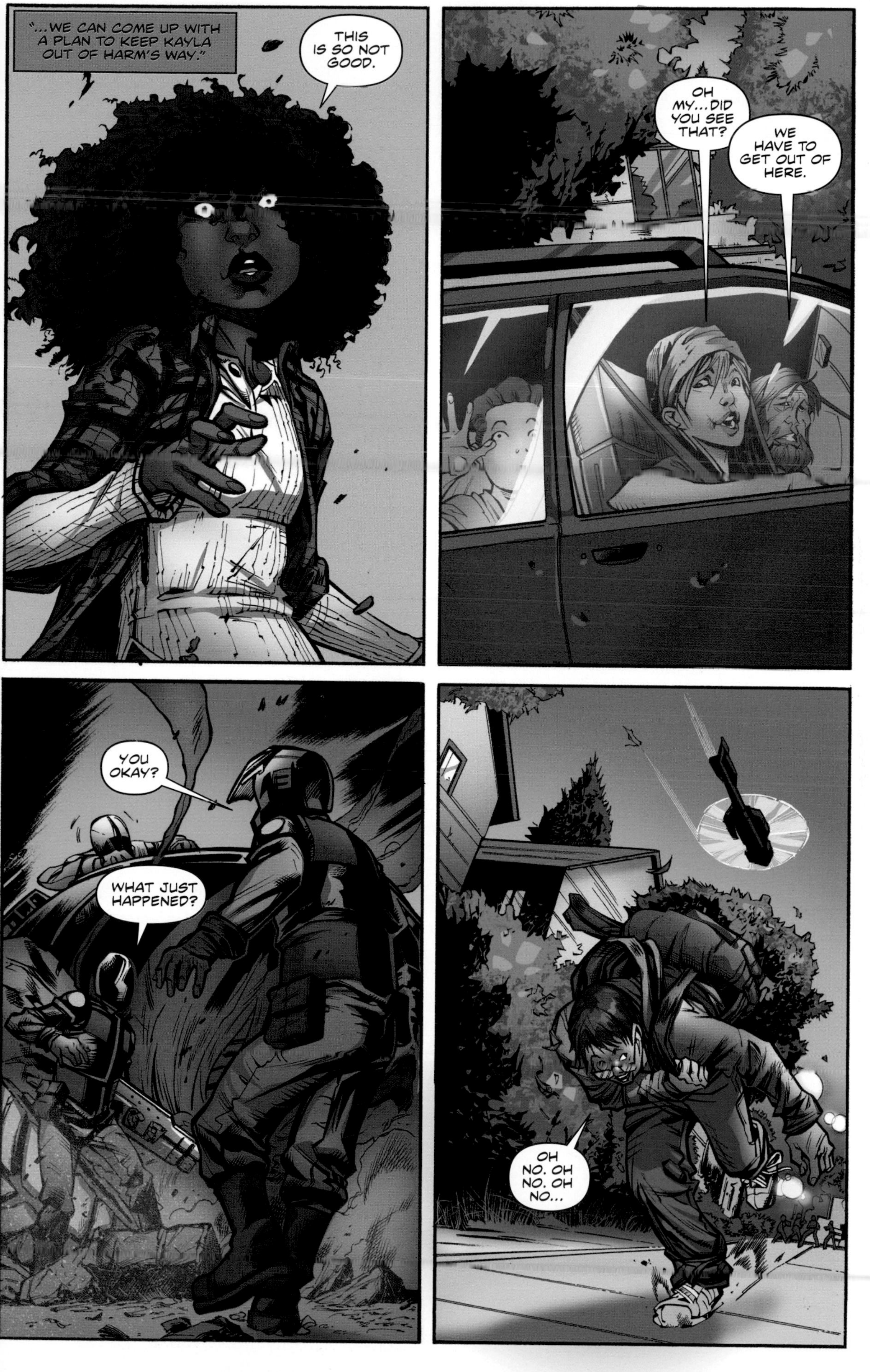
"...WE CAN COME UP WITH A PLAN TO KEEP KAYLA OUT OF HARM'S WAY."
THIS IS SO NOT GOOD.
OH MY...DID YOU SEE THAT?
WE HAVE TO GET OUT OF HERE.
YOU OKAY?
WHAT JUST HAPPENED?
OH NO. OH NO. OH NO...

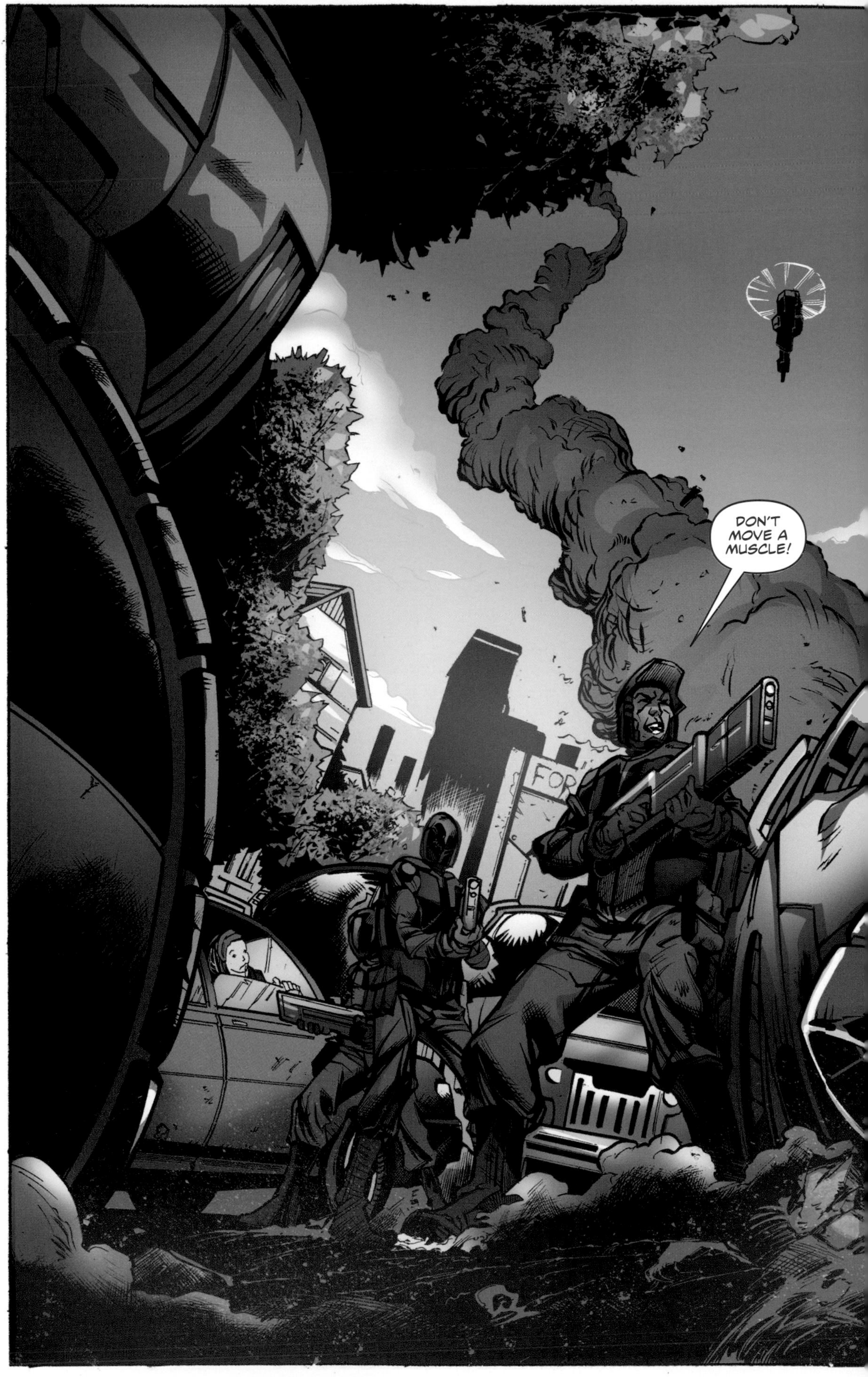
DON'T MOVE A MUSCLE!
FOR

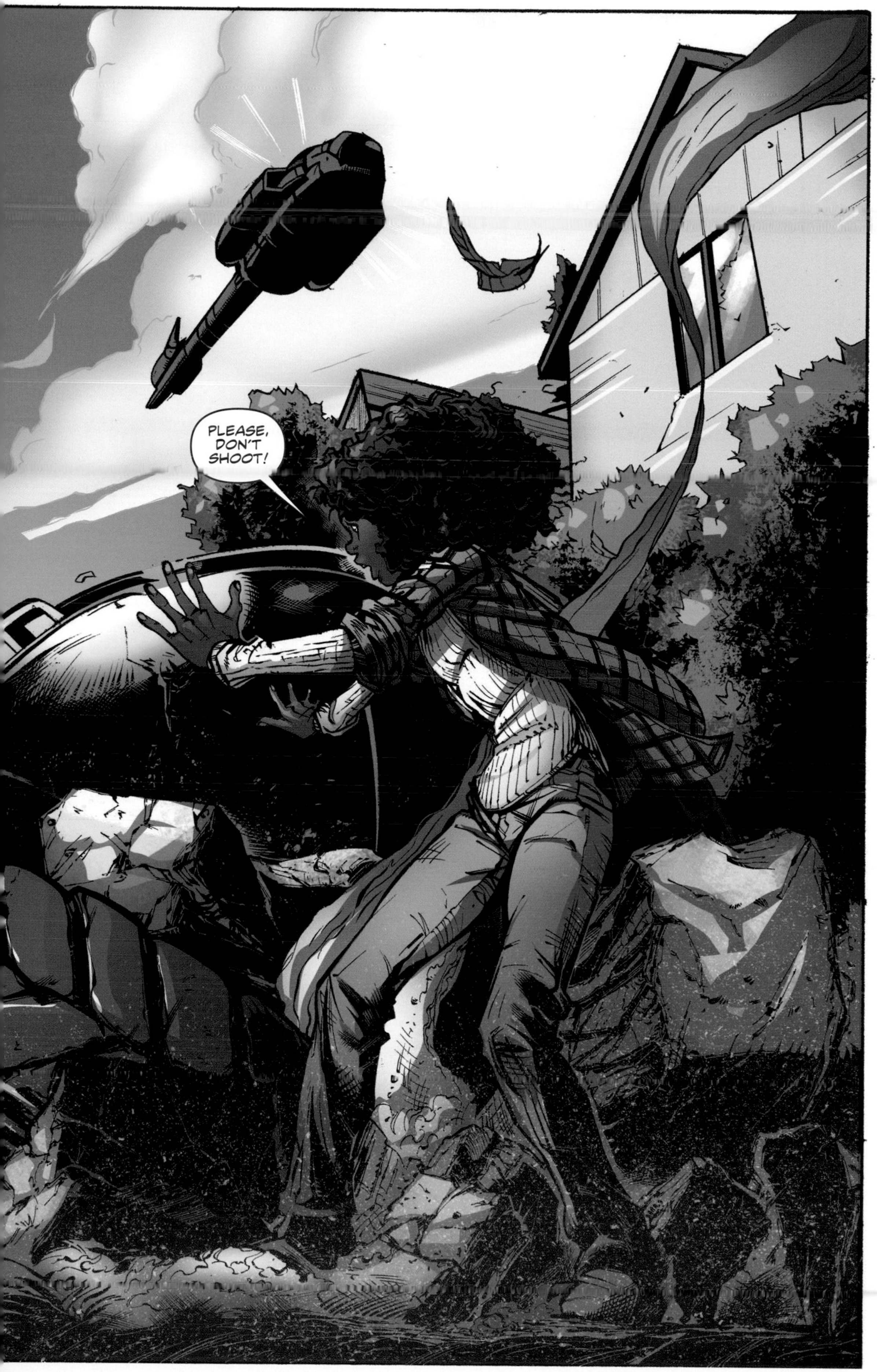
PLEASE, DON'T SHOOT!

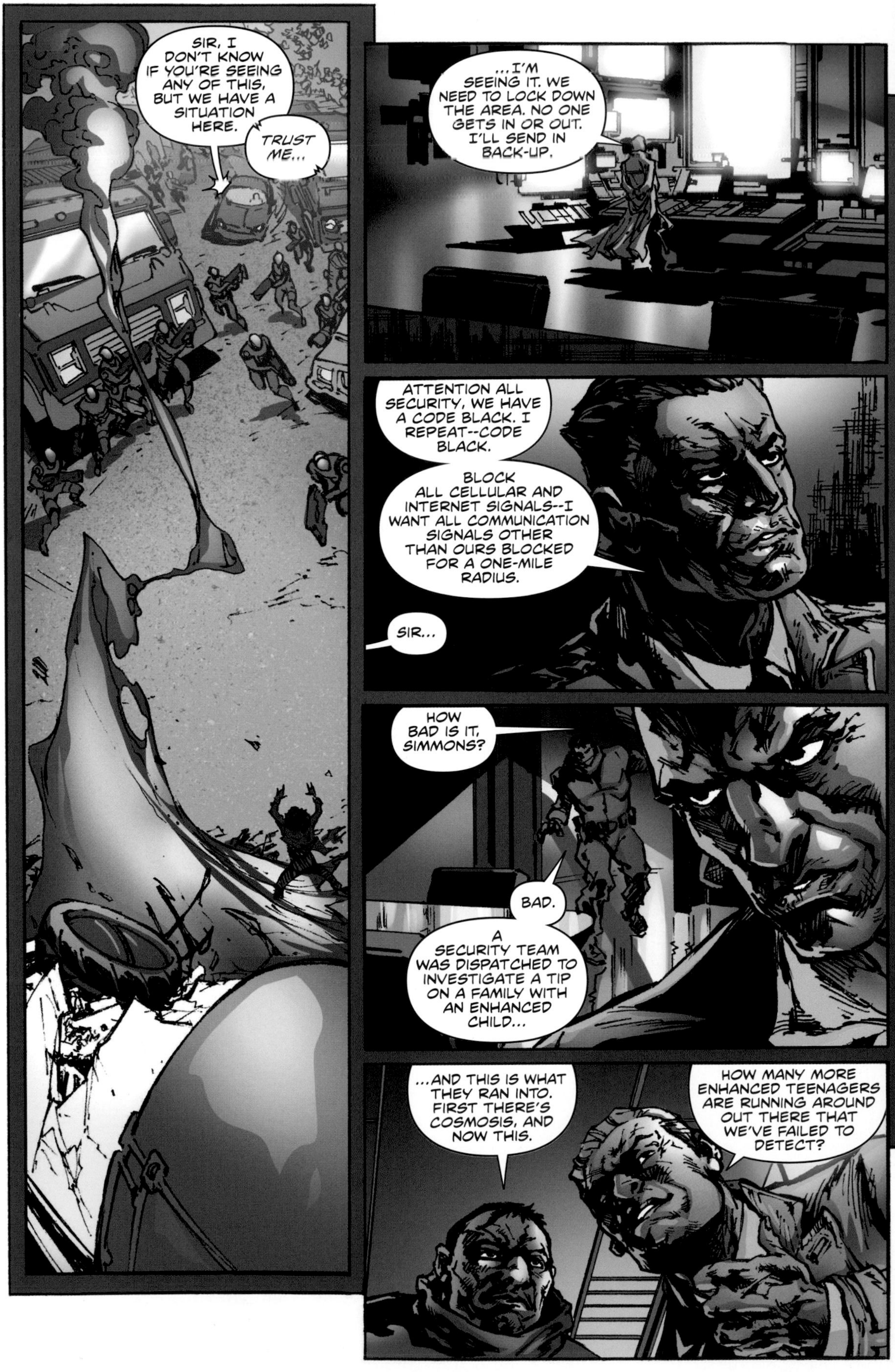
SIR, I DON'T KNOW IF YOU'RE SEEING ANY OF THIS, BUT WE HAVE A SITUATION HERE.
TRUST ME...
...I'M SEEING IT. WE NEED TO LOCK DOWN THE AREA. NO ONE GETS IN OR OUT. I'LL SEND IN BACK-UP.
ATTENTION ALL SECURITY, WE HAVE A CODE BLACK. I REPEAT--CODE BLACK.
BLOCK ALL CELLULAR AND INTERNET SIGNALS--I WANT ALL COMMUNICATION SIGNALS OTHER THAN OURS BLOCKED FOR A ONE-MILE RADIUS.
SIR...
HOW BAD IS IT, SIMMONS?
BAD.
A SECURITY TEAM WAS DISPATCHED TO INVESTIGATE A TIP ON A FAMILY WITH AN ENHANCED CHILD...
...AND THIS IS WHAT THEY RAN INTO. FIRST THERE'S COSMOSIS, AND NOW THIS.
HOW MANY MORE ENHANCED TEENAGERS ARE RUNNING AROUND OUT THERE THAT WE'VE FAILED TO DETECT?

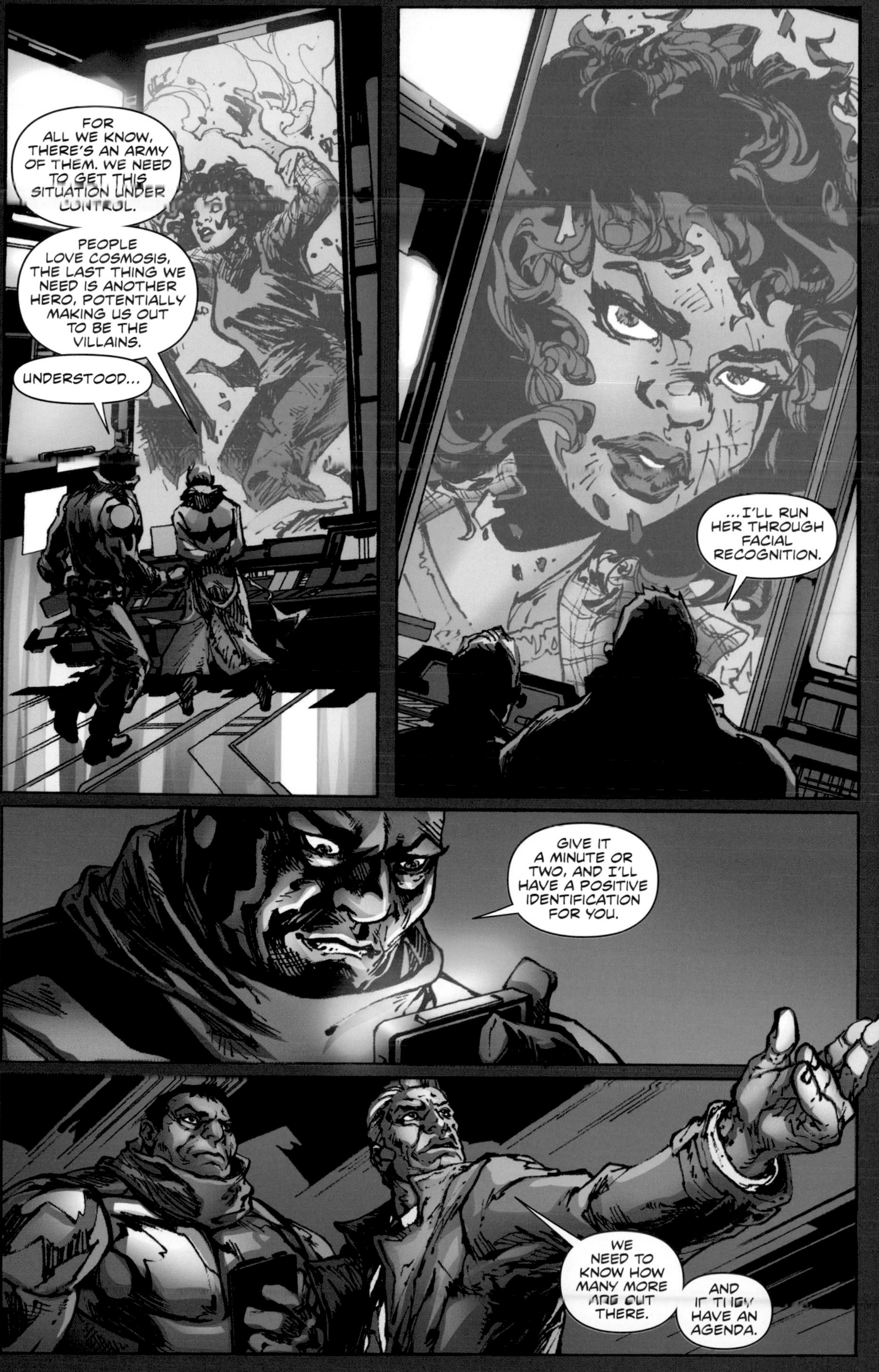
FOR ALL WE KNOW, THERE'S AN ARMY OF THEM. WE NEED TO GET THIS SITUATION UNDER CONTROL.
PEOPLE LOVE COSMOSIS, THE LAST THING WE NEED IS ANOTHER HERO, POTENTIALLY MAKING US OUT TO BE THE VILLAINS.
UNDERSTOOD...
...I'LL RUN HER THROUGH FACIAL RECOGNITION.
GIVE IT A MINUTE OR TWO, AND I'LL HAVE A POSITIVE IDENTIFICATION FOR YOU.
WE NEED TO KNOW HOW MANY MORE ARE OUT THERE.
AND IF THEY HAVE AN AGENDA.

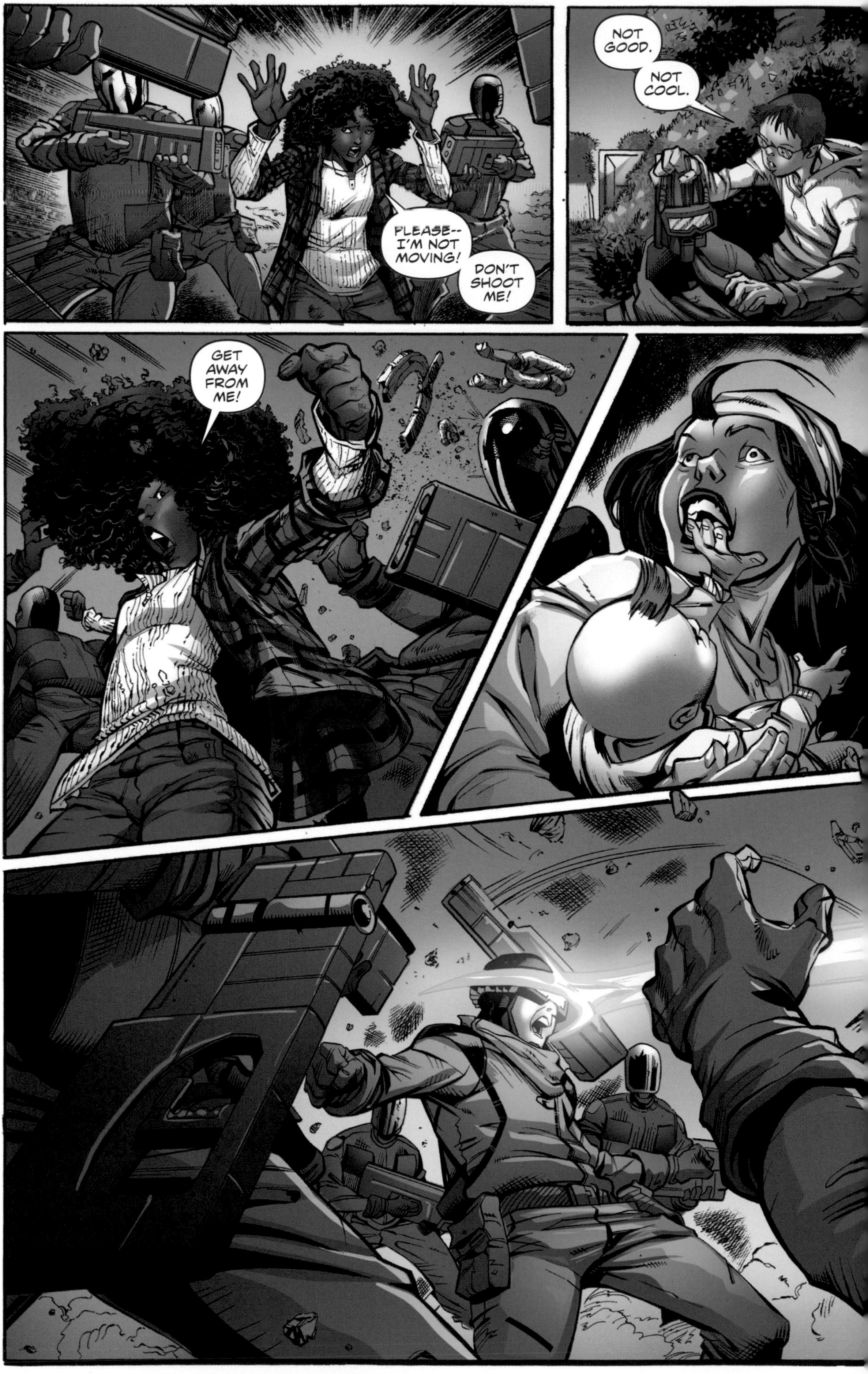
PLEASE-- I'M NOT MOVING!
DON'T SHOOT ME!
NOT GOOD.
NOT COOL.
GET AWAY FROM ME!

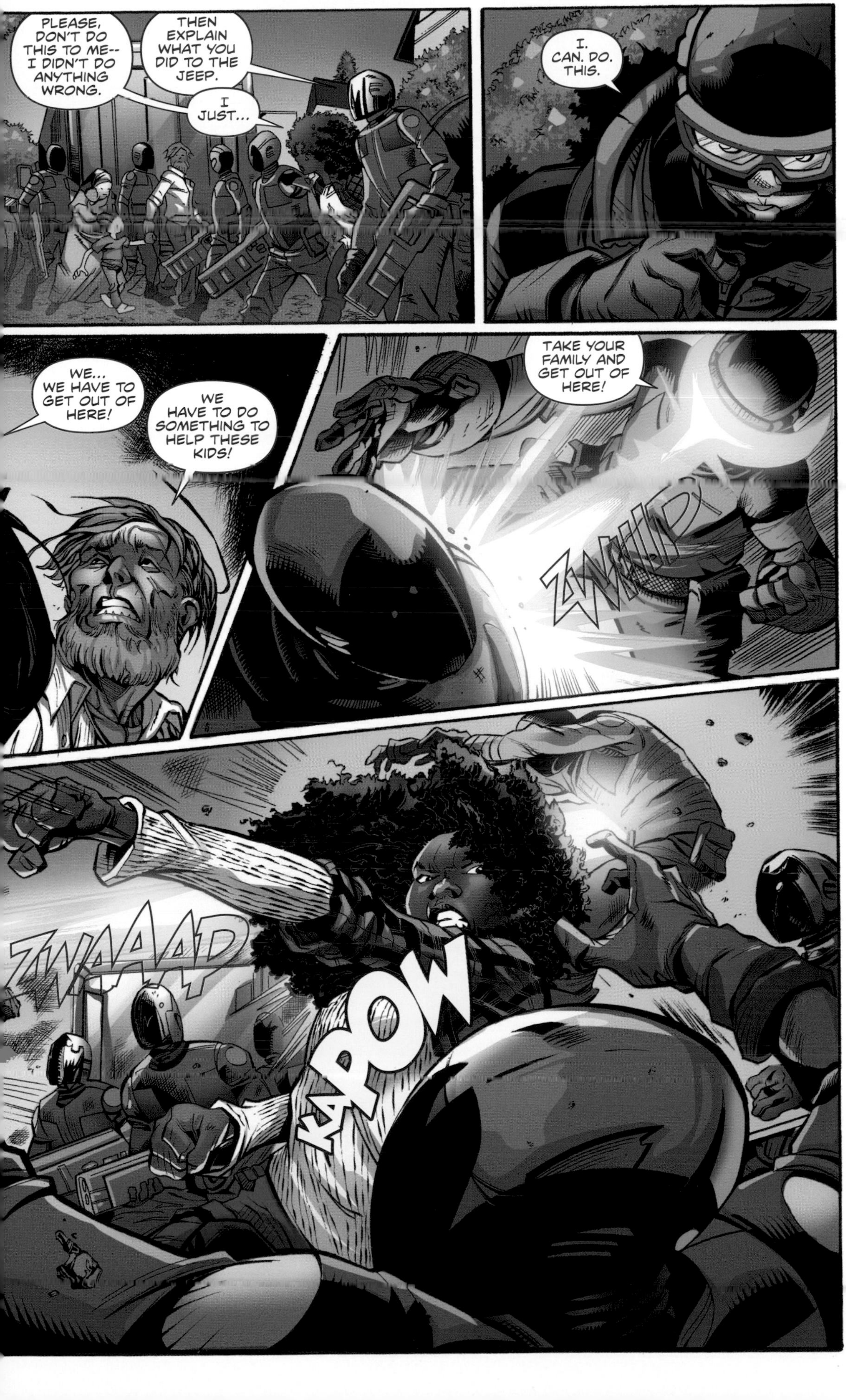
PLEASE, DON'T DO THIS TO ME-- I DIDN'T DO ANYTHING WRONG.
THEN EXPLAIN WHAT YOU DID TO THE JEEP.
I JUST...
I. CAN. DO. THIS.
WE... WE HAVE TO GET OUT OF HERE!
WE HAVE TO DO SOMETHING TO HELP THESE KIDS!
TAKE YOUR FAMILY AND GET OUT OF HERE!
ZWHIP
ZWAAAP
KAPOW

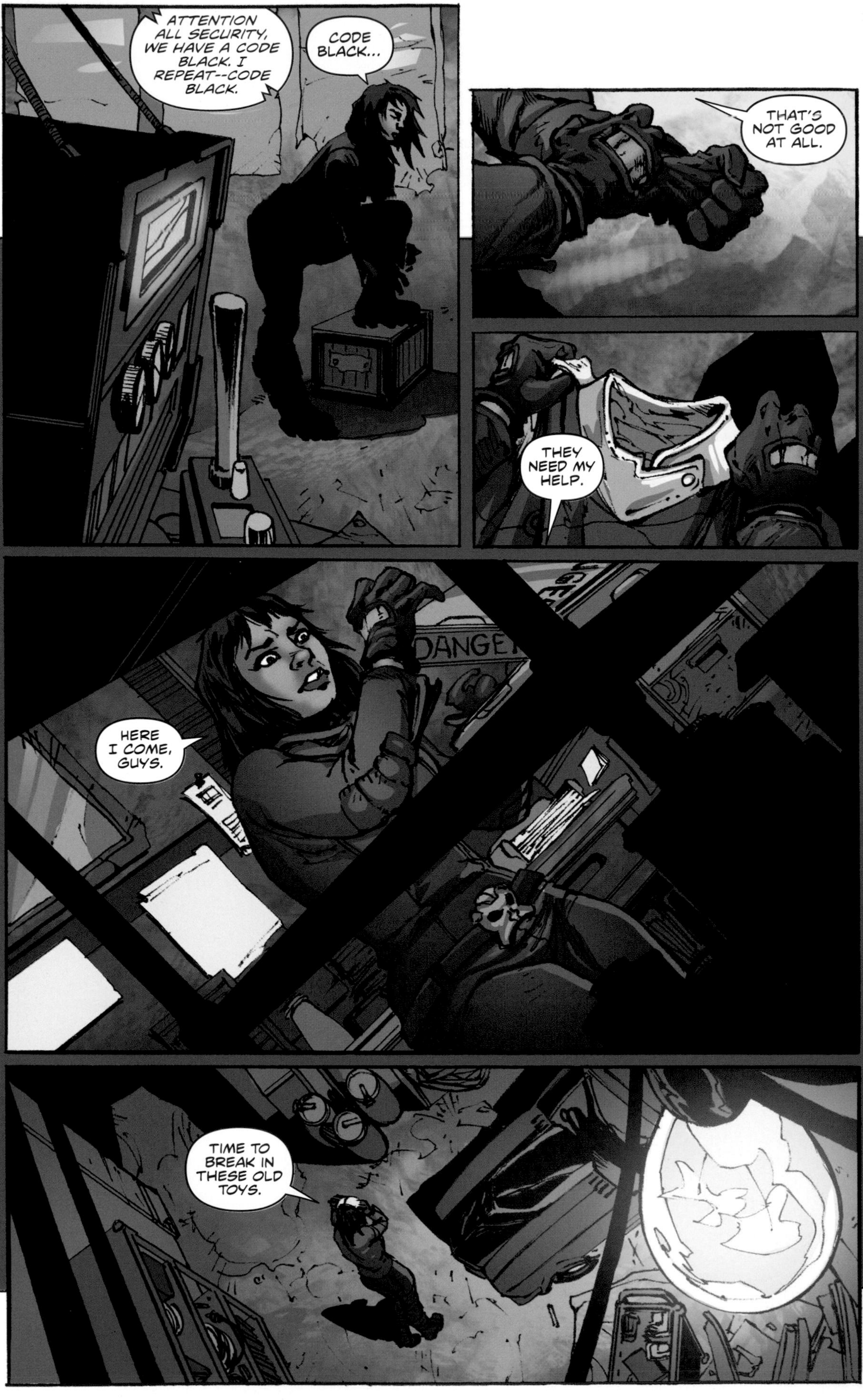

ATTENTION ALL SECURITY, WE HAVE A CODE BLACK. I REPEAT--CODE BLACK.
CODE BLACK...
THAT'S NOT GOOD AT ALL.
THEY NEED MY HELP.
DANGE
HERE I COME, GUYS.
TIME TO BREAK IN THESE OLD TOYS.

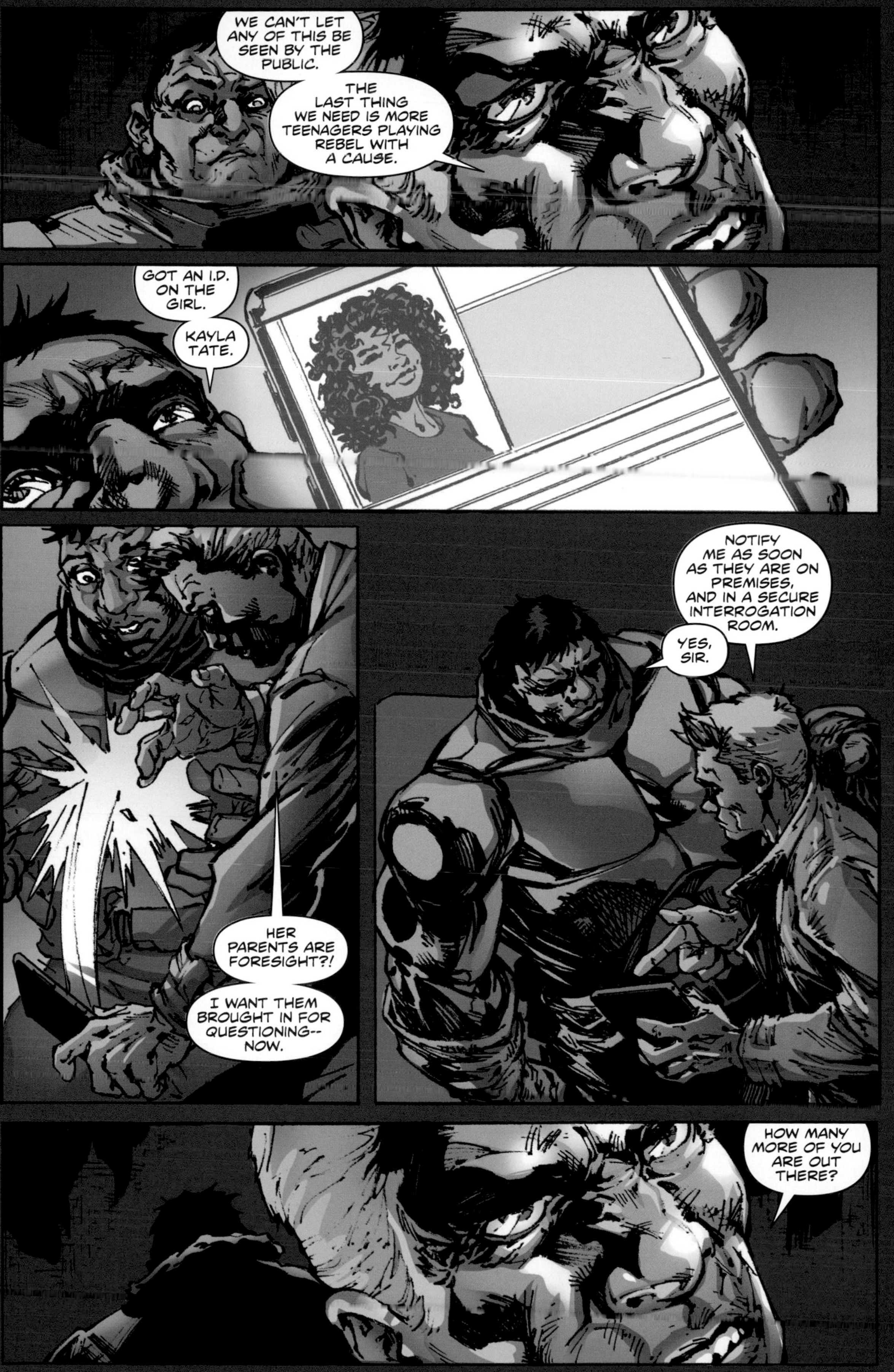
WE CAN'T LET ANY OF THIS BE SEEN BY THE PUBLIC.
THE LAST THING WE NEED IS MORE TEENAGERS PLAYING REBEL WITH A CAUSE.
GOT AN I.D. ON THE GIRL.
KAYLA TATE.
HER PARENTS ARE FORESIGHT?!
I WANT THEM BROUGHT IN FOR QUESTIONING-- NOW.
YES, SIR.
NOTIFY ME AS SOON AS THEY ARE ON PREMISES, AND IN A SECURE INTERROGATION ROOM.
HOW MANY MORE OF YOU ARE OUT THERE?

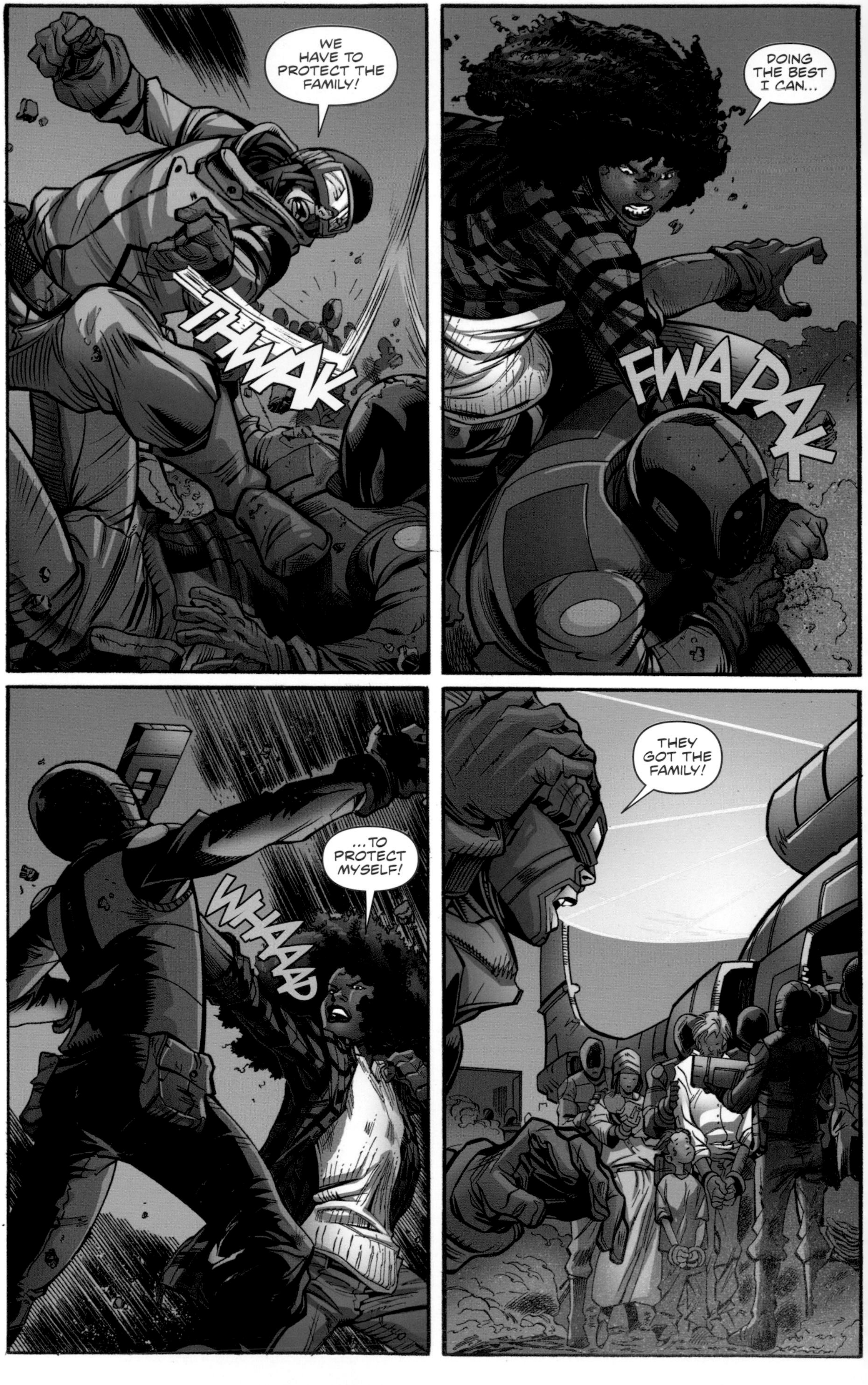
WE HAVE TO PROTECT THE FAMILY!
THWAK
DOING THE BEST I CAN...
FWAPAK
WHAAAP
...TO PROTECT MYSELF!
THEY GOT THE FAMILY!

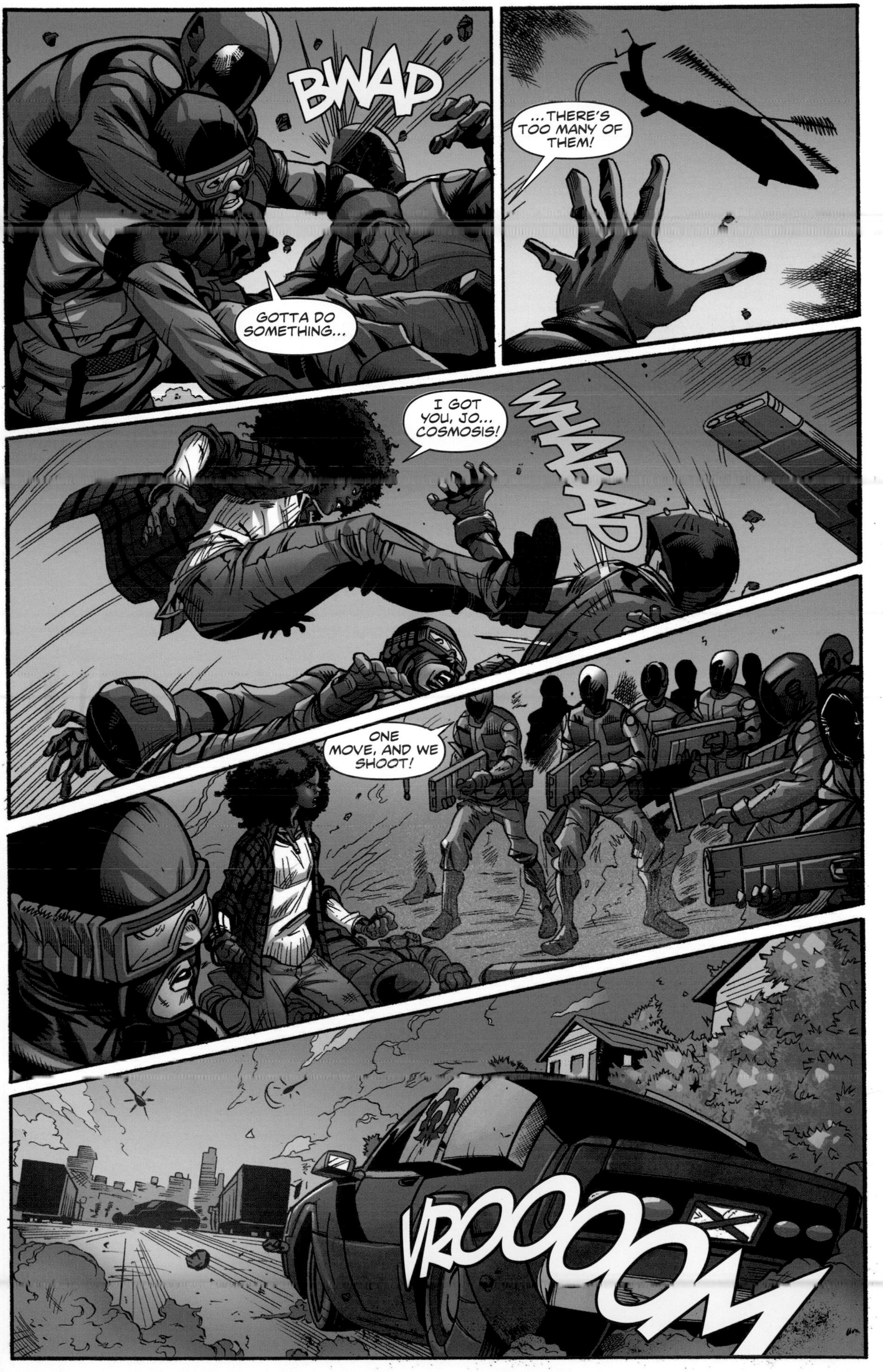
BWAP
GOTTA DO SOMETHING...
...THERE'S TOO MANY OF THEM!
I GOT YOU, JO... COSMOSIS!
WHABAD
ONE MOVE, AND WE SHOOT!
VROOOOOM

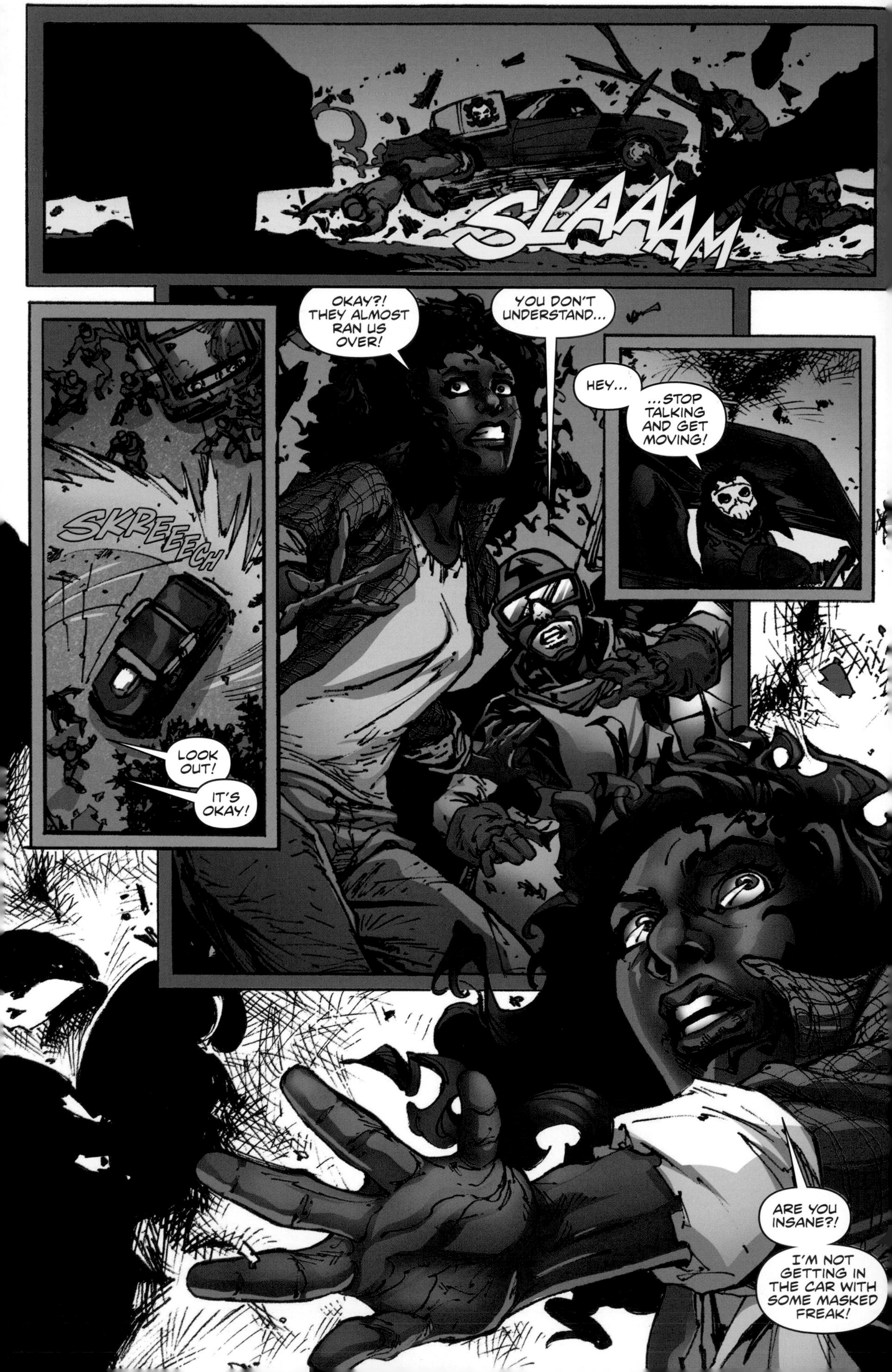
SLAAAM
SKREEEECH
LOOK OUT!
IT'S OKAY!
OKAY?! THEY ALMOST RAN US OVER!
YOU DON'T UNDERSTAND...
HEY...
...STOP TALKING AND GET MOVING!
ARE YOU INSANE?!
I'M NOT GETTING IN THE CAR WITH SOME MASKED FREAK!

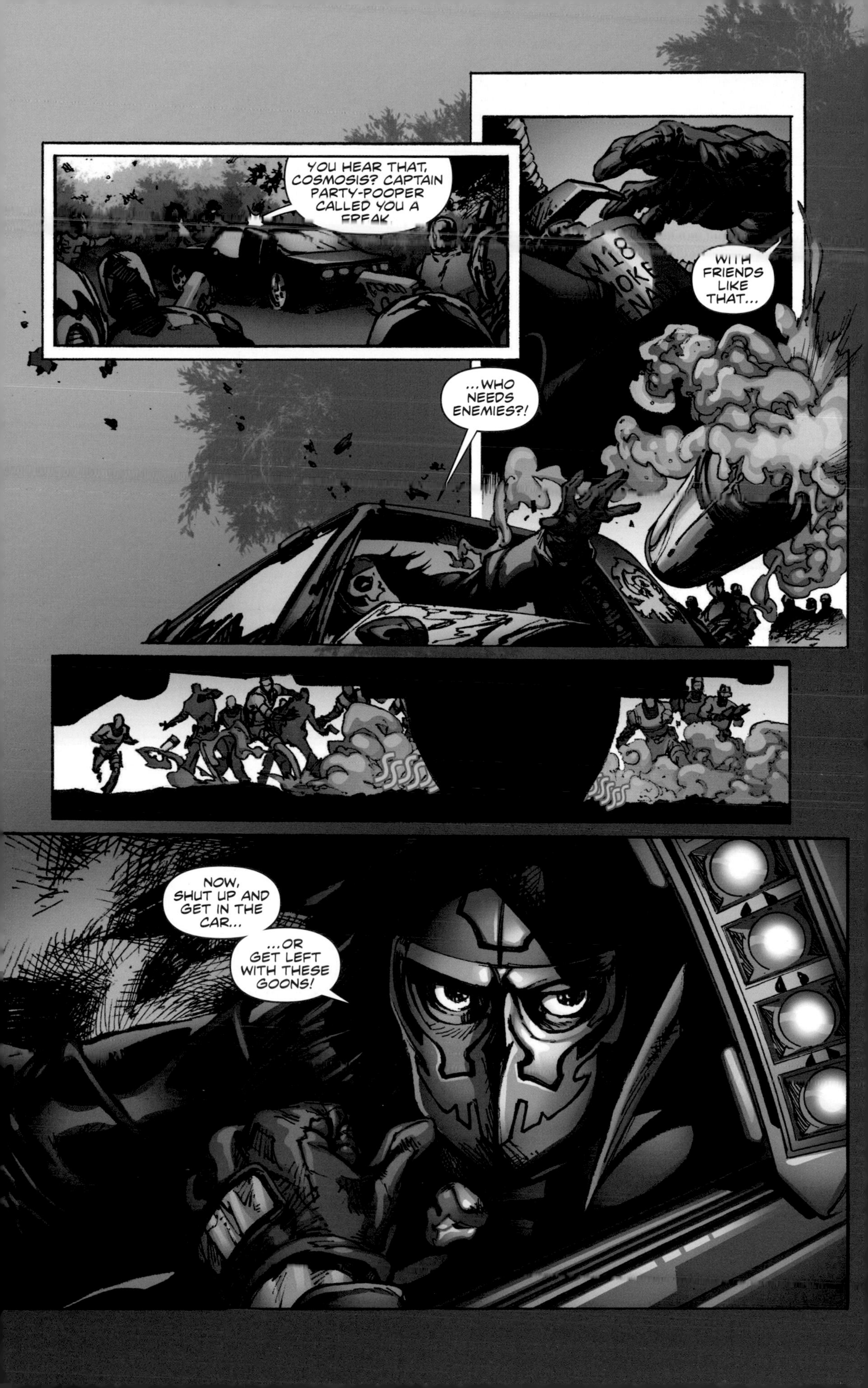
YOU HEAR THAT, COSMOSIS? CAPTAIN PARTY-POOPER CALLED YOU A FREAK.
WITH FRIENDS LIKE THAT...
...WHO NEEDS ENEMIES?!
NOW, SHUT UP AND GET IN THE CAR...
...OR GET LEFT WITH THESE GOONS!

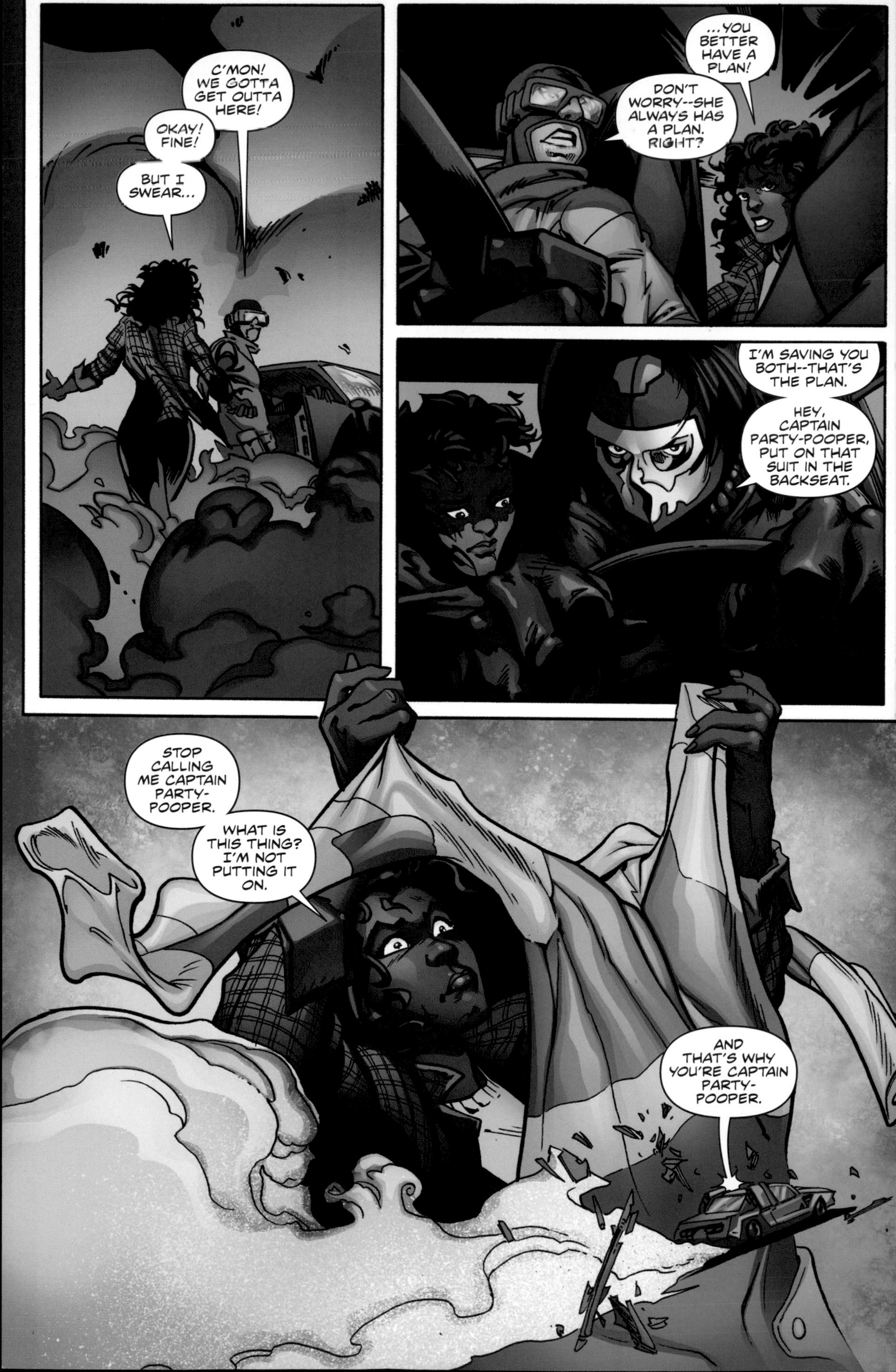
C'MON! WE GOTTA GET OUTTA HERE!
OKAY! FINE!
BUT I SWEAR...
...YOU BETTER HAVE A PLAN!
DON'T WORRY--SHE ALWAYS HAS A PLAN. RIGHT?
I'M SAVING YOU BOTH--THAT'S THE PLAN.
HEY, CAPTAIN PARTY-POOPER, PUT ON THAT SUIT IN THE BACKSEAT.
STOP CALLING ME CAPTAIN PARTY-POOPER.
WHAT IS THIS THING? I'M NOT PUTTING IT ON.
AND THAT'S WHY YOU'RE CAPTAIN PARTY-POOPER.

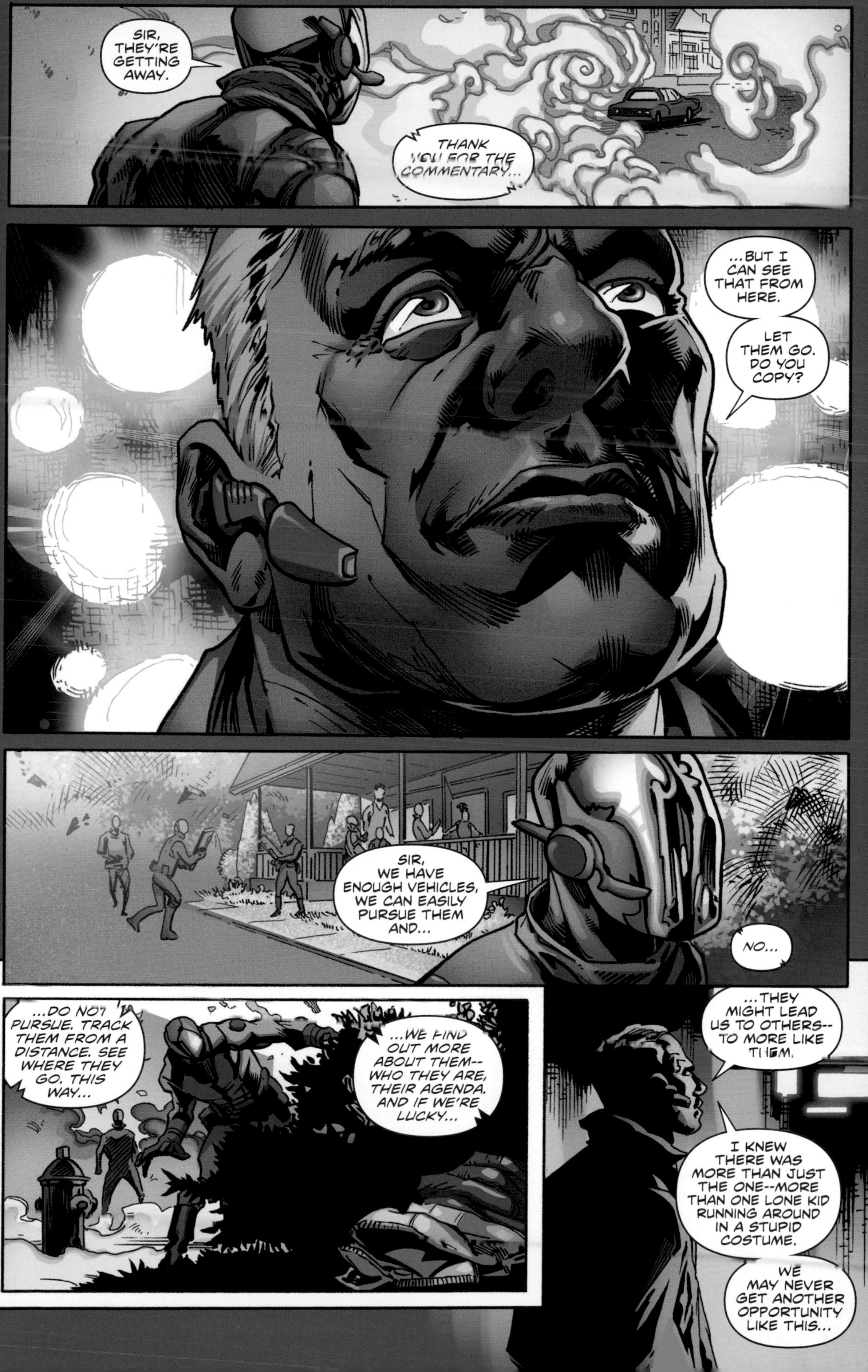
SIR, THEY'RE GETTING AWAY.
THANK YOU FOR THE COMMENTARY...
...BUT I CAN SEE THAT FROM HERE.
LET THEM GO. DO YOU COPY?
SIR, WE HAVE ENOUGH VEHICLES, WE CAN EASILY PURSUE THEM AND...
NO...
...DO NOT PURSUE. TRACK THEM FROM A DISTANCE. SEE WHERE THEY GO. THIS WAY...
...WE FIND OUT MORE ABOUT THEM--WHO THEY ARE, THEIR AGENDA. AND IF WE'RE LUCKY...
...THEY MIGHT LEAD US TO OTHERS--TO MORE LIKE THEM.
I KNEW THERE WAS MORE THAN JUST THE ONE--MORE THAN ONE LONE KID RUNNING AROUND IN A STUPID COSTUME.
WE MAY NEVER GET ANOTHER OPPORTUNITY LIKE THIS...

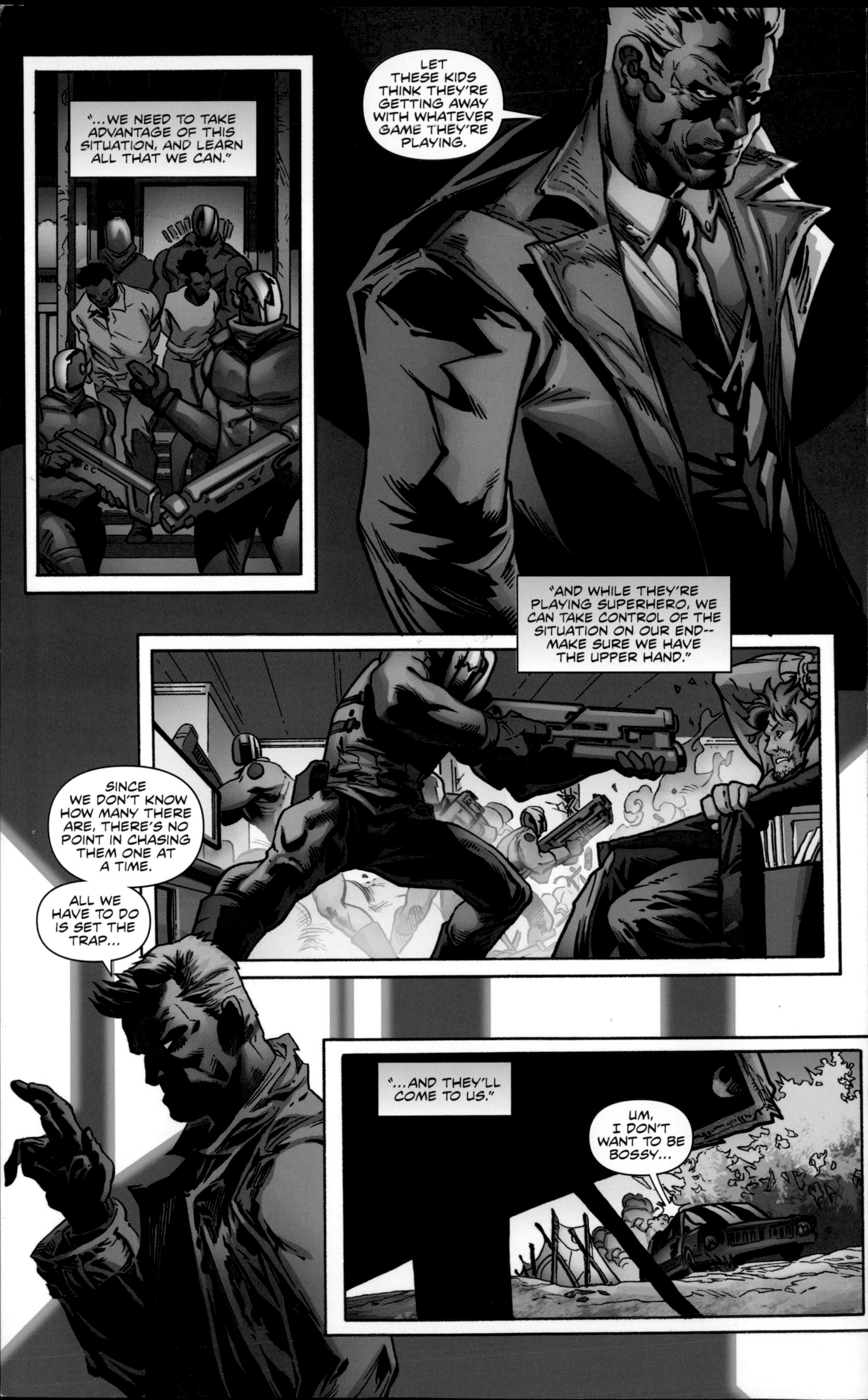
"...WE NEED TO TAKE ADVANTAGE OF THIS SITUATION, AND LEARN ALL THAT WE CAN."
LET THESE KIDS THINK THEY'RE GETTING AWAY WITH WHATEVER GAME THEY'RE PLAYING.
"AND WHILE THEY'RE PLAYING SUPERHERO, WE CAN TAKE CONTROL OF THE SITUATION ON OUR END-- MAKE SURE WE HAVE THE UPPER HAND."
SINCE WE DON'T KNOW HOW MANY THERE ARE, THERE'S NO POINT IN CHASING THEM ONE AT A TIME.
ALL WE HAVE TO DO IS SET THE TRAP...
"...AND THEY'LL COME TO US."
UM, I DON'T WANT TO BE BOSSY...

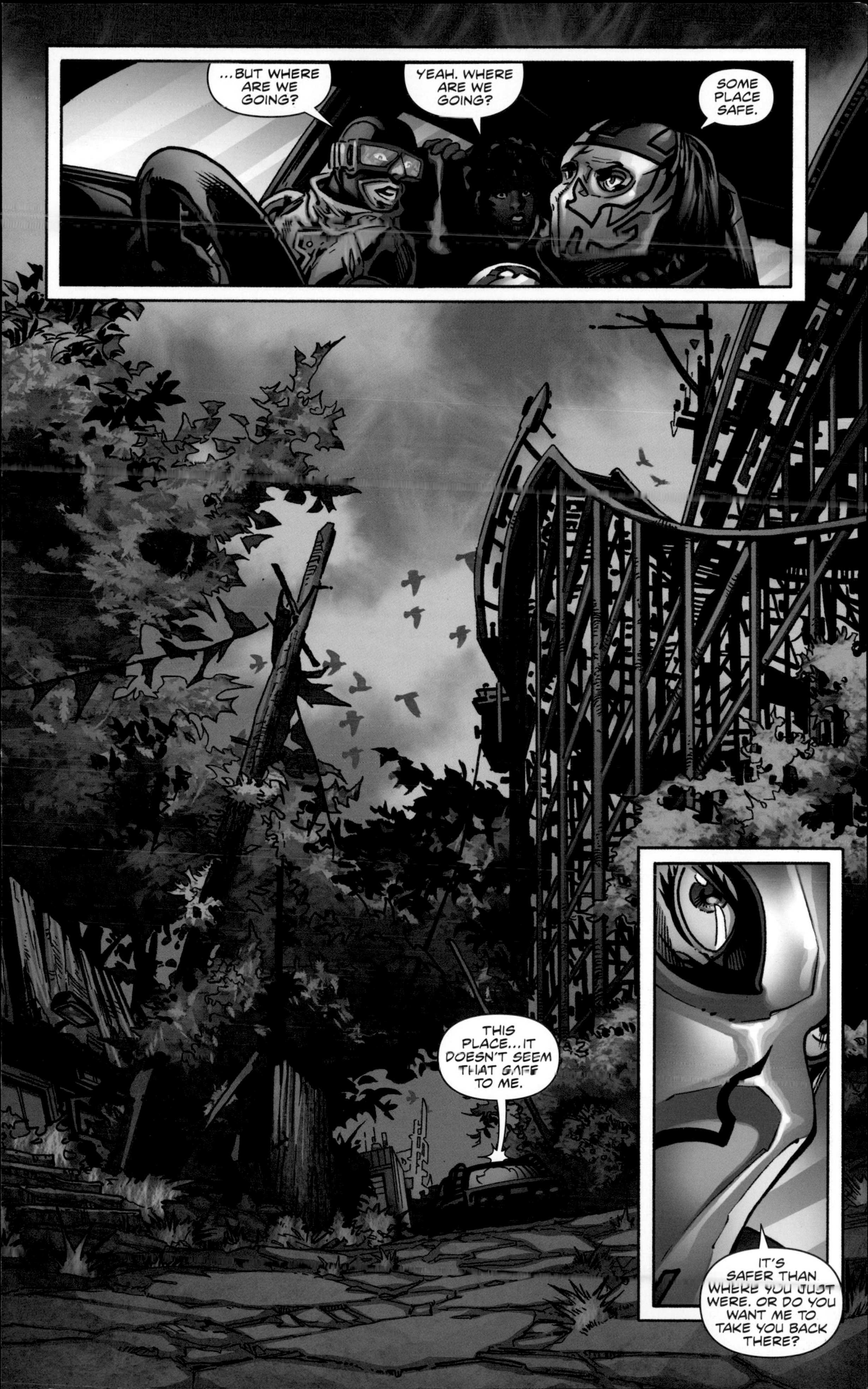
...BUT WHERE ARE WE GOING?
YEAH. WHERE ARE WE GOING?
SOME PLACE SAFE.
THIS PLACE...IT DOESN'T SEEM THAT SAFE TO ME.
IT'S SAFER THAN WHERE YOU JUST WERE. OR DO YOU WANT ME TO TAKE YOU BACK THERE?

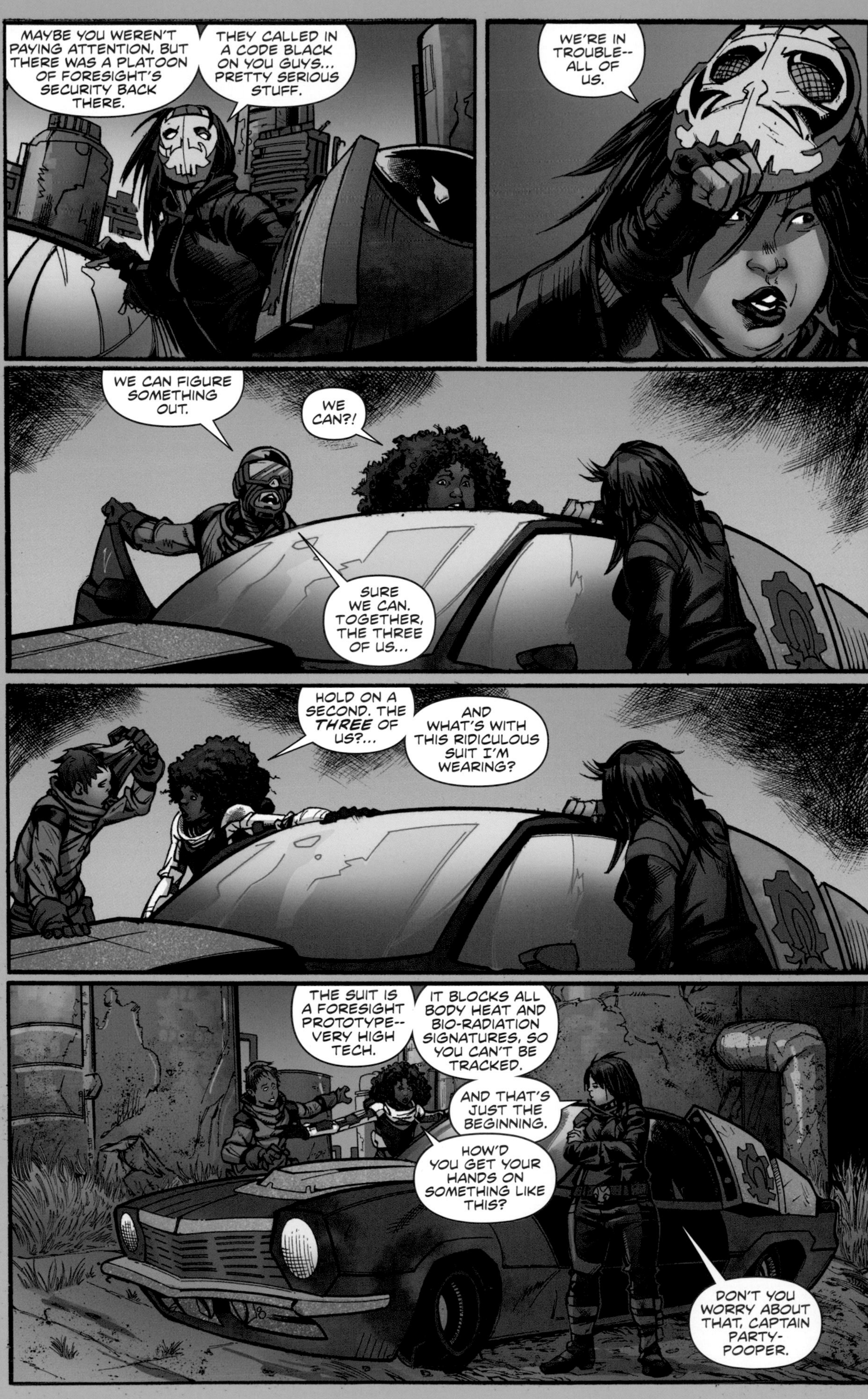
MAYBE YOU WEREN'T PAYING ATTENTION, BUT THERE WAS A PLATOON OF FORESIGHT'S SECURITY BACK THERE.
THEY CALLED IN A CODE BLACK ON YOU GUYS... PRETTY SERIOUS STUFF.
WE'RE IN TROUBLE-- ALL OF US.
WE CAN FIGURE SOMETHING OUT.
WE CAN?!
SURE WE CAN. TOGETHER, THE THREE OF US...
HOLD ON A SECOND. THE *THREE* OF US?...
AND WHAT'S WITH THIS RIDICULOUS SUIT I'M WEARING?
THE SUIT IS A FORESIGHT PROTOTYPE-- VERY HIGH TECH.
IT BLOCKS ALL BODY HEAT AND BIO-RADIATION SIGNATURES, SO YOU CAN'T BE TRACKED.
AND THAT'S JUST THE BEGINNING.
HOW'D YOU GET YOUR HANDS ON SOMETHING LIKE THIS?
DON'T YOU WORRY ABOUT THAT, CAPTAIN PARTY-POOPER.

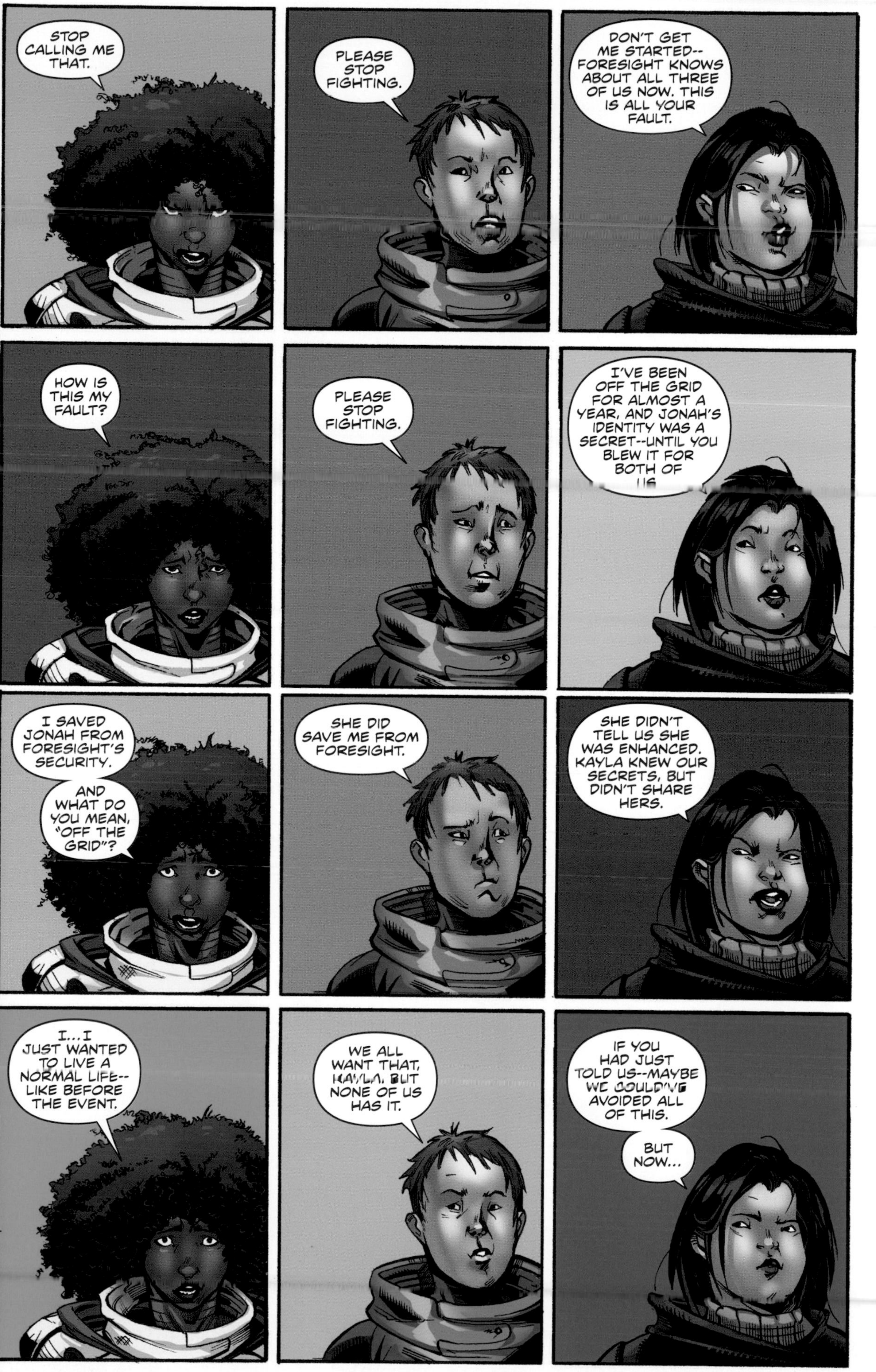

STOP CALLING ME THAT.
PLEASE STOP FIGHTING.
DON'T GET ME STARTED--FORESIGHT KNOWS ABOUT ALL THREE OF US NOW. THIS IS ALL YOUR FAULT.
HOW IS THIS MY FAULT?
PLEASE STOP FIGHTING.
I'VE BEEN OFF THE GRID FOR ALMOST A YEAR, AND JONAH'S IDENTITY WAS A SECRET--UNTIL YOU BLEW IT FOR BOTH OF US.
I SAVED JONAH FROM FORESIGHT'S SECURITY.
AND WHAT DO YOU MEAN, "OFF THE GRID"?
SHE DID SAVE ME FROM FORESIGHT.
SHE DIDN'T TELL US SHE WAS ENHANCED. KAYLA KNEW OUR SECRETS, BUT DIDN'T SHARE HERS.
I...I JUST WANTED TO LIVE A NORMAL LIFE--LIKE BEFORE THE EVENT.
WE ALL WANT THAT, KAYLA. BUT NONE OF US HAS IT.
IF YOU HAD JUST TOLD US--MAYBE WE COULD'VE AVOIDED ALL OF THIS.
BUT NOW...

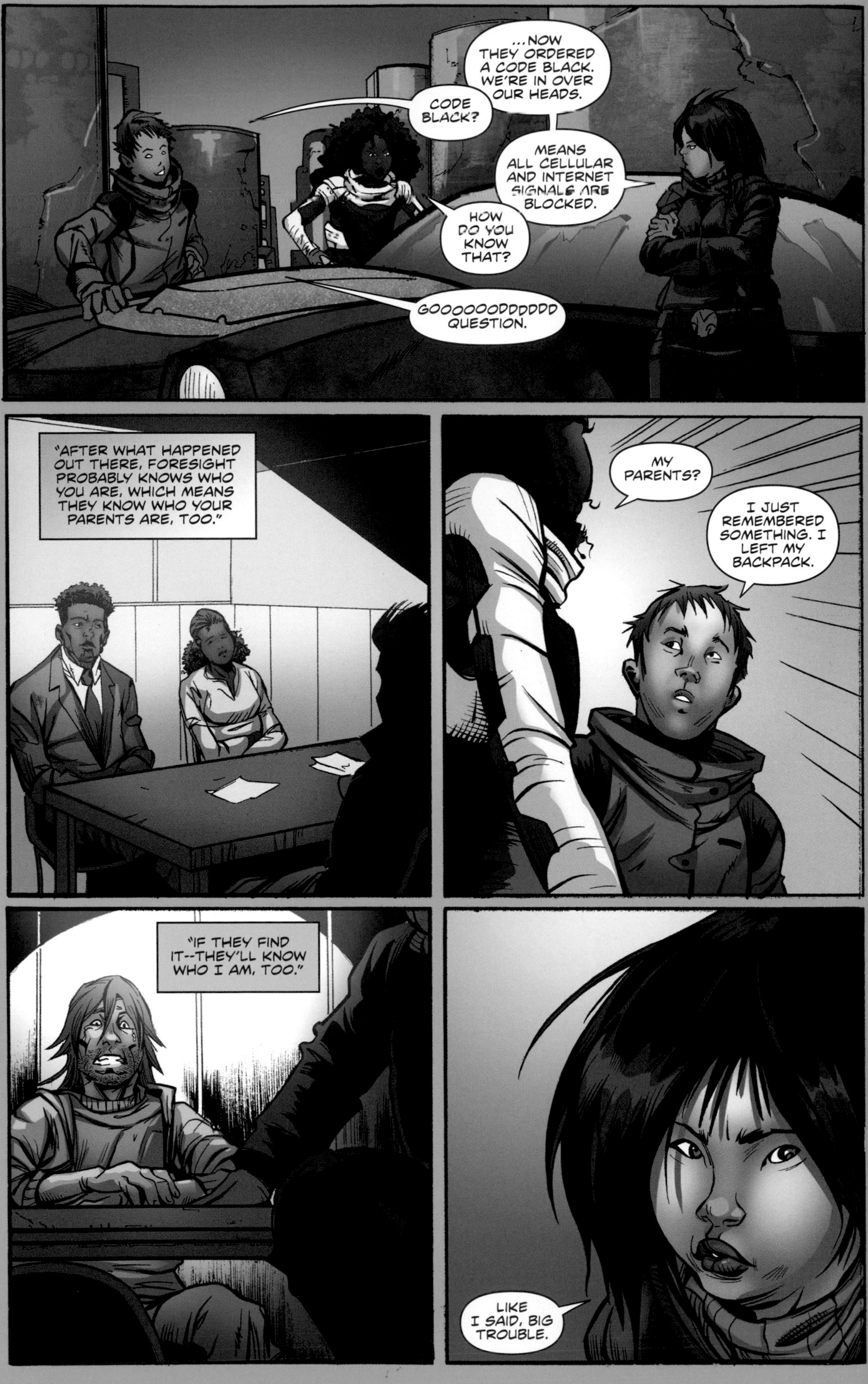
...NOW THEY ORDERED A CODE BLACK. WE'RE IN OVER OUR HEADS.
CODE BLACK?
MEANS ALL CELLULAR AND INTERNET SIGNALS ARE BLOCKED.
HOW DO YOU KNOW THAT?
GOOOOOOODDDDDD QUESTION.
"AFTER WHAT HAPPENED OUT THERE, FORESIGHT PROBABLY KNOWS WHO YOU ARE, WHICH MEANS THEY KNOW WHO YOUR PARENTS ARE, TOO."
MY PARENTS?
I JUST REMEMBERED SOMETHING. I LEFT MY BACKPACK.
"IF THEY FIND IT--THEY'LL KNOW WHO I AM, TOO."
LIKE I SAID, BIG TROUBLE.

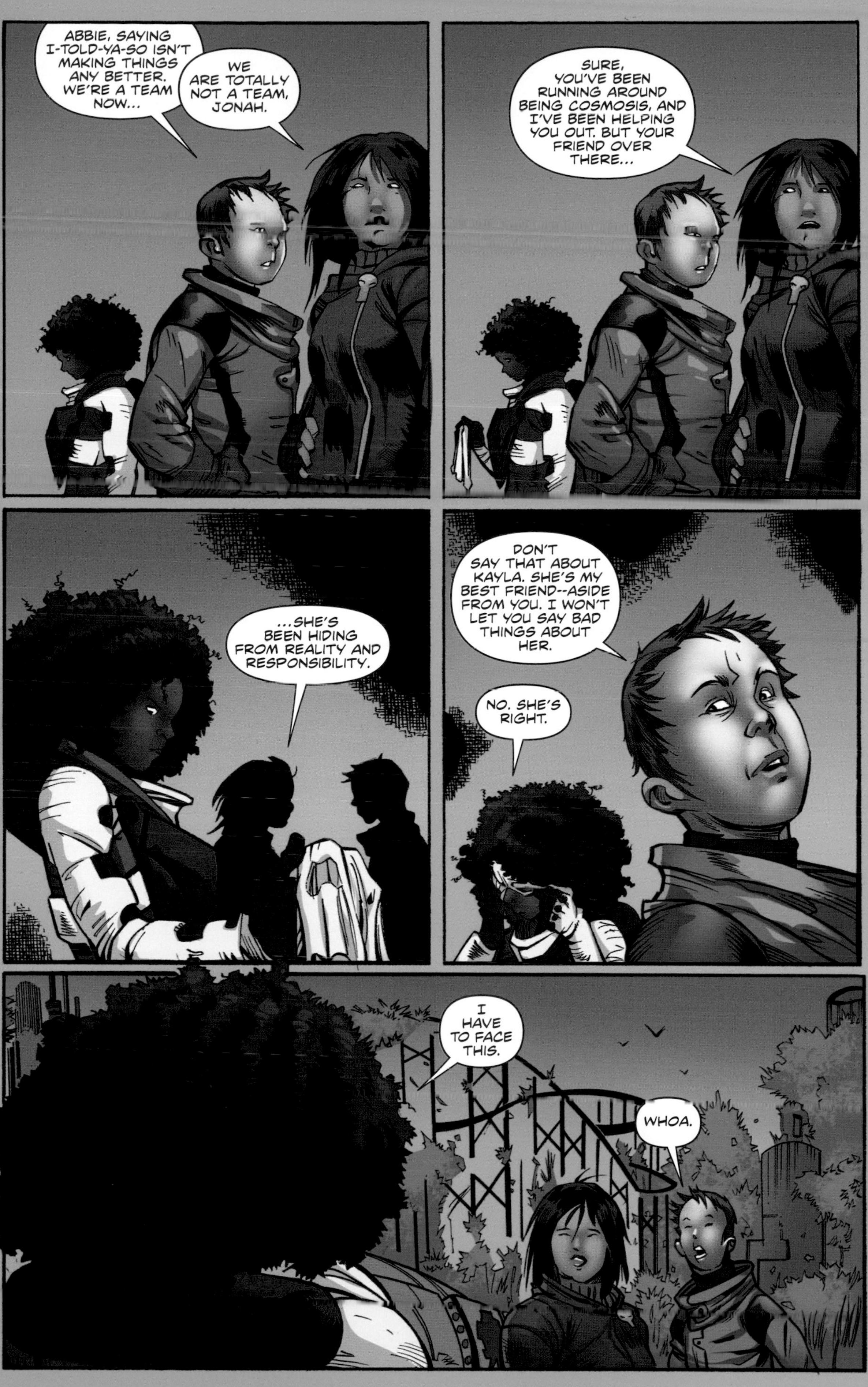
ABBIE, SAYING I-TOLD-YA-SO ISN'T MAKING THINGS ANY BETTER. WE'RE A TEAM NOW...
WE ARE TOTALLY NOT A TEAM, JONAH.
SURE, YOU'VE BEEN RUNNING AROUND BEING COSMOSIS, AND I'VE BEEN HELPING YOU OUT. BUT YOUR FRIEND OVER THERE...
...SHE'S BEEN HIDING FROM REALITY AND RESPONSIBILITY.
DON'T SAY THAT ABOUT KAYLA. SHE'S MY BEST FRIEND--ASIDE FROM YOU. I WON'T LET YOU SAY BAD THINGS ABOUT HER.
NO. SHE'S RIGHT.
I HAVE TO FACE THIS.
WHOA.

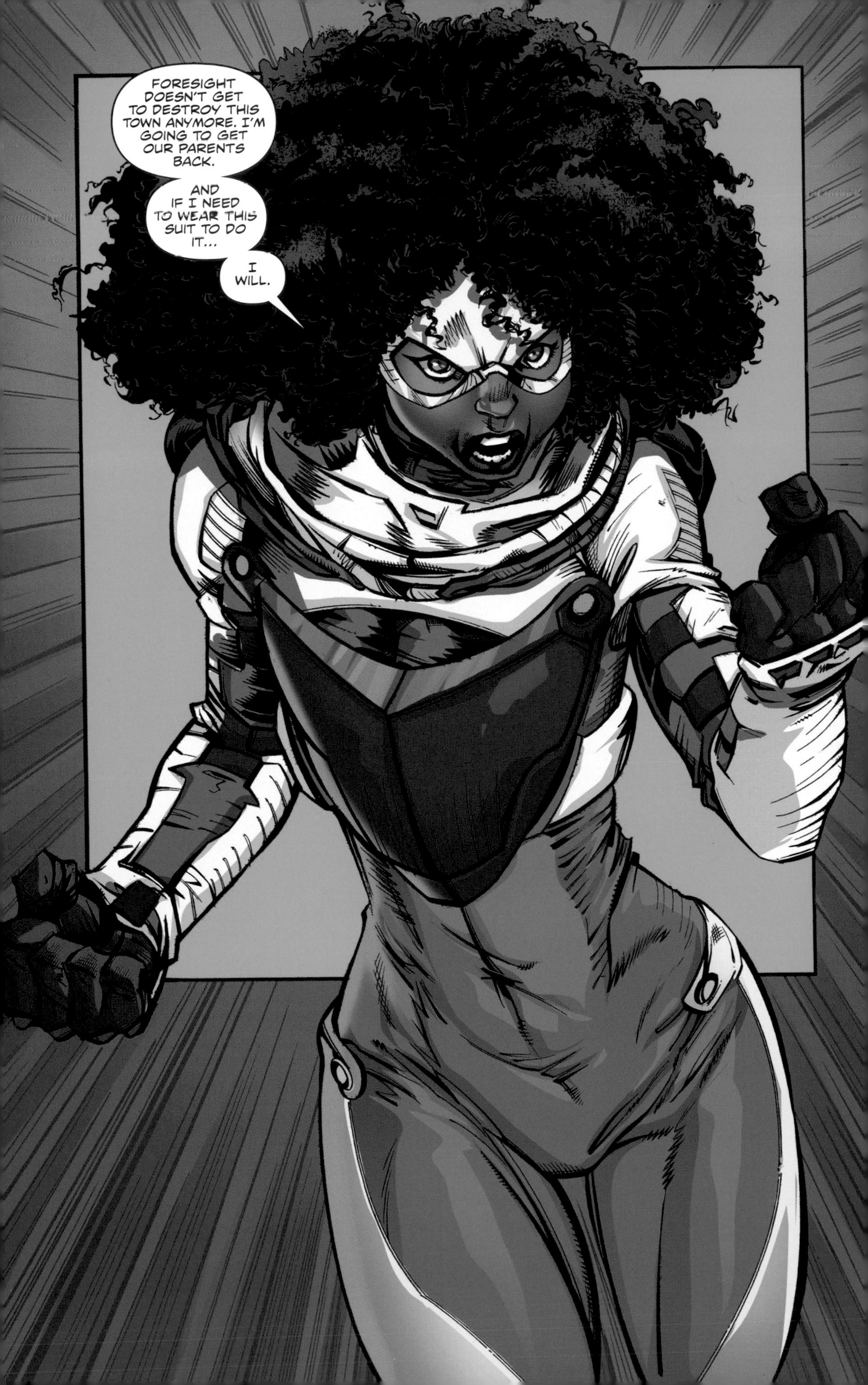
FORESIGHT DOESN'T GET TO DESTROY THIS TOWN ANYMORE. I'M GOING TO GET OUR PARENTS BACK.
AND IF I NEED TO WEAR THIS SUIT TO DO IT...
I WILL.

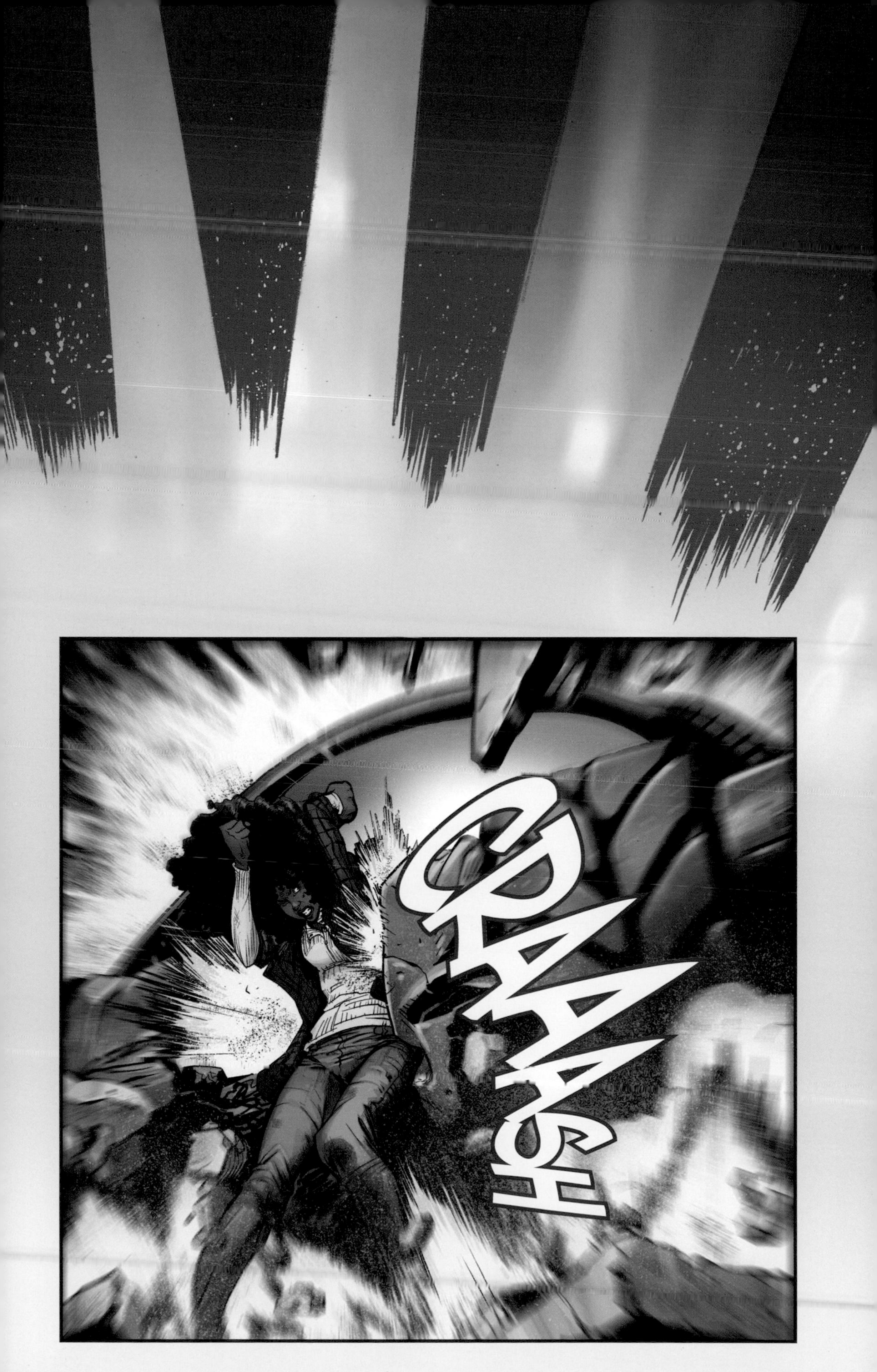
CRAAASH

CATALYST
PRIME

"THE EVENT"

One year before the story of SUPERB, humanity was on the verge of extinction. An asteroid detected in space was on a collision course with Earth.

Foresight Corporation, the world's most advanced high-tech humanitarian company led by CEO Lorena Payan, developed the science and ships needed to destroy the asteroid.

A team of astronauts flew into space on a suicide mission to save the world.

This is the story of that heroic mission, and "The Event" from which a new generation of heroes emerged in the world.

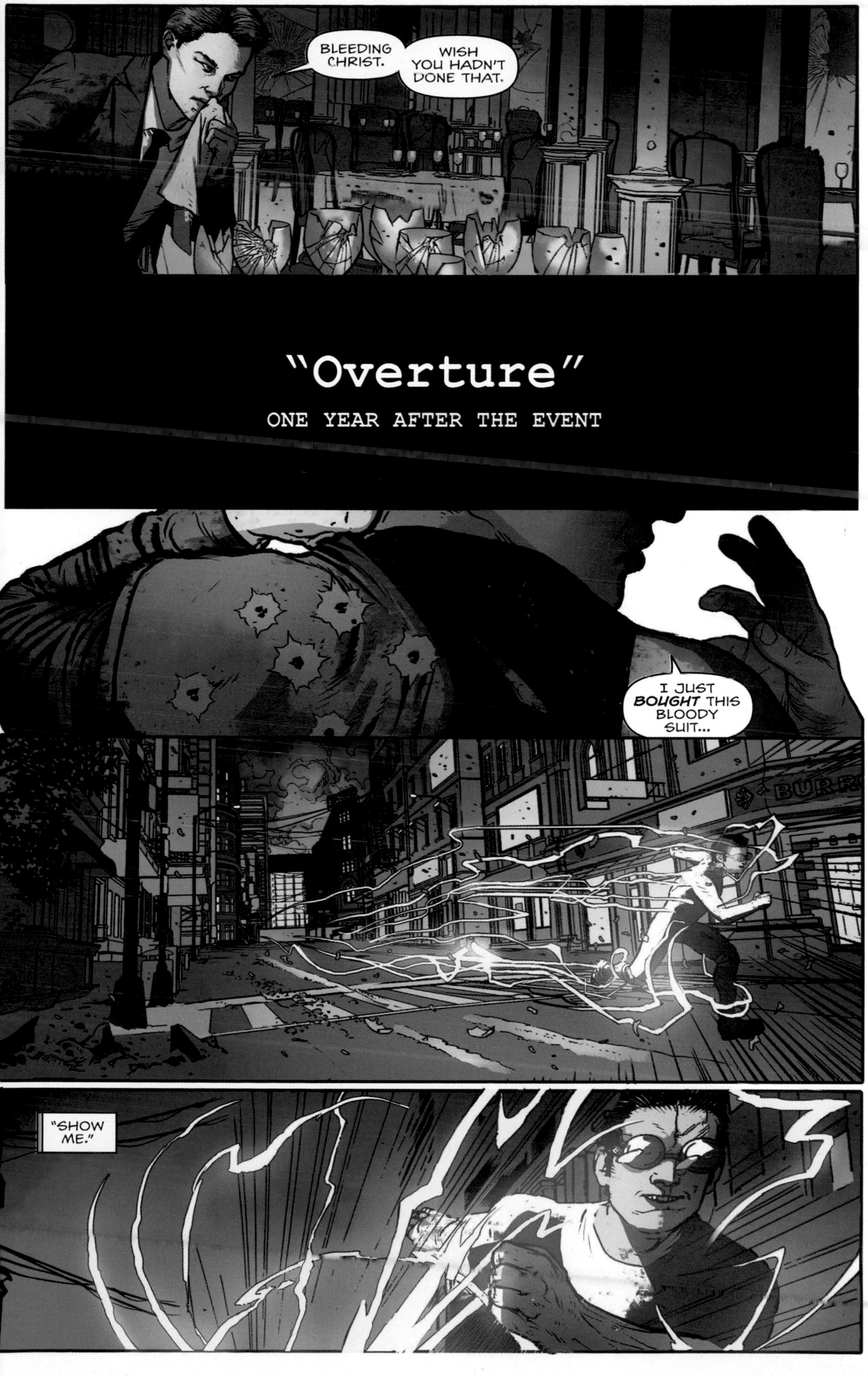
BLEEDING CHRIST.
WISH YOU HADN'T DONE THAT.
"Overture"
ONE YEAR AFTER THE EVENT
I JUST BOUGHT THIS BLOODY SUIT...
BURR
"SHOW ME."

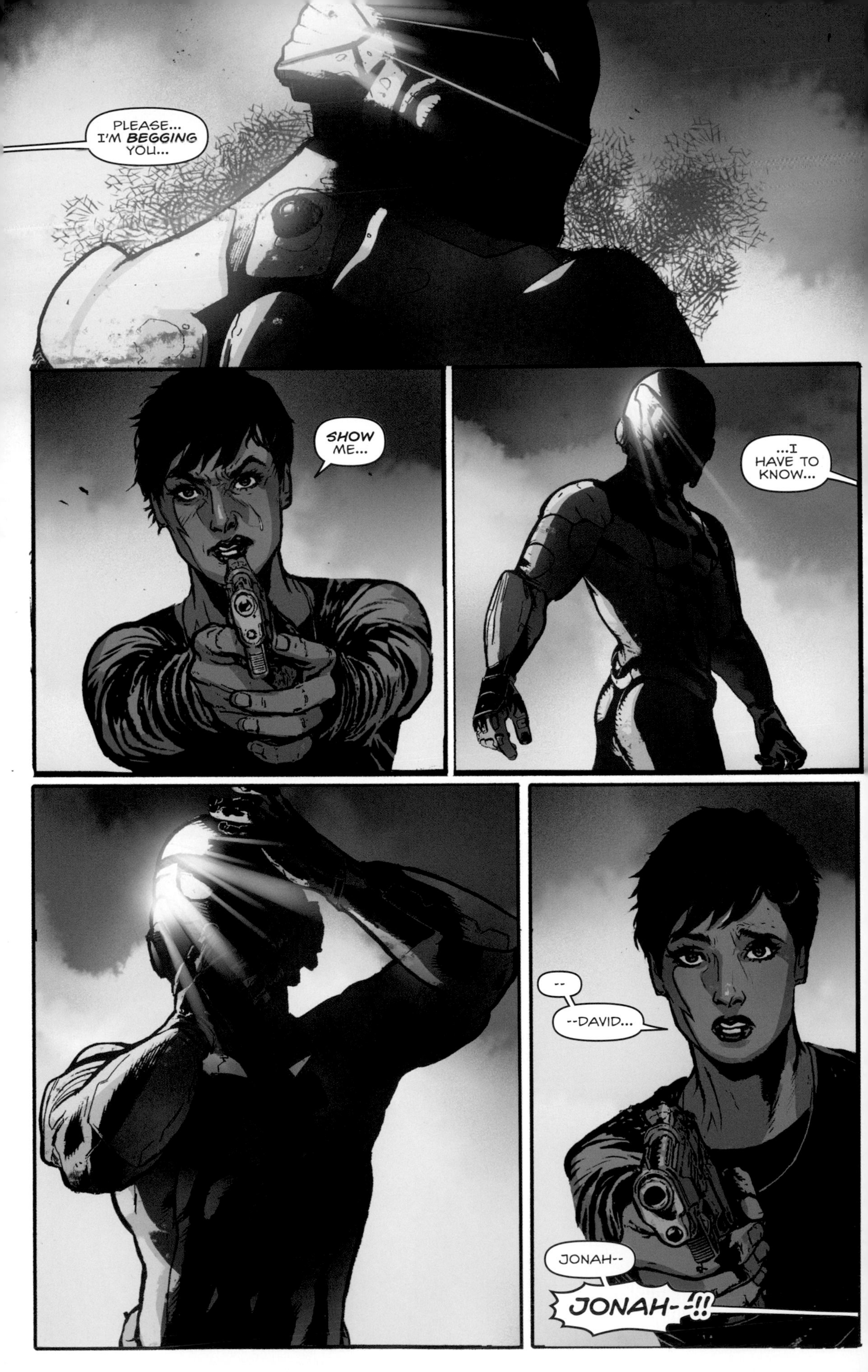
PLEASE... I'M BEGGING YOU...
SHOW ME...
...I HAVE TO KNOW...
--
--DAVID...
JONAH--
JONAH--!!

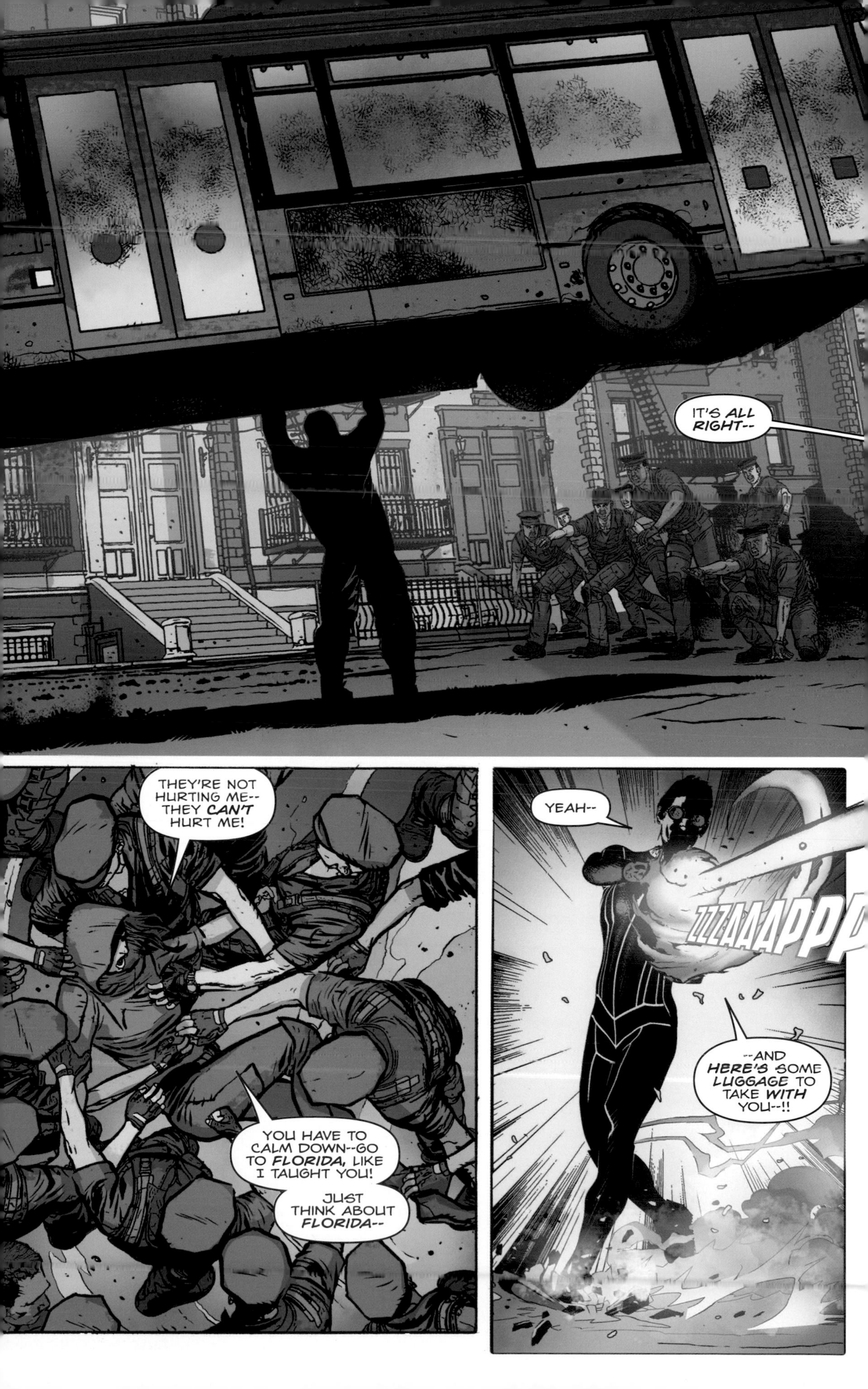
IT'S *ALL RIGHT*--
THEY'RE NOT HURTING ME-- THEY *CAN'T* HURT ME!
YOU HAVE TO CALM DOWN--GO TO *FLORIDA*, LIKE I TAUGHT YOU!
JUST THINK ABOUT *FLORIDA*--
YEAH--
ZZZAAAPPP
--AND *HERE'S* SOME *LUGGAGE* TO TAKE *WITH* YOU--!!

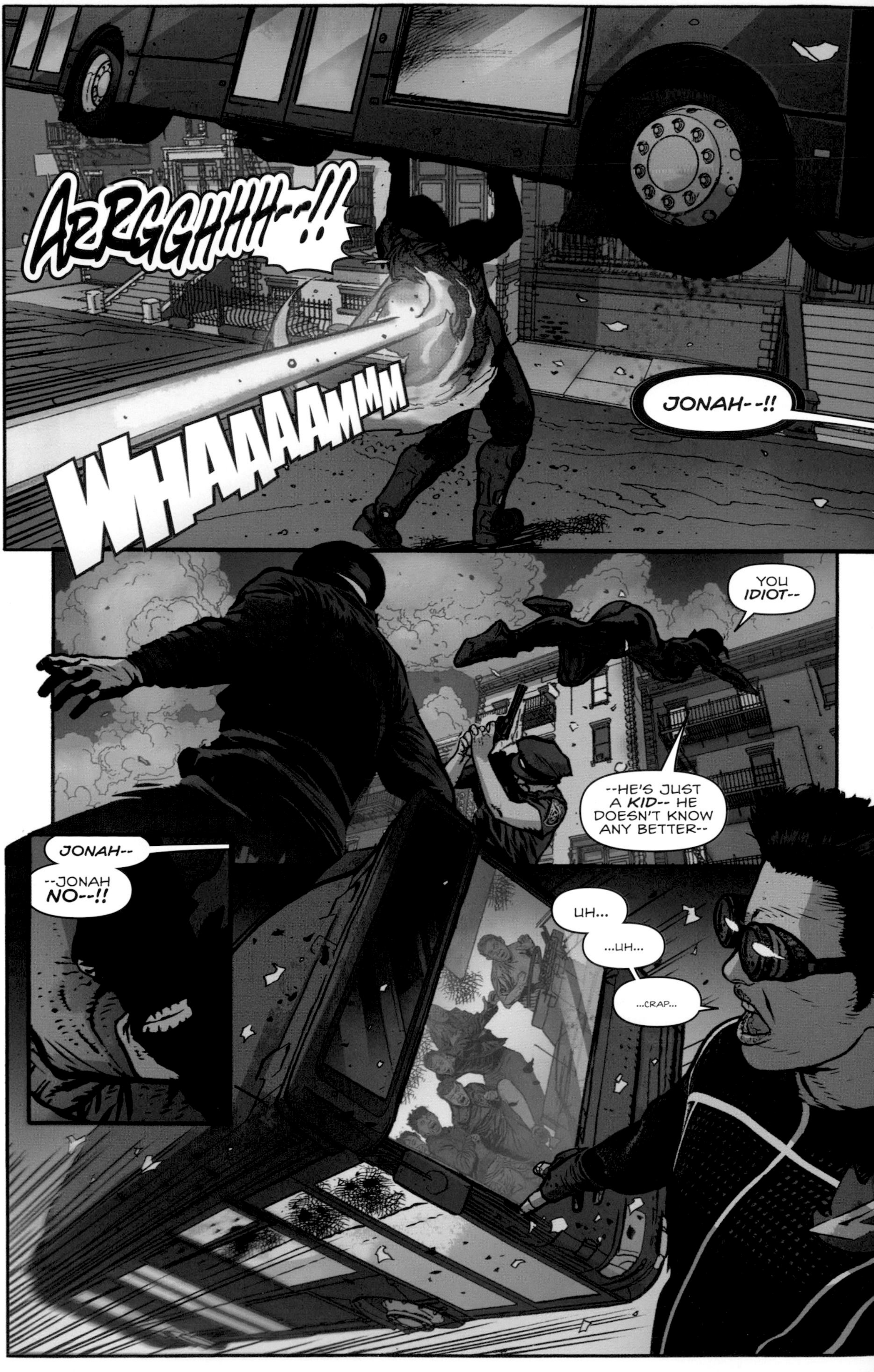
ARRGGHHH--!!
WHAAAAMMM
JONAH--!!
YOU IDIOT--
--HE'S JUST A KID-- HE DOESN'T KNOW ANY BETTER--
JONAH--
--JONAH NO--!!
UH...
...UH...
...CRAP...

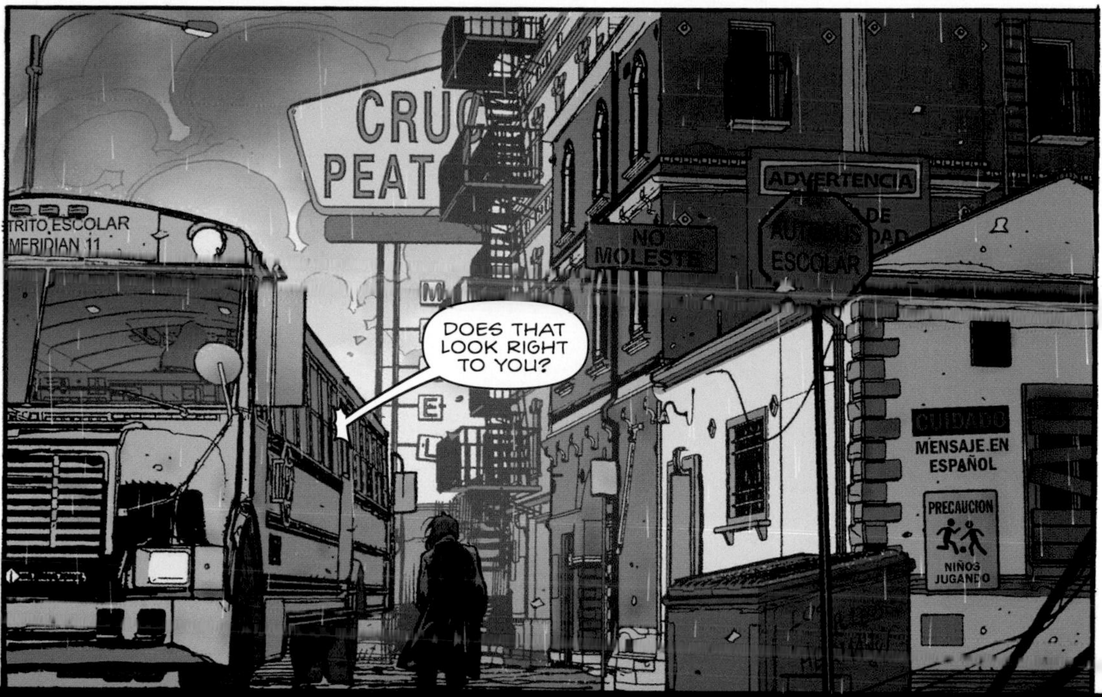

CRUC
PEAT
TRITO ESCOLAR
MERIDIAN 11
ADVERTENCIA
NO MOLESTE
ESCOLAR
CUIDADO
MENSAJE EN ESPAÑOL
PRECAUCION
NIÑOS JUGANDO
DOES THAT LOOK RIGHT TO YOU?

"La Dama en El Autobús"

ONE WEEK BEFORE THE EVENT

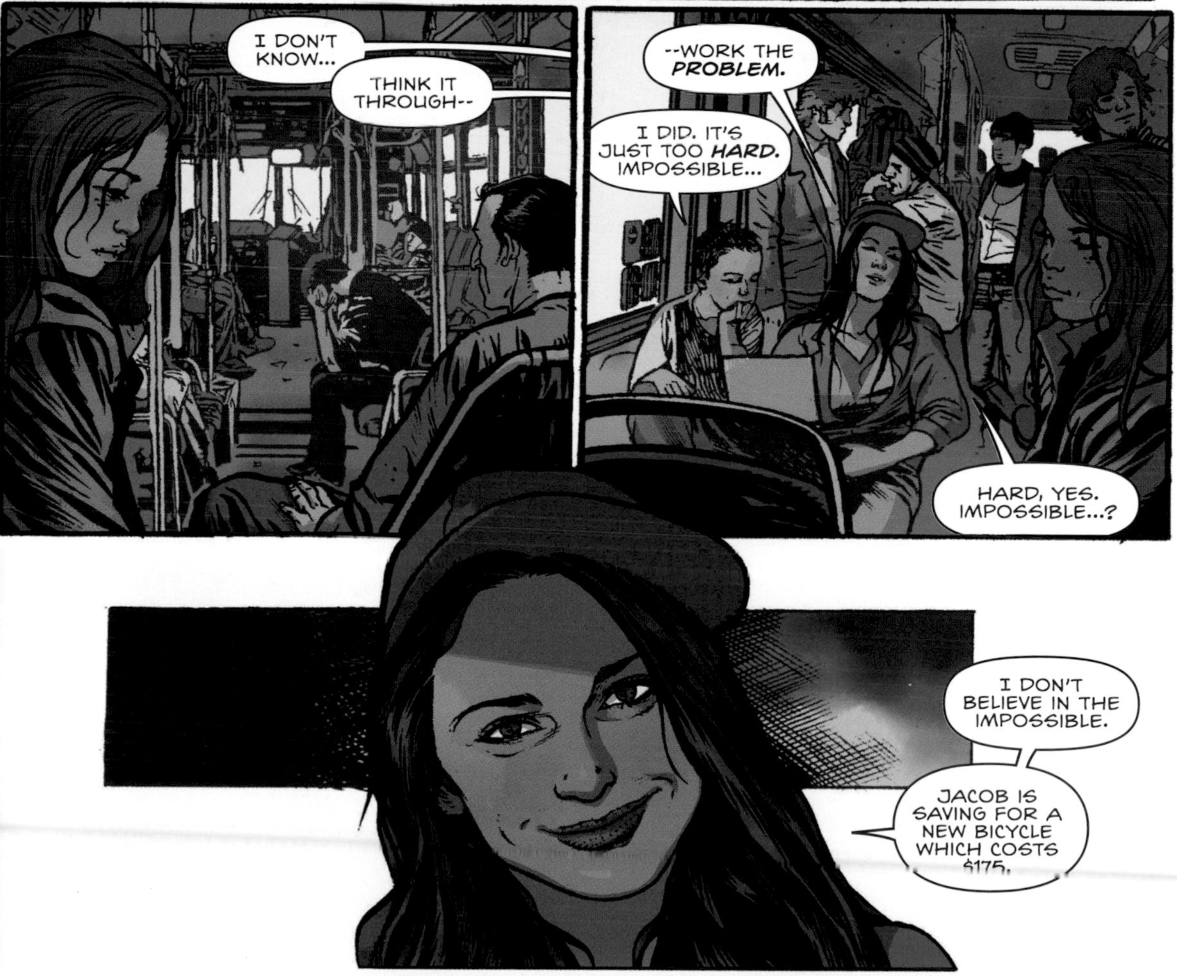

I DON'T KNOW...
THINK IT THROUGH--
--WORK THE ***PROBLEM.***
I DID. IT'S JUST TOO ***HARD.*** IMPOSSIBLE...
HARD, YES. IMPOSSIBLE...?
I DON'T BELIEVE IN THE IMPOSSIBLE.
JACOB IS SAVING FOR A NEW BICYCLE WHICH COSTS $175.

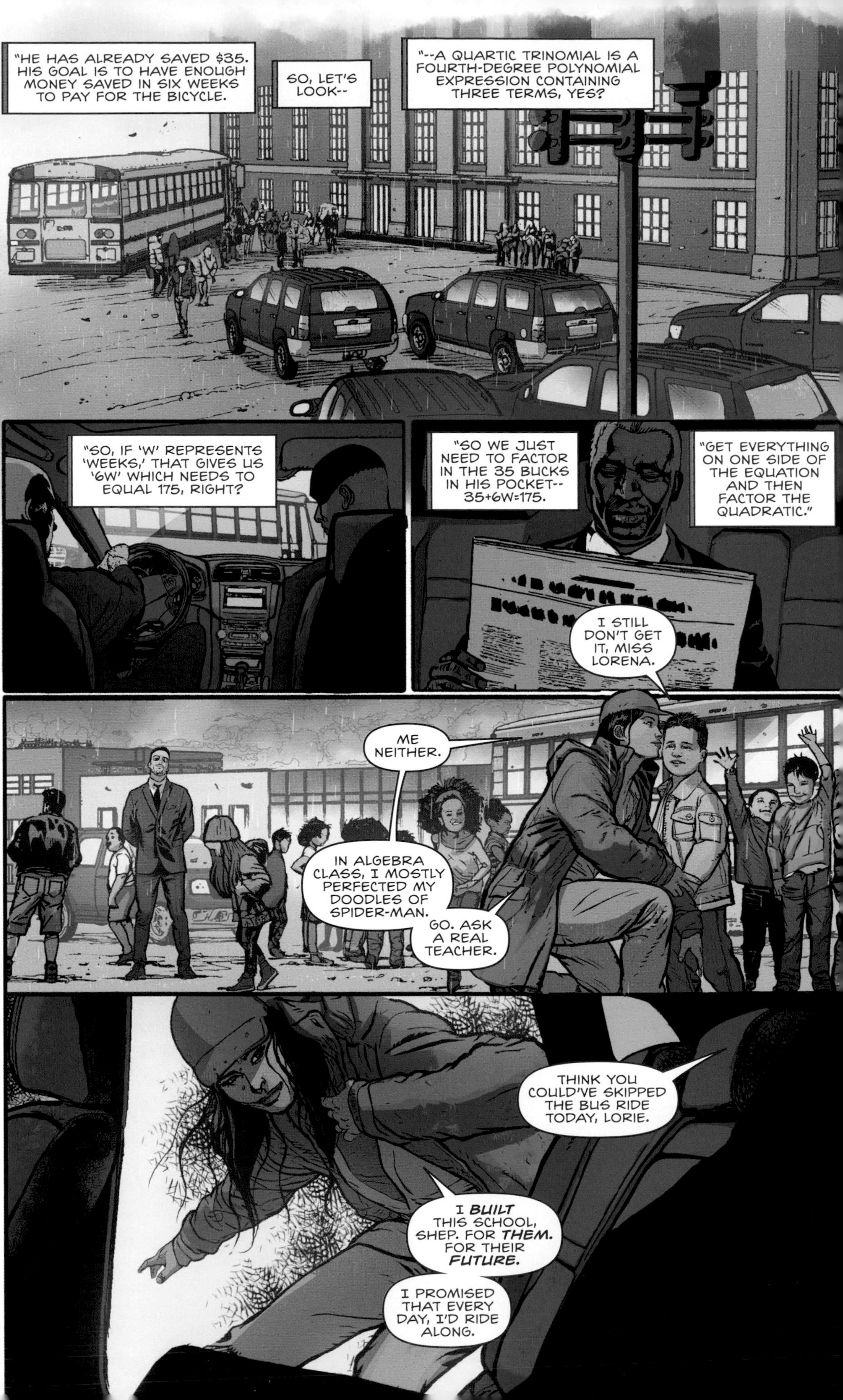
"HE HAS ALREADY SAVED $35. HIS GOAL IS TO HAVE ENOUGH MONEY SAVED IN SIX WEEKS TO PAY FOR THE BICYCLE.
SO, LET'S LOOK--
"--A QUARTIC TRINOMIAL IS A FOURTH-DEGREE POLYNOMIAL EXPRESSION CONTAINING THREE TERMS, YES?
"SO, IF 'W' REPRESENTS 'WEEKS,' THAT GIVES US '6W' WHICH NEEDS TO EQUAL 175, RIGHT?
"SO WE JUST NEED TO FACTOR IN THE 35 BUCKS IN HIS POCKET-- 35+6W=175.
"GET EVERYTHING ON ONE SIDE OF THE EQUATION AND THEN FACTOR THE QUADRATIC."
I STILL DON'T GET IT, MISS LORENA.
ME NEITHER.
IN ALGEBRA CLASS, I MOSTLY PERFECTED MY DOODLES OF SPIDER-MAN.
GO. ASK A REAL TEACHER.
THINK YOU COULD'VE SKIPPED THE BUS RIDE TODAY, LORIE.
I ***BUILT*** THIS SCHOOL, SHEP. FOR ***THEM.*** FOR THEIR ***FUTURE.***
I PROMISED THAT EVERY DAY, I'D RIDE ALONG.

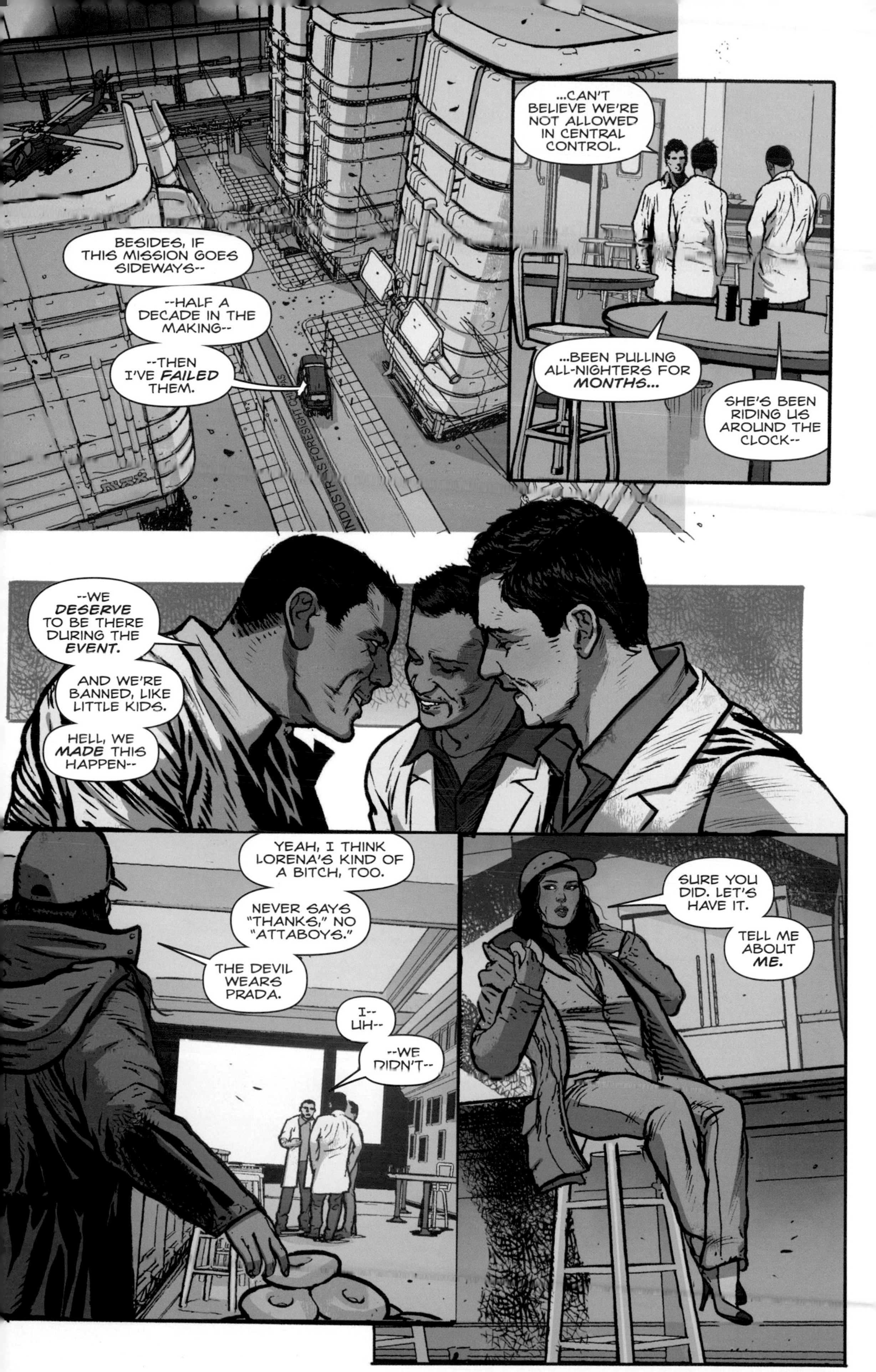
BESIDES, IF THIS MISSION GOES SIDEWAYS--
--HALF A DECADE IN THE MAKING--
--THEN I'VE FAILED THEM.
INDUSTRIES FORESIGHT
...CAN'T BELIEVE WE'RE NOT ALLOWED IN CENTRAL CONTROL.
...BEEN PULLING ALL-NIGHTERS FOR MONTHS...
SHE'S BEEN RIDING US AROUND THE CLOCK--
--WE DESERVE TO BE THERE DURING THE EVENT.
AND WE'RE BANNED, LIKE LITTLE KIDS.
HELL, WE MADE THIS HAPPEN--
YEAH, I THINK LORENA'S KIND OF A BITCH, TOO.
NEVER SAYS "THANKS," NO "ATTABOYS."
THE DEVIL WEARS PRADA.
I-- UH--
--WE DIDN'T--
SURE YOU DID. LET'S HAVE IT.
TELL ME ABOUT ME.

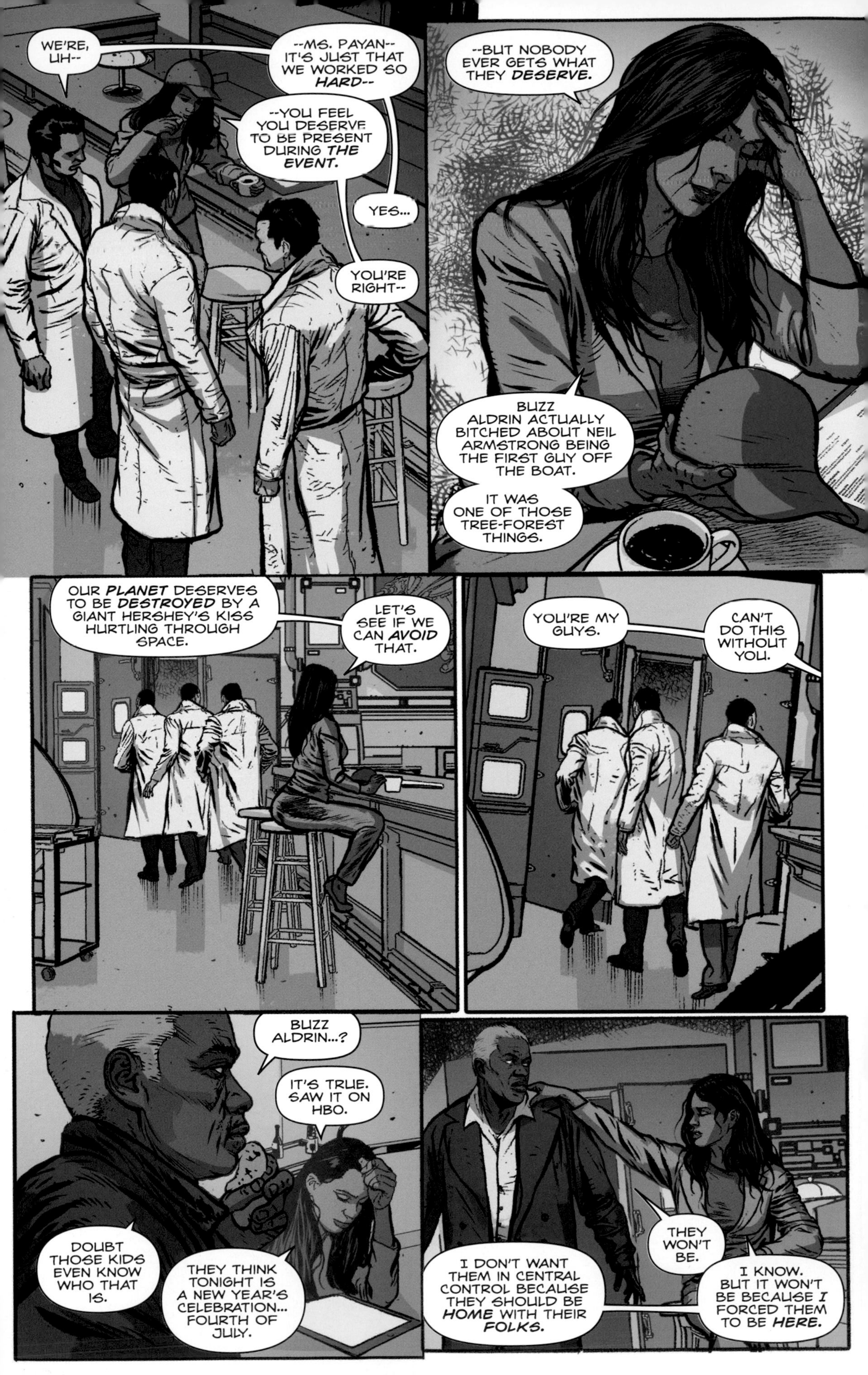
WE'RE, UH--
--MS. PAYAN-- IT'S JUST THAT WE WORKED SO HARD--
--YOU FEEL YOU DESERVE TO BE PRESENT DURING THE EVENT.
YES...
YOU'RE RIGHT--
--BUT NOBODY EVER GETS WHAT THEY DESERVE.
BUZZ ALDRIN ACTUALLY BITCHED ABOUT NEIL ARMSTRONG BEING THE FIRST GUY OFF THE BOAT.
IT WAS ONE OF THOSE TREE-FOREST THINGS.
OUR PLANET DESERVES TO BE DESTROYED BY A GIANT HERSHEY'S KISS HURTLING THROUGH SPACE.
LET'S SEE IF WE CAN AVOID THAT.
YOU'RE MY GUYS.
CAN'T DO THIS WITHOUT YOU.
BUZZ ALDRIN...?
IT'S TRUE. SAW IT ON HBO.
DOUBT THOSE KIDS EVEN KNOW WHO THAT IS.
THEY THINK TONIGHT IS A NEW YEAR'S CELEBRATION... FOURTH OF JULY.
THEY WON'T BE.
I DON'T WANT THEM IN CENTRAL CONTROL BECAUSE THEY SHOULD BE HOME WITH THEIR FOLKS.
I KNOW. BUT IT WON'T BE BECAUSE I FORCED THEM TO BE HERE.

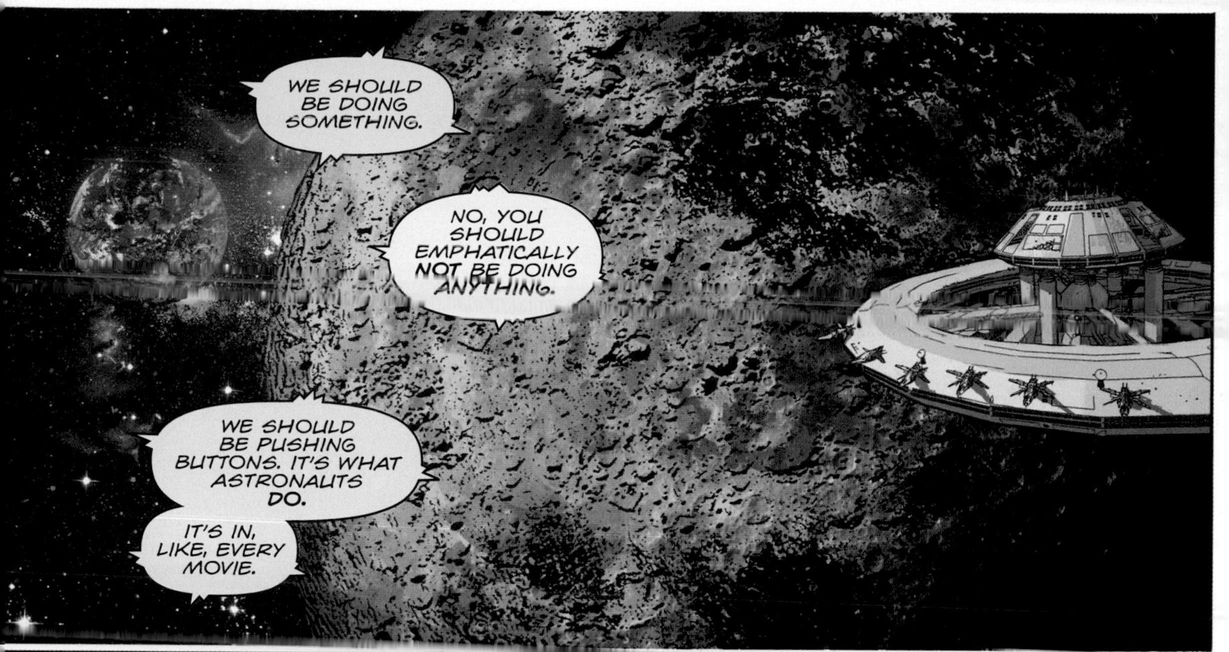
WE SHOULD BE DOING SOMETHING.
NO, YOU SHOULD EMPHATICALLY NOT BE DOING ANYTHING.
WE SHOULD BE PUSHING BUTTONS. IT'S WHAT ASTRONAUTS DO.
IT'S IN, LIKE, EVERY MOVIE.

"Monkeys"

FORESIGHT AMERICO LUNAR PLATFORM
ONE WEEK BEFORE THE EVENT

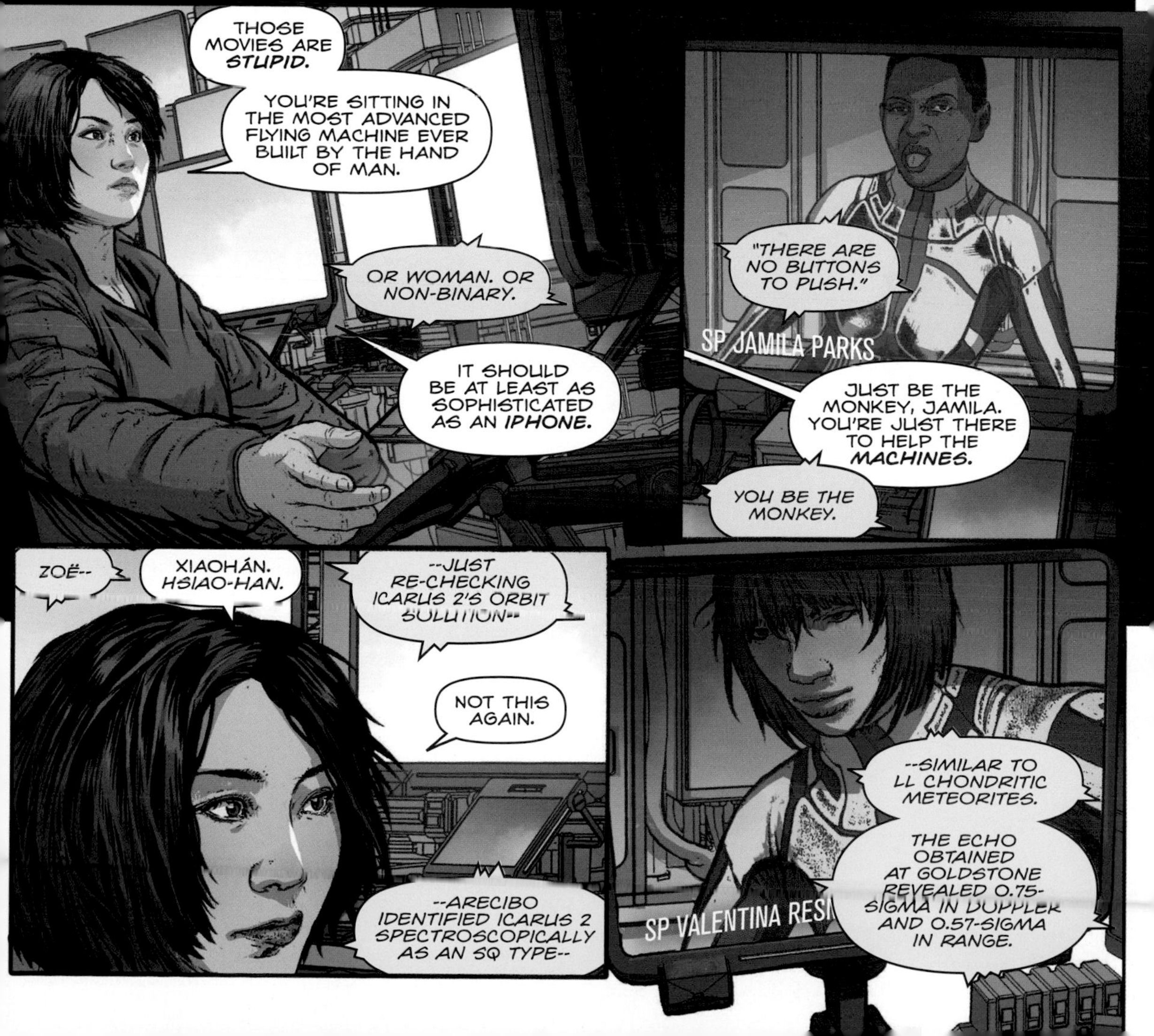
THOSE MOVIES ARE STUPID.
YOU'RE SITTING IN THE MOST ADVANCED FLYING MACHINE EVER BUILT BY THE HAND OF MAN.
OR WOMAN. OR NON-BINARY.
IT SHOULD BE AT LEAST AS SOPHISTICATED AS AN IPHONE.
"THERE ARE NO BUTTONS TO PUSH."
SP JAMILA PARKS
JUST BE THE MONKEY, JAMILA. YOU'RE JUST THERE TO HELP THE MACHINES.
YOU BE THE MONKEY.
ZOË--
XIAOHÁN. HSIAO-HAN.
--JUST RE-CHECKING ICARUS 2'S ORBIT SOLUTION--
NOT THIS AGAIN.
--ARECIBO IDENTIFIED ICARUS 2 SPECTROSCOPICALLY AS AN SQ TYPE--
--SIMILAR TO LL CHONDRITIC METEORITES.
THE ECHO OBTAINED AT GOLDSTONE REVEALED 0.75-SIGMA IN DOPPLER AND 0.57-SIGMA IN RANGE.
SP VALENTINA RESM

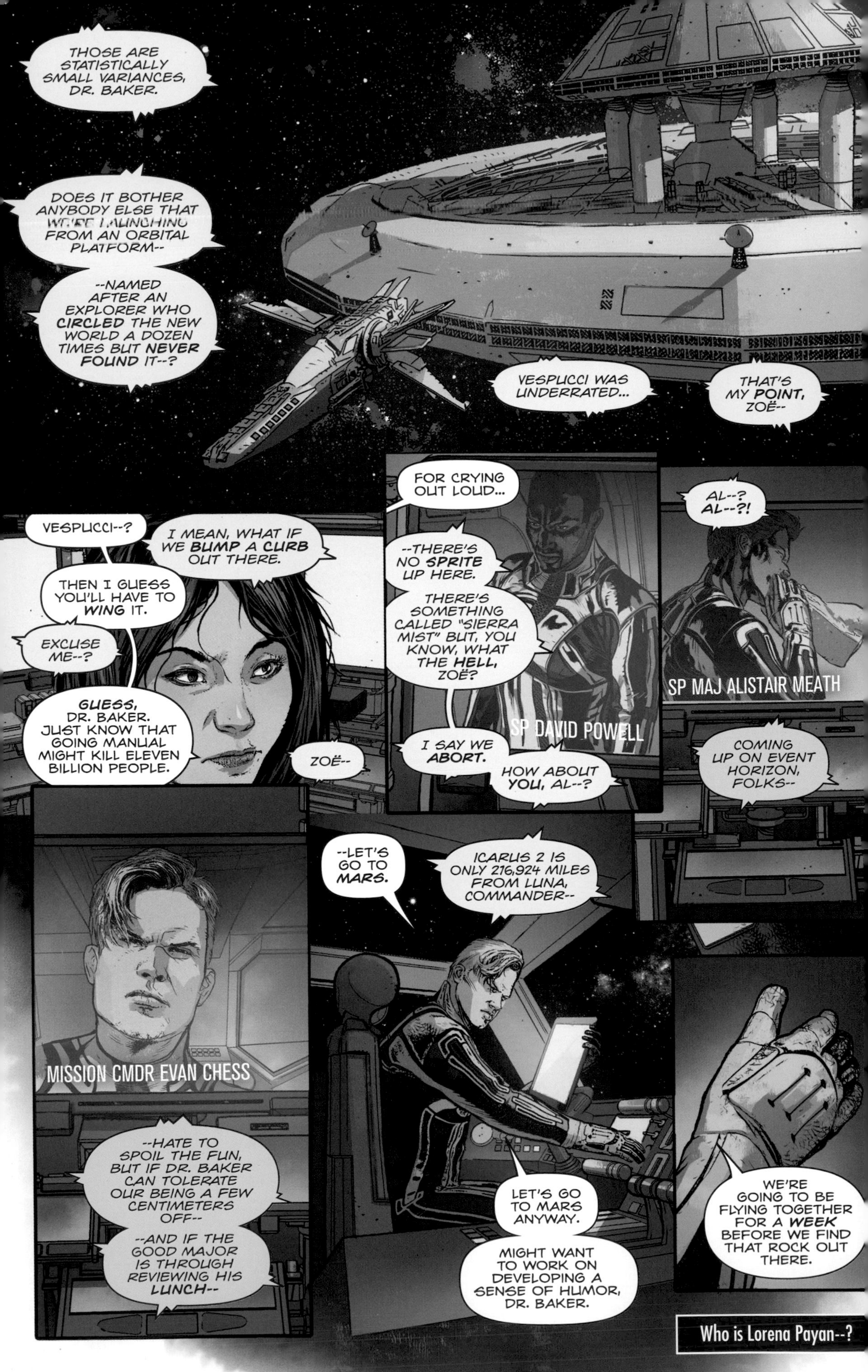
THOSE ARE STATISTICALLY SMALL VARIANCES, DR. BAKER.
DOES IT BOTHER ANYBODY ELSE THAT WE'RE LAUNCHING FROM AN ORBITAL PLATFORM--
--NAMED AFTER AN EXPLORER WHO CIRCLED THE NEW WORLD A DOZEN TIMES BUT NEVER FOUND IT--?
VESPUCCI WAS UNDERRATED...
THAT'S MY POINT, ZOË--
VESPUCCI--?
I MEAN, WHAT IF WE BUMP A CURB OUT THERE.
THEN I GUESS YOU'LL HAVE TO WING IT.
EXCUSE ME--?
GUESS, DR. BAKER. JUST KNOW THAT GOING MANUAL MIGHT KILL ELEVEN BILLION PEOPLE.
ZOË--
FOR CRYING OUT LOUD...
--THERE'S NO SPRITE UP HERE.
THERE'S SOMETHING CALLED "SIERRA MIST" BUT, YOU KNOW, WHAT THE HELL, ZOË?
SP DAVID POWELL
I SAY WE ABORT.
HOW ABOUT YOU, AL--?
AL--? AL--?!
SP MAJ ALISTAIR MEATH
COMING UP ON EVENT HORIZON, FOLKS--
MISSION CMDR EVAN CHESS
--HATE TO SPOIL THE FUN, BUT IF DR. BAKER CAN TOLERATE OUR BEING A FEW CENTIMETERS OFF--
--AND IF THE GOOD MAJOR IS THROUGH REVIEWING HIS LUNCH--
--LET'S GO TO MARS.
ICARUS 2 IS ONLY 216,924 MILES FROM LUNA, COMMANDER--
LET'S GO TO MARS ANYWAY.
MIGHT WANT TO WORK ON DEVELOPING A SENSE OF HUMOR, DR. BAKER.
WE'RE GOING TO BE FLYING TOGETHER FOR A WEEK BEFORE WE FIND THAT ROCK OUT THERE.
Who is Lorena Payan--?

GLOBAL **NOW**

LORENA

HOW THE FATE OF THE WORLD CAME TO REST IN HER HANDS

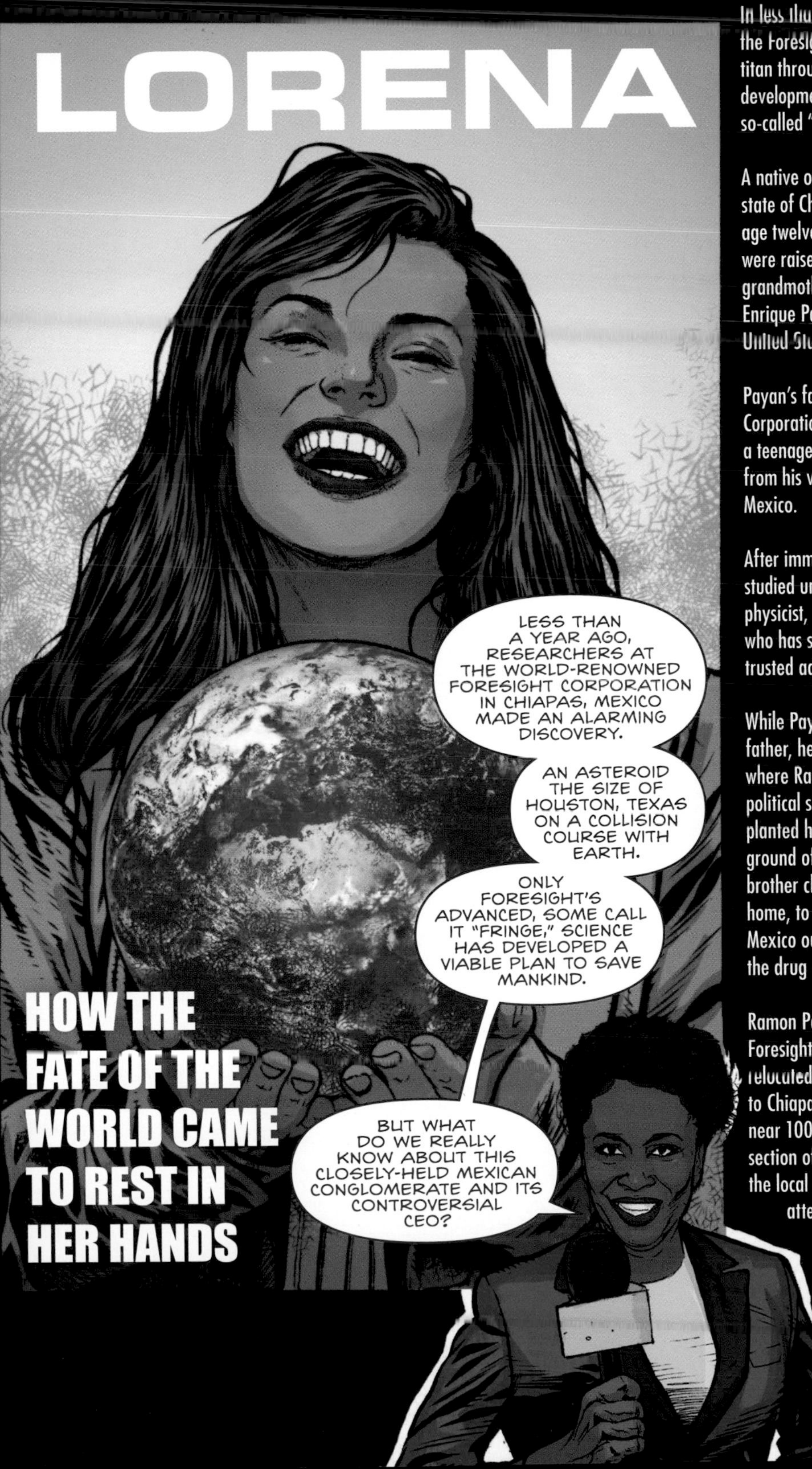

LESS THAN A YEAR AGO, RESEARCHERS AT THE WORLD-RENOWNED FORESIGHT CORPORATION IN CHIAPAS, MEXICO MADE AN ALARMING DISCOVERY.
AN ASTEROID THE SIZE OF HOUSTON, TEXAS ON A COLLISION COURSE WITH EARTH.
ONLY FORESIGHT'S ADVANCED, SOME CALL IT "FRINGE," SCIENCE HAS DEVELOPED A VIABLE PLAN TO SAVE MANKIND.
BUT WHAT DO WE REALLY KNOW ABOUT THIS CLOSELY-HELD MEXICAN CONGLOMERATE AND ITS CONTROVERSIAL CEO?

In less than ten years, Lorena Payan built the Foresight Corporation into a global titan through innovations in aerospace development, space exploration, and so-called "fringe" science.

A native of the impoverished Mexican state of Chiapas, Payan lost her mother at age twelve. She and her brother Ramon were raised by their paternal grandmother Isabel, while their father Enrique Payan attended M.I.T. in the United States.

Payan's father founded the Foresight Corporation in Silicon Valley when she was a teenager, using wealth accumulated from his various business ventures in Mexico.

After immigrating to America, Payan studied under the tutelage of the eminent physicist, Dr. Parker "Shep" Bingham, who has served as her mentor and most trusted advisor.

While Payan lived in America with her father, her brother returned to Mexico, where Ramon Payan rose within the political structure. While Enrique Payan planted himself and his daughter in the ground of the American Dream, Lorena's brother chose to fight for his people back home, to work within the system to pull Mexico out of corruption and save it from the drug cartels.

Ramon Payan inherited the leadership of Foresight upon their father's death and relocated the corporation's central office to Chiapas. The Payan siblings hired a near 100% Mexican labor force in every section of the company and revolutionized the local economy while bringing global attention to the plight of Chiapas's indigenous tribes and social conflicts. Lorena Payan assumed control of Foresight after her brother was killed in a car bombing.

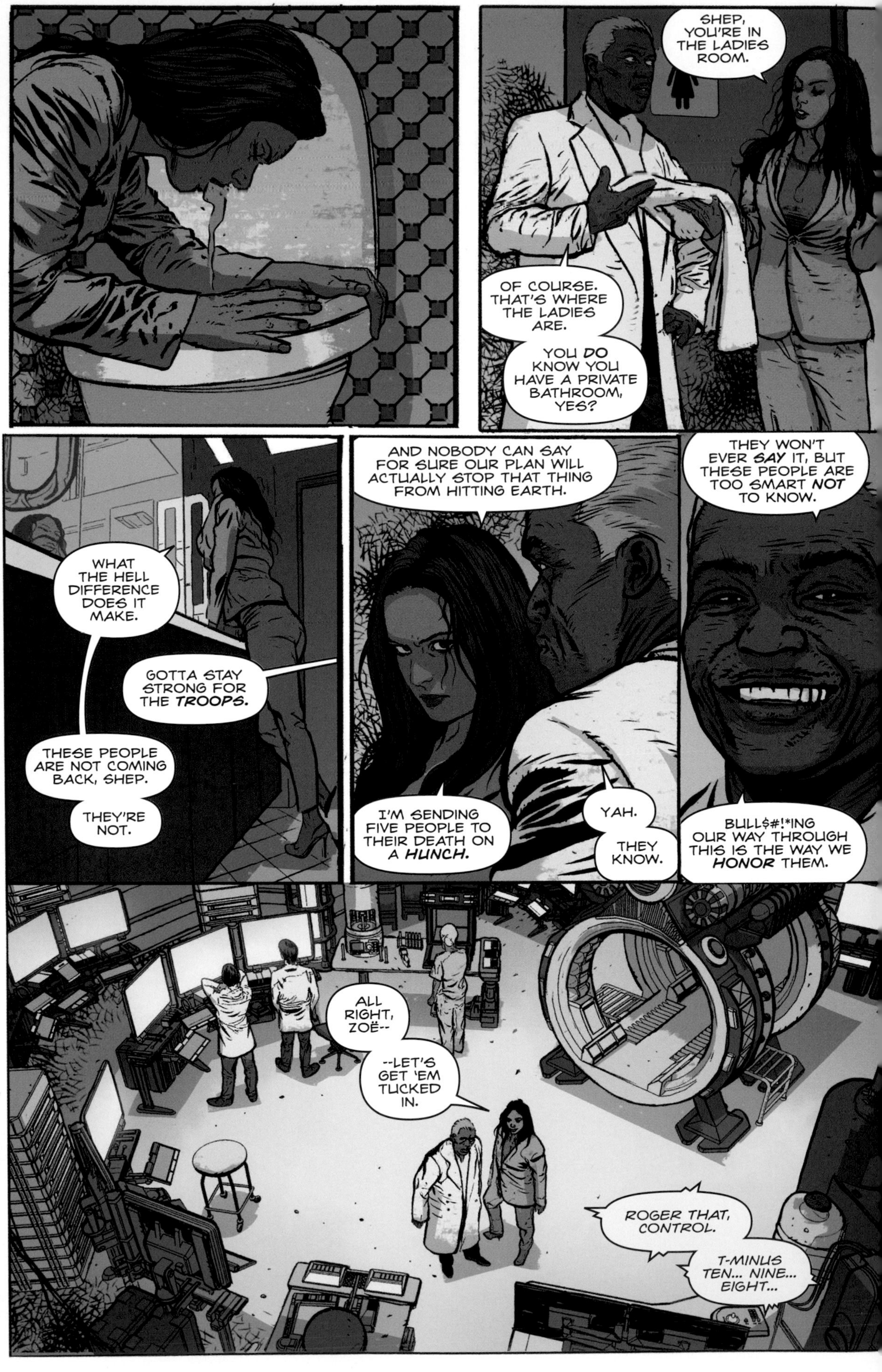
SHEP, YOU'RE IN THE LADIES ROOM.
OF COURSE. THAT'S WHERE THE LADIES ARE.
YOU DO KNOW YOU HAVE A PRIVATE BATHROOM, YES?
WHAT THE HELL DIFFERENCE DOES IT MAKE.
GOTTA STAY STRONG FOR THE TROOPS.
THESE PEOPLE ARE NOT COMING BACK, SHEP.
THEY'RE NOT.
AND NOBODY CAN SAY FOR SURE OUR PLAN WILL ACTUALLY STOP THAT THING FROM HITTING EARTH.
I'M SENDING FIVE PEOPLE TO THEIR DEATH ON A HUNCH.
YAH.
THEY KNOW.
THEY WON'T EVER SAY IT, BUT THESE PEOPLE ARE TOO SMART NOT TO KNOW.
BULL$#!*ING OUR WAY THROUGH THIS IS THE WAY WE HONOR THEM.
ALL RIGHT, ZOË--
--LET'S GET 'EM TUCKED IN.
ROGER THAT, CONTROL.
T-MINUS TEN... NINE... EIGHT...

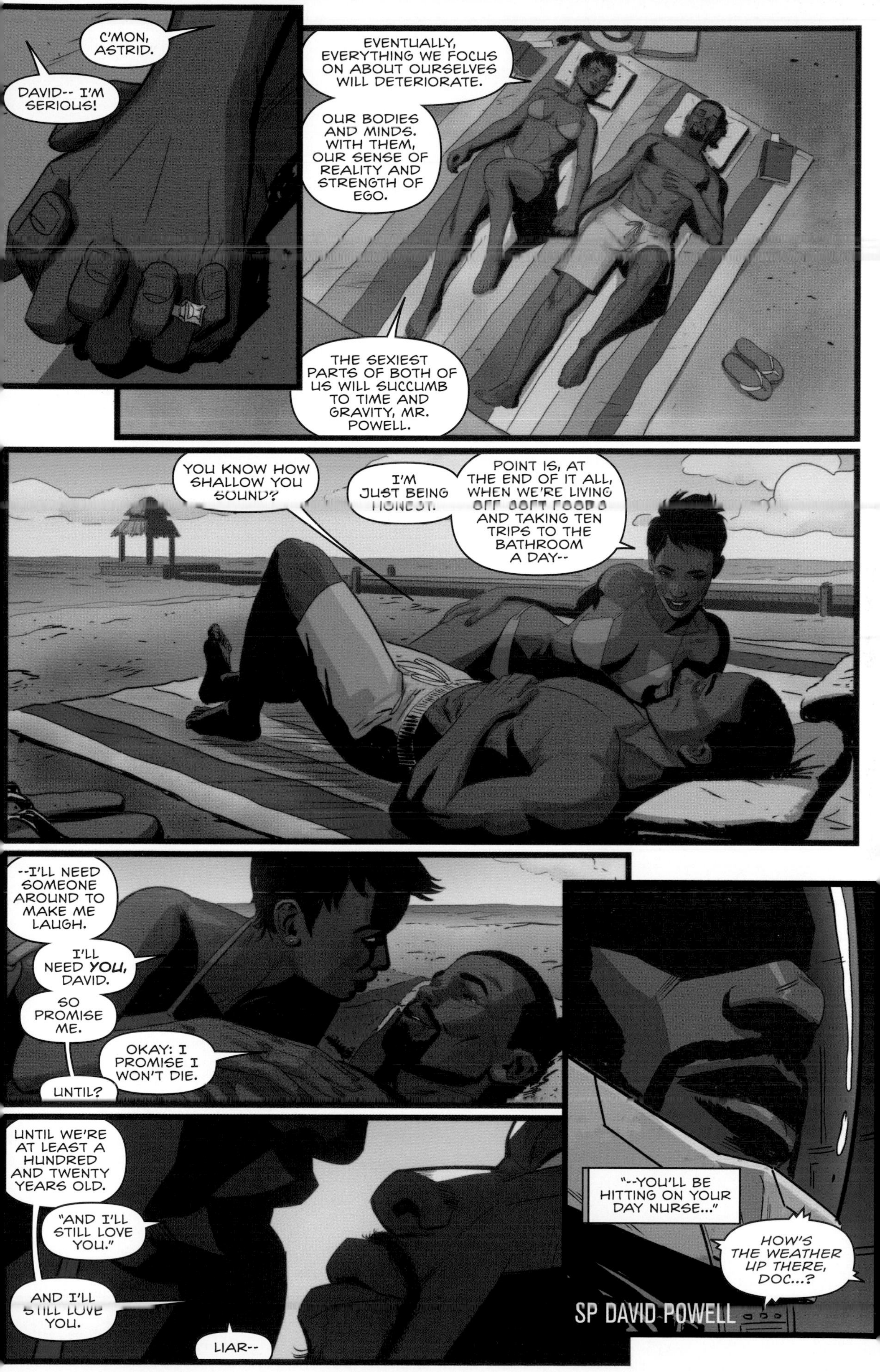
C'MON, ASTRID.
DAVID-- I'M SERIOUS!
EVENTUALLY, EVERYTHING WE FOCUS ON ABOUT OURSELVES WILL DETERIORATE.
OUR BODIES AND MINDS. WITH THEM, OUR SENSE OF REALITY AND STRENGTH OF EGO.
THE SEXIEST PARTS OF BOTH OF US WILL SUCCUMB TO TIME AND GRAVITY, MR. POWELL.
YOU KNOW HOW SHALLOW YOU SOUND?
I'M JUST BEING HONEST.
POINT IS, AT THE END OF IT ALL, WHEN WE'RE LIVING OFF SOFT FOODS AND TAKING TEN TRIPS TO THE BATHROOM A DAY--
--I'LL NEED SOMEONE AROUND TO MAKE ME LAUGH.
I'LL NEED **YOU,** DAVID.
SO PROMISE ME.
OKAY: I PROMISE I WON'T DIE.
UNTIL?
UNTIL WE'RE AT LEAST A HUNDRED AND TWENTY YEARS OLD.
"AND I'LL STILL LOVE YOU."
AND I'LL STILL LOVE YOU.
LIAR--
"--YOU'LL BE HITTING ON YOUR DAY NURSE..."
HOW'S THE WEATHER UP THERE, DOC...?
SP DAVID POWELL

"Icarus"

THIRTY MINUTES BEFORE THE EVENT

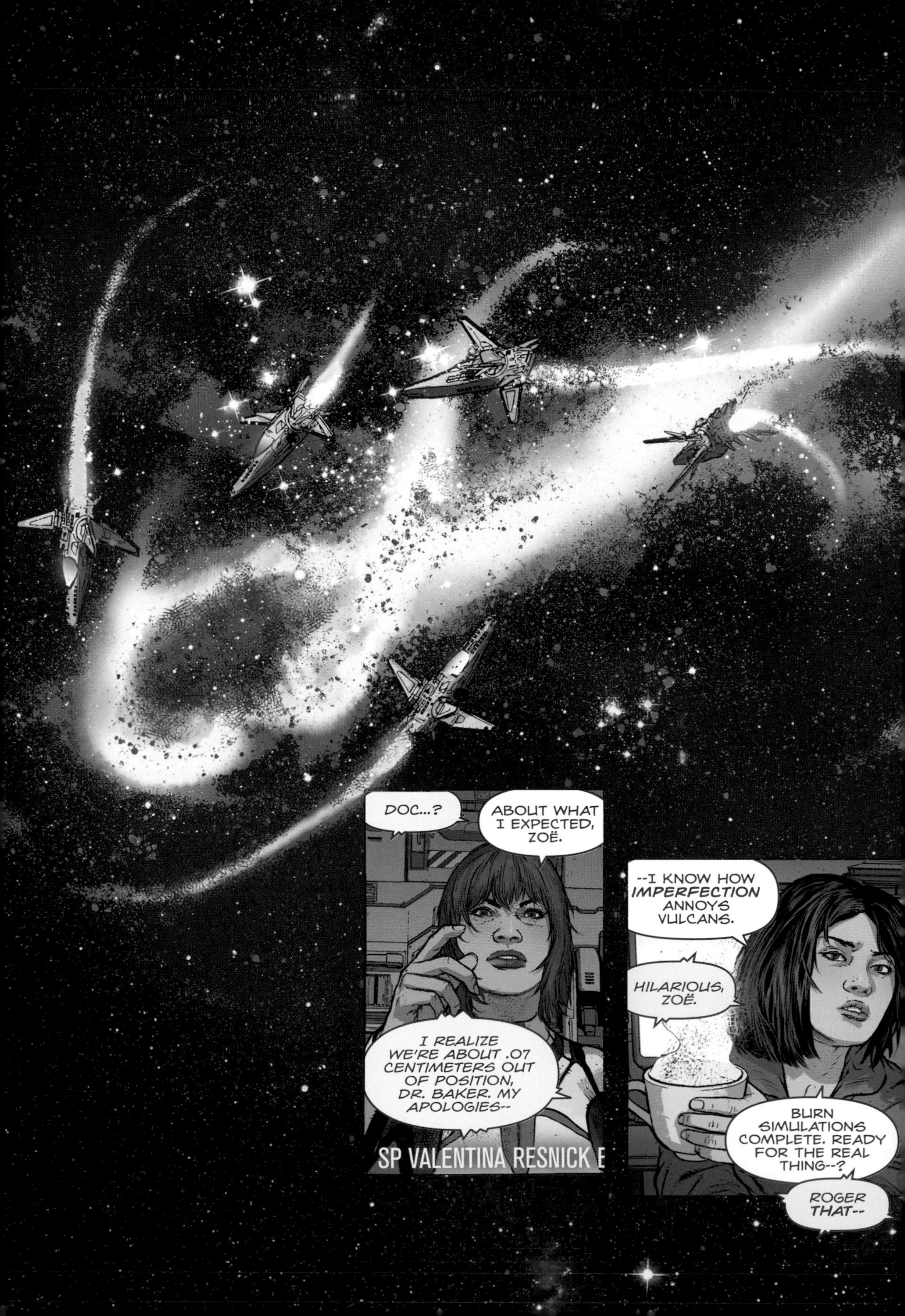
DOC...?
ABOUT WHAT I EXPECTED, ZOË.
I REALIZE WE'RE ABOUT .07 CENTIMETERS OUT OF POSITION, DR. BAKER. MY APOLOGIES--
SP VALENTINA RESNICK E
--I KNOW HOW *IMPERFECTION* ANNOYS VULCANS.
HILARIOUS, ZOË.
BURN SIMULATIONS COMPLETE. READY FOR THE REAL THING--?
ROGER *THAT*--

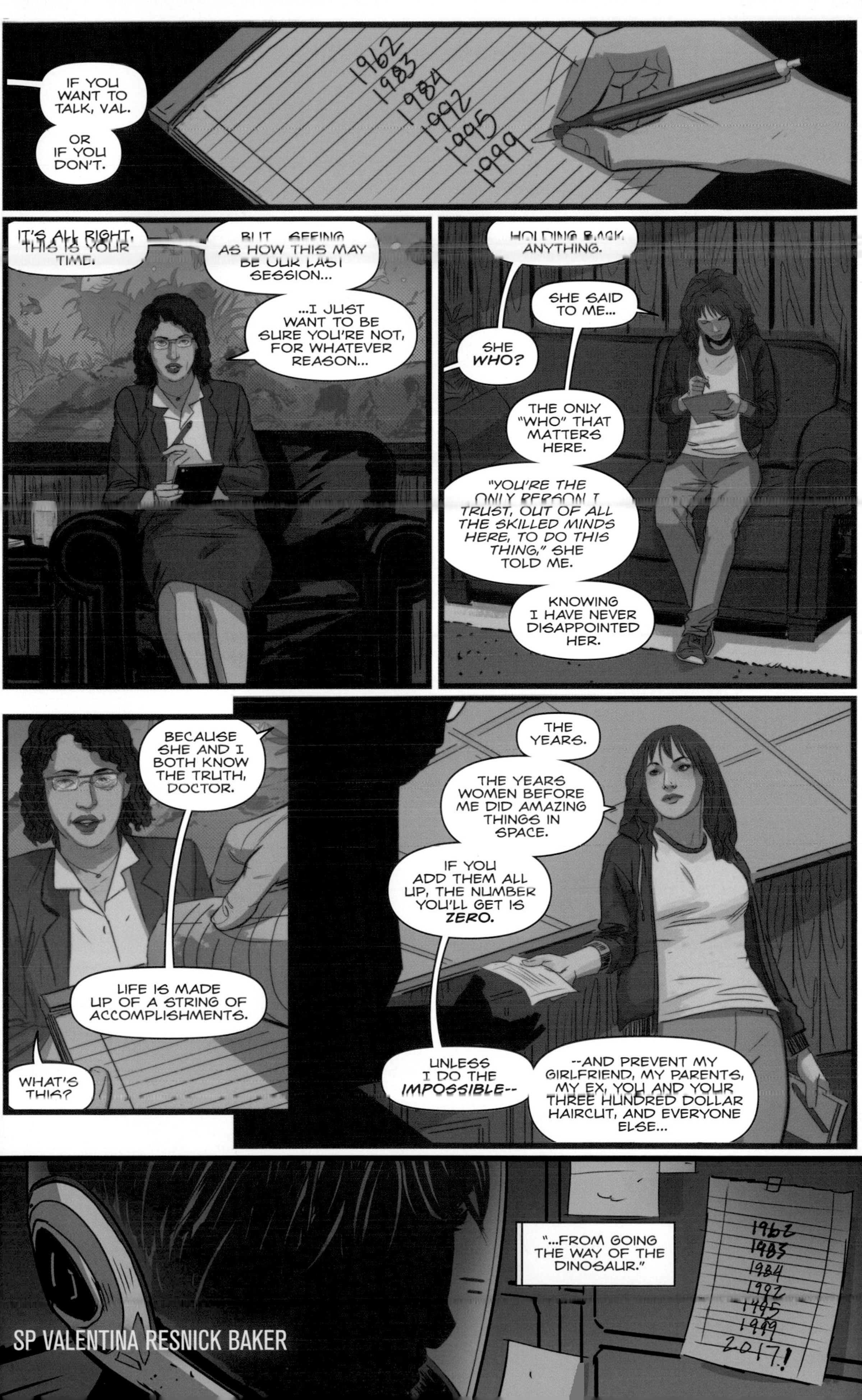
IF YOU WANT TO TALK, VAL.
OR IF YOU DON'T.
1962 1983 1984 1992 1995 1999
IT'S ALL RIGHT. THIS IS YOUR TIME.
BUT... SEEING AS HOW THIS MAY BE OUR LAST SESSION...
...I JUST WANT TO BE SURE YOU'RE NOT, FOR WHATEVER REASON...
HOLDING BACK ANYTHING.
SHE SAID TO ME...
SHE WHO?
THE ONLY "WHO" THAT MATTERS HERE.
"YOU'RE THE ONLY PERSON I TRUST, OUT OF ALL THE SKILLED MINDS HERE, TO DO THIS THING," SHE TOLD ME.
KNOWING I HAVE NEVER DISAPPOINTED HER.
BECAUSE SHE AND I BOTH KNOW THE TRUTH, DOCTOR.
LIFE IS MADE UP OF A STRING OF ACCOMPLISHMENTS.
WHAT'S THIS?
THE YEARS.
THE YEARS WOMEN BEFORE ME DID AMAZING THINGS IN SPACE.
IF YOU ADD THEM ALL UP, THE NUMBER YOU'LL GET IS ZERO.
UNLESS I DO THE IMPOSSIBLE--
--AND PREVENT MY GIRLFRIEND, MY PARENTS, MY EX, YOU AND YOUR THREE HUNDRED DOLLAR HAIRCUT, AND EVERYONE ELSE...
"...FROM GOING THE WAY OF THE DINOSAUR."
1962 1983 1984 1992 1995 1999 2017!
SP VALENTINA RESNICK BAKER

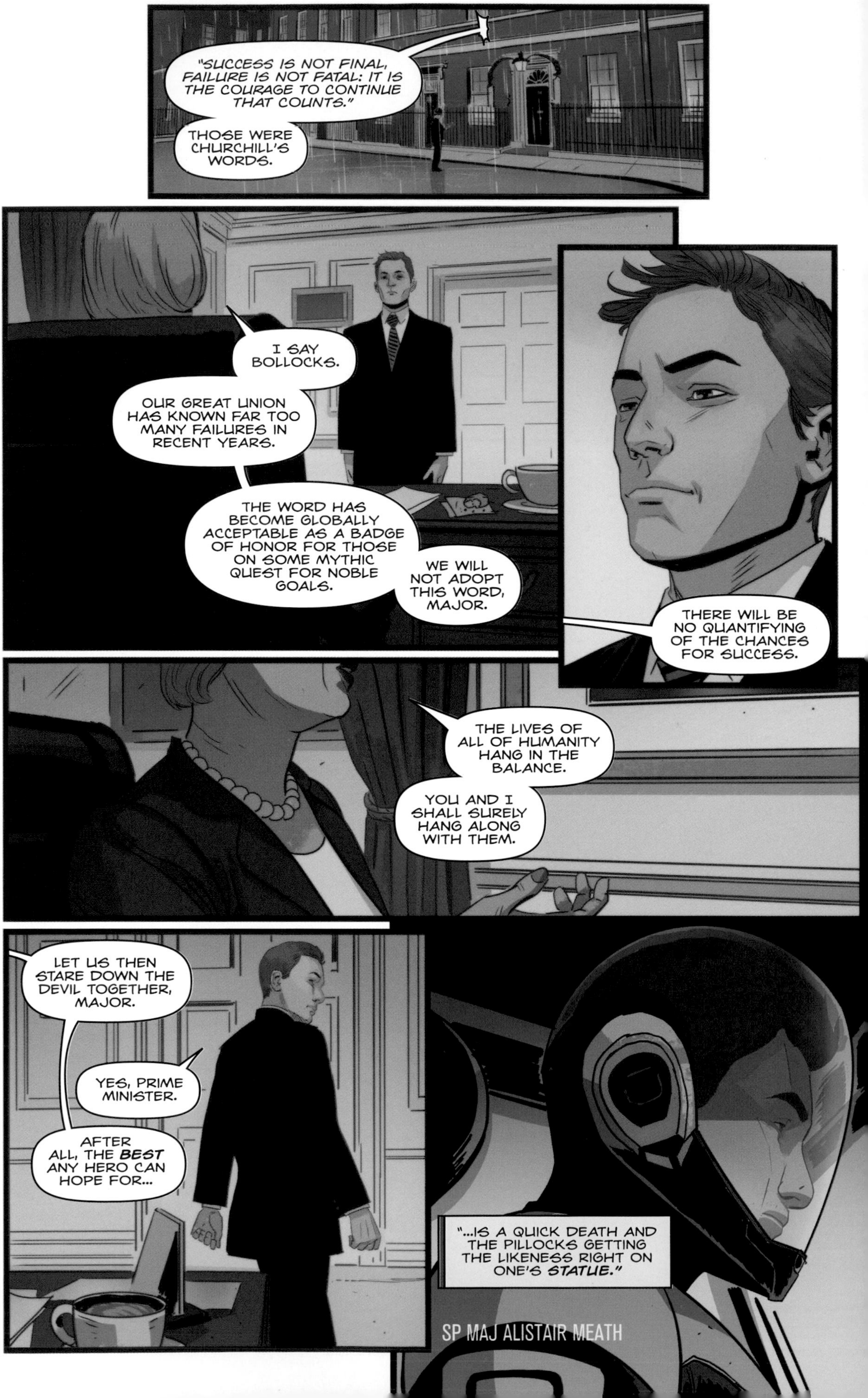
"SUCCESS IS NOT FINAL, FAILURE IS NOT FATAL: IT IS THE COURAGE TO CONTINUE THAT COUNTS."
THOSE WERE CHURCHILL'S WORDS.
I SAY BOLLOCKS.
OUR GREAT UNION HAS KNOWN FAR TOO MANY FAILURES IN RECENT YEARS.
THE WORD HAS BECOME GLOBALLY ACCEPTABLE AS A BADGE OF HONOR FOR THOSE ON SOME MYTHIC QUEST FOR NOBLE GOALS.
WE WILL NOT ADOPT THIS WORD, MAJOR.
THERE WILL BE NO QUANTIFYING OF THE CHANCES FOR SUCCESS.
THE LIVES OF ALL OF HUMANITY HANG IN THE BALANCE.
YOU AND I SHALL SURELY HANG ALONG WITH THEM.
LET US THEN STARE DOWN THE DEVIL TOGETHER, MAJOR.
YES, PRIME MINISTER.
AFTER ALL, THE ***BEST*** ANY HERO CAN HOPE FOR...
"...IS A QUICK DEATH AND THE PILLOCKS GETTING THE LIKENESS RIGHT ON ONE'S ***STATUE***."
SP MAJ ALISTAIR MEATH

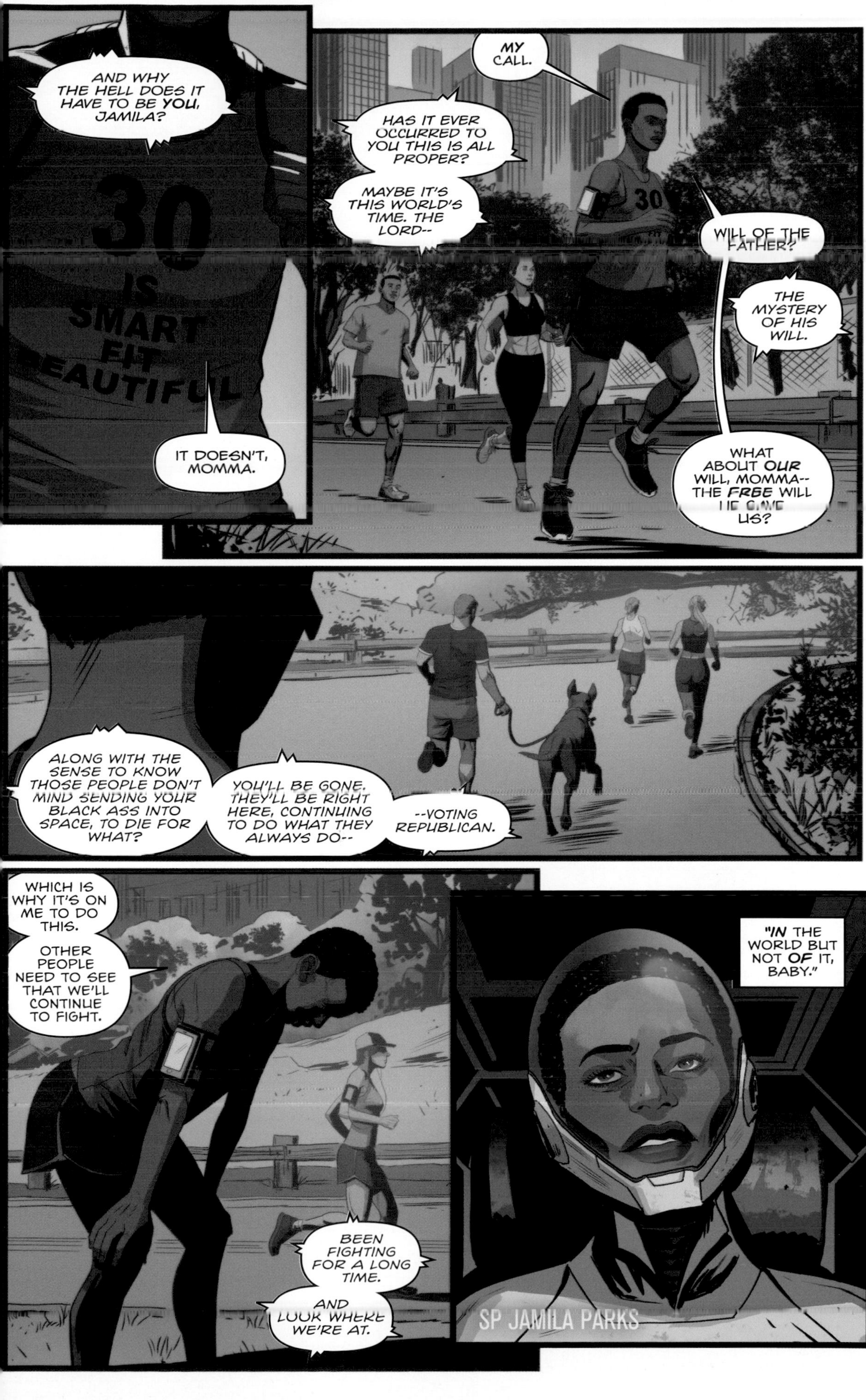
AND WHY THE HELL DOES IT HAVE TO BE YOU, JAMILA?
30 IS SMART FIT BEAUTIFUL
IT DOESN'T, MOMMA.
MY CALL.
HAS IT EVER OCCURRED TO YOU THIS IS ALL PROPER?
MAYBE IT'S THIS WORLD'S TIME. THE LORD--
30
WILL OF THE FATHER?
THE MYSTERY OF HIS WILL.
WHAT ABOUT OUR WILL, MOMMA-- THE FREE WILL HE GAVE US?
ALONG WITH THE SENSE TO KNOW THOSE PEOPLE DON'T MIND SENDING YOUR BLACK ASS INTO SPACE, TO DIE FOR WHAT?
YOU'LL BE GONE. THEY'LL BE RIGHT HERE, CONTINUING TO DO WHAT THEY ALWAYS DO--
--VOTING REPUBLICAN.
WHICH IS WHY IT'S ON ME TO DO THIS.
OTHER PEOPLE NEED TO SEE THAT WE'LL CONTINUE TO FIGHT.
BEEN FIGHTING FOR A LONG TIME.
AND LOOK WHERE WE'RE AT.
"IN THE WORLD BUT NOT OF IT, BABY."
SP JAMILA PARKS

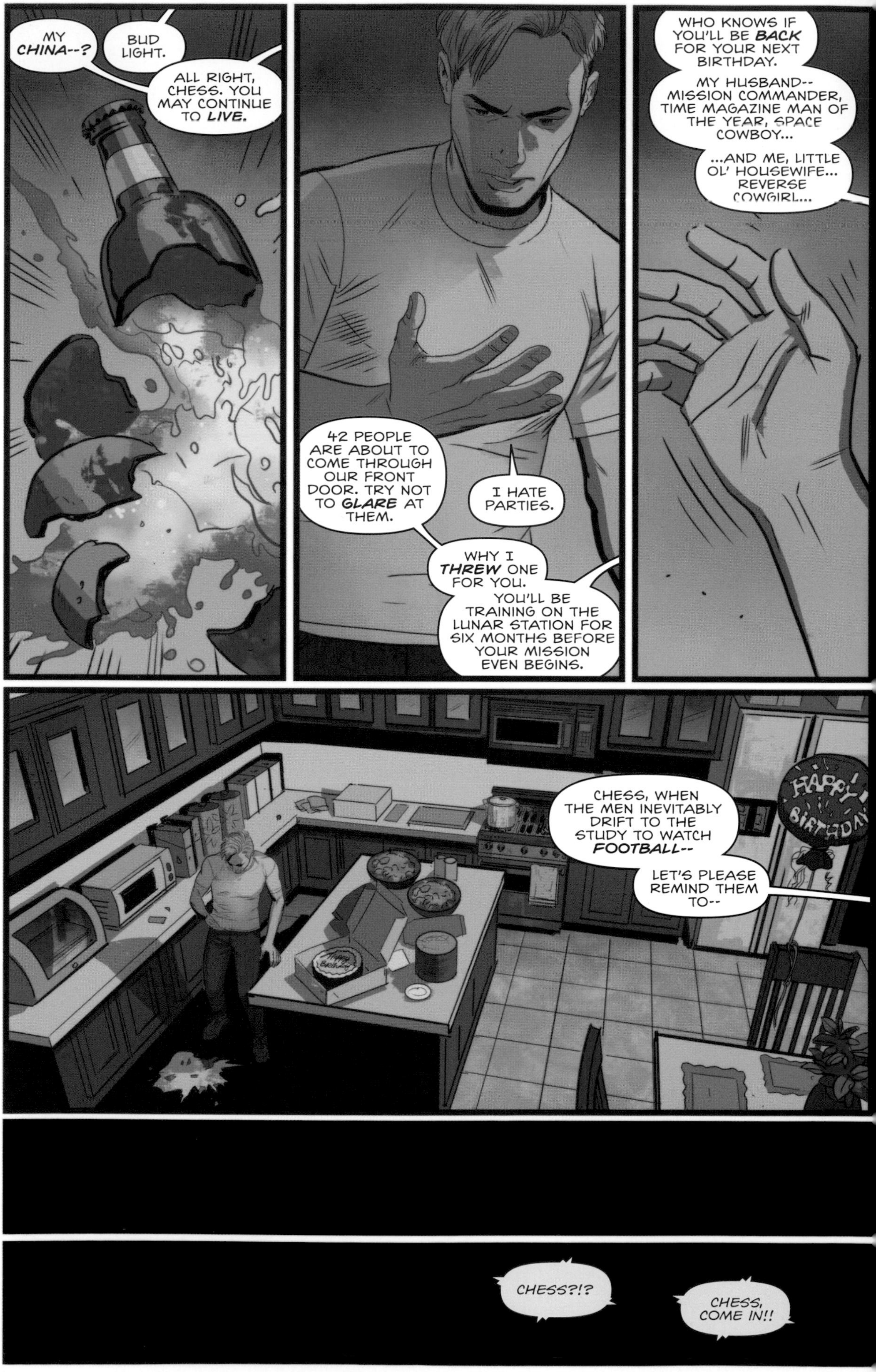
MY CHINA--?
BUD LIGHT.
ALL RIGHT, CHESS. YOU MAY CONTINUE TO LIVE.
42 PEOPLE ARE ABOUT TO COME THROUGH OUR FRONT DOOR. TRY NOT TO GLARE AT THEM.
I HATE PARTIES.
WHY I THREW ONE FOR YOU.
YOU'LL BE TRAINING ON THE LUNAR STATION FOR SIX MONTHS BEFORE YOUR MISSION EVEN BEGINS.
WHO KNOWS IF YOU'LL BE BACK FOR YOUR NEXT BIRTHDAY.
MY HUSBAND-- MISSION COMMANDER, TIME MAGAZINE MAN OF THE YEAR, SPACE COWBOY...
...AND ME, LITTLE OL' HOUSEWIFE... REVERSE COWGIRL...
CHESS, WHEN THE MEN INEVITABLY DRIFT TO THE STUDY TO WATCH FOOTBALL--
LET'S PLEASE REMIND THEM TO--
CHESS?!?
CHESS, COME IN!!

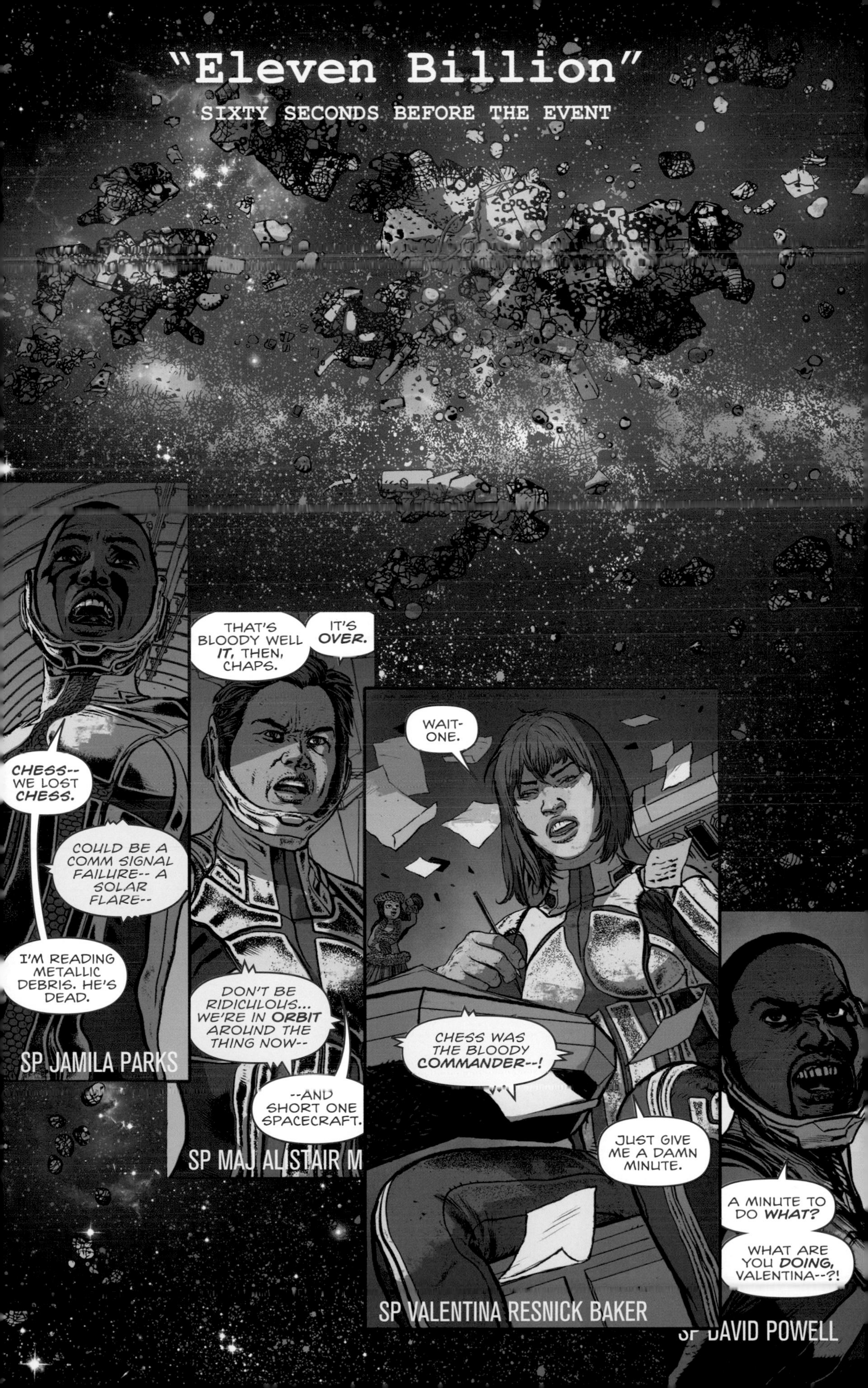
"Eleven Billion"
SIXTY SECONDS BEFORE THE EVENT
CHESS-- WE LOST CHESS.
COULD BE A COMM SIGNAL FAILURE-- A SOLAR FLARE--
I'M READING METALLIC DEBRIS. HE'S DEAD.
SP JAMILA PARKS
THAT'S BLOODY WELL IT, THEN, CHAPS.
IT'S OVER.
DON'T BE RIDICULOUS... WE'RE IN ORBIT AROUND THE THING NOW--
--AND SHORT ONE SPACECRAFT.
SP MAJ ALISTAIR M
WAIT- ONE.
CHESS WAS THE BLOODY COMMANDER--!
JUST GIVE ME A DAMN MINUTE.
SP VALENTINA RESNICK BAKER
A MINUTE TO DO WHAT?
WHAT ARE YOU DOING, VALENTINA--?!
DAVID POWELL

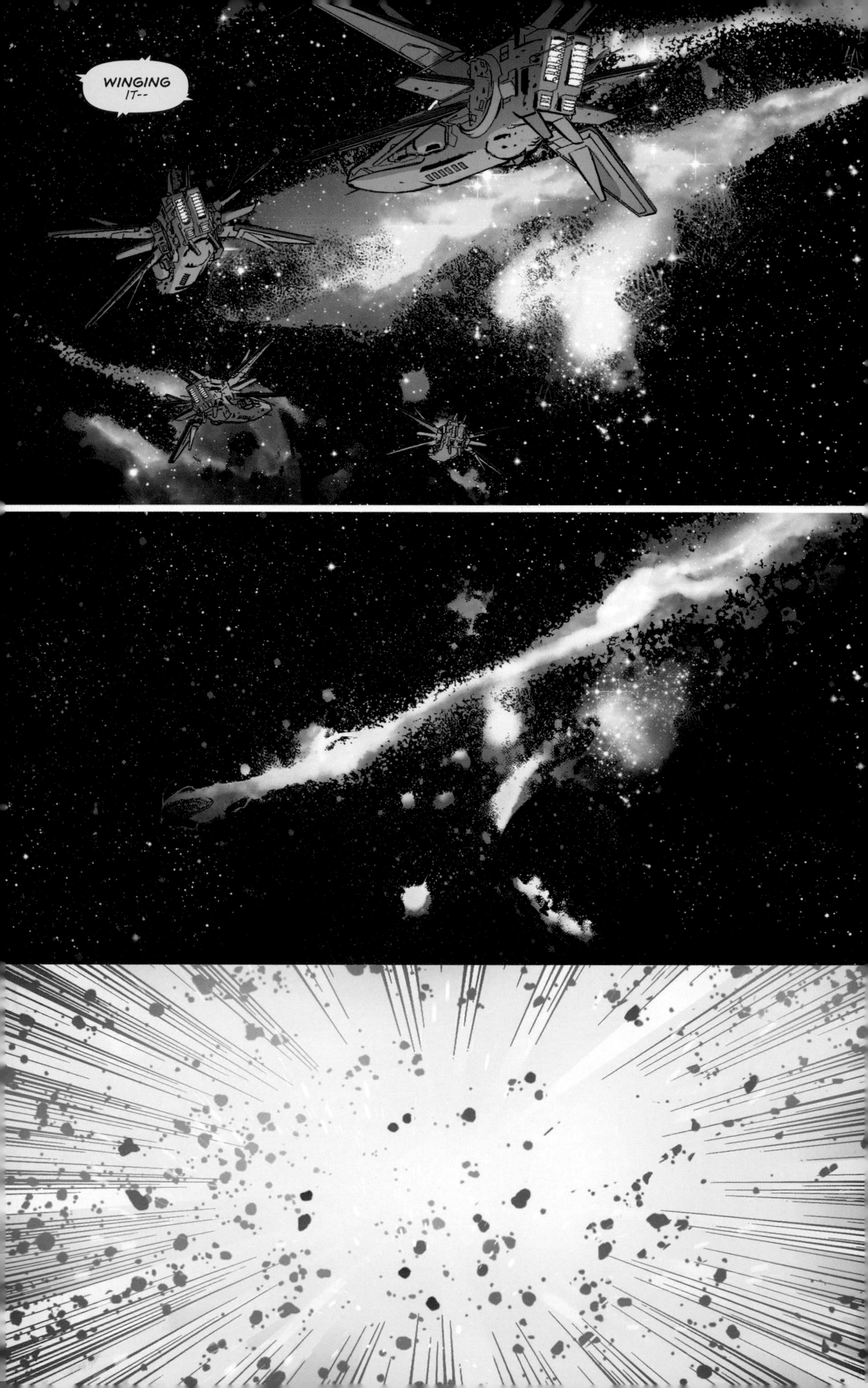
WINGING IT--

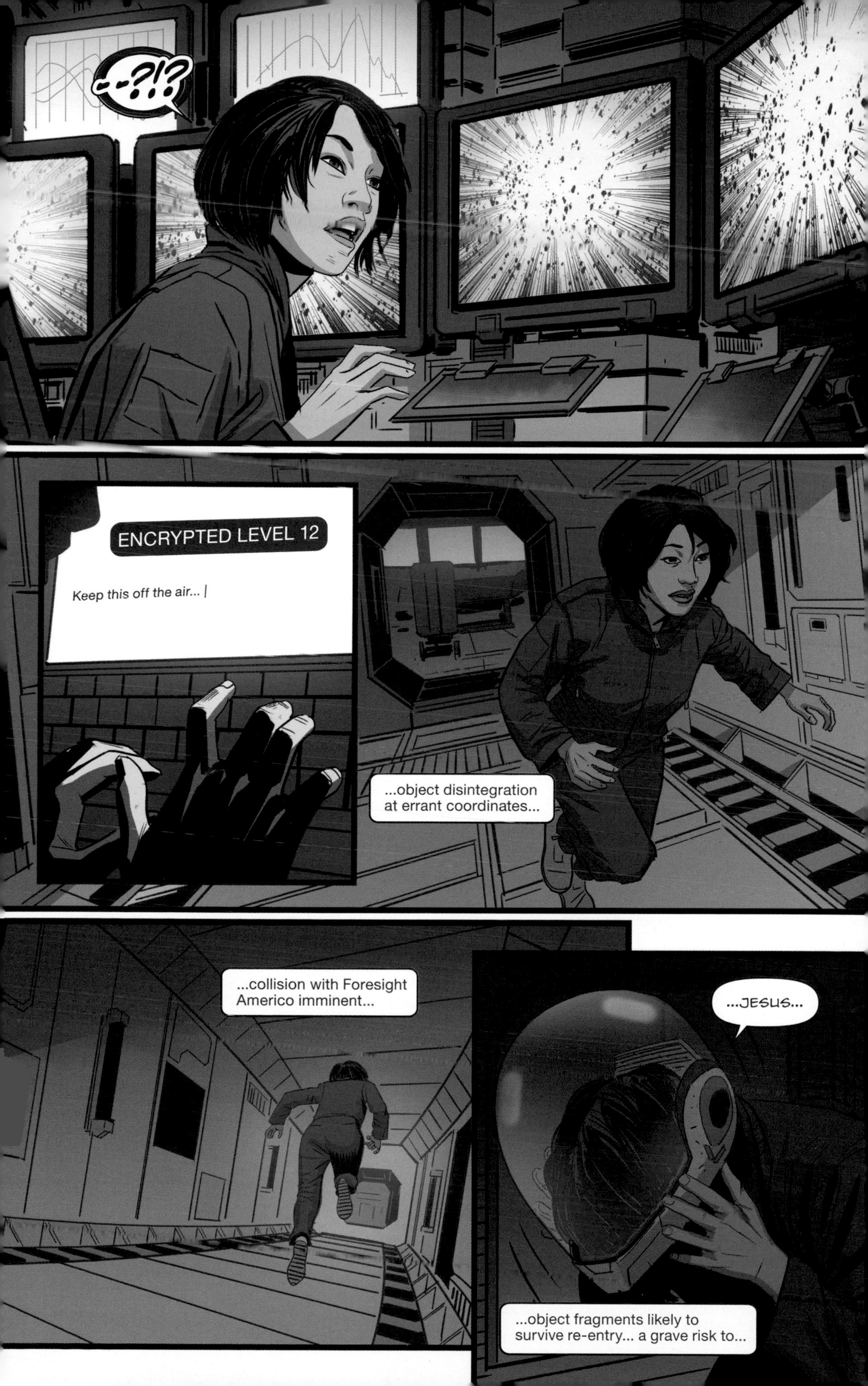
--?!?
ENCRYPTED LEVEL 12
Keep this off the air... |
...object disintegration at errant coordinates...
...collision with Foresight Americo imminent...
...JESUS...
...object fragments likely to survive re-entry... a grave risk to...

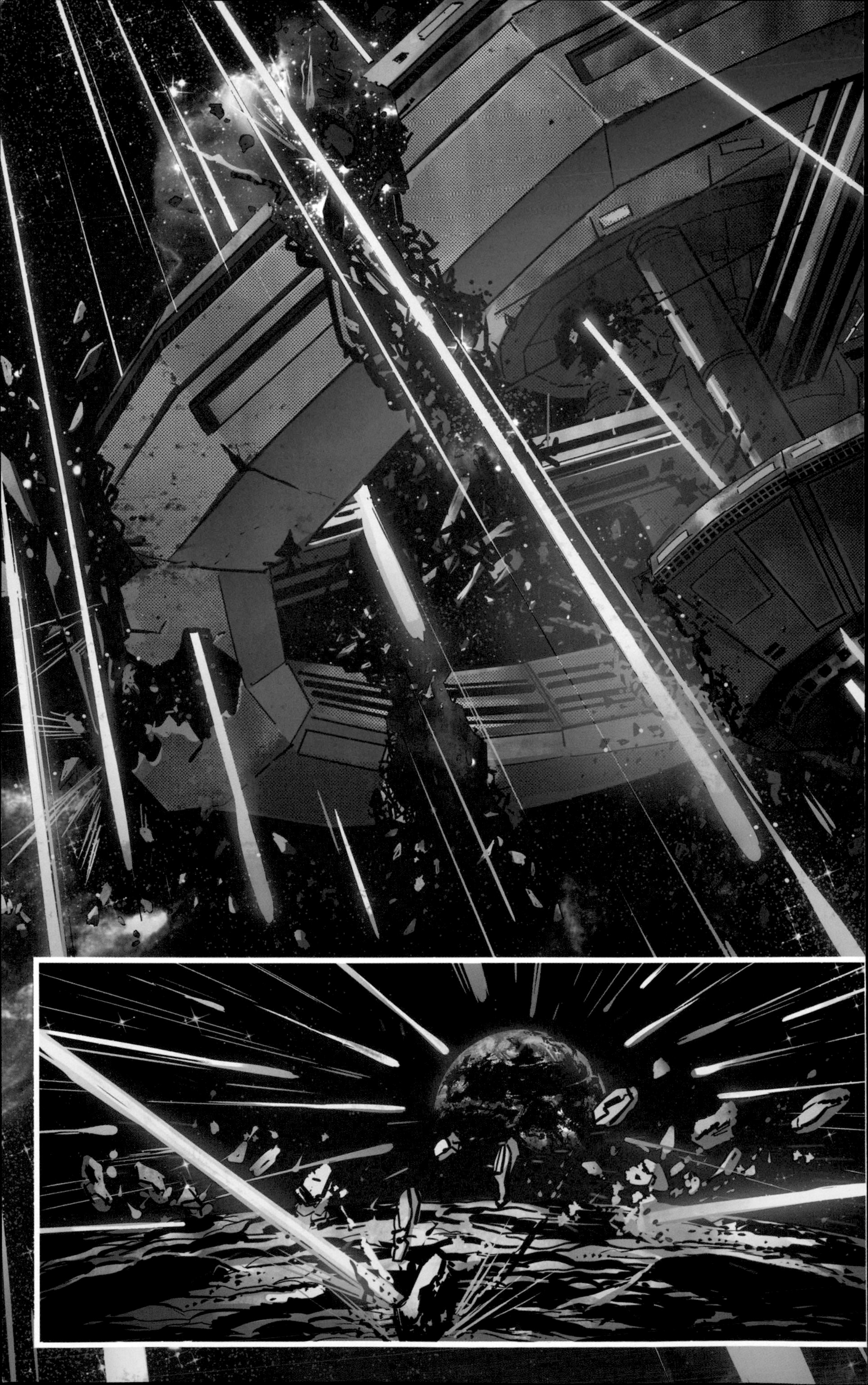

"The Beginning"

THE EVENT

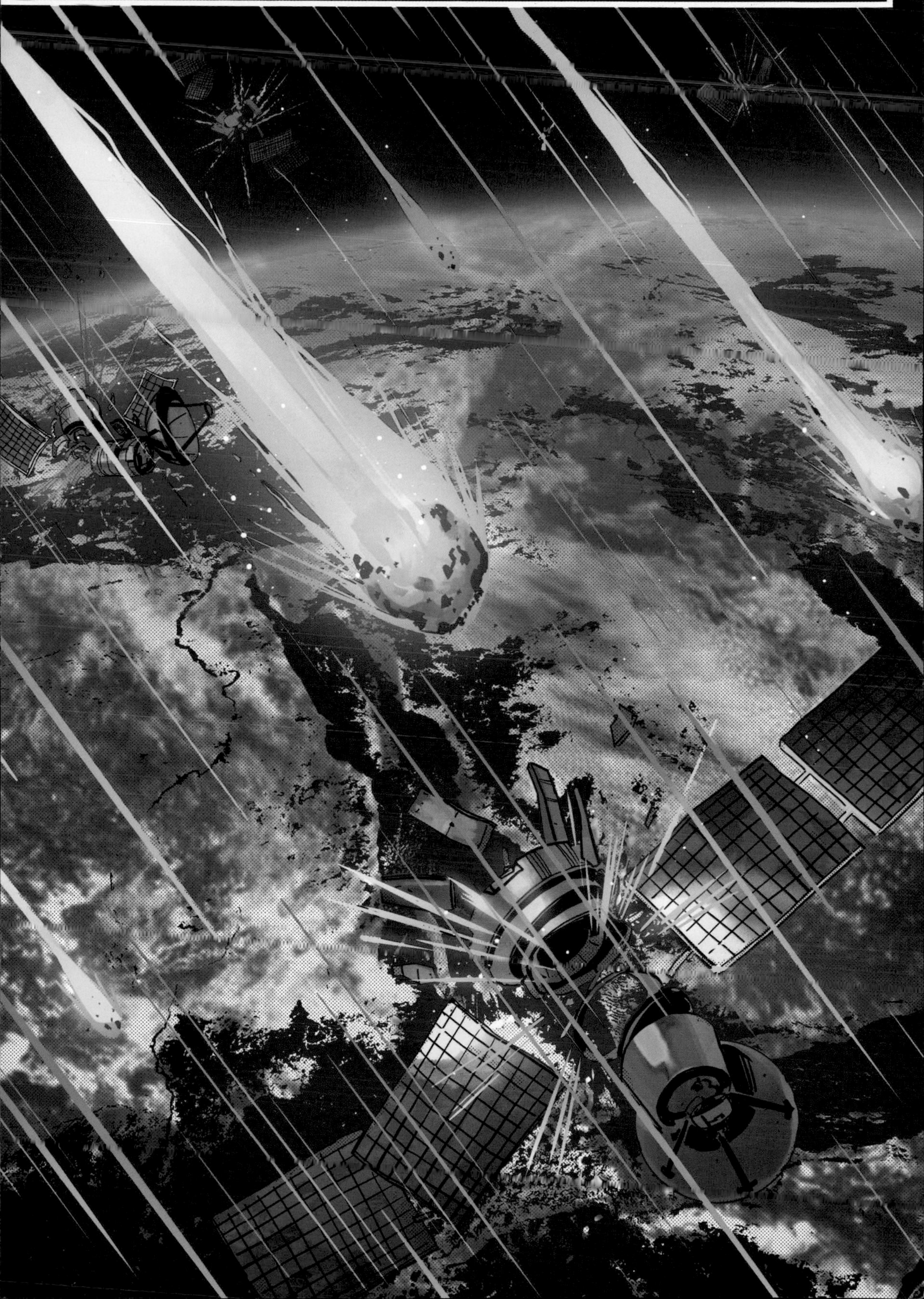

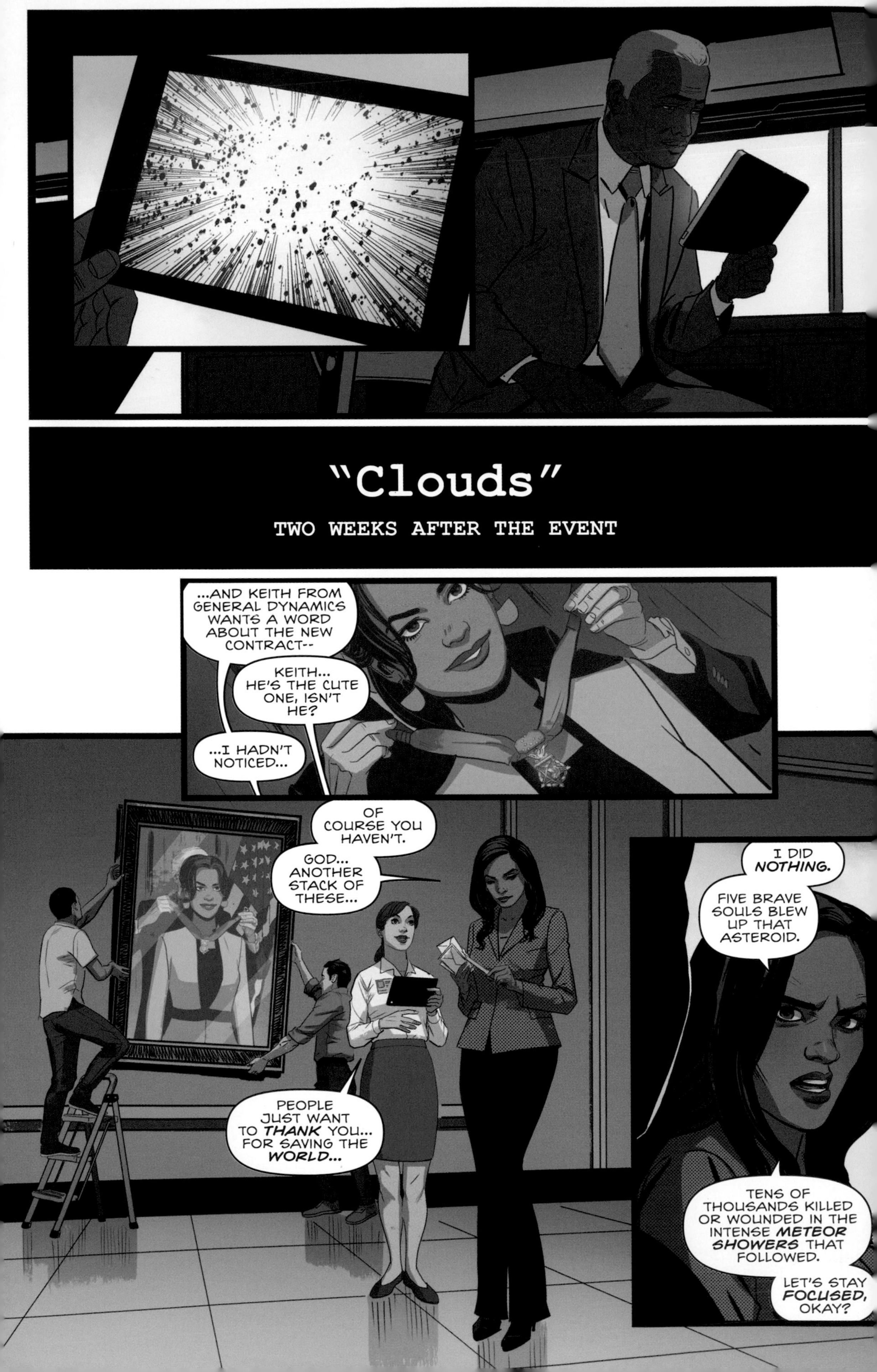
"Clouds"
TWO WEEKS AFTER THE EVENT
...AND KEITH FROM GENERAL DYNAMICS WANTS A WORD ABOUT THE NEW CONTRACT--
KEITH... HE'S THE CUTE ONE, ISN'T HE?
...I HADN'T NOTICED...
OF COURSE YOU HAVEN'T.
GOD... ANOTHER STACK OF THESE...
PEOPLE JUST WANT TO THANK YOU... FOR SAVING THE WORLD...
I DID NOTHING.
FIVE BRAVE SOULS BLEW UP THAT ASTEROID.
TENS OF THOUSANDS KILLED OR WOUNDED IN THE INTENSE METEOR SHOWERS THAT FOLLOWED.
LET'S STAY FOCUSED, OKAY?

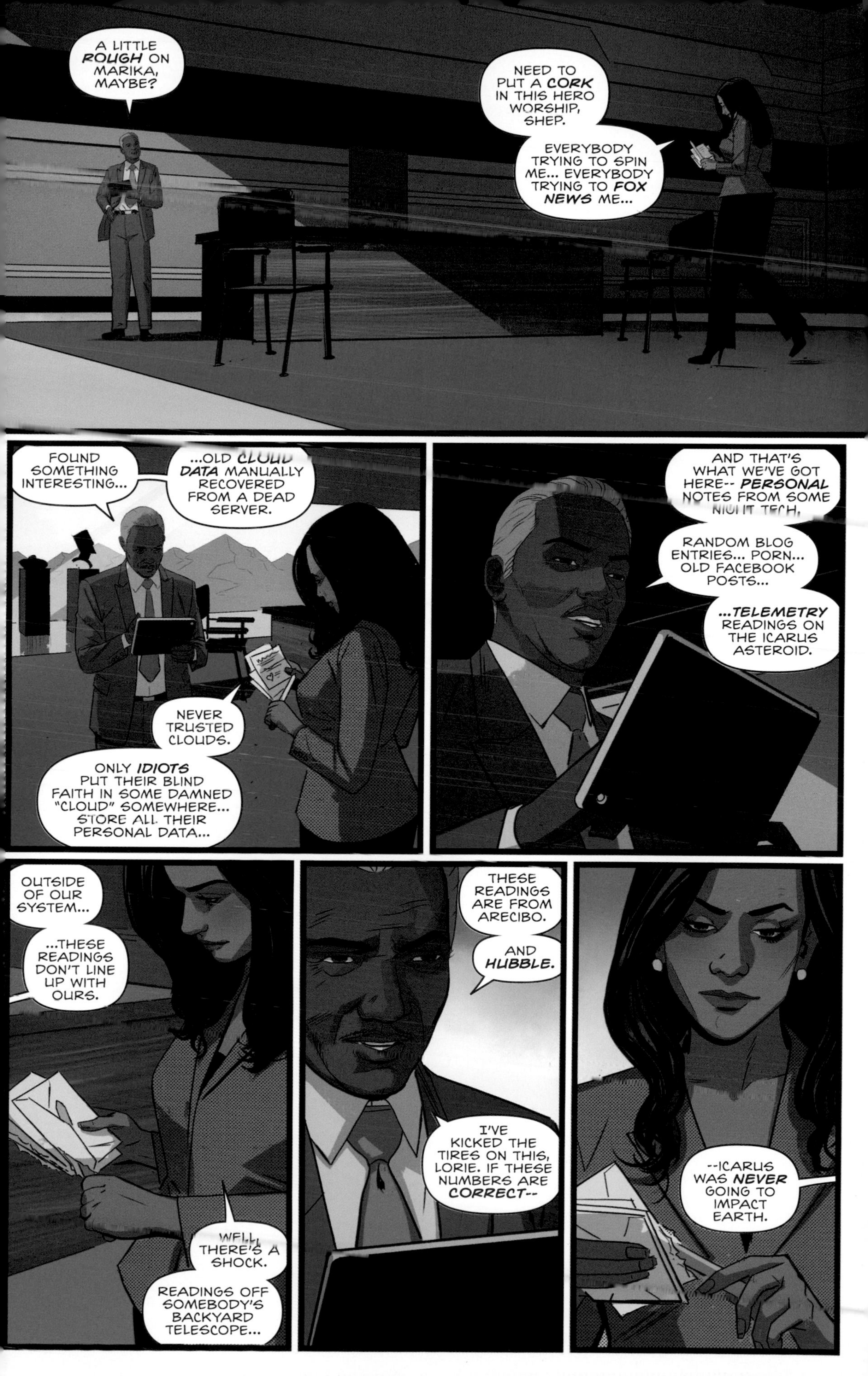
A LITTLE ***ROUGH*** ON MARIKA, MAYBE?
NEED TO PUT A **CORK** IN THIS HERO WORSHIP, SHEP.
EVERYBODY TRYING TO SPIN ME... EVERYBODY TRYING TO ***FOX NEWS*** ME...
FOUND SOMETHING INTERESTING...
...OLD ***CLOUD DATA*** MANUALLY RECOVERED FROM A DEAD SERVER.
NEVER TRUSTED CLOUDS.
ONLY ***IDIOTS*** PUT THEIR BLIND FAITH IN SOME DAMNED "CLOUD" SOMEWHERE... STORE ALL THEIR PERSONAL DATA...
AND THAT'S WHAT WE'VE GOT HERE-- ***PERSONAL*** NOTES FROM SOME NIGHT TECH.
RANDOM BLOG ENTRIES... PORN... OLD FACEBOOK POSTS...
...TELEMETRY READINGS ON THE ICARUS ASTEROID.
OUTSIDE OF OUR SYSTEM...
...THESE READINGS DON'T LINE UP WITH OURS.
WELL, THERE'S A SHOCK.
READINGS OFF SOMEBODY'S BACKYARD TELESCOPE...
THESE READINGS ARE FROM ARECIBO.
AND ***HUBBLE.***
I'VE KICKED THE TIRES ON THIS, LORIE. IF THESE NUMBERS ARE ***CORRECT--***
--ICARUS WAS ***NEVER*** GOING TO IMPACT EARTH.

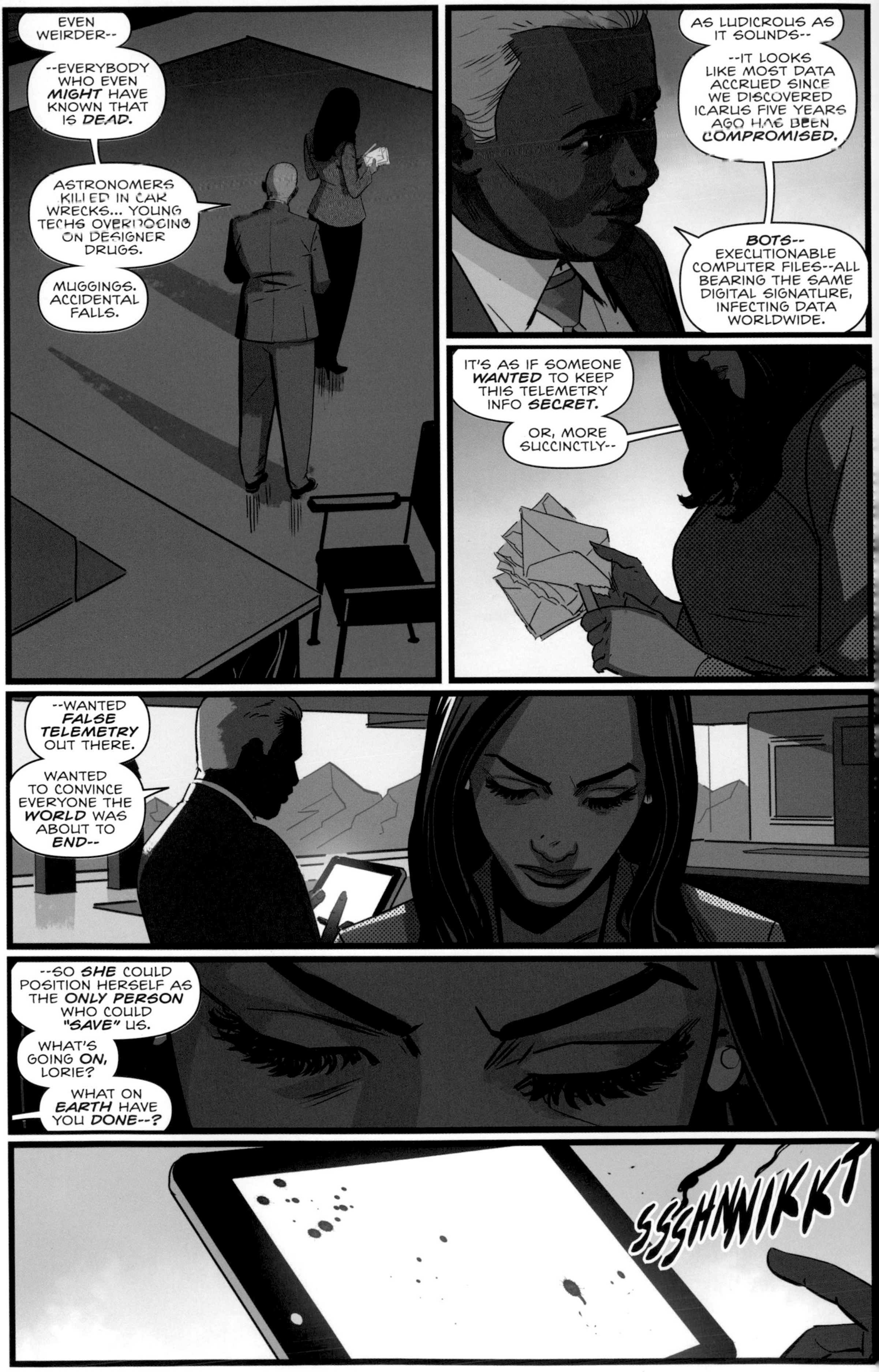
EVEN WEIRDER--
--EVERYBODY WHO EVEN MIGHT HAVE KNOWN THAT IS DEAD.
ASTRONOMERS KILLED IN CAR WRECKS... YOUNG TECHS OVERDOSING ON DESIGNER DRUGS.
MUGGINGS. ACCIDENTAL FALLS.
AS LUDICROUS AS IT SOUNDS--
--IT LOOKS LIKE MOST DATA ACCRUED SINCE WE DISCOVERED ICARUS FIVE YEARS AGO HAS BEEN COMPROMISED.
BOTS--EXECUTIONABLE COMPUTER FILES--ALL BEARING THE SAME DIGITAL SIGNATURE, INFECTING DATA WORLDWIDE.
IT'S AS IF SOMEONE WANTED TO KEEP THIS TELEMETRY INFO SECRET.
OR, MORE SUCCINCTLY--
--WANTED FALSE TELEMETRY OUT THERE.
WANTED TO CONVINCE EVERYONE THE WORLD WAS ABOUT TO END--
--SO SHE COULD POSITION HERSELF AS THE ONLY PERSON WHO COULD "SAVE" US.
WHAT'S GOING ON, LORIE?
WHAT ON EARTH HAVE YOU DONE--?
SSSHNNIKKT

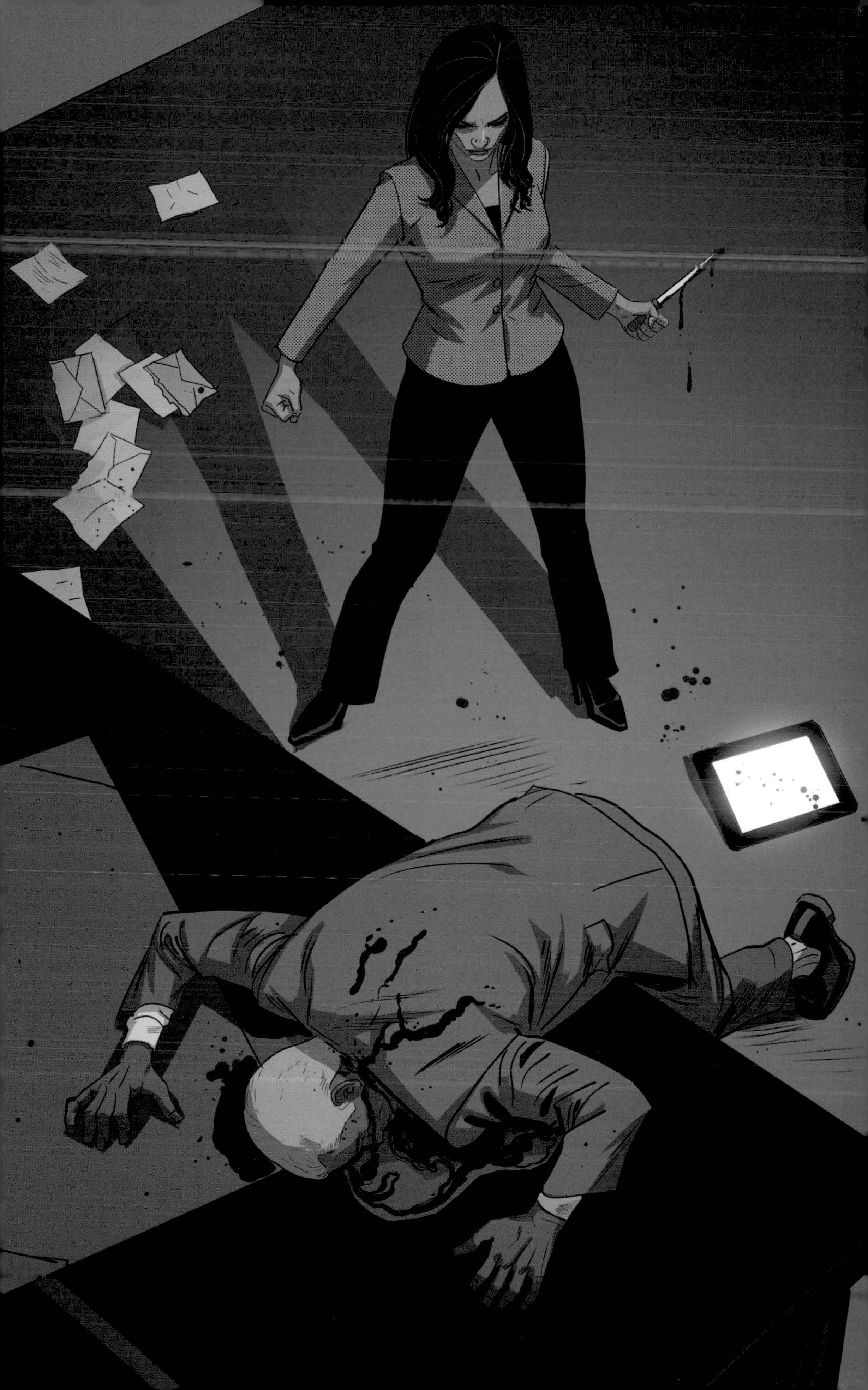

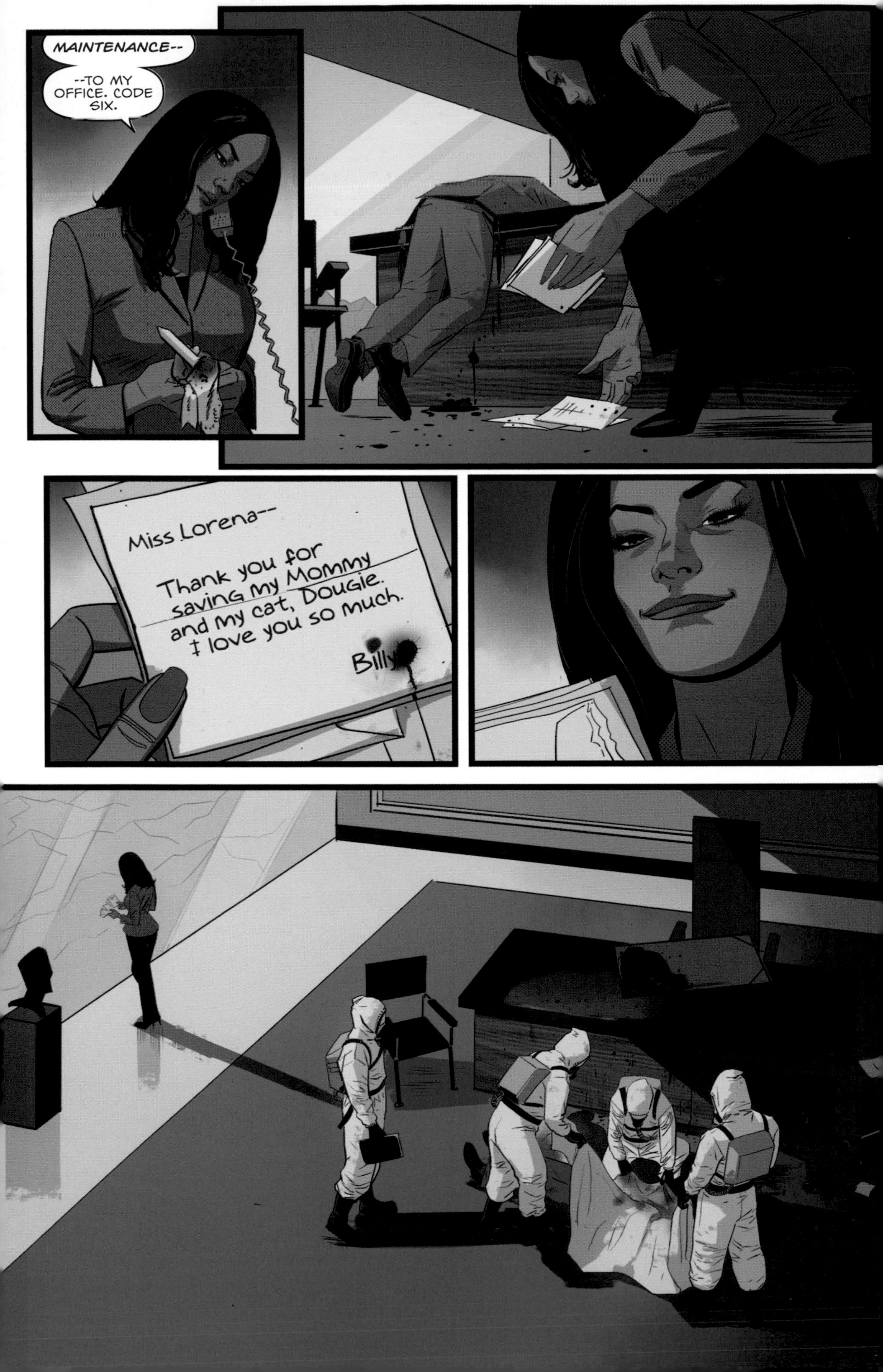
MAINTENANCE--
--TO MY OFFICE. CODE SIX.
Miss Lorena--
Thank you for saving my Mommy and my cat, Dougie. I love you so much.
Billy

A LETTER FROM THE NDSS

national down syndrome society

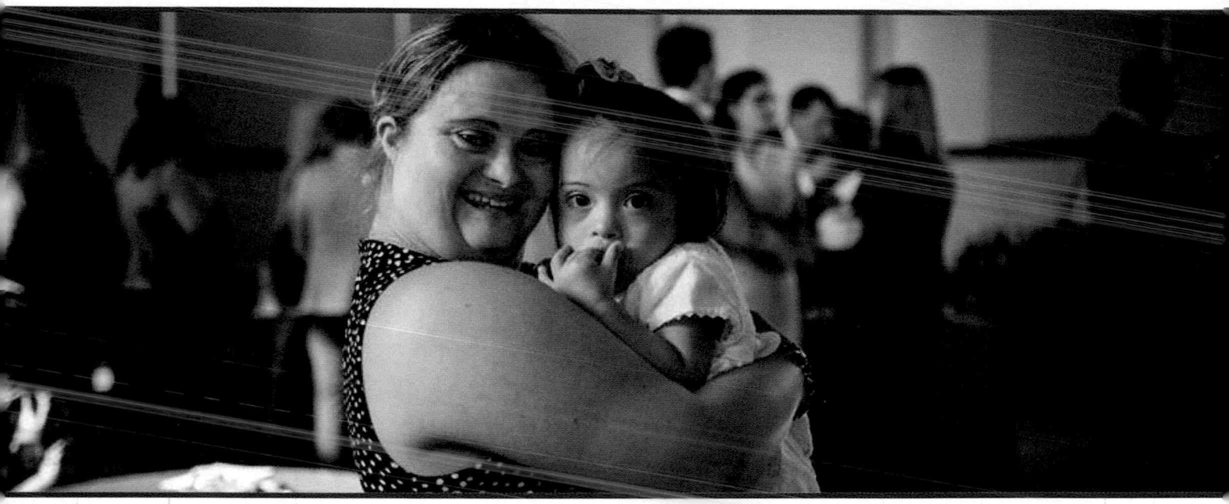

The National Down Syndrome Society is the leading human rights organization for all individuals with Down syndrome. NDSS provides state-of-the-art, comprehensive programing to all individuals with Down syndrome and their families with four main areas of programming which include: the National Advocacy & Policy Center, the National Inclusive Health & Sports Program featuring our National Buddy Walk® Program, Community Outreach and Resources and Public Awareness. NDSS envisions a world in which all people with Down syndrome have the opportunity to enhance their quality of life, realize their life aspirations, and become valued members of welcoming communities.

Superb is continuing to prove to the world that individuals with Down syndrome are heroes and can positively contribute to society! NDSS is thrilled to continue to share Jonah's adventure to encourage the value, acceptance, and inclusion of the superheroes we know exist within all people with Down syndrome.

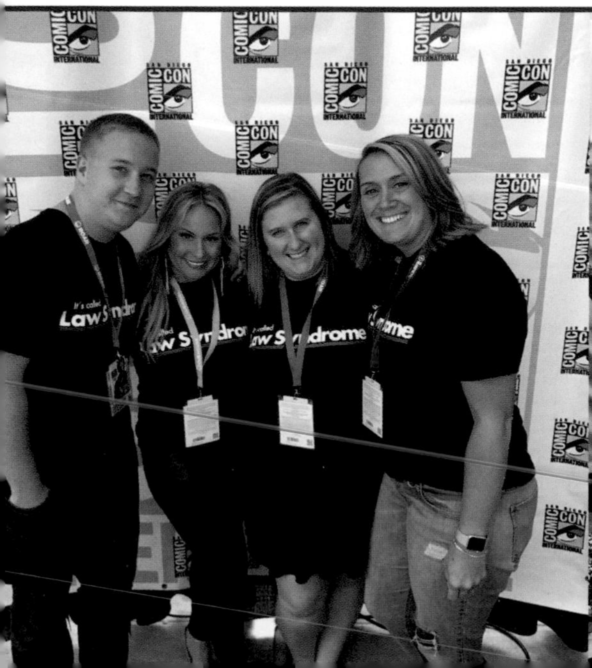
COMIC CON
INTERNATIONAL

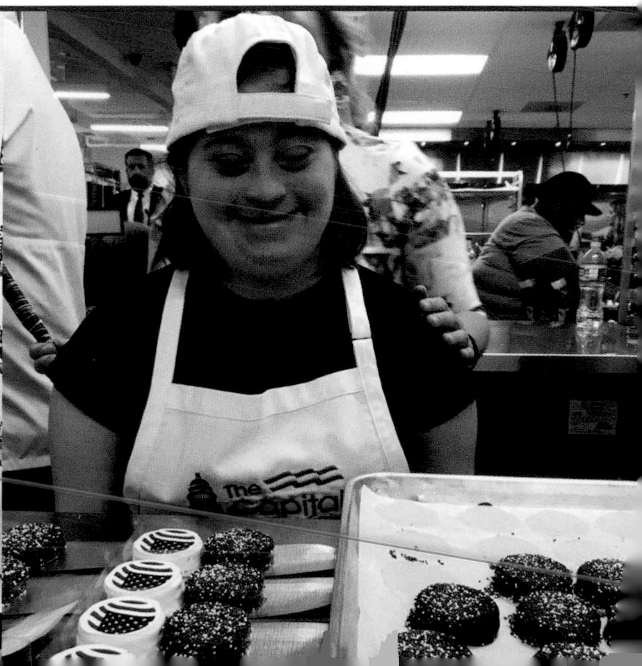

COVER GALLERY

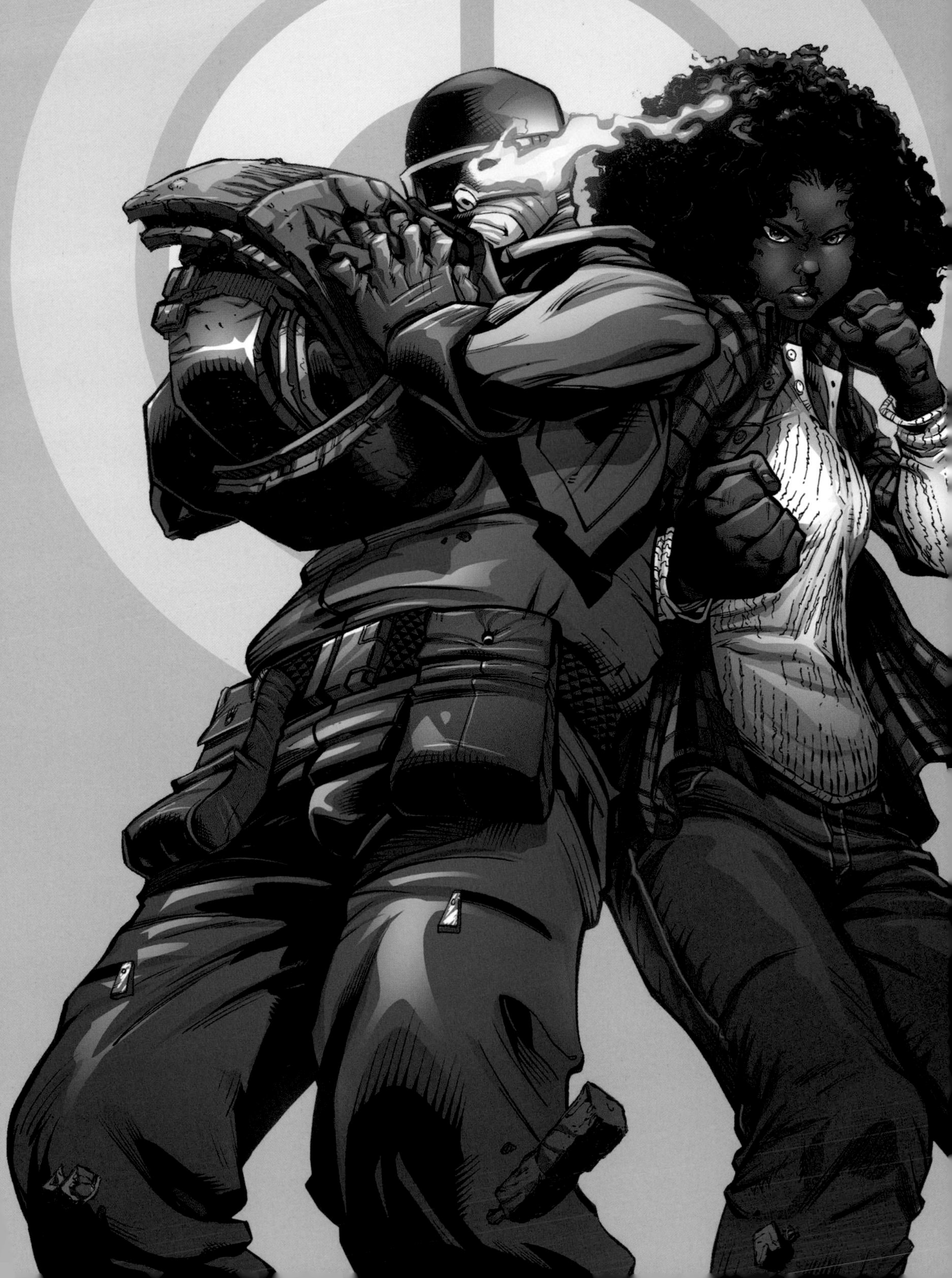

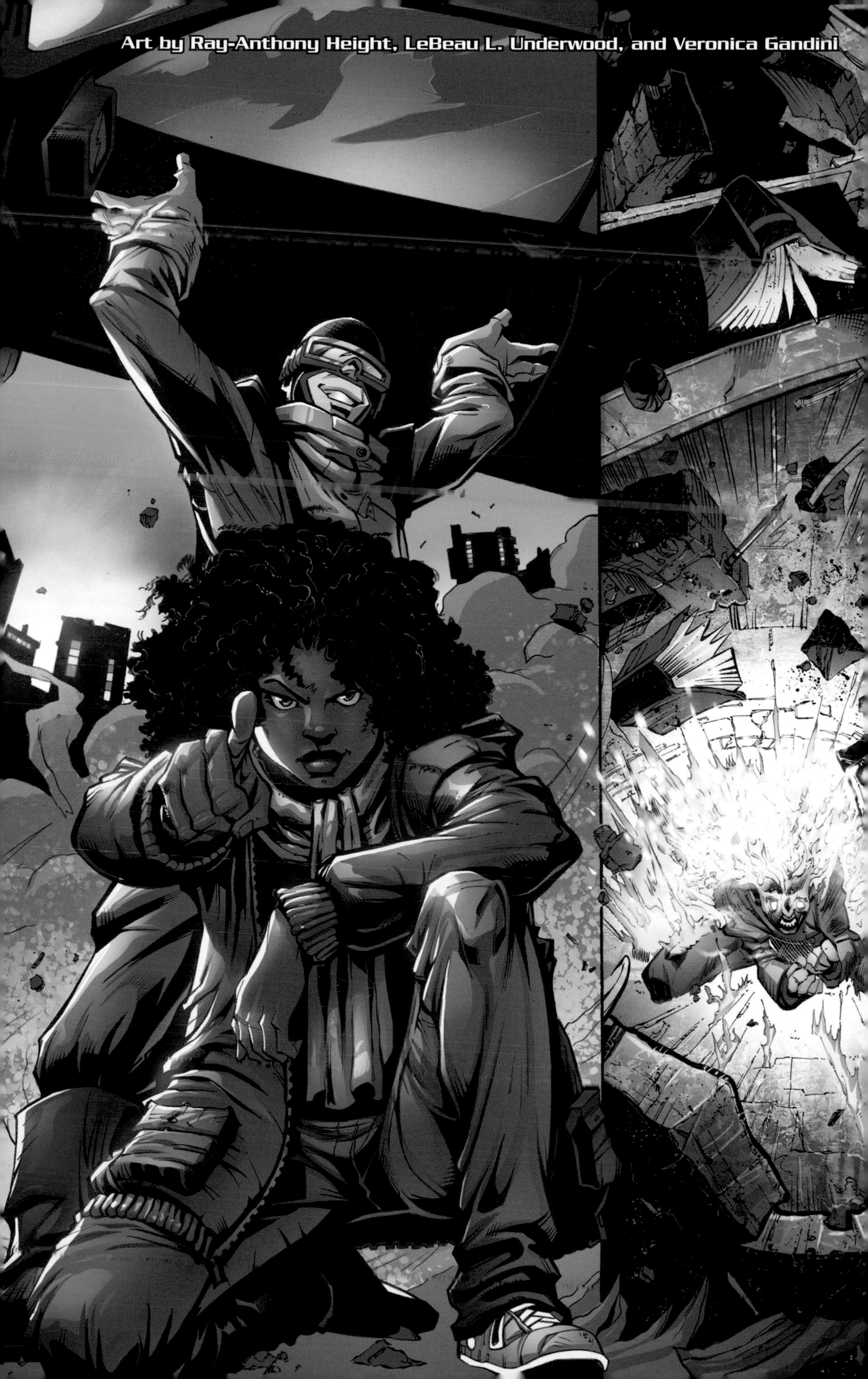
Art by Ray-Anthony Height, LeBeau L. Underwood, and Veronica Gandini

Art by Khary Randolph and Emilio Lopez

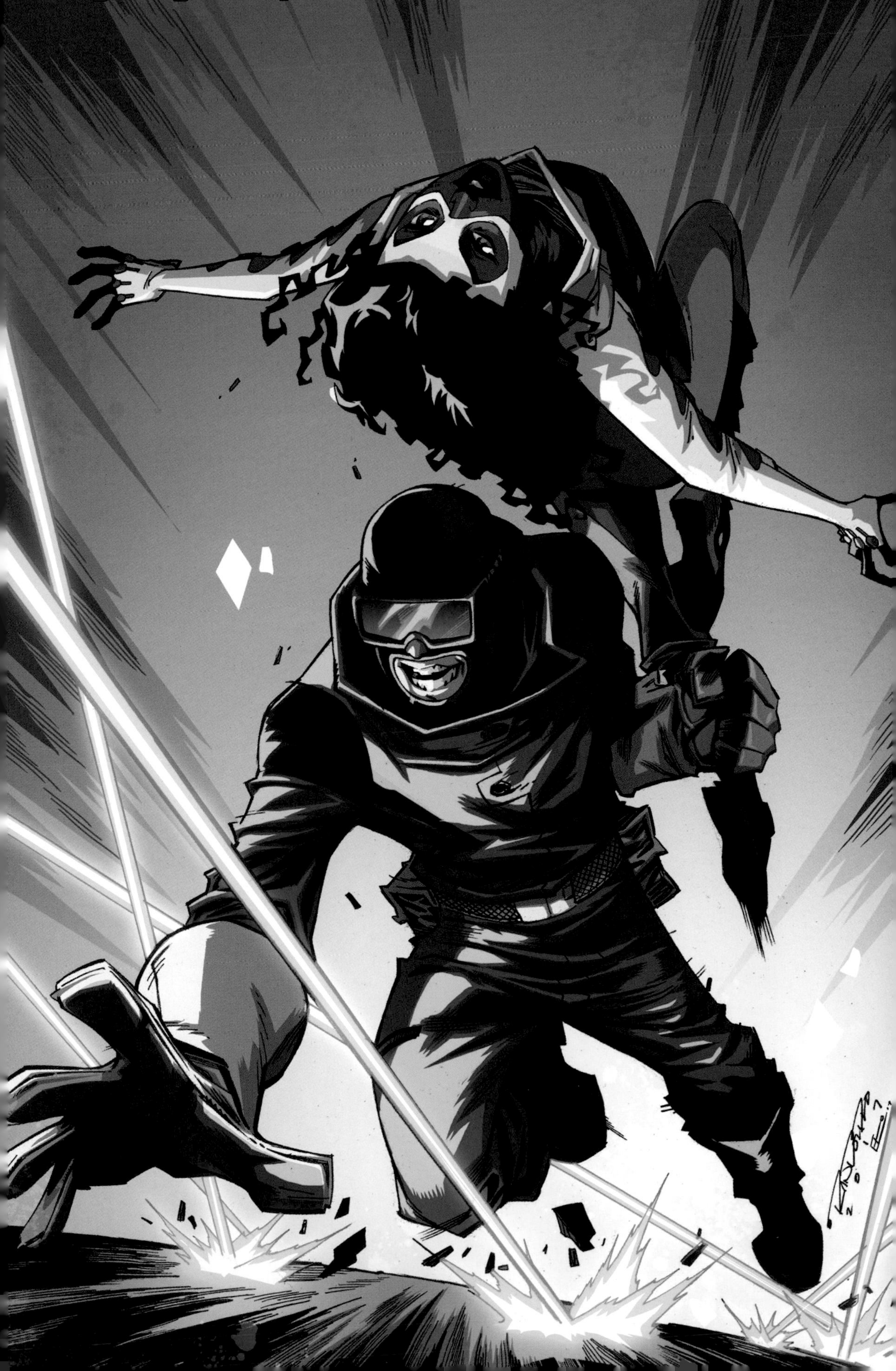

Art by John Cassaday and Laura Martin

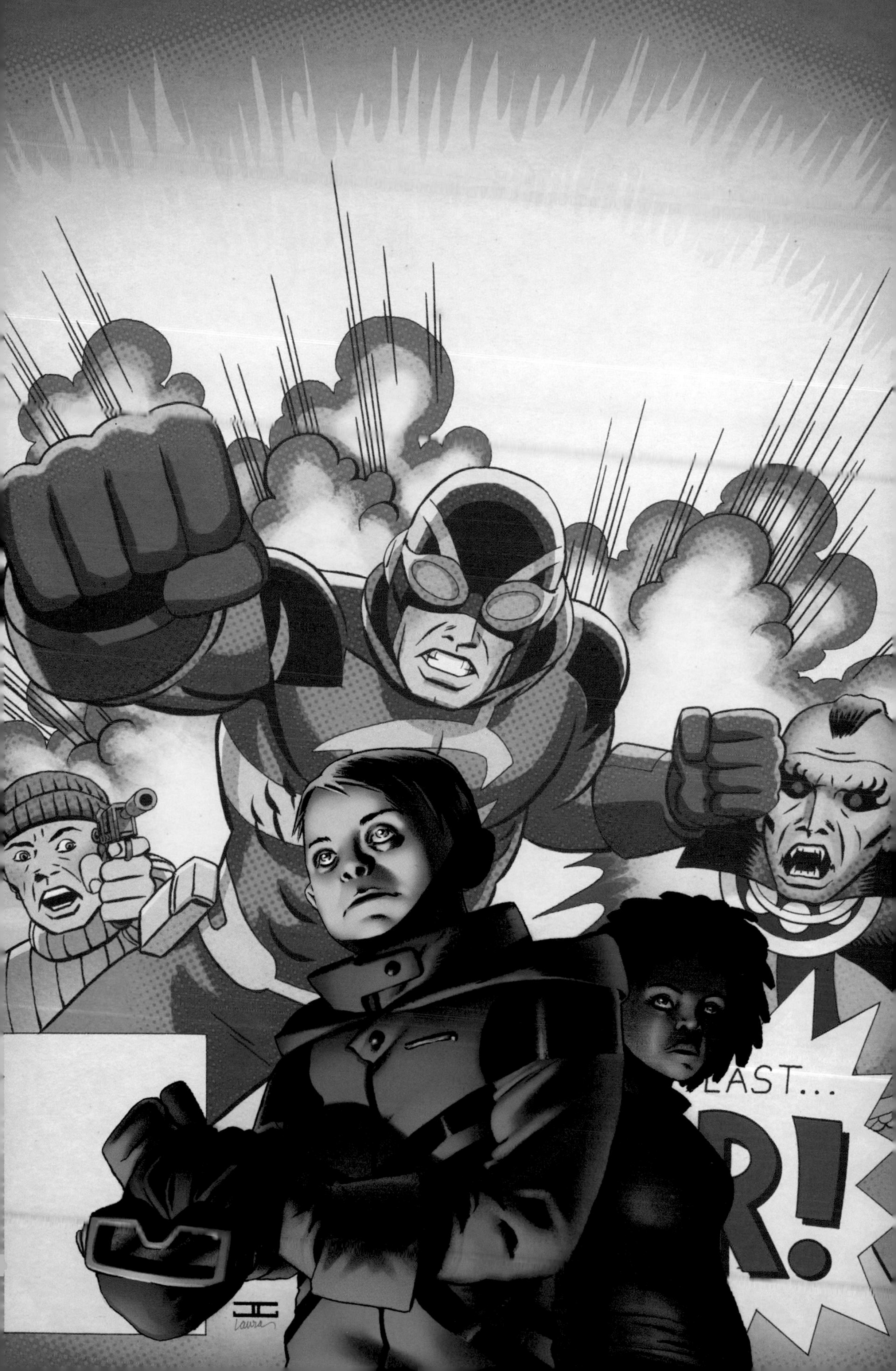
LAST...

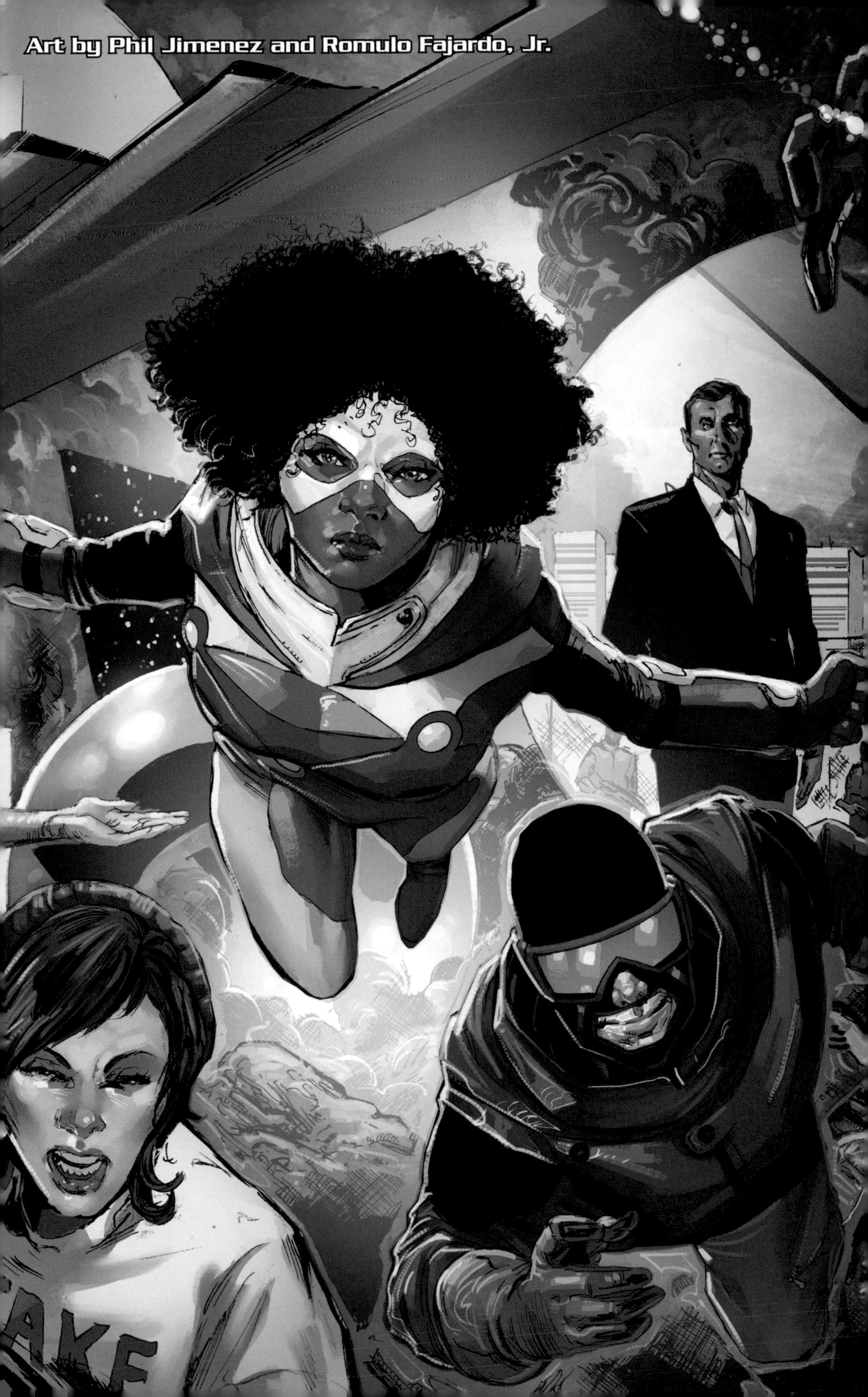

Art by Phil Jimenez and Romulo Fajardo, Jr.

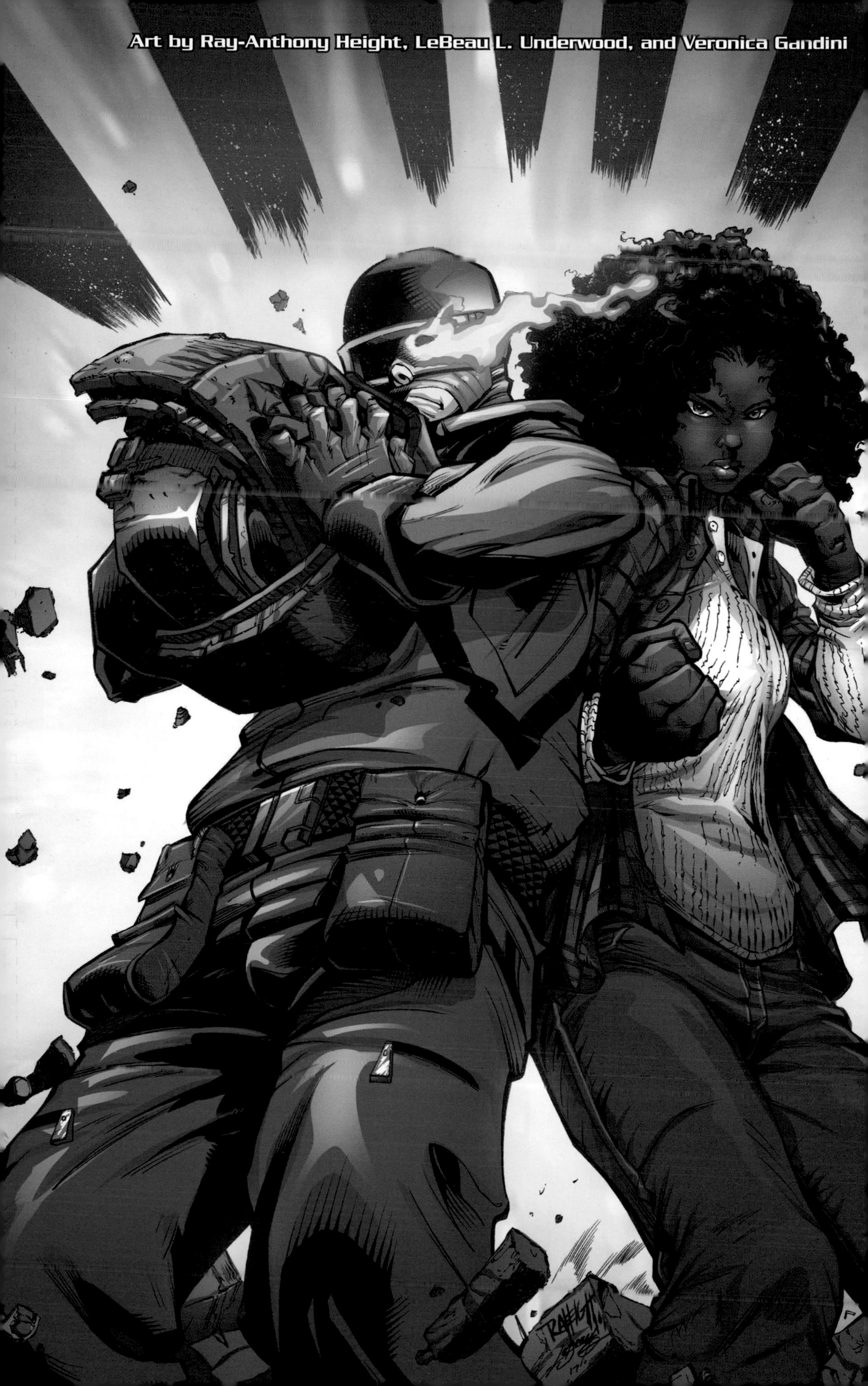

Art by Ray-Anthony Height, LeBeau L. Underwood, and Veronica Gandini

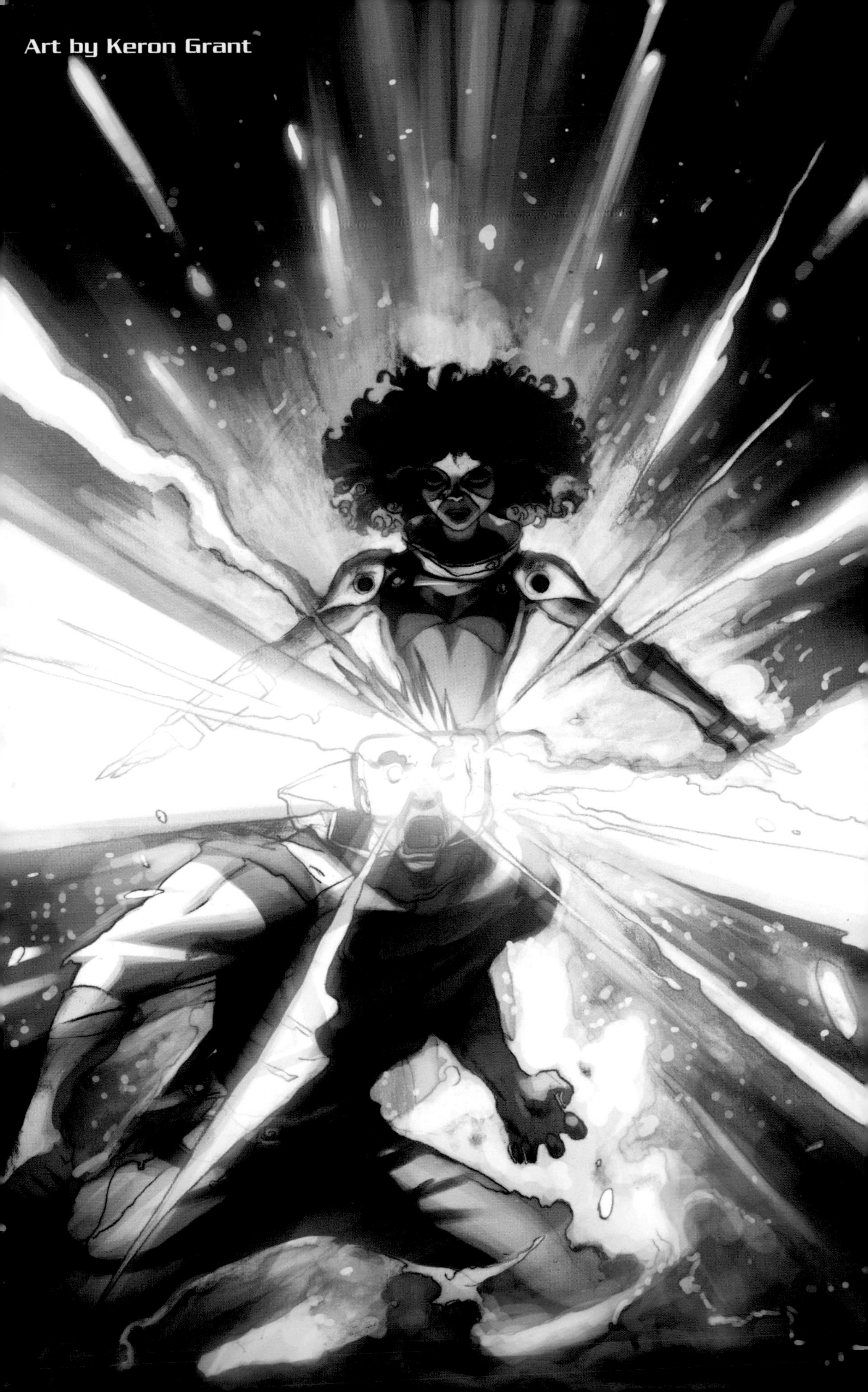

Art by Keron Grant

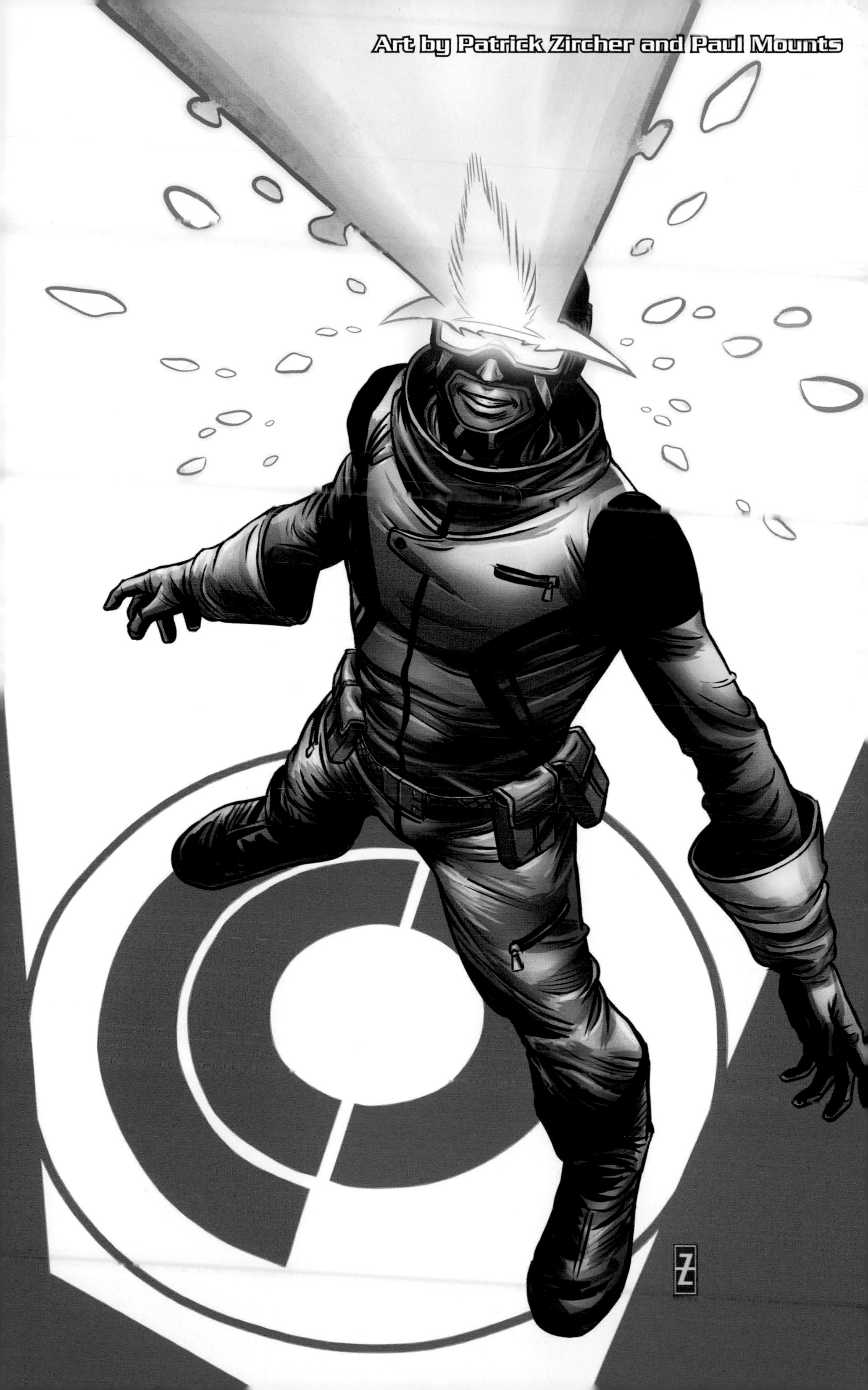

Art by Patrick Zircher and Paul Mounts

Art by Ray-Anthony Height, LeBeau L. Underwood, and Veronica Gandini

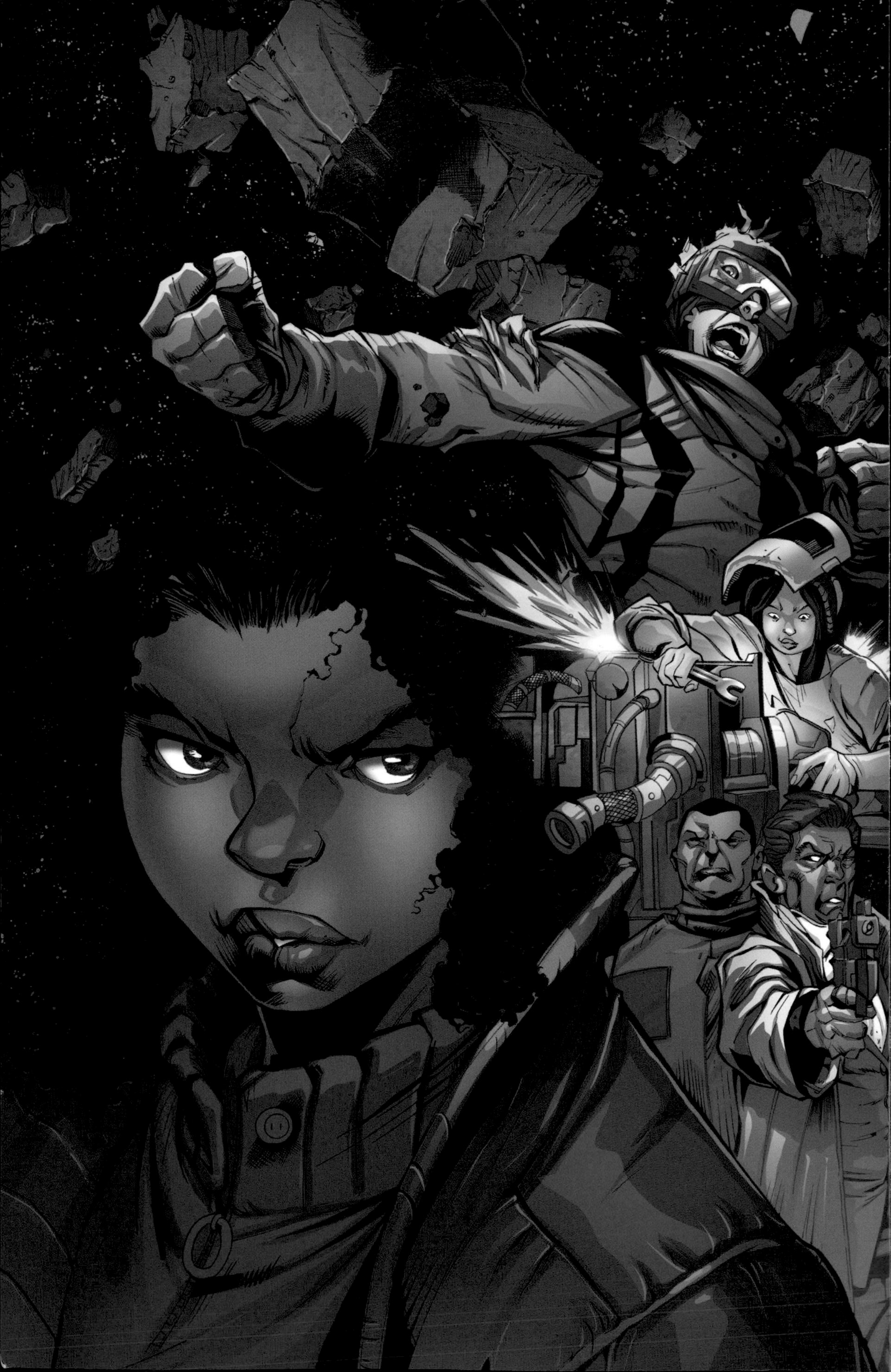

Art by Ray-Anthony Height, LeBeau L. Underwood, and Veronica Gandini

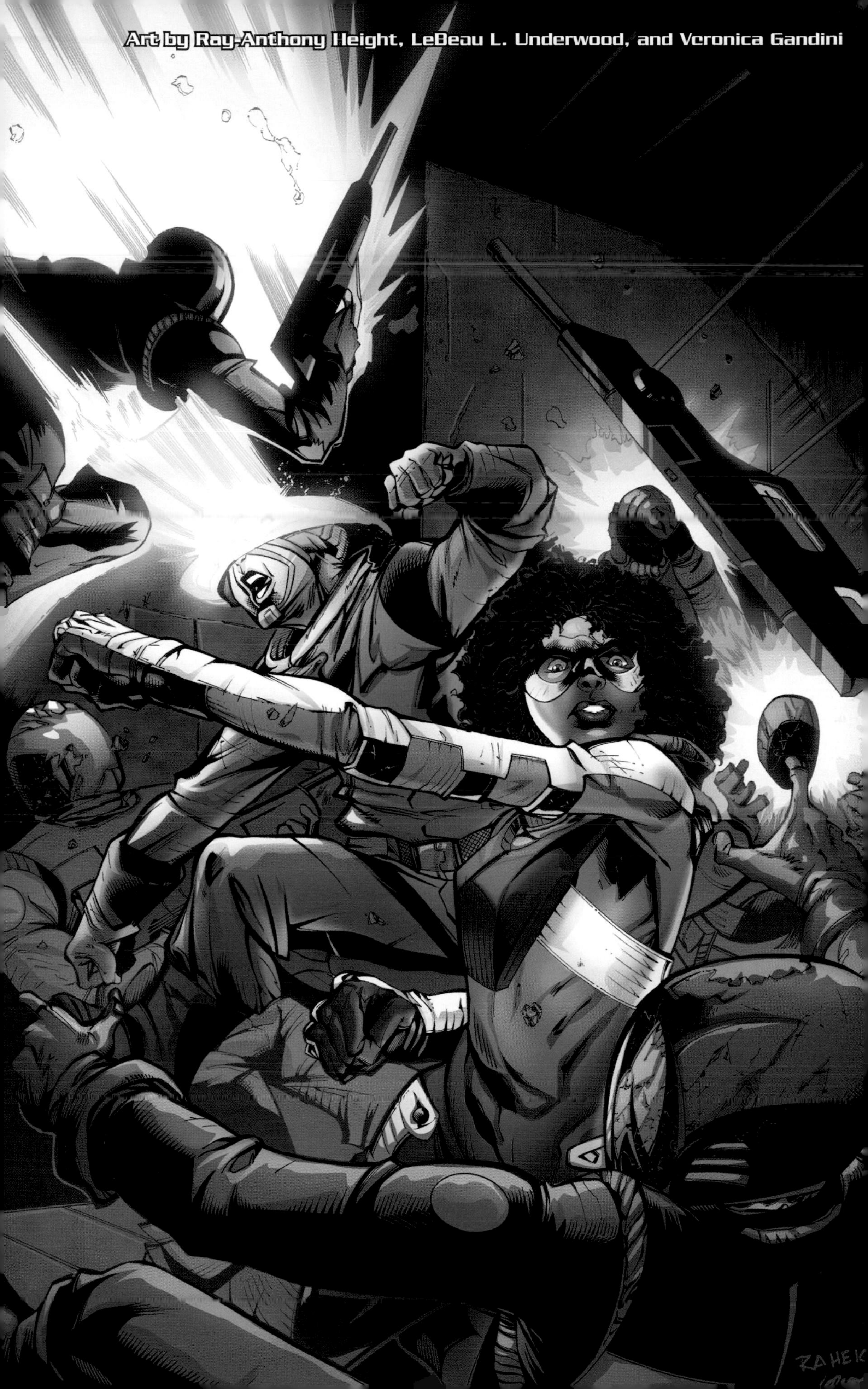

Art by Alitha Martinez

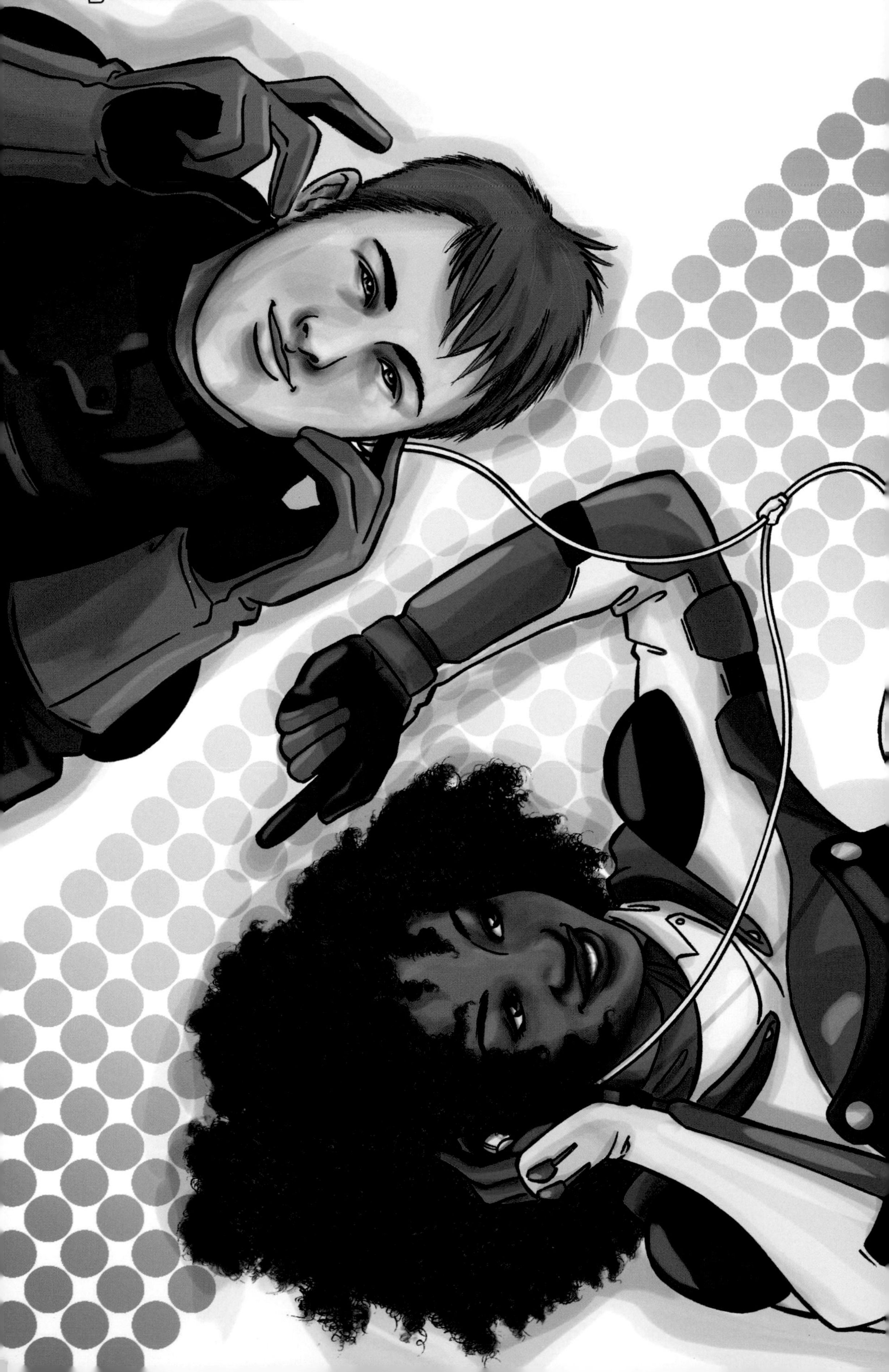

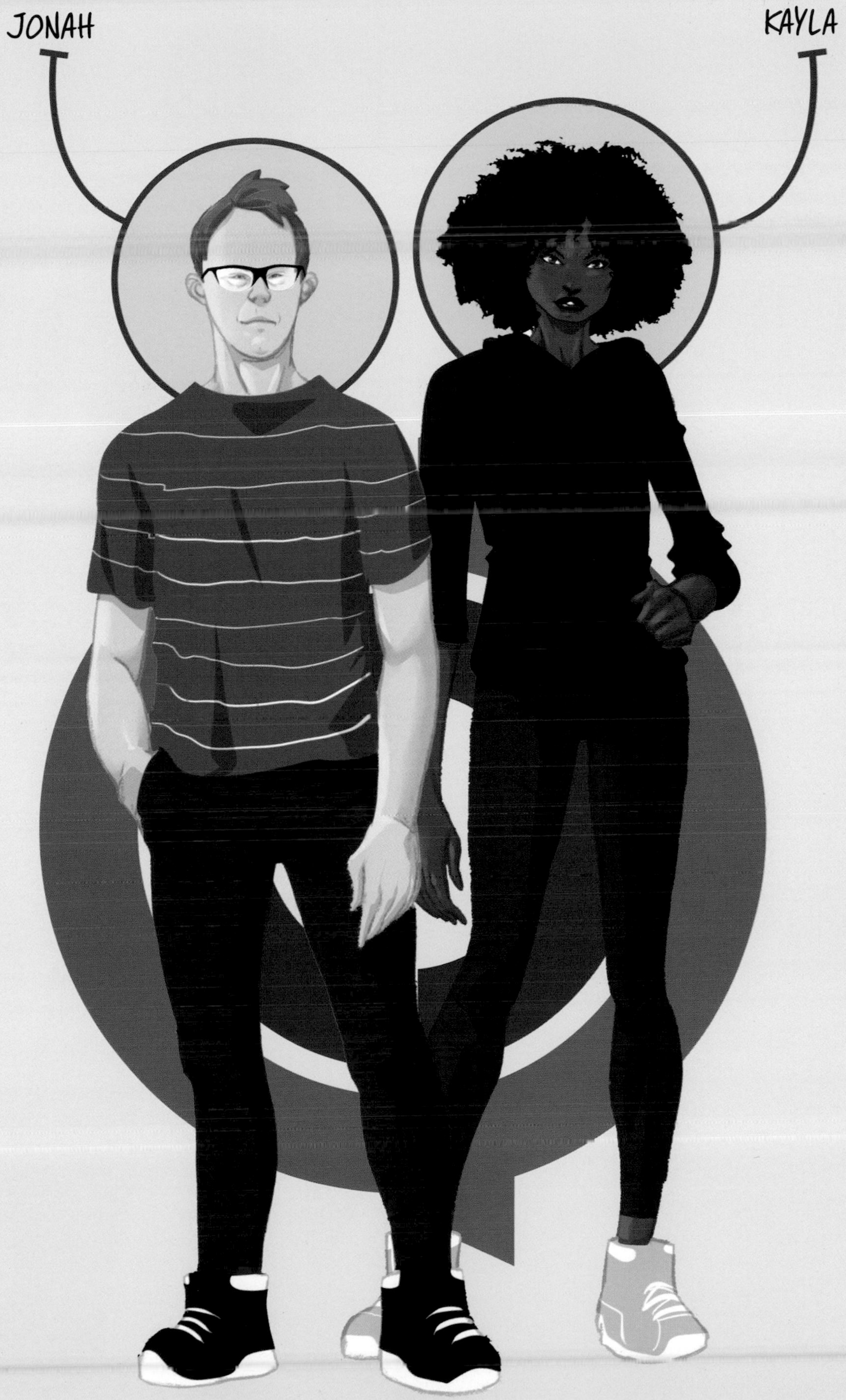
JONAH
KAYLA

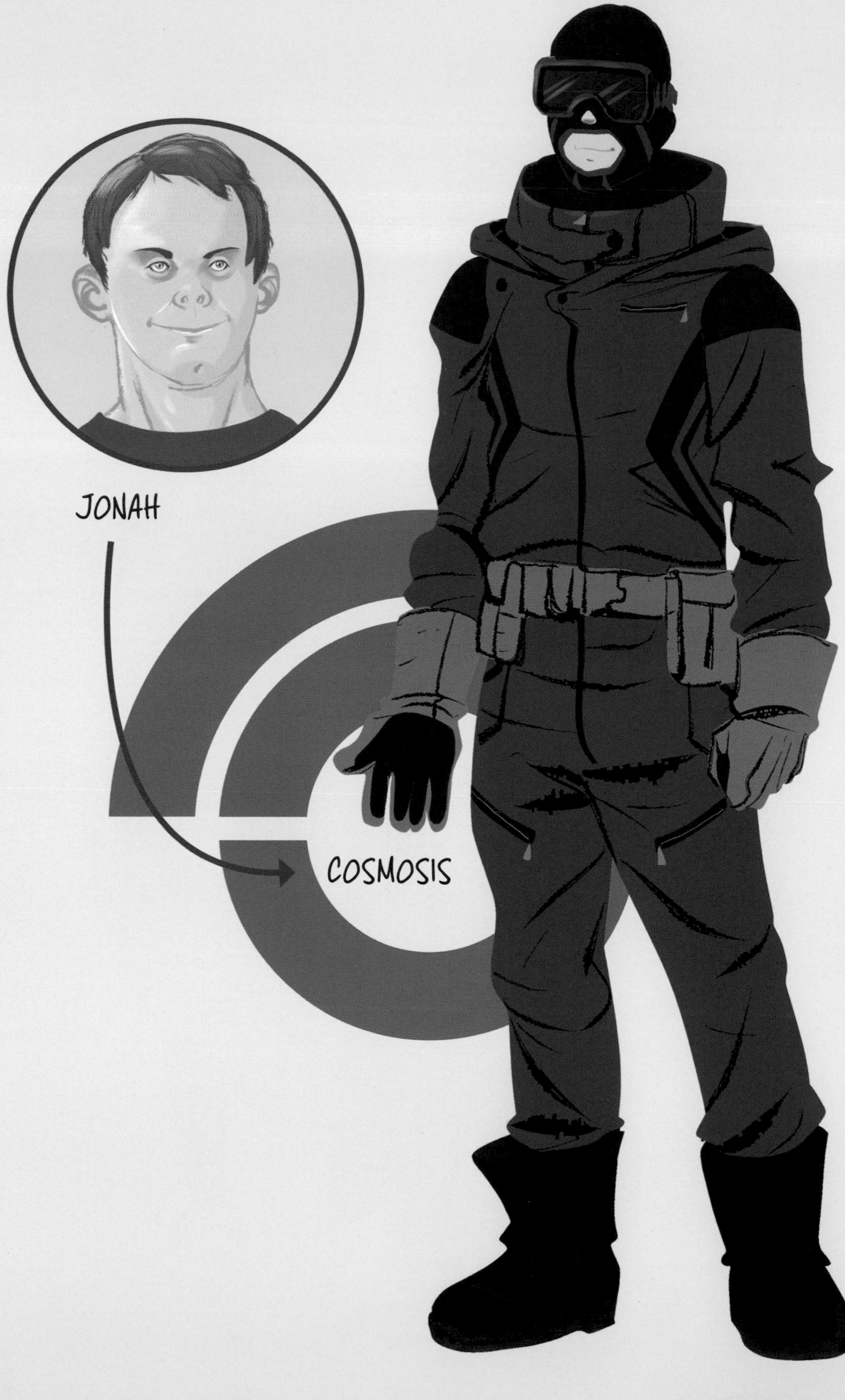
JONAH
COSMOSIS